D0435565

WITHDRAWN

THE
PEACEMAKERS

ALSO BY BRUCE W. JENTLESON

American Foreign Policy: The Dynamics of Choice in the 21st Century

The End of Arrogance: America in the Global Competition of Ideas
(with Steven Weber)

With Friends Like These: Reagan, Bush, and Saddam, 1982–1990

THE
PEACEMAKERS

LEADERSHIP LESSONS FROM TWENTIETH-CENTURY STATESMANSHIP

BRUCE W. JENTLESON

W. W. NORTON & COMPANY
Independent Publishers Since 1923
New York | London

To Barbara Ann, and Our We

At crucial moments, at turning points . . . individuals and their decisions and acts . . . can determine the course of history.

ISAIAH BERLIN

CONTENTS

RECONCILING THE POLITICS OF IDENTITY

ADVANCING FREEDOM AND PROTECTING HUMAN RIGHTS

FOSTERING GLOBAL SUSTAINABILITY

My Students Got Me Thinking

Toward the end of the U.S. foreign policy course I taught in the early 1980s at the University of California-Davis, I'd ask the students their thoughts on the future. "Well, Professor Jentleson," one earnest young man said, "I think the Cold War will end, and end peacefully." From another bright-eyed one, "Apartheid will end and South Africa will transition to a black majority democracy." My responses were along the lines of it's nice to be young, naïve, and California dreaming, but let's be realistic.

The Cold War did end, and without a shot fired. Apartheid did end, and the political transition that followed was impressively civil. While many factors came into play in both situations, the extraordinary leadership provided by Mikhail Gorbachev and Nelson Mandela was the crucial one.

In graduate school we were steered away from focusing on individual leaders. International affairs, the canon held, were driven largely by systemic forces and such timeless dynamics as national interest and balance of power. Yet as Oxford's eminent Soviet expert Archie Brown put it, no "politically conceivable alternative candidate for the General Secretary-ship in the mid-1980s [other than Gorbachev] would have acted in the same way." British Prime Minister Margaret Thatcher, typically so conservative and dour, was struck by how Gorbachev's "personality could not have been more different from the wooden ventriloquism of the average Soviet *apparatchik*." Mandela's commitment to reconciliation, hardly a given for someone who'd spent 27 years as a political prisoner, nurtured the rebirth of his own nation and presented the world with a very different model from retribution and revenge. As James Joseph, U.S. ambassador to South Africa in the Mandela years and a noted expert on leadership (and a colleague at Duke) put it, "once I got to know him [Mandela], I felt that he even exceeded the myth—which is rare about a human being." This didn't have me invoking "Great Man" theories of history, but it did call to mind Isaiah Berlin's insight that "at crucial moments, at turning points . . . individuals and their decisions and acts . . . can determine the course of history."

So over the years I got thinking about two other questions. First: Who else in the twentieth century was a "profile in statesmanship"— a global counterpart to John F. Kennedy's *Profiles in Courage*—shaping a major breakthrough for peace? The leaders I include in the book were not totally successful, but all sought to be transformational in the ways that Isaiah Berlin speaks to, whether in forging rapprochement between major powers or promoting reconciliation of peoples, or in such other ways crucial to international peace and justice as building international institutions, advancing freedom and human rights, and protecting global sustainability. And as we'll see, I consider not only leaders of countries but also leaders of key international institutions and pioneering nongovernmental organizations (NGOs) who did for peace and justice what governments could not or would not do.

A second question followed from the first: What can we learn from twentieth-century statesmanship for the twenty-first century? For a while in the late 1980s and early 1990s, it seemed like the world was going in a positive direction. The Cold War was ending peacefully. Dictatorships were falling to democracy. Globalization appeared to be spreading the wealth. History was said to be over with world affairs so harmonious as to be downright boring.

And yet the end of the Cold War has not meant the end of war. U.S. relations with both Russia and China have grown tense and tenuous. That democratic wave has broken up on some rocky shores. Globalization has had losers as well as winners. History has come roaring back, its ancient hatreds fueled by modern venom. Climate change is speeding up. Global health pandemics are spreading. Cyber and other emerging technologies are in need of rules of the game but aren't getting them. Indeed, it's a lot easier to name a global problem that's been growing worse than one on which progress is being made.

Meeting these and other twenty-first-century challenges has many dimensions. Some bottom-up solutions will be generated by the "people power" of protest movements. Others will be middle-out answers from science, technology, economics, education, and other fields. But much must come top-down from global leaders who are able and willing to try to be transformational, to break out of narrow tunnel-vision thinking and myopic focus on today but not tomorrow. For just as the world is so interconnected that, as Thomas Friedman put it, "weak leadership in one country now deeply impacts so many others," so too can bold and visionary leadership have global impact.

This was my thinking even before Donald Trump was elected president of the United States. All along I've intended this book to draw lessons from twentieth-century statesmanship to help shape and motivate the peace and security breakthroughs our twenty-first-century era so crucially needs. Trump, as I come back to in the Epilogue, has made this all the more urgent. Others, such as Vladimir Putin, do as well. In so many ways we are at one of those "crucial moments, turning points" that Isaiah Berlin spoke to at which leaders will determine the next course history takes—for the worse or for the better.

Does History Make Statesmen or Do Statesmen Make History?

ny proper study of political leadership has to start with this question. At one end of the debate is the nineteenth-century Scottish philosopher Thomas Carlyle's heroic conception that "the history of what man has accomplished in this world, is at bottom the History of the Great Men who have worked here . . . all things that we see standing accomplished in the world are properly the outer material result, the practical realization and embodiment of Thoughts that dwell in the Great Men sent into the world." At the other end is his English contemporary Herbert Spencer deriding the "universal love of personalities" going back well before *People* magazine and *Yahoo! Celebrity* to when "round the camp-fire assembled savages tell the events of the day's chase and he among them who has done some feat of skill or agility is duly lauded." Carlyle is too much the romanticist and overstates the role of individuals while undervaluing conducive conditions that create opportunities for leadership. Spencer is too much the sociologist, overstating social processes and context and undervaluing what the twentieth-century American philosopher Sidney Hook calls the "individual to whom we can justifiably attribute preponderant influence in determining an issue or event whose consequences would have been profoundly different if he had not acted as he did."

The academic literature digs deeper than the latest who's up and who's down, but with some notable exceptions too often stays at a level of abstraction that glosses over the impact that leaders do have. The talk inside the DC Beltway and among journalists can get too caught up in personalities but often does consider critical decision making. Analytic balance requires a "3 C's" approach: recognizing that history and broad social forces create *constraints* as well as *conducive conditions* but don't determine the *choices* that are made. Although no individual is so extraordinary as to achieve transformational impact irrespective of the context, it also is not a given that any and all leaders would have been able to pull off comparable statesmanship accomplishments. It's a matter of man or woman and moment, fit and timing, bounded by constraints and conducive conditions with choices to be made.

We actually think this way a lot when it comes to "bad guy" leaders. Take Adolf Hitler and Nazi Germany. Deep sociopolitical dynamics and a severe economic crisis in Germany in the 1920s and 1930s fed instability and resentment, but the particular road Germany took, from the pursuit of continental conquest to the perpetration of the Holocaust, had much to do with who the leader was. Similarly, policies such as the Soviet Great Terror of 1937–1938 and the deliberate starvation of Ukrainians, as Princeton historian David Bell writes, were a function of "Stalin's character and his particular strategies for seizing and maintaining power for himself." And in Cuba, decades of repression and corruption made the country ripe for revolution, but Fidel Castro put his own stamp on the kind of revolution it was.

In deciding on which twentieth-century "peacemakers" to focus on, I've had three main criteria in mind:

Transformational statesmanship more than transactional diplomacy: Drawn from scholars such as James MacGregor Burns and Joseph S. Nye, Jr., this distinction is between efforts at making major breakthroughs in global peace and security and efforts at diplomacy geared to managing and resolving issues in the normal course of events. While transactional diplomacy is often undervalued for its day-to-day, issue-by-issue utility, our focus here instead is on those crucial moments and turning points at which, as in the opening quote from Isaiah Berlin, "individuals and their decisions and acts . . . can determine the course of history." If our criterion were full transformational success, it would yield a rather brief book. Still these are critical junctures, breakthroughs marked by significant progress on issues long thought intractable. They make further progress possible but cannot guarantee it. Backlashes and backsliding may follow. We draw lessons both from what was achieved and what wasn't.

Statesmanship "moneyball": The wins-against-replacement-player statistic (WARP), which calculates how much one player contributes to team victories over alternative players at the same position, is one of the most useful parts of the Moneyball craze in Major League Baseball. Scholarly studies of political leadership use more formal language, such as "actor indispensability," where a leader acts significantly differently than another leader in the same situation would have acted. Actor indispensability has been shown to bear especially on situations such as transformational statesmanship when, as political scientist Fred Greenstein put it, "the more demanding the political act . . . the greater the likelihood that it will be influenced by personal characteristics of the actor." While there is no neat diplo-ball "statesman-above-replacement-leader" ("SARL") sabermetric, evidence can be marshaled to make the same point: who the player or leader is makes a big difference—and not only with some already prominent figures but also with some lesser-known ones.

Impact had—not position held: Typically, when we think of statesmanship we turn to presidents and prime ministers, secretaries of state and ministers of foreign affairs, and other leaders of nation-states. While emphasizing national leaders, I also include transformational leaders from international institutions, social movements, and nongovernmental organizations (NGOs) who did for peace and justice what governments were unable or unwilling to do.

To get a handle on "international peace and security," I break it out into the following five component dimensions: (1) *Managing Major Power Rivalries*: limiting the geopolitical competition and conflict between major powers that historically has been a leading cause of war; (2) *Building International Institutions*: creating and strengthening global bodies for preventing conflict with the United Nations as the principal example; (3) *Reconciling the Politics of Identity*: fostering reconciliation of peoples whose historically rooted hatreds have fed deadly conflicts; (4) *Advancing Freedom and Protecting Human Rights*: ending colonization, democratizing countries from both communist rule and military regimes, and protecting individuals and groups from repression; and (5) *Fostering Global Sustainability*: promoting global development, environmental protection, and public health as matters of peace and security, not just economics and equity.

As I thought about which twentieth-century leaders met the three criteria, I cast a wide net. In giving talks at various universities and other venues in the United States and internationally, I'd ask colleagues, students, and other audiences for their nominees. I mused about a social media game. The nominees' list was becoming quite long. So I shifted to focusing on representative examples for each of the five dimensions of international peace and security.

Who then are the profiles? Here's a quick preview:

MANAGING MAJOR POWER RIVALRIES

HENRY KISSINGER AND ZHOU ENLAI, for the seminal breakthrough in U.S.-China relations

MIKHAIL GORBACHEV, for his most crucial role in ending the Cold War

BUILDING INTERNATIONAL INSTITUTIONS

WOODROW WILSON, for his initial efforts at a global institution

FRANKLIN D. ROOSEVELT, for the founding of the United Nations

DAG HAMMARSKJÖLD, the secretary-general who showed how impactful the United Nations can be

RECONCILING THE POLITICS OF IDENTITY

NELSON MANDELA, for leading the fight to end apartheid through peaceful means and the global icon he became

YITZHAK RABIN, for his pursuit of Arab-Israeli peace

BETTY WILLIAMS AND MAIREAD CORRIGAN, founders of Northern Ireland Women for Peace

ADVANCING FREEDOM AND PROTECTING HUMAN RIGHTS

MAHATMA GANDHI, for fighting colonialism while embodying nonviolence

LECH WALESA, for blazing the path to ending Eastern European communism

AUNG SAN SUU KYI, for her defiant leadership of the political movement to end Burma's military dictatorship

PETER BENENSON, founder of Amnesty International, the first contemporary human rights advocacy NGO

FOSTERING GLOBAL SUSTAINABILITY

GRO HARLEM BRUNDTLAND, for advancing sustainable development and global public health

BILL AND MELINDA GATES FOUNDATION, for its work on global public health and exemplifying the increasing significance of philanthropy statesmanship

I offer three qualifiers about the profiles selected. First, selection is based on particular peacemaking roles, not leaders' overall foreign policies or other politics. Henry Kissinger is included for his China statesmanship, notwithstanding criticisms of his role in the Vietnam War, the 1970–1973 destabilization of Chile, and some other aspects of his foreign policy. Aung San Suu Kyi's role in the 2017

Rohingya crisis, an ethnic cleansing against this Muslim minority, has been at sharp variance with her earlier role in bringing democracy to Myanmar. Such intra-profile contrasts are brought into the discussion, including ways that help get at the factors explaining such stark variation.

Second, in many of our cases other leaders also had roles and impact: for example, Ronald Reagan along with Gorbachev, Yasir Arafat with Rabin, F. W. de Klerk with Mandela. But whereas Kissinger and Zhou had essentially equal roles and are thus made a paired profile, I bring those other leaders into the stories but don't find comparable proportionality or high SARL actor indispensability.

Third, the full set of profiles is heavily Western and mostly male. I've thought about these a great deal, and others have raised them at seminar and colloquium presentations. While it would be disingenuous to claim pure selection objectivity, these imbalances reflect the nature of an international system that for the last century has largely been dominated by the West and run by men. I take this up in the Epilogue, including some indications of change in the geography and gender of global leadership.

Genus leadership, species statesmanship: Who-why-how-what framework

"Leadership is," as James MacGregor Burns put it, "one of the most observed and least understood phenomena on earth." We have basic generic definitions like "the capacity of an individual, or group, to change the thoughts, feelings and actions of a significant number of individuals." Beyond that it is, as noted author and public intellectual Walter Isaacson puts it, an "elusive quality." Harvard's Barbara Kellerman cites close to 40 theories of leadership. International relations scholar Gabriel Sheffer starts his book with the expectation that there would be "a large and well-defined body of theoretical and analytical literature" only to conclude that there is much less such work.

That's not for lack of trying. Books abound. Some are about political leadership. Some are about business leadership. Some are philosophical, some are how-to. There are books for virtually every domain of human activity. Walking through Heathrow Airport on a recent trip, the most prominent display in WHSmith was for *Leading* by Alex Ferguson, longtime manager of Manchester United football/soccer club. The *Washington Post* provides a reading list "for strengthening your leadership chops." An Amazon search brought up 191,637 books for keyword *leadership*, 79,455 for *political leadership*, and 611 for *statesmanship*. One social science study provides a "periodic table of leadership" with 53 "elements" (not quite the 118 of the natural world, but still).

Nor is there a shortage of university-based leadership programs. Harvard has its Advanced Leadership Institute, New York University its Center for Leadership in Action, Duke its Hart Leadership Program, University of Virginia its Batten School of Leadership and Public Policy, Claremont-McKenna College its Kravis Leadership Institute, and Stanford its Knight-Hennessy Scholars Program for a "new generation of global leaders." You can even get a Ph.D. in leadership and change. And not just U.S. universities: for example, leadership studies courses also can be found at the Sheikh Fatima bint Mubarak Program for Leadership at Zayed University in the United Arab Emirates. In the corporate world a 2014 study estimated that $14 billion had been spent over the prior two decades on leadership development, twice as much as previously. Yet 75 percent of study respondents deemed the programs ineffective.

People talk about leadership all the time, in many contexts, but with the same "we need leadership" and "how do we get it?" mantras. For all this attention, one gets a sense of both fascination and frustration: fascination in how, time and again, explanations of success and failure in such a range of professions and pursuits hone in on leadership as a key factor; and frustration in how difficult it is to define the elements of leadership with any degree of consistency, let alone to teach and cultivate them.

Through a mix of muddling through and mining leadership studies and leadership programs, four lines of analysis emerge:

- *Who* were leaders as individuals?
- *Why* did they make the crucial choices they did?
- *How* did they pursue their goals?
- *What* was (and wasn't) achieved?

This who-why-how-what framework both provides insights into the individual profiles and brings out patterns across them that help establish lessons going forward.

Who: "A man's rootage," as Woodrow Wilson once said, "means more than his leafage." We look at our leaders' early lives and other shaping effects, getting a sense for their personas, with three caveats. First, there are no born leaders. There are more early signs of leadership in some cases than others, but in none is there anything akin to a statesmanship equivalent of Mozart, the five-year-old prodigy, or LeBron James with NBA-level skills coming straight out of high school. As they develop into leaders we do see that, as work by Margaret Hermann shows, "the higher the position held . . . the more likely personal characteristics come into play." Second, no indulging in hero worship where leaders get so idealized as to become like "talismans with a strong emotional tone . . . [that] approaches the religious." None of these leaders were perfect people: FDR was unfaithful to his wife; Gandhi's moralism had its internal contradictions; Mandela had problematic relations with some of his own children.

Third, avoid both one-size-fits-all models and laundry lists. There isn't a single persona type that works in all places at all times. Political psychology research has identified many factors that contribute to effective political leadership. But as Isaacson states at the outset of his *Profiles in Leadership* book, "There is no one recipe for great leadership." One study provides an all-of-these list of "integrity, intelligence, articulateness, collegiality, shrewd judgment, a questioning mind, willingness to seek disparate views, ability to absorb information, flexibility, courage, vision, empathy, boundless energy." Another presents a five-factor model that "meta-analyzed" 222 correlations from 73 samples to determine which personality traits were most significant. While such extensive inventories are valuable for their comprehensiveness, they are less helpful for honing in on key qualities.

Two key "who" traits come through in varying combinations in our profiles. One is *personal capital*, meaning qualities the leader brings to the position separate from those inherent to it that strengthen the capacity to be transformational. Personal capital is distinct from social capital, which is more about bonds of shared identity within a broad community, and from political capital, which is more about resources to be distributed and rewards to be conferred. For leaders whose statesmanship requires broad popular support, personal capital has a strong moral dimension, a sense of commitment to the cause validated by family roots, sacrifices made and courage shown, charisma exuded, and other such personal bona fides that provide authenticity. In cases where the breakthroughs for peace are achieved more through formal diplomacy, professional stature is a key source of personal capital. This is a mix of expertise, prior achievements and service, and overall prestige that the individual brings to the position held.

Political skills also are a key trait. It's not enough to have that personal capital; it has to be wielded effectively. Nan Keohane, former president of Duke and author of a book on leadership, emphasizes being able to devise the right combination of incentives, consequences, persuasion, and inspiration. Some of this is being adept at the inside game of working within the relevant policy arena, as Elizabeth Saunders emphasizes in her studies. Some is the outside game of mobilizing popular support. Much is about what Daniel Goleman dubbed "emotional intelligence," a sense for what people are feeling and how to connect with them. The particulars vary situationally but being able to ensure support for one's leadership is always crucial.

Why: Woodrow Wilson was a college professor. Dag Hammarskjöld was widely viewed as the kind of faceless bureaucrat who would just go along with the major powers. Mairead Corrigan was a secretary at a Guinness brewery, Lech Walesa a dockworker, Peter Benenson a middling barrister, and Bill Gates didn't show signs of interest in much beyond the techie-business world. Yet each came to possess a guiding vision that provided the "why" for transformation.

A vision is really a story, a political one akin in form and functions to what we think of more broadly as narratives. It tells us "where we want to go," it is "about the future." It "guides action . . . defines meaning" while also being "goal oriented." It "reminds us who we are, is simultaneously backward looking and aspirational; it accentuates what we hope to achieve." To do all this successfully, whether politically or otherwise, a vision/narrative has to have three aspects: analytic, identifying the problem of what's wrong with the present; prescriptive, providing a solution for a better future; and normative, doing so while avoiding deeply rooted cultural taboos. All three elements are crucial: the first as motivating, the second as direction setting, and the third as legitimizing. Laying this analytic-prescriptive-normative template onto our profiles helps us see why some statesmanship visions get more traction than others.

How: The "how" question gets at the politics and strategy—"the art of finding the means to achieve the ends set forth in one's vision," as Joseph Nye puts it—for getting from noble motivations and good ideas to actual achievements. This aspect has an international dimension of negotiation strategies and maneuvering with foreign leaders and other international actors. And it always involves politics, whether those of democratically elected leaders (Wilson, FDR, Rabin, Mandela), autocratic leaders still subject to political rivalries and opposition (Zhou, Gorbachev), movement leaders (Gandhi, Williams and Corrigan, Walesa, Aung San Suu Kyi), diplomats serving in national governments (Kissinger), or leaders of international organizations (Hammarskjöld, Brundtland) or NGOs (Benenson, Gates). Transformational leaders can't just be visionaries; they also have to be "navigators," charting the course for change. Leadership theorist Elizabeth Samet sees this as identifying an opportunity and then "harnessing its energy." Among the keys to doing so is what Harvard's Ronald Heifetz and Marty Linsky see as "orchestrating" the transformation by "controlling the temperature," raising the heat enough so that people sit up and pay attention as well as lowering it when necessary to avert counterproductive tension, and "keeping the opposition close," weakened but not so alienated that it resorts to extreme action—advice not sufficiently heeded by Wilson, Gorbachev, or Rabin.

What: "There is nothing more difficult to carry out, nor more doubtful of success, nor more dangerous to handle," Machiavelli warned, "than to initiate a new order of things." Change is hard, transformational change especially so. Vested interests resist. Traditional beliefs are called into question. Fearmongering can quash hope. Cases that qualify as fully made peace are, as lamented earlier, few if any. But the balance sheet in all our cases is positive in four respects.

First, while constraints and conducive conditions come into play, the choices that the leaders made were not a given: the 3 C's all taken into account. Second, those choices would not likely have been made by another leader: the diplo-ball SARL ranking. Third, while acknowledging roles and allocating credit to other leaders (e.g., Reagan with Gorbachev, Arafat with Rabin, de Klerk with Mandela), the most critical roles were played by the principals of the profiles: the notion of actor indispensability. Fourth, while there has been backsliding and backlash in some of these cases—for example, U.S.-Russian relations, Israeli-Palestinian peace, Burma-Myanmar Rohingya—the situations would be much worse had these peacemaking breakthroughs not occurred.

Book structure and goals

The book is organized into five sections corresponding to the five policy areas of global peace and security, each with chapters on the relevant leaders.* The who-why-how-what framework structures each profile. Each section ends with a forward-looking discussion of lessons to be drawn from twentieth-century statesmanship, as both inspiration and strategies for the twenty-first-century agenda.

---

* Dates in the chapter titles indicate the principal period of focus.

The Epilogue integrates the five sections, highlighting similarities as well as differences. It delves into the particular challenges statesmanship faces in the twenty-first century. There is no anointing this or that person. Had someone tried to do that with many of our twentieth-century profiles along the way, they would have missed quite a few. Being a peacemaker is difficult. But as we will see, it is possible. And as we are reminded every day, it is so necessary.

MANAGING MAJOR POWER RIVALRIES

THROUGHOUT HISTORY, CONFLICTS AMONG MAJOR POWERS OF the era have been the greatest threat to world peace. In the twentieth century two breakthroughs in managing major power rivalries stood out: the seminal "opening" in U.S.-China relations engineered in 1971–1972 by **Henry Kissinger** and **Zhou Enlai** (Chapter 1), and the end of the Cold War and the role of **Mikhail Gorbachev** (Chapter 2).

No statesman, as Niall Ferguson put it with only some hyperbole, was "as reviled or revered" as Kissinger. Notwithstanding warranted criticisms of other aspects of his foreign policy, the opening to China was Kissinger at his best. It entailed realpolitik strategizing of great power politics. It required the face-to-face diplomacy, back channels, and secret meetings that his persona suited so well. Zhou Enlai was very much an equal partner. He was that extraordinary mix of committed revolutionary, pragmatic diplomat, and what some have called the last Mandarin bureaucrat in the Confucian tradition. President Richard Nixon and Chairman Mao Zedong were, of course, also major players—and they did get the opera—but Kissinger and Zhou worked the statecraft.

With Gorbachev, as biographer William Taubman framed it, while "admirers marvel at his vision and his courage" and critics "accuse him of everything from naiveté to treason . . . the one thing they all agree upon is that he almost single-handedly changed his country and the world." While some credit goes to Ronald Reagan and others, it was Gorbachev who made the key decisions that brought the Cold War to an end. As bad as things were for the Soviet Union—the Afghanistan war, the crumbling economy, restiveness all over Eastern Europe—it is not a given that another Soviet leader would have made the same decisions Gorbachev did. While he was eliminated from the Russian political scene, his impact endured, ending the Cold War that had lasted more than 40 years and that, Vladimir Putin notwithstanding, is still over.

As the twentieth century ended and the twenty-first century began, for a while it seemed like the "great game" of major power politics might be a thing of the past. Russian and American leaders were embracing (Bill Clinton and Boris Yeltsin), peering into each other's eyes and "getting a sense of his soul" (George W. Bush after his first meeting with Vladimir Putin), and declaring a "reset" to get relations back on track (Barack Obama and Dmitry Medvedev). The interweaving of China into the global economy was supposed to temper the country's rise. The United States claimed to be playing its leadership role in ways that were in the interest of the overall international community.

Sure hasn't worked out that way. Russia has been more aggressive than at any time since the Cold War. China has been flexing its muscles in Asia. The United States has veered from Bush unilateralism to Obama multilateralism to Trump's America First. If U.S.-Russia and U.S.-China relations are to get on a better track, some lessons need to be drawn from the Kissinger-Zhou and Gorbachev breakthroughs.

Henry Kissinger, Zhou Enlai, and the U.S.-China Opening, 1971–1972

I n the 1950s and 1960s, Americans didn't call that large country with lots of people over in Asia "China" or the "People's Republic of China": it was "Red China." The Soviets were dangerous. The Chinese were sinister. Let's tune back in to a 1958 CBS News Special Report, "The Face of Red China," hosted by Walter Cronkite, the iconic television newsman of that era. "Russia, which pretends it is heading toward 'true communism,' actually is backing away from it," a correspondent reassured Americans watching at home. China, though, "is rapidly becoming a *real* Marxist state . . . This is what makes the story of 650 million people so fascinating—and so *terrifying* . . . The most terrifying change is not the physical regimentation but the regimentation of men's minds. When these people are not pounding the earth, their minds are being pounded with the slogans of communism. At least an hour of indoctrination a day." Then came footage of children outside their "communal nursery": "the face of Red China tomorrow. In return for the promise of security, the peasant is also surrendering his child to the state, for a massive experiment in indoctrination that makes the Soviet example seem amateurish in comparison." The broadcast won both Emmy and Peabody Awards.

The following year, a U.S. Senate committee dedicated an entire hearing to the testimony of Edward Hunter, a self-styled expert on psychological warfare who claimed to have invented the term "brain-washing." As bad as Soviet collective farms were, taking property and freedom away from farmers, Hunter avowed, China's were "those of a slave society." Actually, even worse: "Is it a human ant heap?" the Senate committee chief counsel asked. "It so closely approximates an ant heap," Mr. Hunter replied, "that I would have difficulty telling the difference, except in size." Anti-Americanism was part and parcel of this arrangement, "an integral part of Communist doctrine in China. Chinese communism imposes the obligation to keep hate for the United States within one's perspective at all times."

Such views were fomented and enforced by the China Lobby. The fervent anticommunism of 1950s' McCarthyism was especially targeted at those said to be sympathetic, or worse, to Red China. For not extending the Korean War to China, Senator Joe McCarthy attacked President Harry Truman as "a rather sinister monster." Secretary of State Dean Acheson was accused of appeasement. McCarthyite pressure prompted the purge of the State Department Foreign Service "China hands," their warnings that Chiang Kai-shek was going to lose the Chinese civil war twisted into being supportive of Mao Zedong. Then Congressman Richard Nixon went on to win his California Senate race in large part by painting his opponent as pro–Red China. Groups such as the Committee to Defend America by Aiding Anti-Communist China flexed their political muscles. George Kennan, the era's most esteemed foreign policy strategist, was told that whatever the strategic savvy of his ideas for initial overtures to China as a way of getting leverage over the Soviet Union, domestic political opposition was too intense. "I hope that someday history will record this as an instance of the damage done to our foreign policy by the irresponsible and bigoted interference of the China Lobby and its friends in Congress," Kennan wrote in his diary in July 1950.

Over in China it wasn't just Maoist ideology. The bill of particulars against the United States went further back. While American military forces did not join with the British in the 1839–1842 Opium Wars,

American merchants had been part of the opium trade before the war and benefited from commercial concessions imposed on China. While portrayed in American history books as standing up for China against the Europeans carving spheres of influence, the "Open Door Policy" of the late nineteenth century was more about the United States getting its share. U.S. soldiers were part of the 20,000 troops that intervened in 1898–1900 against the Boxer Rebellion. Back in the United States, Chinese immigrants faced discrimination and worse. In 1885, white mobs attacked Chinese workers in Rock Springs, Wyoming, killing 28 and looting and burning Chinese businesses and homes. The 1888 Scott Act restricted Chinese immigration. The 1892 Geary Act stripped Chinese already in the United States of substantial legal rights, requiring them to carry at all times papers showing legal residency or face hard labor or deportation. The 1924 National Origins Act virtually excluded all new Asian immigration. It was, they were, the "yellow peril."

There were some positives. Christian missionaries in China materially helped the communities in which they were proselytizing. YMCA programs helped raise literacy rates. Hospitals were built. American charities raised $50 million during the 1920–1921 North China famine. The Rockefeller Foundation provided support for a new medical college in Peking. Between 1900 and 1920, 2,400 Chinese students entered American universities, many of whom returned to China after graduating to become part of the new elite.

But on the big issues the United States sided with Japan against China. President Theodore Roosevelt (1901–1909) made a number of agreements reinforcing Japanese interests in Manchuria, a key province in northeastern China. At the end of World War I, Chinese leaders had their hopes raised by President Woodrow Wilson and his Fourteen Points. The top American diplomat in China cabled back that Wilsonian principles about self-determination had entered "deeply and directly into the hearts of the Chinese people." So when Wilson allowed Japan to keep its colonial claim on Shandong province in eastern China, the sense of betrayal ran deep. "China has received the vibration of the sound but not the application of the principles," as one publication put it. On Sunday, May 4, 1919, an estimated 3,000 people mobilized in Tiananmen Square in Beijing calling this National Humiliation Day and excoriating the American president as a liar.

Among those who organized the protest and kept it alive as the May Fourth Movement was a 21-year-old student named Zhou Enlai.

WHO was Zhou Enlai?

He was "the most superior brain I have so far met in the field of foreign politics," observed Dag Hammarskjöld, United Nations secretary-general (1953–1961). "Urbane, infinitely patient, extraordinarily intelligent, subtle. . . one of the two or three most impressive men I have ever met," was Henry Kissinger's take based on their joint statesmanship.

Zhou Enlai (Enlai, "the advent of grace") was born March 5, 1898, into a prominent clan in the village of Baoyuqizo in east-central China to Zhou Yineng and Wan Donger. While one biographer characterizes his childhood as "turbulent," it also strengthened his character. His father was weak and often absent. He had in effect three mothers: his natural mother, his aunt who became his adopted mother,* and his wet nurse. At 12 years old he was sent to Manchuria to live with another uncle. There he attended a series of schools that combined traditional Confucian teachings with Western subjects, including one modeled after the august Phillips Academy (Andover, Massachusetts). He excelled in school and showed the first signs of a broader political consciousness. "As to all of our schoolmates, who are we?" he wrote in a prize-winning essay. "Aren't we the citizens who will be responsible for the future of our country?" By senior year he was editor in chief of the school newspaper, *Xiaofeng.* Later in life he would reflect on how

---

* Soon after his birth, in the name of *chongxi*, the superstition that the birth of a son would cure serious illness, his mother and father gave him up for adoption to his father's seriously ill younger brother Zhou Yigan. The younger brother died anyway.

the move away from home "was a key to the transformation of my life and my thoughts."

The May Fourth Movement was the beginning of Zhou's political activism. A few months later he cofounded the Awakening Society, melding demands for internal reform and opposition to concessions to Japan. A nationwide boycott of Japanese goods was organized. When Zhou and other students went to deliver a petition to the local Chinese governor, they were arrested. He was held in prison for six months.

Soon after his release Zhou received a scholarship for study in Europe, where he would spend most of the next four years. This turned out to be less a period of formal study—he never made it to the University of Edinburgh—than of political education. In 1921 in Paris he joined a small Chinese Communist cell. The following year he became one of the founders of the Chinese Youth Communist Party in Europe. He exhibited diplomatic tact early on. He drafted the party charter. He was made publisher of the party journal *Youth* (and brought on the slightly younger Deng Xiaoping as a printer). As one colleague wrote, "We depended on him to prepare all our public statements, either orally or in writing, because once he handled them they were sure to be accepted by all groups involved."

He made a strong enough impression in Europe that the Chinese Communist Party (CCP) brought him back to China in 1925. Still in his late twenties, he quickly rose to party secretary-general and member of the Politburo. He also was appointed head of the CCP's military committee. At the time the CCP and the Kuomintang, led by Chiang Kai-shek, were working together against the warlords and concessions to Japan. Inherently an alliance of convenience, one of the incidents over which it broke apart was the March 1927 general strike in Shanghai shutting down industries, seizing police headquarters and the railway station, and proclaiming a "citizen's government." Rather than providing support as promised, Chiang Kai-shek allied with Shanghai's underworld secret societies against the CCP strikers, killing an estimated 5,000 people. A $200,000 bounty was posted for the capture or killing of Zhou Enlai. Zhou managed to escape.

In his own right Zhou could be quite ruthless. In 1931, he ordered the execution of the entire family of a party member who under police interrogation had provided sensitive information. In 1934, at the beginning of the Long March, Zhou was the one designating the unreliables to be executed or abandoned into Chiang's grasp.

Even before the Long March, the Zhou-Mao relationship evidenced the mix of rivalry and mutual need that would characterize it for the next 40 years and more. They first met in 1931 in rural Jiangxi Province, where the CCP was rebuilding. Zhou initially had the upper hand, but during the 1934 Long March, Mao gained greater control. In 1935, and not for the last time, Mao tried to push Zhou out—and not for the last time, Zhou maneuvered around him. Mao kept having to acknowledge that he could not run the party or country without the tactical and organizational skill of Zhou. In the civil war with Chiang Kai-shek, as one observer put it, "the Communists are winning the mainland not through combat, but across the negotiating table with Zhou at the other side." For his part Zhou recognized Mao's leadership capacity. When the People's Republic of China (PRC) was proclaimed on October 1, 1949, Mao was named chairman of the party and Zhou was named premier and foreign minister.

Over the next quarter-century Zhou would do what it took to maintain his position and influence. Even though he opposed Mao's Great Leap Forward (1958–1961), Zhou took charge of efforts to get grain out to the countryside for famine relief while deflecting some of the blame for the massive failure from Mao to himself. Zhou saw that Mao's Cultural Revolution launched in 1966 was pushing the country into even greater chaos: "Never in my wildest dreams did I think anything like this could happen," Zhou confided. "Whenever I think about it shivers go down my spine, and my whole body breaks into a cold sweat." But he also knew the ancient Chinese adage that "going with the flow is easier than opposing it." This included not intervening when the Red Guards seized and then killed his own adopted daughter. He "rode the tiger during the Red Guard terror," as a Chinese scholar put it, and came out with even greater position and power. Among other things, he reinstated Deng Xiaoping, who had been purged by Mao, as deputy premier.

Zhou's personal capital came from his professional stature. It's hard to speak of moral capital for someone who, while less so than Mao, had plenty of brutality on his own record. What he had was his long history as a PRC founder and defender and, in particular, as the principal hand guiding foreign relations. We've seen the political skills he showed along the way. The havoc the Cultural Revolution had wreaked on the PRC's diplomatic relations provided another opportunity. All but one Chinese ambassador had been recalled and put into re-education "study classes." Leftists who took charge of the Foreign Ministry were largely interested in propaganda—we Chinese communists are "the only revolutionaries." Zhou prepared a report showing how "extreme leftist thinking . . . sabotage[d] our foreign relations." Mao approved the report, even he having to admit that "now we are isolated." With this fluidity at home and heightened threats internationally—including increased tensions in relations with the Soviet Union—conditions were somewhat conducive for a major new diplomatic initiative.

WHO is Henry Kissinger?

Heinz Alfred Kissinger was born May 27, 1923, in Fürth, Germany, close to Nuremberg, in Bavaria. His family was middle class, his father, Louis, a teacher. The family belonged to an Orthodox Jewish congregation. Heinz was bar mitzvahed there. He studied at a Jewish school until the equivalent of high school age. But by the time he was ready to apply to the local state system *gymnasium*, Jews had been barred. In 1938, amid mounting Nazi anti-Semitism, the family emigrated to the United States; at least 13 family members would perish in the Holocaust. Yet over his career Kissinger would minimize his Jewish identity, referring to his childhood and family as "typical middle-class German."

The family settled in New York City. Henry (his name Americanized) attended George Washington High School. Always studious, he was singled out by one teacher as the "most serious and mature of the German refugee students," even while working part time for a company that made shaving brushes. Like many immigrant youth of the day, he enrolled in City College. He did so thinking he'd be an accountant.

In 1943, World War II and the draft interrupted his studies. He was selected for Army counterintelligence, first stateside and then in Europe. He was stationed in Germany, promoted to sergeant, and made commandant of a district. His unit was involved in the December 1944 Battle of the Bulge. He taught a course on German paramilitary organizations at the newly established European Command Intelligence School in Oberammergau. When the war was over, he did get back to Fürth. Only one childhood friend was to be found, the only member of his family to survive the concentration camps.

Back in the United States in 1947, no longer interested in studying accounting and with the support of the GI Bill, Kissinger was accepted at Harvard and majored in government studies. He graduated summa cum laude, his honors thesis, "The Meaning of History," bold in its scope (Kant, Spengler, Toynbee) and so long (383 pages) as to lead to the "Kissinger rule" limiting the length of future honors theses. Kissinger stayed at Harvard for doctoral studies, culminating in his Ph.D. dissertation, "A World Restored: Metternich, Castlereagh and the Problems of Peace 1812–22," on the diplomacy that brought order back to Europe after Napoleon. He was offered a faculty position at Harvard, although not the prestigious Society of Fellows to which he aspired. This was in part due to the reputation he was developing among peers and faculty as arrogant and overly ambitious. Biographer Walter Isaacson tells of Kissinger going to the dean, McGeorge Bundy (who a few years later would become President John F. Kennedy's national security advisor), with the "cheeky request" that he receive tenure early. There were numerous other incidents that even when filtered for jealousies and other subjectivities can be read fairly as less than admirable qualities, in some instances bordering on deceitfulness.

Kissinger also had shown interest beyond academia, looking to the policy world. While still a graduate student, he was appointed assistant to the director of a major project on nuclear weapons strategy at the elite Council on Foreign Relations. He got himself positioned to write the book that came out of the project, *Nuclear Weapons and Foreign Policy*. The book not only was well received by policy experts but also was a Book-of-the-Month selection. Then Vice President Richard Nixon was photographed carrying a copy.

These efforts didn't yield the job offer that Kissinger had hoped for from the Kennedy administration. He took on various advisory positions and consulting assignments while staying on the Harvard faculty. On the Republican side—these were the days of overarching foreign policy bipartisanship—he was developing his relationship with Nelson Rockefeller, Republican governor of New York and scion of the famously wealthy family. When Rockefeller ran for the Republican presidential nomination in 1964, Kissinger was a top foreign policy advisor. Rockefeller, the epitome of what then were Republican moderates/liberals, lost the nomination to conservative Arizona Senator Barry Goldwater. Lyndon Johnson, who had become president upon Kennedy's assassination in November 1963, won in a landslide. Kissinger became a consultant to the Johnson administration working on Vietnam, which included some back-channel diplomacy exploring possible terms for a peace agreement.

When Rockefeller again sought the Republican presidential nomination in 1968, Kissinger signed back on. When Rockefeller lost, this time to Richard Nixon, Kissinger was uncharacteristically blunt and public about his feelings. "My view," he told an interviewer, "was very deeply that Rockefeller was the only candidate at this time who could unite the country." He had "grave doubts" about Nixon. But as the campaign went on, he leaked information to the Nixon campaign about Johnson's plans for a Vietnam bombing halt, trying to counter any "October surprise" boost for Democratic candidate Hubert Humphrey.

Nixon won the election. A few weeks later, while Kissinger and Rockefeller were having lunch, a phone call came through inviting Kissinger to sit down with the president-elect. Richard Nixon told

Henry Kissinger that he wanted him to be his national security advisor. Some saw it as an odd match, the son of a small-town California grocer turned hard-nosed politician and the German refugee, now leading foreign policy intellectual. Some saw it as a worrisome combination of Nixon's dark-side insecurities and Kissinger's arrogance and ambition. Others saw it more positively: the *New York Times*' James Reston, the leading columnist of the day, deemed it "reassuring." Whatever the anticipatory assessment, no president–national security advisor combination has more greatly impacted American foreign policy and the world, before or since.

For Kissinger, like Zhou, personal capital was a matter of professional stature, although in his case less from a long track record than what he acquired through the power and prestige he built once in government. In his first book Professor Kissinger was quite biting about the dysfunctional impact of bureaucratic infighting, "reflect[ing] the attainable consensus among sovereign departments rather than a sense of direction." He applied this thinking in ways that marginalized Cabinet members like Secretary of State William Rogers and redefined the position of national security advisor as the center of the foreign policy process. Those who opposed Nixon's foreign policies made Kissinger a main target for criticism, but all the approbation was testimony to his stature. Indeed, he not only had the political skills to master the bureaucratic game but also to become the leading "wonk" celebrity in the broader media.

WHY the opening with China?

When major powers have complementary visions of the possibility and desirability of transformation of their relationship, even if they have not yet made that choice, statesmen have conducive conditions with which to work.

Kissinger hailed from the "Realpolitik School" of international relations and held fast to its core precepts. One was the balance of power, being a "statesman of the equilibrium," as he had praised Metternich and Castlereagh in his doctoral dissertation, "seeking a security in a balance of forces." He applied this to his world as the need to move American foreign policy away from "the assumption that technology plus managerial skills gave us the ability to reshape the international system . . . Political multipolarity makes it impossible to impose an American design." He wrote in a speech for the 1968 Rockefeller campaign, "In a subtle triangle of relations between Washington, Peking, and Moscow, we improve the possibilities of accommodations with each as we increase our options towards both." Just before his July 1971 secret trip to China, when meeting with Soviet Ambassador Anatoly Dobrynin to finalize a U.S.-Soviet summit, Kissinger privately noted, "It was comforting to hold cards of which the other side was unaware."

A pragmatic focus on interests, not ideology, was the second core realpolitik precept. Communists didn't need to be transformed ideologically in order to find shared interests. "We will judge other countries, including Communist China," Kissinger stated at a December 1969 press conference, "on the basis of their actions and not on the basis of their domestic ideology." This was all the more striking coming from someone whose family had fled an ideologically driven regime, and those who didn't flee suffered horrific consequences. But following Otto von Bismarck, the late nineteenth-century Prussian statesman who was another one of Kissinger's heroes, "foreign policy had to be based not on sentiment but on an assessment of strength." The monolithic view of communism was more about American moralism than hardheaded strategic analysis and was a "dead weight" from which U.S. foreign policy had to be freed. Once that happened, then "each Communist superpower would have greater inducement to deal with us constructively" and our options toward them would be "greater than their options toward each other." Once in office, one of the first studies he ordered was of U.S. policy toward China and possible shifts in strategy. A few months later he initiated another study particularly focused on Sino-Soviet relations and how the United States could play that subtle triangle.

Kissinger also was realistic enough to recognize U.S. weakness. The isolation of China was being punctured more and more. In 1964, France granted the PRC diplomatic recognition. Canada did so in 1970. Despite U.S. opposition, most NATO members either voted for or abstained from voting on a 1971 UN resolution expelling Taiwan and granting the PRC UN membership and the permanent seat and veto power on the Security Council.

The Vietnam War also was a part of the calculus. It was not going well militarily on the ground or politically at home. Perhaps Beijing would be more willing than Moscow to lessen support for the North Vietnamese and Vietcong communists. Regardless, the statesman image Nixon could gain from a breakthrough with China might at least partially offset Vietnam's political negatives and help him avoid Lyndon Johnson's fate of a one-term presidency.*

Zhou had his own vision for the possibility of U.S.-China rapprochement.

Whereas Kissinger was interested in better relations with China as diplomatic leverage over the Soviet Union, Zhou was interested in better relations with the United States as protection from a serious Soviet military threat. Contrary to the notion of monolithic global communism, Sino-Soviet relations had a long, tense history. While Joseph Stalin did sign the 1950 Sino-Soviet Treaty of Friendship, Alliance and Mutual Security, providing some support to Mao's fledgling regime, the terms provided much less aid than requested and retained Soviet operations in northwestern China and Mongolia. Relations improved for a while after Stalin's death, but by 1959 the Sino-Soviet split had opened up. A decade later the Soviets had built up military forces along the border with China to over one million troops. In early 1969, Chinese and Soviet forces clashed along the border at the Ussuri River.

---

* We would later find out in the Watergate scandal how far Nixon and his political operatives were prepared to go to find other means for countering anti-Vietnam politics, which helped him get reelected but would force him to become the first president in American history to resign from office.

Though minor clashes had occurred before, these were recurring and escalating, including an all-day battle in August in which Chinese forces suffered hundreds of casualties. At one point, Mao even said, "We must get ready for war." Intelligence reports came through of the Soviets even considering bombing Chinese nuclear facilities.

As manifestation of his own realpolitik orientation, Zhou had initiated a study on the "international strategic situation." While the United States saw China as a "potential threat," the Soviet Union saw China "as its leading enemy, so it [the Soviet Union] is a greater threat to China's security than American imperialism." And in their own chess game move: "the United States tries to take advantage of the contradictions between China and the Soviet Union, and the Soviet Union tries to take advantage of the contradictions between China and the United States. So we should intentionally take advantage of the contradictions between the Soviet Union and the United States." Pursuing talks with the United States, the report concluded, was "a tactical action [that] may achieve strategic success."

The ideologist in Zhou did see some signs of U.S. decline in the changing international landscape and the albatross of Vietnam. Improving relations with the United States thus was its own opportunity to continue the "struggle against imperialist expansion and hegemonism." His overall view of the United States, though, never had been as deeply negative as that of Mao. Zhou had worked with General Joseph Stilwell during World War II against the Japanese and when Stilwell had tried to shift U.S. policy away from blanket support for Chiang Kai-shek. Zhou worked after the war with General George Marshall, who also had tried to broker intra-China unity. In 1953–1954 he negotiated indirectly through UN Secretary-General Dag Hammarskjöld the release of some American prisoners after the Korean War (see Chapter 4).

Zhou also had his own politics with which improved relations with the United States could help. The mutual respect manifested by a U.S.-China rapprochement would show that China's century of humiliation going back to the Opium Wars was over. China was no longer on its knees. It was negotiating with a world superpower on an equal footing. Opening China up also could help prevent another inward turn and the dangers that could pose to him personally and to his country's future. This also was why Maoist radicals kept opposing the opening and the transformation it could catalyze.

HOW was the opening achieved?

On both sides visions were taking shape for why improved relations were in Sino-American mutual interests. Conditions were more conducive than earlier in the Cold War. But constraints remained. Continued confrontation was still an option. Making the decision to pursue an "opening" was not a given; making it work wasn't either. It took the kind of statesmanship that created space for a transformation.

First, the Minuet

While both sides were making similar strategic calculations, many years of limited communication meant that neither could be sure the other was doing so. Low-level talks had been held on and off in Warsaw since 1955 but with little traction: as Kissinger put it, "the longest continual talks that could not point to a single important achievement." Even these had been suspended in 1968 as fallout from the Cultural Revolution.

Various signals were sent, intriguingly but cautiously. In his 1969 inaugural address President Nixon stated that he was open to relations with China. Mao in turn told the *People's Daily* to publish Nixon's inaugural address in full, although offset with another article calling Nixon the latest "puppet" chosen by the "monopoly bourgeoisie clique." Nixon did his own offsetting in citing the nuclear threat from China as a main rationale for one of his first major defense policy initiatives, the antiballistic missile (ABM) system.

On July 7, 1969, the United States reduced some trade and travel restrictions. Three days later, China freed two American yachtsmen who recently had been seized after they had capsized off the coast of Hong Kong and their lifeboat had floated into Chinese waters. In November while reaffirming its commitment to defend Taiwan, the United States reduced its naval presence in the Taiwan Strait. On the one hand, this was couched as part of a general cutback in defense spending. On the other hand, to make sure the signal wasn't missed, Kissinger authorized a leak to Chinese officials in Hong Kong.

On December 3, on orders from Kissinger, Ambassador to Poland Walter Stoessel used the occasion of a fashion show at the Warsaw Palace of Culture to pull aside a Chinese diplomat and tell him the United States was interested not just in reconvening the Warsaw talks but also in arranging more serious and higher-level talks. Three days later, Zhou announced the release of two other wayward American citizens who had inadvertently strayed into Chinese waters. The following week Ambassador Stoessel was invited to the Chinese embassy in Warsaw and told to come through the front door, not the back door, which was Zhou's way of making sure the Soviets knew. The Nixon administration's 1970 Foreign Policy Annual Report called the Chinese "a great and vital people." Zhou responded with instructions to the Chinese delegation in the Warsaw talks to change the language from "willing to consider" receiving a U.S. delegation to "willing to receive."

But when the United States invaded Cambodia in May 1970 as an extension of the Vietnam War, China suspended the Warsaw talks. A rally of 500,000 people was staged in Beijing welcoming Prince Norodom Sihanouk, the Cambodian leader deposed by the United States. Mao called on the oppressed peoples of the world to rise up against American imperialism and its "running dogs." This would be his last major public statement full of anti-U.S. invective.

Meanwhile the "intricate minuet," as Kissinger characterized it, continued. Pakistani President Yahya Khan had been serving as a quiet back channel between Washington and Beijing, taking advan-

tage of his country's position as both a U.S. ally and friend of China.*
On December 9, his ambassador to Washington delivered a handwritten note from Zhou Enlai: "a special envoy of President Nixon's will be
most welcome in Peking." The agenda was stated as specifically about
Taiwan. The U.S. response pushed for a broader agenda. In back-and-
forth messages, some signals were perceived as intended. Some were
missed. Concern mounted that momentum was being lost. And then
came "Ping-Pong diplomacy."

In early April 1971, the U.S. and Chinese national Ping-Pong (table
tennis) teams were in Japan competing in the world championship.
Ping-Pong had a long tradition in China. In a partly random, partly
strategized sequence, Zhou arranged for a Chinese player to invite the
American team to play an exhibition in China. The head of the team
asked the American diplomat at hand in Japan if the team could accept
the invitation. Citing the annual foreign policy report that the White
House had issued a few months earlier and the statement that "the
US is open to educational, cultural and educational exchanges with
the PRC," the diplomat said yes. Within days the American team was
in China, playing to packed stadiums. Zhou, who still played Ping-
Pong himself, personally oversaw the schedule. When he met with
the American team, he congratulated both teams for having "opened

---

* Controversy rages over whether the price for reliance on Yahya for the channel to
China was, as Princeton Professor Gary Bass argues in his book *The Blood Telegram:
Nixon, Kissinger and the Forgotten Genocide*, a blind eye to the mass atrocities Yahya and
his forces were inflicting on the East Pakistanis, particularly the genocidal targeting
of the Hindu minority. My assessment, based on Bass's research and other sources, is
that while the China channel was a factor, others were more significant. India tilted to
the Soviet Union in the Cold War geopolitics of the day, while Pakistan was a U.S. ally.
Nixon in particular had a strident antipathy toward India as well as a buddy-ish attitude
toward Yahya. Nor was this the only time Nixon and Kissinger stuck to a "he-may-be-
an-SOB-but-he's-our-SOB" policy. So while I agree with Bass that the China channel
"added to their unwillingness to speak up" (107), even without it Nixon and Kissinger
likely would have pursued largely the same policy. I make these points as explanation,
not justification.

a new page in the relations of the Chinese and American people. I am confident that this beginning again of our friendship will almost certainly meet with the approval and support of the great majority of our two peoples." Back in the United States media coverage was huge.

A few days later, on April 27, a message from Zhou arrived at the White House inviting "a special envoy of the President of the US (for instance, Mr. Kissinger)." On July 9, under the cloak of secrecy with the trip code name "Polo," Henry Kissinger arrived in Beijing.

The Breakthrough

Had Las Vegas bookies known about the Kissinger-Zhou meeting—representing two countries that had been enemies for more than 20 years, that regularly demonized one another politically and culturally, and that had burning issues like U.S. support for Taiwan and Chinese aid to North Vietnam—no doubt the betting odds would have been on breakdown. The breakthrough can be traced to three key factors: personal rapport, policy, and politics.

Kissinger and Zhou developed genuine mutual trust and respect. At their very first encounter Kissinger immediately offered his hand for a handshake. This harked back to Secretary of State John Foster Dulles's refusal to shake hands with Zhou at the 1955 Geneva conference ratifying partition of Vietnam into the communist North and noncommunist South. Dulles had been cordial to Soviet Foreign Minister Vyacheslav Molotov but not to that Red Chinese. "That was unforgivable," Kissinger apologized. Zhou would later comment on how much this meant to him.

Over the ensuing two days they held 17 hours of meetings, some with aides but much one-on-one (with translators only). In the follow-up visit over four days in October (Polo II) they held another 10 meetings, totaling 23 hours and 40 minutes. The meetings had "a depth that one experiences only in the presence of a great man," as Kissinger put it with regard to Zhou. "Very intelligent, indeed a Doctor!" Zhou said of Kissinger.

They engaged as fellow intellectuals, not just following stilted talking-points exchanges. Early on Kissinger gave a sense of his historical perspective by acknowledging that the People's Republic was part of, not an aberration from, China's long traditions and achievements. Zhou showed how knowledgeable he was of world history and of American history in particular. At times they jousted, with different views over the lessons of history, how societies should organize themselves, and other questions that while deeply philosophical also bore on the agenda at hand. At one point, for example, Zhou framed his case for Taiwan noting that it had been part of China longer than Long Island had been part of the United States.

A friendly humor added to the atmosphere. Kissinger had been on a trip to Pakistan when he secretly diverted to Beijing for Polo I, the traveling press corps told he was ill and resting in a state guesthouse up in the hills. The press wasn't buying. A few stories were published along the lines of "where is Henry?" So as they first met Zhou smiled and said, "There's special news this afternoon—you are lost!"

They also found camaraderie in shared distaste for bureaucracies. Zhou: "You don't like bureaucracy, either." Kissinger: "Yes, and it's mutual; the bureaucracy doesn't like me. . . . Our bureaucracy would like to try acupuncture on me to see how many needles they can put into me, and they will not do it as delicately as the Chinese doctors." Another telling instance involved James Reston, the eminent *New York Times* columnist scheduled to arrive in Beijing soon thereafter. Suddenly a local Chinese communist party official told him his trip to Beijing would be delayed a few days. Once he had arrived, Kissinger requested that Zhou please not tell Reston that he was there or what they talked about, or he would be forced to ask for a job in Zhou's Foreign Ministry. The transcript notes "considerable laughter" on the Chinese side.

Even with the tight schedule and extensive meetings, visits to the Imperial Palace and to the Great Wall were arranged. The banquets were sumptuous, Peking duck and other food were bountiful, the beverages flowed freely, and the toasts were more genuine than the usual clichés. Over one of their meals Zhou spoke remarkably candidly about the Cultural Revolution. It had been necessary, he held the line, for purging and de-bureaucratization. But he also acknowledged excesses.

Not all was forthright and friendly; some was frank and contentious. At one point in the October meetings, after a day of apparent progress, the next morning Zhou delivered a hard-hitting critique of overall American Cold War foreign policy. Kissinger pushed back. But even this was within the context of the trust and respect the two statesmen had fostered. "You probably thought the Chinese communist party had three heads and six arms," Zhou said, "but lo and behold I am like you, someone who you can talk reason with and talk honestly." Zhou showed a "largeness of spirit," Kissinger wrote Nixon. He was an extraordinary man, "equally at home in philosophic sweeps, historical analysis, tactical jousting, hard bargaining, light repartee." "Come back soon," was Zhou's farewell to Kissinger, "for the joy of talking." When he did come back with Nixon, Zhou would greet him, "Ah, old friend."

The personal level can only take things so far without common policy ground. The second key factor in breakthrough rather than not breakdown was that *they made the transactional serve the transformational.* Often in diplomacy the latter is dependent on the former: we can only have a new relationship if we first fully resolve the specific issues between us. In some instances, though, those very issues may become more resolvable, the transactions more open to compromise, if the overall relationship at least begins to be transformed. Zhou spoke precisely to this when in one of their first meetings he assessed the failure of the Warsaw talks as having focused too heavily on particular issues of contention. "Only the settlement of fundamental questions first can lead to the settlement of other questions."

In this vein Kissinger early on made two key points departing from prior U.S. policy. "A strong and developing PRC poses no significant threat to any US interest": that is, we no longer are locked into seeing you as our enemy. "We do not deal with Communism in the abstract but with specific Communist states on the basis of their specific actions towards us, and not as an abstract crusade": that is, the anticommunist crusade is over. Similar strategic thinking is evident in Zhou's handwritten remarks on a Foreign Ministry memo, "We will adhere to principles but make flexible adjustments if circumstances require. We will be ready for bargaining with the American side." Both sides had a keen sense of the opportunity to lay the foundations for a fundamentally new relationship.

This transformational context made for a mutual willingness to compromise on the transactional issues. On Taiwan the initial Chinese position was for resolution as a precondition to any other progress. Resolution meant the United States would end diplomatic recognition, withdraw all military forces, and abrogate the mutual defense treaty. In their first meeting Zhou pushed very hard on this issue. Kissinger agreed that the United States would not support the idea of "two Chinas," or a Taiwanese independence movement ("one China, one Taiwan"), and that it would remove some military forces from Taiwan. There was more that we could do, Kissinger hinted, but as Kissinger put it a number of times alluding to the China Lobby back home, we could not yet end all relations with Taiwan and fully normalize relations with the PRC.

Zhou continued to push, reflecting his own politics including Mao's views. He questioned whether the CIA was behind the Taiwanese independence movement. Why had the Republican governor of California, Ronald Reagan, gone to Taiwan and embraced Chiang Kai-shek? In between their first meeting, when Kissinger had stated U.S. policy as "one China," and their second meeting, the State Department had made a more ambiguous statement on Taiwan's future. Kissinger reassured Zhou that the CIA was not covertly maneuvering for Taiwan's independence, that Governor Reagan was not coordinating with President Nixon, and that there would be no more objectionable State Department statements.

China compromised sufficiently to have Taiwan dealt with as parallel constructions rather than a joint position in the February 1972 Shanghai Communiqué. The Chinese stated their views: that Taiwan is a province of China, that its liberation was an internal matter "in which no other country has a right to interfere," that all U.S. military forces had to withdraw, and that Taiwan remained the crucial issue obstructing U.S.-PRC normalization. For its part the United States "acknowledges that all Chinese on either side of the Taiwan Strait maintain there is but one China and that Taiwan is a part of China," and that "the U.S. government does not challenge that position." This went further than past U.S. policy, but to acknowledge and not challenge was not the same as to accept and endorse. So too on the American military presence, full withdrawal was affirmed as an "ultimate objective," and even initial reductions were linked to "as the tension in the area diminishes."

So while U.S. policy did shift, the greater transactional compromise came from the PRC. "We have already let the Taiwan issue remain for 22 years," Zhou later remarked, "and can still afford to let it wait there for a time." It would have to be resolved before there could be full normalization, but it was not a precondition for the strategic relationship to start building. By some accounts Kissinger and then Nixon in his meetings with Mao made pledges to resolve the Taiwan issue and establish full diplomatic relations with the PRC during the second term they expected Nixon to have.

On the other main issue of Vietnam, the United States made the greater compromises. Kissinger and Nixon wanted Beijing to pressure North Vietnamese leader Ho Chi Minh in ways that Moscow had not. The war had been intensifying and spreading. At home antiwar politics were ratcheting up political pressure. Kissinger tried to make the case that the United States was prepared to end the war but that it had to be done in ways that preserved U.S. dignity and credibility. He made various proposals, including backing off the insistence that Nguyen Van Thieu remain South Vietnamese president after a settlement, discussing limits on U.S. military aid, and offering reconstruction money inclusive of North Vietnam.

As part of its rivalry with the Soviets, as well as with a touch of ideological solidarity, China resisted pressuring North Vietnam to move toward a peace agreement. The state-run news was still publishing articles declaring that China would continue to support North Vietnam and calling for the unconditional withdrawal of all U.S. troops. Zhou was quite frank in his view that the U.S. intervention was the problem in what he continued to see as a classic struggle for liberation. The compromise he came to was that China would not provide excessive support for continued war or discourage North Vietnam from seeking peace.

On Vietnam, as on Taiwan, the Shanghai Communiqué follows a parallel agree-to-disagree structure. The U.S. section: our priority is a negotiated solution; the eight-point U.S.-South Vietnamese proposal is the way to get there; if there's not a negotiated agreement we will only withdraw our troops "consistent with the aim of self-determination for each country of Indochina." The Chinese section: "wherever there is oppression, there is resistance"; firm support for the people of Vietnam, Cambodia, and Laos; no foreign troops; and support for the alternative peace proposal from the Provisional Revolutionary Government of South Vietnam (the Vietcong).

One issue on which the Shanghai Communiqué was more joint than parallel was the Soviet Union. It was obvious who was in mind in the statement that neither the United States nor China would seek hegemony in the Asia-Pacific region "and each is opposed to any other country or group of countries seeking to establish such hegemony." Two sentences later is their joint opposition to major countries "divid[ing] up the world into spheres of interest." Kissinger made clear that the United States would continue to seek détente with the Soviets, while also being quite explicit that "we do not accept the proposition that one country can speak for all Socialist countries." He and Nixon also provided China with intelligence on Soviet forces along the Chinese border and pledged that nuclear arms control and various other agreements reached with the Soviet Union would apply only to the two of them. For his part Zhou emphasized that the PRC would seek improved relations with Moscow, although he did also note that China had been receiving "much unasked for advice from other countries, especially one other country in recent months."

So the personal was cultivated. The policy was strategized. But if the *politics* couldn't be managed, these wouldn't suffice. And both sides had their politics.

On the Chinese side Mao, while not as locked into his ideology as often portrayed, was less convinced than Zhou of the strategic opportunity. Nothing could have proceeded without his approval. Zhou, who checked in with Mao nightly and often many times a day, came back into some meetings with Kissinger taking a harder line than the night before or even a few hours earlier. When Zhou came in with a firm position to offer, such as the compromises on Taiwan, it was evident that Mao had signed off.

Kissinger's October visit came right after the Lin Biao incident. The April 1969 Ninth Party Congress had designated General Lin Biao, longtime minister of defense, as Mao's successor. Lin still was an advocate of forging a front of the "revolutionary peoples of Asia" to drive the United States out. In September 1971, prompted in part by the Kissinger-Zhou talks and more than ample personal ambition, he attempted a coup against Mao. Accounts vary, some reporting that there was an actual assassination attempt against Mao. Accounts also vary as to how Lin met his demise; an airplane crash as he attempted to flee to the Soviet Union was the official story. Kissinger and team felt the aftereffects. The initial greeting at the airport, this time a more public one, was less warm. When they arrived at the guesthouse, they found propaganda pamphlets in their rooms with phrases calling for the "overthrow of the American imperialists and their running dogs." Kissinger had his aides collect all the pamphlets and gave them to one of the Chinese officials, stating that surely a previous visitor must have left them. Whether Zhou knew about it and needed to let it be done to assuage political opponents or it was done behind his back, he told Kissinger "to observe Peking's actions, not its rhetoric; the anti-American propaganda was 'firing an empty cannon.'" Mao struck a similar note in his first meeting with Nixon, saying, "In our country also there is a reactionary group which is opposed to our contact with you. The result was that they got on an airplane and fled abroad."

On the American side oppositional politics intensified even within the Nixon administration. The CIA's assessment stuck to the view that Chinese policy toward the United States would only change post-Mao. Right when the initial invitation for talks was in the works, Secretary of State William Rogers stated in a television interview that China remained "expansionist" and "rather paranoiac" toward the outside world and that no presidential trip was foreseeable until China complied "with the rules of international law." Nixon's own vice president, Spiro Agnew, told the press that the United States took "a propaganda beating." Even Rose Mary Woods, Nixon's faithful longtime secretary, lashed out the night of the big Nixon-Mao banquet when told she was running late, saying "Don't rush me. As long as we have sold out to these bastards, it doesn't make any difference."

The China Lobby struck back through the media and its congressional connections. At one point Kissinger remarked to Zhou that it was hard to tell which had become more vituperative: left-wing, anti-Vietnam protests or right-wing, anti–China opening efforts. Kissinger negotiating with Zhou was akin, William Buckley excoriated, to "if Sir Hartley Shawcross had suddenly risen from the prosecutor's stand at Nuremberg and descended to embrace Goering and Goebbels and Doenitz and Hess, begging them to join with him in the making of a better world." Nixon's own right-wing, anticommunist credentials helped deflect some of the opposition, giving rise to the generic "Nixon goes to China" for how leaders with hawkish credentials can pursue peace.

WHAT: Balance Sheet

The February 21, 1972, banquet welcoming President Nixon to China drew a TV audience second only to the July 20, 1969, first Moon landing. Zhou had the orchestra play "America, the Beautiful." Toasts were made, although Nixon was advised by the advance team to stick to the wine and avoid the "white lightning" mao-tais. Gifts were exchanged then and throughout the trip, including Ling-Ling and Hsing-Hsing,

the two Chinese pandas that became top attractions at the Washington National Zoo. The door that Henry Kissinger and Zhou Enlai had
opened now swung wide.

Margaret MacMillan, in her book on Nixon and Mao, called it
the week that shook the world. Mao and Nixon did meet and, like
Kissinger and Zhou, their transcript shows some playful exchanges
interspersed.

MAO: I "voted" for you during your election . . . I like rightists.
NIXON: I think the important thing to note is that in America, at
    least at this time, those on the right can do what those on the left
    talk about.

Substantively they discussed strategic issues very much along the
lines Kissinger and Zhou had. But when Nixon raised more particular issues, like Taiwan and Vietnam, that would have to go into
the Shanghai Communiqué, Mao insisted that while the two leaders
would be the ones to sign it, they would leave these issues to Kissinger
and Zhou. This was in part because Mao was ill by then and in part a
manifestation of how the Mao-Zhou partnership long had worked. It's
also why even MacMillan concludes that the Nixon trip was largely
"confirming what had already been negotiated."

So, yes, Nixon and Mao got the opera. Kissinger and Zhou did
the statecraft. Both scored high on the diplo-ball SARL (statesman-
above-replacement-leader) index. "There was no assurance that it
would work out," Kissinger aide Winston Lord reflected. "It was still
somewhat of a gamble." With the signing of the Shanghai Communiqué on the penultimate day of the Nixon visit (February 27), the
gamble paid off. The document acknowledged that discussions had
been "extensive, earnest and frank . . . present[ing] candidly to one
another their views on a variety of issues." There still were "essential differences between China and the United States in their social
systems and foreign policies." Parts of the document on issues like
Taiwan and Vietnam follow the parallel structure of agreement tem-

pered with agreeing to disagree for now. But having acknowledged all that, these two bitter Cold War adversaries affirmed the fundamental transformation that they would "conduct their relations on the principles of respect . . . nonaggression . . . without resorting to the use of force . . . peaceful coexistence . . . broaden the understanding between the two peoples." And "the two sides expressed the hope that the gains achieved during this visit would open up new prospects for the relations between the two countries. They believe that the normalization of relations between the two countries is not only in the interest of the Chinese and American peoples but also contributes to the relaxation of tension in Asia and the world."

Zhou's toast at the celebratory banquet captured the essence of what had been accomplished. "The social systems of China and the United States are fundamentally different, and there exist great differences between the Chinese Government and the United States Government," he realistically acknowledged. "However, these differences should not hinder China and the United States from establishing normal state relations. . . . Still less should they lead to war . . . We hope that, through a frank exchange of views between our two sides to gain a clearer notion of our differences and make efforts to find common ground, a new start can be made in the relations between our two countries." A breakthrough had been achieved. A basis for peace had been established.

Quasi-embassies, known as liaison offices, were opened in Washington and Beijing; the diplomat David Bruce was the first head of the U.S. office, in 1974 George H. W. Bush the second. Educational exchanges were initiated. Trade started to develop. But politics on both sides slowed down full diplomatic relations. In the United States the Watergate scandal, which broke a few months later with the first story by Bob Woodward and Carl Bernstein in the *Washington Post*, had by August 1974 forced President Nixon's resignation. In China not only did Mao's illness grow worse and more weakening, but also Zhou was diagnosed with bladder cancer shortly after the Nixon visit. Zhou's last major public appearance was September 30, 1974, the day

before the twenty-fifth anniversary of the Chinese Communist revolution. He died in January 1976. Mao died the following September.

Still, the next steps did come. On January 1, 1979, with Jimmy
Carter as U.S. president and Deng Xiaoping rehabilitated and now
in charge in China, full diplomatic relations were established. Over
the decades since, many aspects of the relationship have been developed. China and the United States have cooperated on some issues.
They have conflicted on others, including some testy crises. And they
have an uncertain future that needs its own comparable twenty-first-
century statesmanship on both sides.

Mikhail Gorbachev: Ending the Cold War, 1985–1991

The individual who made the most profound impact
on world history in the second half of the twentieth century.
—*Oxford Professor Archie Brown*

A great man, a giant in modern history,
but who also had shortcomings and failures.
—Washington Post *Moscow Bureau Chief Robert Kaiser*

WHO is Mikhail Gorbachev?

Mikhail Sergeyevich Gorbachev was born in 1931, making him the first general secretary of the Soviet Communist Party to be born after Lenin's 1917 revolution. His family was hit hard by the Stalinist purges, his paternal grandfather exiled to Siberia in 1933 for failing to meet collective farm quotas and his maternal grandfather imprisoned on inflated charges. When years later as general secretary of the Soviet Communist Party he viewed the previously banned anti-Stalin movie *Repentance* (which would go on to win awards at the Cannes Film Festival), he "choked back tears during several of the scenes."

During his law studies at the University of Moscow, young Mikhail read widely: Roman law, Hobbes, Rousseau, Aquinas, Machiavelli, Montesquieu. He was interested in Marxism as the basis for a system that while not perfect was perfectible. But he also was playing the game the way it needed to be played. He joined the Communist Party in 1952. He became head of the law student chapter of Komsomol (the Young Communist League).

It also was at Moscow University that he met Raisa Maksimovna Titorenko, a student in philosophy, whose family also had suffered in the purges of the 1930s. At the university Mikhail got good grades; Raisa got even higher ones and went on to complete the equivalent of a Ph.D. in sociology. They were married in 1953. Raisa was a confidante and advisor during Mikhail's rise and very much part of his public profile during his years in power. Stylish and educated, she broke the Soviet first lady mold in ways that were seen quite positively in the West but had more mixed reviews at home.

After graduation Gorbachev returned to Stavropol, in his home region in the North Caucasus about 900 miles south of Moscow, for a position in the office of the procurator (prosecutor), which in the Soviet system was mostly about keeping people toeing the party line. From the start Gorbachev didn't take well to this role. Work one summer was "disgusting," he wrote Raisa, particularly "the manner of life of the local bosses . . . the acceptance of convention, subordination, with everything predetermined, the open impudence of officials . . . When you look at one of the local bosses you see nothing outstanding apart from his belly."

Nevertheless he kept advancing through the party hierarchy and honing his political skills, as biographers Dusko Doder and Louise Branson put it, to "pass readily from the rural banter to the realm of ideas." In 1962, Fedor Kulakov, the regional party boss, put him in charge of party cadres, which gave him patronage power for lots of appointments. When in 1970 Kulakov went to Moscow as a member of the Central Committee and agriculture secretary, Gorbachev succeeded him as regional party first secretary. He went about his work as "an honest and unpretentious man seemingly determined to do a good job," a rarity among party officials so many of whom were part of the stagnation and corruption that increasingly pervaded the Soviet system under General Secretary Leonid Brezhnev. He also was different from peers in seeking out opportunities for travel to the West, even turning a 1975 official trip to France into an opportunity to bring Raisa and stay on and drive all over the country in a rented Renault. He would later reflect that these trips revealed the disconnect between Soviet propaganda and what the West really was like. "The question haunted me: why was the standard of living in our country lower than in other developed countries?"

Stavropol proved to be a useful locale for developing relations with two other Kremlin power brokers. Mikhail Suslov, a member of the Central Committee since 1949 and the Politburo since 1955, also was from the area; indeed back in 1939–1944 he had held the same regional party first secretary position. When Fedor Kulakov died in 1978, Suslov was instrumental in getting Gorbachev appointed Central Committee secretary for agriculture, then the following year as a candidate member of the Politburo, and in 1980 a full member—and at 49 years old, the youngest.

Gorbachev also had nurtured relations with Yuri Andropov, long-time head of the KGB, who would become Brezhnev's successor in 1982. Andropov also was from the Stavropol region and came back frequently to visit the spas. Gorbachev took advantage of a party protocol that the regional first secretary host Moscow dignitaries upon their arrival. With Andropov these became longer and more intensive conversations. Andropov admired Gorbachev's sharp mind and contempt for the petty corruption that Andropov could see was eating away at the Soviet economy. While Andropov was viewed in the West as the real-life version of John le Carré's master spy Karla, at home he also was a reformist seeking to save the Soviet system from itself. Toward that end he gave Gorbachev access to information that revealed how bad the economic situation was. He also made him senior personnel secretary with influence over party appointments. He had him create working groups that included intellectuals and policy experts from outside the party and state, many of whom Gorbachev would later draw into his own administration. They were impressed with him: "He was smart; he listened to them; he asked provocative questions."

Andropov died of kidney disease in February 1984; indeed he had been bedridden months earlier. He had tried to position Gorbachev as his successor, expanding his protégé's formal policy portfolio from agriculture to the overall economy and having him chair Politburo meetings when he could not be present. But more conservative factions within the Kremlin threw their support to the Brezhnev-like Konstantin Chernenko.

Gorbachev played his cards shrewdly, supporting Chernenko sufficiently to not further antagonize the old guard. Of course, he also could calculate less than favorable actuarials for a 73-year-old lifelong heavy smoker with a medical history of emphysema and pulmonary disease. Even in his inaugural speech from atop Lenin's tomb Chernenko ran short of breath. As the military parade paid tribute, he couldn't hold a salute. Within a month of taking power, he started going in and out of the hospital. Meanwhile Gorbachev was building his circles of like-minded thinkers and party allies. This also was when he made his trip to Great Britain in which arch-conservative Prime Minister Margaret Thatcher remarked, "I like Mr. Gorbachev. We can do business together." As she later wrote in her memoirs, *The Downing Street Years*:

> His personality could not have been more different from the wooden ventriloquism of the average Soviet *apparatchik*. He smiled, laughed, used his hands for emphasis, modulated his voice, followed an argument through and was a sharp debater . . .
> It was the style far more than the Marxist rhetoric which expressed the substance of the personality beneath.

Chernenko died on March 10, 1985. The very next day Mikhail Gorbachev was selected general secretary. It wasn't as straightforward, though, as that might imply. Before his death, Chernenko had signaled that Viktor Grishin, longtime Moscow first secretary, was his choice. Grigory Romanov, who oversaw the vast military-industrial complex, was another rival. When Chernenko died, three of the Brezhnevites were away from Moscow. By pushing for the vote to be held that evening, under the guise of the importance of showing the outside world a rapid succession, Gorbachev got the "unanimous" vote he wanted. He maneuvered to convince Andrei Gromyko, who had been foreign minister even longer than Brezhnev had been general secretary, to give the nominating speech. Among the attributes Gromyko cited was Gorbachev's ability to "grasp the essence of processes going on outside our country, in the international arena."

"Gorbachev," the man reflected upon himself in third-person language to biographer William Taubman, "is hard to understand." Even Taubman, after working for more than 10 years on a 900-page biography, is left asking, "How did Gorbachev become Gorbachev?" yet not being able to answer more definitively than "his character is hard to define." In our personal capital–political skills terminology, we see some interesting patterns. Gorbachev would not have gotten to the top of the Kremlin at such a young age were it not for the combination of his own career accomplishments and those high-level patrons who both enhanced his personal capital and honed his political skills. Roald Sagdeev, a leading Soviet scientist, observed how few were those "who did not fall under the spell of Gorbachev's personal charm and the magnetism of his verbal talent." His reforms created more of a sense of progress than the Soviet people had felt for a long time. They also gave him an international stature unprecedented for a Soviet leader. He was to be the leader who saved the Soviet Union from itself and brought it back into the international community. But this proved to be more difficult and more contentious than anticipated. Opponents were more determined to stop him than supporters were able to buttress him. Gorbachev grew overconfident that, just as Sagdeev had qualified his compliment about Gorbachev's charm and magnetism, "he could persuade anyone in the Soviet Union about anything." While having brought him to a position to be transformational, his personal and political skills proved not as well suited to managing the forces unleashed.

WHY "New Thinking"?

For all the rungs climbed up the party ladder, Gorbachev never was a strict apparatchik. Zdenek Mlynar, a Czech friend from his Moscow University days, recounts that Gorbachev "didn't have the ingrained bureaucratic nature—the inflexibility, narrowness and incapacity for independent thought." But that open-mindedness and flexibility existed within a fundamental belief in the Soviet system. Unlike Brezhnev, he recognized the flaws of the system. But unlike Boris Yeltsin, he wasn't seeking to end it.

Gorbachev's "New Thinking" vision had three core elements: *perestroika* (economic restructuring), *glasnost* (political openness), and transformation to a post–Cold War world. Early on he called for a "profound perestroika of planning and administration" (June 1985), declaring that "radical reform is necessary" (February 1986). His plans included putting economic efficiency and productivity over the privileges of the *nomenklatura*, the party elite. He kept hitting at "an atmosphere of complacency . . . stagnation . . . economic retardation" not only damaging the economy but also causing "a gradual erosion of the ideological and moral values of our people." Perestroika was not about moving to capitalism, it was about perfecting socialism. Lenin and his 1921 New Economic Policy were cited as "an ideological source of perestroika." The West, while admired for many of its economic achievements, still had the ills of inequality, unemployment, and a moneyed class that exerted excessive power for its own interests.

Signs of what later would be called *glasnost* occur early in Gorbachev's story when as Stavropol first secretary Gorbachev made some party documents public. He conducted regular briefings for the press. He even told the editor of the local official newspaper *Pravda* to make his own decisions on what to publish without routinely checking with the party leadership. "Wide, prompt and frank information," Gorbachev would later elaborate, "is evidence of confidence in the people and respect for their intelligence and feelings, and for their ability to understand events for themselves." Censorship was relaxed. Previously banned movies were released. Books such as *Dr. Zhivago* were put back in print. Magazines like *Ogonyok*, one of the oldest weeklies, reappeared and with independent editorial control, quickly built circulation into the millions.

In a particularly dramatic measure Gorbachev freed the internationally esteemed dissident Andrei Sakharov from internal exile. Sakharov, whom Brezhnev had confined incommunicado to the closed city of Gorki, tells the story of authorities showing up at his home on December 15, 1986, to install a telephone (he had been denied one as part of his confinement) and telling him that he'd get a call the next morning from Mikhail Sergeyevich. "You can return to Moscow. The decree of the Presidium of the Supreme Soviet will be rescinded." Gorbachev sprang this on likely opponents in the Politburo and pulled it off without tipping off the KGB.

Unlike perestroika and glasnost, Gorbachev had given few hints that he had fundamental changes in mind for Soviet foreign policy. In his acceptance remarks to the Politburo he spoke of increasing "the economic and military might of the motherland." This sounded a lot like Andropov who, notwithstanding traces of glasnost and perestroika, had held that peace "can only be upheld by relying on the invincible might of the Soviet armed forces." Foreign Minister Gromyko was known as "Mr. Nyet" for his skepticism about cooperation with the United States. But Gorbachev knew that the domestic system could not be revitalized as long as Cold War policies were pursued abroad: "Perestroika and the fundamental reform of both our economic and political systems would have been impossible without the corresponding changes in Soviet foreign policy and the creation of propitious international conditions . . . This understanding was the starting-point for everything."

Those changes in Soviet foreign policy were to be nothing less than the end of the Cold War. Four elements were integral to the vision: ending the nuclear arms race, getting out of Afghanistan, liberalizing/liberating Eastern Europe, and laying the basis for a post–Cold War world. Although none of these actions were altruistic, none were the tactical deception that American and other skeptics claimed of making the Soviets leaner and meaner and ever more equipped to pursue malicious interests. The Gorbachev worldview, with concepts such as humanistic universalism, was very much the statesmanship of shared, not just national, interests. "We want a world free of war, without arms races, nuclear weapons and violence; not only because this is an optimal condition for our internal development. It is an objective global requirement that stems from the realities of the present day."

HOW Gorbachev played the key role in ending the Cold War

The late 1970s through the early 1980s had seen the Cold War heat up. The December 1979 invasion of Afghanistan was the first Soviet use of overt military force since the 1968 invasion of Czechoslovakia. President Jimmy Carter suspended Senate ratification of the second Strategic Arms Limitation Treaty (SALT II), signed with Brezhnev just months earlier. He imposed economic sanctions including those on grain exports, which amid Soviet harvest failures had come to account for 80 percent of Soviet grain imports. He withdrew the American team from the upcoming 1980 Moscow Summer Olympics. He proclaimed the Carter Doctrine and threatened to respond militarily to any Soviet incursions further into the Persian Gulf region.

Notwithstanding such toughening up, and with domestic economic stagflation (high unemployment and high inflation) a major factor, Carter lost his November 1980 bid for reelection to Ronald Reagan. Reagan made clear that he was not interested in détente, be it the Carter or the Nixon-Kissinger-Ford version. The Soviets "lie and cheat," President Reagan baldly put it in his very first press conference. They were "unrelenting" in their military buildup. Their hand was in "all the unrest that is going on. If they weren't engaged in this game of dominoes, there wouldn't be any hot spots in the world." In powerful rhetorical flourishes, he declared that the Soviets were headed for "the ash heap of history" (June 1982 speech to the British Parliament) and that they were "the focus of evil in the modern world" (March

1983 speech to the National Association of Evangelicals). His defense policies set out to close the "window of vulnerability" that he claimed had been opened up by the combined effects of the Soviet nuclear buildup and defense neglect under Carter. This included the Strategic Defense Initiative (SDI) for building an ostensibly impenetrable nationwide defense umbrella against nuclear attack. Secretary of State George Shultz recounts that "relations between the superpowers were not simply bad, they were virtually non-existent." Able Archer '83, a NATO exercise simulating a nuclear war in Europe, was seen in the Kremlin as cover for a nuclear surprise first strike, setting off counter-maneuvers that brought the countries close to the nuclear brink.

Nor was concern about the risks of war only on the Soviet side. Peace movements spread in the West declaiming this "American cowboy" recklessness. Within the United States the nuclear freeze movement gained traction, including a June 1982 protest with 750,000 people marching in New York City from the United Nations to Central Park. *The Day After*, a made-for-television movie about life after a nuclear war, was watched by over 100 million people and still stands as the most viewed television movie ever. Yet Reagan was reelected in 1984 by a landslide. "The Bear in the Woods," showing a prowling grizzly bear with the ominous narration "Some say the bear is tame. Some say it is vicious. Since no one knows, isn't it smart to be as strong as the bear, if there is a bear?" was one of his most successful television ads.

In April 1985, a few months after Reagan's reelection—and a month after Gorbachev came to power—the Pentagon issued the study "Soviet Military Power," which was full of exaggerated estimates and worst-case scenarios. In June the CIA reported that Gorbachev and his team might be new but they "are not reformers and liberalizers either in Soviet domestic or foreign policy." In this context, as one Soviet official put it, Gorbachev "needed courage to reverse the dominant mood in the top political echelon of the Soviet leadership."

The intra-Kremlin mood was to just ride out Reagan's second term. But with his sense of so much of his perestroika and glasnost agenda depending on at least a thaw in the Cold War, Gorbachev was determined to probe the possibilities even with Reagan. He moved quickly to establish his own team. By July 1985, "Mr. Nyet" had been replaced as foreign minister with Eduard Shevardnadze, a like-minded political ally and someone temperamentally able to deal with Western counterparts. New Thinking aides, such as Alexsandr Yakovlev, Anatoly Chernyaev, and Georgy Shakhnazarov, were brought in. Included also was Yevgeny Velikhov, a leading nuclear physicist in the Soviet Academy of Sciences recently named to Pope John Paul II's commission on the dangers of nuclear war. More of the "old think" were pushed out of the Kremlin and the military. Gorbachev worked the 27th Party Congress in March 1986 to get close to a 40 percent change in the Central Committee, including reformers as secretaries in key ministries such as industry and ideology.*

With his foreign policy team in place and a sense of a somewhat more receptive party, Gorbachev set out on his foreign policy agenda.

Ending the Nuclear Arms Race

Within a month of taking charge, Gorbachev took an initial arms control step, suspending deployment of Soviet SS-20 intermediate-range nuclear missile deployments aimed at Western Europe ("Euromissiles"). He next proposed 50 percent cuts in Soviet and American overall nuclear arsenals. These proposals were on the table when in November 1985, breaking the longest interval in over 20 years without a U.S.-Soviet summit, Gorbachev and Reagan met in Geneva. While no specific agreement was reached, they did issue a joint statement that "a nuclear war cannot be won and must never be fought." Given the tensions that had built up, this was important in reestablishing some common ground. And the two leaders hit it off better than many

---

* He did, though, make other appointments, such as elevating Yegor Ligachev within the Politburo and Boris Yeltsin as Moscow first secretary, who would over time turn against him.

expected. At the closing press conference Gorbachev stressed how "a great deal of time was spent in the private sessions [that] enable us to discuss a wide range of issues, looking one another straight in the eye." Back home Reagan told a group of newspaper columnists, "I think I'm some judge of acting, so I don't think he was acting. He, I believe, is just as sincere as we are."

The next Gorbachev-Reagan summit, held October 11–12, 1986, in Reykjavik, Iceland, did not go as well. Gorbachev came, as James Goldgeier put it, "armed with a surprise." Well beyond what had been discussed at Geneva, he proposed not just percentage cuts but the total elimination of nuclear weapons by the year 2000 as long as the United States agreed to limit efforts to develop the Strategic Defense Initiative (SDI). This was quite extraordinary. SALT and other prior arms control treaties had been largely to limit rates of growth in nuclear arsenals. Now total nuclear disarmament was on the table. SDI was the stumbling block. Gorbachev's concerns about SDI were not simply, as often contended, that this reputed technological leap would give the United States nuclear superiority. Even if the Soviets couldn't match the SDI technology, they could develop asymmetric countermeasures with decoys and chaff that would significantly reduce any confidence the United States could have in the reliability of its defensive shield. For Gorbachev, it was the larger vision of how nuclear disarmament would make both sides more secure and the world more peaceful.

The Reykjavik summit broke up with a sense of disarray, in the moment an ominous sense of crisis. "I was very disappointed—and *very* angry," Reagan wrote. Gorbachev was of the same sentiment. "My first, overwhelming intention had been to blow the unyielding American position to smithereens," which was what the Politburo had set as plan B. "If the Americans rejected the agreement, a compromise in the name of peace, we would denounce the U.S. administration and its dangerous policies as a threat to everyone in the world." Instead Gorbachev gave a masterful performance at the concluding press conference—with "flying colors," the German newsmagazine *Der Spiegel* characterized it—seizing the high ground

as he stressed his own determination to reach nuclear arms control
agreements.

Gorbachev and team kept going. Marshal Sergey Akhromeyev, military chief of staff, had undertaken a far-reaching review of Soviet military doctrine. Shortly after Reykjavik, in a speech at the Academy of
the General Staff, Akhromeyev revealed new doctrine by which "we are
prepared to dismantle the mechanism of military confrontation with
the United States and NATO in Europe" and "we stand for complete
liquidation of nuclear weapons in the world." The reaction among the
assembled officers was "incomprehension, bewilderment and alarm."
Even with the prestige Akhromeyev carried, including having served
with distinction on the Leningrad front during World War II, "accu-
sations just short of treason were hurled at me." *Krasnaya Zvezda* (*Red
Star*), the Soviet armed forces newspaper, editorialized against "the
illusions of people who, despite facts to the contrary, still believe ...
that the U.S. administration is capable of heeding the voice of reason."

Over in Washington, even though Reagan had held firm on SDI,
hawks were concerned that he seemed to share the vision of a world
free of nuclear weapons. Assistant Secretary of Defense Richard Perle
railed that his own president shared this "dream of a world without
nuclear weapons" but that such thinking was "a disaster, a total delu-
sion." The Joint Chiefs of Staff claimed that in a world without nuclear
weapons, they would need more Army divisions, more Navy antisub-
marine warfare capabilities, and more Air Force bombers and cruise
missiles. "The naysayers were hard at work, even in my own building,"
Secretary of State George Shultz would later lament.

Still Gorbachev persisted in trying to end the nuclear arms race.
He offered to de-link the Euromissiles issue from SDI and go for the
"zero option." The Soviet Union would remove all of its SS-20s and
other missiles aimed at Europe if the United States would remove all
of its missiles based there. Negotiations ultimately resulted in the
Intermediate-Range Nuclear Forces (INF) Treaty signed by Gorbachev and Reagan in December 1987 at a summit in Washington.
While the United States claimed victory based on how many more

missiles the Soviets cut, the INF Treaty also served Gorbachev's purposes. First, the weapons he gave up were targeted at U.S. allies, while
the weapons the United States gave up were targeted at the Soviet
Union itself, which helped with his hawks at home. Second, eliminat-
ing the Euromissile SS-20s removed a problem in efforts to improve
Soviet-European relations. Third, the willingness to make concessions
substantiated how serious Gorbachev was about broader nuclear arms
control.

Gorbachev also used the Washington summit to burnish his image
among the American public. Raisa's stylishness got much media
attention. Mikhail jumped out of his limousine along Connecticut
Avenue to shake hands with folks on the street. He also made the
media rounds and met with groups of academics, businesspeople,
celebrities, and the like. He chatted with Steven Spielberg and signed
a baseball for Joe DiMaggio. The rapport between him and Reagan,
tarnished at Reykjavik, was again growing. Their press conferences
were more joint than dueling. The banquet toasts went well beyond
token appreciation.

Nevertheless, American hawks kept insisting that Gorbachev
wasn't for real. Memos still came to the Oval Office like that from
CIA Deputy Director Robert Gates insisting that it still was "hard
to detect fundamental changes, currently or in prospect, in the way
the Soviets govern at home or in their principal objectives abroad."
As Reagan readied for his May 1988 reciprocating trip to Moscow,
briefing papers kept attributing Gorbachev's cooperative foreign policy principally to the Soviet domestic economic burden, shortchanging
the extent to which Gorbachev was seeking to end the Cold War. Reagan, to his credit, didn't totally buy in. When asked while he and Gorbachev were touring Red Square whether he still considered the Soviet
Union the evil empire, he responded "No." Sure, he had called them
that a few years before, but that was "another time, another era." He
still met with dissidents, gave a speech at Moscow State University on
freedom, and otherwise conveyed his critique of the communist way
of life. But as he boarded Air Force One to head home, he told the

Soviet Union general secretary how he and his wife Nancy not only "are grateful to you and Mrs. Gorbachev, but want you to know we think of you as friends."

Many observers believed that arms control would move ahead quickly when George H. W. Bush, who had been Reagan's vice president, won the 1988 presidential election. They were wrong. Some of the delay was to appease right-wing conservatives who had gotten worked up even against Reagan, let alone the more moderate Bush. It also reflected the extent to which the Bush team still held the skeptical is-he-for-real view of Gorbachev. Condoleezza Rice, then the National Security Council senior director for the Soviet Union, acknowledged the purpose was "to slow down what was widely seen as Ronald Reagan's too-close embrace of Mikhail Gorbachev." The policy review dragged out for most of the year, yielding little more than studies that even Secretary of State James H. Baker III dismissed as "mush." This was despite a May 1989 Gorbachev proposal to eliminate an entire class of tactical nuclear weapons in Europe and a unilateral withdrawal of 500 warheads (pledging more if the United States reciprocated), despite another proposal for major conventional arms reductions, despite the Soviet withdrawal from Afghanistan, and despite warnings from U.S. Ambassador Jack Matlock in Moscow that Soviet hawks were using Bush's foot-dragging against Gorbachev. "Washington Fumbles" is how Matlock titles this chapter of his memoirs; "The Lost Year" is Gorbachev aide Chernyaev's chapter title. Just as when Gorbachev had been doing well with the United States it helped him at home, when he wasn't it hurt him. This lost year for nuclear arms control also was when economic problems mounted, revolution swept Eastern Europe, and some of the Soviet republics grew restive. Old Brezhnevites on the right were pulling Gorbachev to slow down, Boris Yeltsin on the left pushing him to speed up.

Finally in December 1989, Bush and Gorbachev met off the coast of the Mediterranean island of Malta. But it would not be until July 1991 that they finalized the Strategic Arms Reduction Treaty (START), making deep cuts in offensive nuclear weapons. While these were unprecedented cuts, they were well short of the 50 percent that had been on the table in the Gorbachev-Reagan talks, let alone full disarmament.

Getting out of Afghanistan

Afghanistan was not a heroic defense of comrades; it was, Gorbachev bluntly stated in a February 1986 speech to the 27th Party Congress, a "bleeding wound." The imagery was intentionally chosen to convey what the war was doing to the Soviet body politic as a whole. Casualties approached 75,000 (comparison: American casualties in Vietnam were about 58,000). Red Army morale was battered. Jihadists were crossing into Central Asian republics. The UN General Assembly condemned the war. In New Thinking terms getting out was "a reflection of our current political thinking, our new up-to-date vision of the world . . . If the arms race, which we are so insistently seeking to halt—with some success—is mankind's insane rush to the abyss, then regional conflicts are bleeding wounds capable of causing spots of gangrene on the body of mankind."

Gorbachev did initially escalate, telling the military it had a year to achieve victory. But this was more political maneuvering than strategic direction. He carefully avoided saying the war was a mistake from the beginning. But to make his point that continuing it would be even worse, he read the Politburo some heartbreaking letters from soldiers and their families: "International duty? In whose name? . . . Is it worth the lives of our boys, who don't even know why they were sent there, what they are defending, killing old people and children? And how can you (the Soviet leadership) send green recruits against professional killers, well trained and armed?" He met with Afghan Communist leader Babrak Karmal, telling him it was time for an Afghanization of the war, with Soviet aid but not troops. Karmal resisted and was soon replaced by Mohammad Najibullah. On February 9, 1988, Gorbachev went on Soviet television announcing that troop withdrawal would begin in May and all troops would be out within a year. The last Soviet combat troops left Afghanistan on February 15, 1989.

The argument is frequently made that CIA aid to the Afghan *muja-hideen*, particularly surface-to-air Stinger missiles, forced the Soviets to get out of Afghanistan. U.S. aid did make the bleeding wound bleed all the more, but the Stingers weren't as target effective as the popular image conveyed, "a mixed bag at best" according to the authoritative *Jane's Defense Weekly*. Moreover, while the decision to supply Stingers was made in 1985, they weren't operational until spring 1987, by which time the chain of decisions leading to withdrawal was well on its way. And given what has happened in Afghanistan in the years since, with the safe haven provided to Al Qaeda and Osama bin Laden for the planning of 9/11 and the longest war in U.S. history that has followed, it is hard to argue that the United States won.

Liberalizing/Liberating Eastern Europe

The Brezhnev Doctrine, as laid out in August 1968 when Soviet military forces invaded Czechoslovakia to crush the Prague Spring, was that a threat to any socialist country was "a threat to the security of the socialist commonwealth as a whole." As a member of the delegation Brezhnev sent to Prague, Gorbachev toed the line. Privately, though, he told Zdenek Mlynar, his Czech friend from university days and a Prague Spring activist, that "different countries have the possibility to proceed along their own specific roads of development." As general secretary he sent early signals that while he had to go along with the Brezhnev Doctrine back then, he was not going to abide by it now.

Relations with Eastern Europe must change, he told his Ministry of Foreign Affairs in a May 1986 confidential speech. He delivered the same message later that year directly to Warsaw Pact leaders at a Moscow summit. Subsidizing the satellite states was yet another economic drain on perestroika. It would be that much harder to keep pushing glasnost at home if he helped out old-line communists in Eastern Europe. And they were a political liability for forging "a common European home" uniting West and East, as well as his broader vision for a post–Cold War world.

So on August 22, 1988, against the resistance of Polish communist leaders to a coalition government with Lech Walesa and Solidarity, Gorbachev told them to proceed. When days later the Hungarian foreign minister floated the tentative decision to open the border with Austria as a back door for East Germans seeking to transit to West Germany, Moscow did not object. The message was loud and clear when on October 25 Foreign Ministry spokesman Gennadi Gerasimov publicly stated that Moscow had shifted from the Brezhnev Doctrine to the "Sinatra Doctrine"—that bloc countries could "do it their way." The massive cuts Gorbachev ordered in the Soviet military presence in Eastern Europe of withdrawing 500,000 troops and disbanding six tank divisions were tangible reinforcement. And then on that fateful night of November 9, 1989, when the Berlin Wall came down, Soviet troops were under orders to stay in their barracks. Along with the hosannas in the Western press came this statement from the official Soviet news agency Tass: "The pulling down of the Berlin Wall, which has symbolized the division of Europe for many years, is surely a positive and important fact."

President George H. W. Bush showed admirable restraint the night the Berlin Wall fell. As the *Washington Post*'s Don Oberdorfer recounted, "Bush called reporters to the Oval Office for an on-camera reaction that was positive but so restrained in comparison with the almost delirious joy that was seen on television that his questioners and viewers found it odd. With Gorbachev in mind, Bush said, 'We are handling it in a way where we are not trying to give anybody a hard time.'" There was to be no dancing on the Berlin Wall, at least not by the president of the United States.

The toughest and most telling issue was German unification. The legacy of World War II was especially powerful with regard to the country that had invaded the Soviet Union. By February 1990, Gorbachev told German Chancellor Helmut Kohl that unification was up to the Germans to decide. When the official unification ceremonies were held November 9, 1990, the one-year anniversary date of the fall of the Berlin Wall, Gorbachev was in attendance. Gorbachev admits in his memoirs that he didn't foresee "the course of events and the problems the German question would eventually create." He wanted reform; he got revolution. His intent had been to liberalize Eastern Europe, not necessarily liberate it. Kremlin hard-liners who had been concerned over Poland, Hungary, and Czechoslovakia were outraged over a unified Germany, the country that within their lifetime had invaded theirs, inflicting over 20 million deaths, becoming a member of NATO. Still Gorbachev stuck to nonintervention and conciliation.

No doubt U.S. and Western European responses would have been much more oppositional if Gorbachev had tried to crack down. But here, too, he did have choices. Had he not given the signals he did before 1989, the revolutions may not have happened when they did and how they did. The pressures were there, the economies in distress, the people growing restive, the old guard leaders more and more out of touch. But this would not have been the first time countries with problems managed to keep going. Even if that had only been for a few years, who knows what the dynamics would have been? Gorbachev created the more permissive environment that was conducive to, if not an incentive for, Eastern European peoples to have the courage to take to the streets. Once they did and began to go faster and further than he had intended, Gorbachev could have tried to limit things. He may not have succeeded. But he could have tried. He didn't. He really meant it when he said the Brezhnev Doctrine was over, that people had freedom of choice, and that every nation had that inalienable right to determine its own future independently.

Laying the Basis for a Post–Cold War World

The 1970s' nuclear arms negotiations were about limiting the arms race, thus the label Strategic Arms *Limitation* Talks and acronym SALT. The 1980s and 1990s were about reducing and even ending nuclear weapons, thus the label Strategic Arms *Reduction* Talks (START). And whereas the détente of the 1970s was about the relaxation of East-West tension, the effort of the 1980s and 1990s was toward fuller normalization of East-West relations. Tracing back to impressions formed through his earlier life travels, Gorbachev just did not see the West as an inveterate adversary. The rapport he developed with President Reagan and other Western leaders reinforced this sense of commonality.

Soviet cooperation against Saddam Hussein's August 1990 invasion of Kuwait was especially telling. On the day that Saddam invaded Kuwait, Secretary of State Baker and Soviet Foreign Minister Shevardnadze happened to be in the Siberian city of Irkutsk for formal meetings and a fishing trip. At their hastily called joint press conference Shevardnadze was quite candid. Saddam had been a longtime Soviet ally, making this "a rather difficult decision for us." But "this aggression is inconsistent with the principle of new political thinking and in fact with the civilized relations between nations." In his memoirs Baker reflected on how extraordinary it was that the Soviet Union was "actively engaging in joining the United States in condemning one of its staunchest allies." It was as if "the world had just turned upside down." Even though Iraq had been a longtime Soviet ally, Gorbachev instructed his UN ambassador to vote for UN Security Council Resolution 678 authorizing the use of force if Iraq did not withdraw from Kuwait by January 15. He did try to dissuade President Bush from resorting to force and dispatched his foreign policy aide Yevgeny Primakov to Baghdad for eleventh-hour diplomacy on terms that differed from the U.S. position. Overall, though, Soviet cooperation with the United States against one of its own allies, on an issue in which U.S. interests were more threatened than its own, was an enormous indication of not just ending the old conflict but also of forging a broader and deeper basis for cooperation.

Taking this new cooperation further, the United States and the Soviet Union cosponsored a broad Arab-Israeli Middle East peace conference in Madrid, Spain, in October 1991. For decades the two superpowers had vied for influence in the Middle East. During the October 1973 Yom Kippur War, they had come close to nuclear war. Now here they were writing a joint letter of invitation to Israel and its Arab adversaries: "The United States and the Soviet Union are prepared to assist the parties to achieve a just, lasting and comprehensive peace settlement . . . Toward that end, the president of the U.S. and the president of the USSR invite you to a peace conference, which their countries will co-sponsor, followed immediately by direct negotiations."

All along Gorbachev had seen relations with Western Europe as having their own value, not as simply a subset of relations with the United States. "We are Europeans," Gorbachev stated. "The history of Russia is an organic part of the great European history." He kept a busy schedule of meetings with European leaders. He praised British Prime Minister Thatcher for "honestly trying to help us mobilize the West's help for perestroika." He worked with French President François Mitterrand on a number of European issues. He was close with Felipe Gonzalez, Spanish prime minister and Socialist Party leader, who influenced his thinking in a social democratic direction. He found that common ground with German Chancellor Kohl. The Treaty on Conventional Armed Forces in Europe (CFE), signed in November 1990 in Paris, was the troops and armor complement to the INF treaty. These negotiations traced back to the 1970s, but without much progress until the Gorbachev era. Conventional forces weren't taken down to zero; countries needed their armies for reasons other than the East-West rivalry. But they were ratcheted down to levels that reflected the end of the Cold War. The reference in Gorbachev's 1989 speech to the European Parliament speech to "a vast economic space from the Atlantic to the Urals" was a sense of the potential benefits of greater economic interchange.

Gorbachev also had in mind a broader agenda. In the new "dialectics of present-day development," it was less about Marxist-Leninist class conflict than "the growing tendency towards interdependence of the states of the world community." In his memoirs Secretary of State Shultz quoted from Gorbachev's toast at a State Department luncheon during the 1987 Washington summit:

> Urging us on is the will of hundreds of millions of people, who are beginning to understand that as the twentieth century draws to a close, civilization has approached a dividing line, not so much

between different systems and ideologies, but between common sense and mankind's feelings of self-preservation on the one hand, and irresponsibility, national egoism, prejudice—in short, the old thinking—on the other.

In another statement Gorbachev sounded downright Wilsonian:

Mankind has realized that it has had enough wars and it is time to put an end to them for good. Two World Wars, the exhausting Cold War and the minor wars which have cost and are still costing millions of lives—this is more than a sufficient price to pay for adventurism, ambition and the neglect of the other's rights and interests.

And well before Al Gore:

Another no less obvious reality of our time is the . . . critical condition of the environment, of the air basin and the oceans, and of our planet's traditional resources which have turned out not to be limitless.

And more of what we have come to know as the twenty-first-century global agenda:

I mean old and new awful diseases and mankind's common concern: how are we to put an end to starvation and poverty in vast areas of the Earth? I mean the intelligent joint work in exploring outer space and the world ocean and the use of the knowledge obtained to the benefit of humanity.

No wonder when he pulled much of this together in his December 1988 speech to the United Nations General Assembly that the *Washington Post* called this speech "as remarkable as any ever delivered at the UN . . . changes the rules the world has lived by for four decades."

Mikhail Gorbachev would keep working to help build this post–Cold War era throughout the rest of his life. But he would have less time than he thought to keep doing so as president of the Soviet Union.

The same day he was giving the UN speech, a massive earthquake hit Armenia. Gorbachev dashed home. As he toured the stricken area, he was asked by a reporter his views on Armenia-Azerbaijan tensions over Nagorno-Karabakh, a self-contained territory within Azerbaijan with a majority Armenian population. Rather than simply deflecting with praise for the heroic rescuers and reiterating his pledge to provide aid, he delved into the politics of the Nagorno-Karabakh issue, criticizing the Armenian position. He went back to Moscow and made little effort to stay in public view and otherwise show concern and commitment for the tens of thousands killed and an estimated 400,000 left homeless. Amid such death and displacement, this was not the time for a leader to be seen as insensitive and detached. The leadership skills that served him so well in international forums were failing him at home.

Other problems also were mounting. Perestroika was not delivering economically. Prices on basic necessities were being kept steady but only with mounting pressure on the budget: butter was selling at 3 rubles 40 kopecks per kilogram but cost 8 rubles 20 kopecks to produce; beef 1 ruble 50 kopecks but 5 rubles to produce. Per capita income increased only modestly, never getting above half that of Western Europe and only a third of that in the United States. And the gap was growing, as Western economies had started a recovery after years of recession. By early 1991 there were breadlines in Moscow.

Meanwhile nationalism was spreading from one Soviet republic to another. The Baltic republics Lithuania, Latvia, and Estonia were pushing for greater autonomy. In March 1990, Lithuania declared independence. In January 1991, in a secret plot hatched by the KGB and military hard-liners, the tanks that Gorbachev would not let roll in Eastern Europe rolled into the streets of the Lithuanian capital,

Vilnius, led by a special forces unit that massacred dozens. That the Lithuania crackdown was hatched behind Gorbachev's back cut both ways. He too had opposed Lithuanian independence, but not with military force. Public statements like that he only found out about it when it was over, "when they woke me up," added to the sense that he was losing control. Independence rumblings spread to Ukraine, Moldova, Belorussia, Turkmenistan, Tajikistan, Kazakhstan, and other parts of the Union of Soviet Socialist Republics. None of this was sitting well with hard-liners. They'd had their privileges threatened by perestroika, their political power undermined by glasnost, their sphere of influence stripped away by the Sinatra Doctrine, and now their Union of Soviet Socialist Republics was tearing itself apart.

While hard-liners were pushing back against what they saw as too much change too quickly, Boris Yeltsin was mobilizing critics on the left who felt Gorbachev was doing too little too slowly. The public was torn between wanting a better life and worrying about the uncertainties. Opinion polls showed that as late as December 1989 Gorbachev still had 49 percent full approval (plus 32 percent partial approval) in Russia and 52 percent full approval (with 32 percent partial approval) in the overall Soviet Union. But by December 1990 these figures had plummeted: in Russia he had only 14 percent full approval (although 38 percent still partial approval) and only 17 percent full approval (with 39 percent partial approval) in the overall Soviet Union.

On August 18, 1991, while Gorbachev was on his annual Black Sea respite, members of a self-appointed State Committee for the State of Emergency arrived at his villa. They sought to intimidate him into declaring emergency rule, which would turn them loose for "legitimate" repression. Gorbachev refused. They demanded his resignation. He refused. They put him under house arrest while telling the world he had taken so ill that he couldn't carry out his presidential duties. It was a coup. A number of his own appointees were among the *putschists*: KGB head Vladimir Kryuchkov, Defense Minister Dmitri Yazov, his own chief of staff, Valery Boldin. Others included Deputy Defense Minister Valentin Varennikov, who as commanding general of the Soviet forces in Afghanistan had opposed the withdrawal, and Marshal Sergey Akhromeyev, who once had been a strong supporter but became disillusioned—and who when the coup failed took the ultimate step of disillusionment by committing suicide.

In what would be his finest moment Boris Yeltsin took to the streets and rallied citizens against the coup. An iconic photo captured Yeltsin standing on the tank outside the Russian parliament building. The coup was reversed. Gorbachev returned to Moscow. But the political momentum was running against him. On August 21 Latvia declared its independence; on September 6 Estonia, September 21 Armenia, December 1 Ukraine. Yeltsin, having been elected in June to the newly created position of president of Russia, literally moved into the Kremlin alongside Gorbachev. On December 8, Yeltsin and his counterpart presidents of Ukraine and Belorussia (Belarus) declared that the Soviet Union ceased to exist and they would be replacing it with a Commonwealth of Independent States. Gorbachev protested against such a unilateral and unconstitutional move but to no avail. On December 25, Christmas Day, Gorbachev announced his resignation.

WHAT: Balance Sheet

In assessing how much credit goes to Gorbachev for the Cold War ending, three questions must be addressed:

How unique was Gorbachev and would another Soviet leader have made the same policy choices he did?

Oxford's Archie Brown is quite definitive on Gorbachev's high SARL ranking: no "politically conceivable alternative candidate for the General Secretary-ship in the mid-1980s would have acted in the same way." So too William Taubman: "Admirers marvel at his vision and his courage. Detractors . . . accuse him of everything from naiveté to treason. The one thing they all agree upon is that he almost single-handedly changed his country and the world." Andropov was reformist on the economy but his foreign policy views—"If we begin to make concessions, defeat would be inevitable"—reflected his KGB roots. Chernenko had even tried at the last minute to stop Gorbachev's December 1984 perestroika speech. Gorbachev constantly had to push against party vested interests (*nomenklatura*) who resisted giving up their sinecures and privileges. The 1991 massacre of Lithuanian protesters was not the first time the KGB and other hard-liners went behind Gorbachev's back with actions contrary to his policy line—and it would not be the last.

There were qualities of Gorbachev as a person (the "who") and elements of his vision (the "why") that had led to his unique statesmanship. His reformist roots, tracing all the way back to his positions in Stavropol in the 1950s and 1960s, and the sponsorship of the likes of Suslov and Andropov gave him his initial personal capital. The self-confidence always was there, as was the ambition, not unbridled but clearly driving him forward and guiding the way. He was, as his Foreign Minister Aleksandr Bessmertnykh (successor to Shevardnadze) put it, "very intellectual . . . and knowledgeable." Neither was this just in private and with leaders. His charisma was the talk of the 1987 Washington summit, that scene shaking hands on Connecticut Avenue, orchestrating press interviews with aplomb, benefiting also from the impressions his stylish wife, Raisa, made. In Western European countries he was more popular than their own leaders, let alone Ronald Reagan. East Germans greeted him with cheers of "Gorby! Gorby!" while conveying disdain for their own leader, Erich Honecker.

How much credit for the end of the Cold War goes to others, particularly Ronald Reagan?

To say Gorbachev deserves principal credit for ending the Cold War does not deny the roles of others. There were what Cornell's Matthew Evangelista calls "unarmed forces," the European and American peace movements of the early 1980s whose pressure helped temper Reagan's initial hard-line policies. Transnational groups such as Pugwash had built relationships over decades with intellectuals, activists, scientists, and others within the Soviet Union who came into positions of influence under Gorbachev. There were Eastern European leaders such as Lech Walesa and Vaclav Havel whose courage inspired and mobilized their peoples. So too did Pope John Paul II, the "Polish Pope." have an important role, his influence so great that the Brezhnev KGB conspired to assassinate him. There were Western European leaders who had helped to initially validate Gorbachev (British Prime Minister Thatcher), provided some quasi-kindred advice and cooperation (Socialists French President Mitterrand and Spanish Prime Minister Gonzalez), and worked with him on such tough issues as German unification (German Chancellor Kohl). There were the brave Soviet dissidents (Andrei Sakharov, Aleksandr Solzhenitsyn, Yuri Orlov, and numerous others) who kept the pressure on for decades.

And there was Ronald Reagan. Some give Reagan the lion's share of credit. They hold to the view that the pressure Reagan brought meant that any Soviet leader would have had to pursue the same policies. Milestones like Reykjavik were Reagan's triumphs. New Thinking was little more than giving in to U.S. pressure: the zero option on Euromissiles, getting out of Afghanistan, tearing down the Berlin Wall just as Reagan called for in a speech. We won the Cold War. They lost. Pure and simple. Reagan's grand strategy had worked.

At the other end of the spectrum are those who refuse to grant Reagan any credit. He was a warmonger and would have remained so had it not been for the political pressure from the peace movements. His dreamy belief in Star Wars-SDI made Reykjavik a huge missed opportunity, standing in the way of ending the nuclear arms race. The Reagan Doctrine stuck to a blind anticommunism that made many Third World conflicts even more deadly, squandering prospects for peace and keeping the United States on the side of leaders and movements like the Nicaraguan contras that could hardly be characterized as democratic.

Here too objective assessment lies in between. In many respects the Cold War ended the way George Kennan, he of the classic "Mr. X" telegram, had strategized back in 1946–1947, "the patient but firm and vigilant containment of Russian expansive tendencies" that over time would "bring about the gradual mellowing of Soviet power." In that respect every American administration since Truman shares in the credit. The additional squeeze exerted in Reagan's first term did impose added costs and did come at a particularly vulnerable time for Moscow. But economic squeeze is one thing, strangulation quite another. The CIA's own analysis of the Soviet economy was of having substantial problems but not "losing viability . . . an economic collapse in the USSR is not considered even a remote possibility."

Rather it was the shift to a more mixed and moderate strategy for which Reagan deserves his share of the credit. He had to take on some of his own political supporters to do so. His own Defense Secretary Caspar Weinberger and National Security Advisor John Poindexter considered the deep nuclear weapons cuts discussed at Reykjavik "a blunder of the greatest magnitude." The Joint Chiefs of Staff prepared a briefing conveying in no uncertain terms their concerns about the proposal for full elimination of ballistic missiles to which Reagan had come so close to agreeing. Conservatives in Congress and the Republican Party said they were "appalled." Democrats and liberals pushed on a few issues but, as with Nixon going to China, could not but be supportive of Reagan going to Moscow.

The extraordinary personal relationship Gorbachev and Reagan developed played a big part, arguably even more than with Kissinger and Zhou. Gorbachev says that by end of their first summit "I realized . . . that Ronald Reagan too was a man 'you could do business with.'" Reagan in his memoirs speaks to "something very close to a friendship . . . We could—and did—debate from opposite sides of the ideological spectrum. But there was a chemistry that kept our conversations on a man-to-man basis, without hate or hostility." That chemistry was especially poignant when on January 11, 2004, as the recently deceased Ronald Reagan lay in state in the U.S. Capitol rotunda, the honor guard cleared the way for "a vigorous senior citizen with a distinctive birthmark on his bald pate" to pay his respects. "I gave him a pat," Mikhail Gorbachev said, describing how he ran his hand over the Stars and Stripes–draped coffin.

Reagan was "critically important," as noted historian Melvyn Leffler struck the balance, "but Gorbachev was the indispensable agent of change." The choices still were Gorbachev's. He could have let the Soviet economy limp along keeping the *nomenklatura* sated with their own perks and keeping the lid on any political dissonance, just as his predecessors had done and just as all too many leaders in other countries have done. He chose to pursue perestroika and glasnost. He could have kept to 1970s' standard fare nuclear arms control. He chose to be more visionary about how deeply nuclear arsenals could be cut. He could have not sent permissive signals to Eastern Europe and could have intervened militarily. He chose to let Hungary open its borders, let the Berlin Wall come down, and let Germany unify and do so within NATO. He could have kept his agenda to managing the Cold War. He chose to articulate and take steps toward a post–Cold War new world order. In these and other ways, it was Gorbachev's statesmanship that deserves principal credit for the peaceful end of the Cold War.

Why didn't Gorbachev succeed more than he did?

Recall the three aspects we stressed in the Introduction of a vision providing the "why" of transformational change: (1) analytically identifying the problem (i.e., naming what's wrong with the present); (2) prescriptively providing a solution while laying out a better future; and (3) doing so while avoiding deeply rooted cultural taboos that can normatively delegitimize even a sound vision. Gorbachev did the first very well. He did the second pretty well. But he severely violated the third. He allowed his enemies to cast him as being against the Motherland, as not a true patriot. For all their differences, both Yeltsin on the left and the coup plotters on the right played this delegitimizing card. Gorbachev became such a pariah at home that more than 20 years later the Vladimir Putin–led Duma considered a bill to prosecute him for the "crime" of the collapse of the Union of Soviet Socialist Republics.

Gorbachev had three fundamental flaws in how he handled domestic politics. One was the inherent tension between the Communist

Party as his agent of change and its vested interests in the status quo. This was, as Archie Brown so aptly put it, like trying to be both the Pope and Martin Luther. A second was the halfway-ism of perestroika. Gorbachev and his team were indecisive on the scope and role of markets. They would determine some prices some of the time, but it wasn't very clear which ones and when. Private property was partially allowed but with limits and uncertainties. Economic decentralization was to be encouraged in the name of efficiency but this also facilitated profit skimming and black marketeering. Economic reforms were mandated but blocked from implementation. Third was the tension of opening up the political system for a more democratic Soviet Union while trying to keep it from giving license for questioning whether there should still be a Soviet Union. Gorbachev thought that nationalist pulls in the Soviet republics would be subsumed in and tempered by the overall perestroika-glasnost economic progress and greater political freedom. Yet this severely underestimated the potency of nationalism and identity as ideological forces in themselves and as forces manipulated by leaders seeking to ride them for their own power and position.

Gorbachev's case was very much a case of transformational leadership as "a dangerous activity," in the terms of Harvard's Ronald Heifetz and Marty Linsky. "You appear dangerous to people when you question their values, beliefs, or habits of a lifetime. . . Although you may see with clarity and passion a promising future of progress and gain, people will see with equal passion the losses you are asking them to sustain." Perestroika threatened those extracting economic gain from the old system. Nuclear arms control threatened the military-industrial complex. Glasnost undermined those who kept politics reined in. Normalizing relations with the West took the enemy and its manipulative utility away. Ceding Eastern Europe, and a unified Germany within NATO, ran counter to the buffer zone–sphere of influence lessons many drew from history. The crumbling of the Soviet Union itself got at bedrock senses of identity and national pride. For a political culture that so highly valued order, these were far-reaching and profound transformations. They drained the personal capital Gorbachev initially had.

Gorbachev also violated another Heifetz-Lipsky transformational leadership dictum in not keeping the opposition close. Admittedly that would have been hard to do. Those on the hard-line right were used to resorting to subterfuge. Yeltsin on the left had his own agenda and aspirations. Still one is struck by how somebody who had cultivated relationships so well on his way up—Kulakov, Suslov, Andropov—was so unperceptive of the machinations around him. The political skills that had served him so well in the past no longer did. When in June 1991 U.S. Ambassador Jack Matlock passed on a warning about a possible coup, Gorbachev expressed appreciation but reassured him "not to worry. I have everything well in hand." When President Bush personally phoned Gorbachev two nights later, he stuck to the same view, "a thousand percent impossible."

In his Christmas 1991 resignation, he said to his people and to the world:

> When I found myself at the head of the state it was already clear that all was not well in the country . . . The society was suffocating in the vise of the command-bureaucratic system, doomed to serve ideology and bear the terrible burden of the arms race . . . The process of renovating the country and radical changes in the world turned out to be far more complicated than could be expected . . . However, work of historic significance has been accomplished . . . We live in a new world. The Cold War has ended, the arms race has stopped, as has the insane militarization which mutilated our economy, public psyche and morals. The threat of a world war has been removed . . . I am leaving my post with apprehension, but also with hope.

The Cold War did end. Peacefully. As the Norwegian Nobel Committee stated in awarding Gorbachev the 1990 Nobel Peace Prize, this award was made "in recognition of the leading role he has played in the radical changes that have taken place in East-West relations. President Gorbachev has undoubtedly cooperated with other persons and other nations. But we recognize quite clearly that his manifold personal contributions and his efforts . . . have proved decisive."

TRUMP-PUTIN, TRUMP-XI, AND MAJOR POWERS STATESMANSHIP

In both the U.S.-China opening and the end of the Cold War, it was the combination of common policy ground developed, domestic politics effectively managed, and personal relationships forged that led to the breakthroughs. When I was working on this section of the book in the summer and fall of 2016, my thinking (I confess) was on how to make the policy-politics-personal dynamic work for a President Hillary Clinton–President Vladimir Putin relationship. Donald Trump's election as president added to the issues in U.S.-Russian relations. While U.S.-China relations got off to a less rocky start than feared from Trump's campaign China-bashing and transition feelers to Taiwan, tensions still are such that a Harvard professor titled his book *Destined for War*.

U.S.-Russia

As bad as U.S.-Russia relations are, calling it a new Cold War goes way too far. Whatever else the tensions are, they are not global, they are not as intensely ideological, and they are not casting the specter of nuclear war. The collaborative relationship of the mid-1980s through the 1990s and the genuinely warm leader-to-leader relations do seem a distant memory. Both sides have their narrative. On the Russian side: the United States has taken NATO expansion too far and too close to Russia's border, used force largely at its own discretion (Iraq

2003, Libya 2011), sought to overthrow governments of Russian allies (Ukraine, Syria), meddled in Russia itself through the guise of democracy promotion, and engaged in Beltway chest-thumping of Russia having been reduced to a second-rate power with nuclear weapons and oil wells. On the American side: Russia violated bedrock rules of the international system by annexing part of another country (Crimea), militarily intervening in neighboring countries (Georgia, Ukraine) and in support of Assad's brutal regime in Syria, staging military provocations against NATO allies, assassinating dissidents who flee the country, and hacking the U.S. 2016 presidential election.

If Putin continues to pursue the policies that he has over the past few years, there will be further breakdown, not renewed breakthrough. Russian forces remain in Ukraine and Syria. The September 2017 Zapad (West) military exercises were more provocative than exercises a few years earlier. Under the guise of setting orderly rules of the road for cyberspace, Russia pushed a proposal at the United Nations that would actually make authoritarian control and hacking of democracies easier. PBS *Frontline*'s October 2017 "The Putin Files" is a searing account of Putin's modus operandi.

Still, in a number of ways Putin's strategy shows signs of reaching a point of diminishing returns. The Ukraine conflict and provocations against NATO have strained relations, not just with the United States but with much of Europe. Continued military support for Syria's Bashar Assad, while having made some gains in the short run, risks making Russia responsible on an open-ended basis for stability in a country in which about the only long-term certainty is instability. Terrorist blowback from ISIS already has hit—for example, the April 2017 St. Petersburg metro bombing and the December 2016 assassination of the Russian ambassador to Turkey. With Islamist militants returning to Chechnya and elsewhere in the Caucasus, more terrorism may follow. Economically, between declining oil prices and the impact of U.S.-European sanctions, Russian GDP growth rates plunged to −2.8 percent in 2015. Translating this to a per capita basis, the drop was 42.5 percent from a peak of $15,553 to $8,947. Growth turned slightly positive in 2017 but with a long way back that required austerity measures in the 2017–2019 budgets.

That Putin is, as Brookings Institution experts Fiona Hill and Clifford Gaddy see it, "most of all . . . concerned about the economy" and open to collaboration with the West "when there is a mutual strategic interest" suggests a potential policy basis for getting relations back on track. Even that would entail what Georgetown Professor Angela Stent calls "limits of partnership," but even a limited partnership would have its value.

Politically, while Putin's approval rating remains sky high (e.g., 81 percent in a November 2017 poll), this is not without some underlying crosscurrents. His Ukraine policy still gets 63 percent support—but that's down 20 percent from where it was. Despite Kremlin efforts, reports of Russian casualties incurred in Syria keep seeping out, and they show numbers mounting. While it is important not to overstate how economic discontent plays out in a quasi-authoritarian political system, it was a significant factor in the downfall of both Gorbachev and Yeltsin. Those in the middle class with a positive view of their economic prospects dropped from 41 percent (2013) to 22 percent (2016). The percentage of people in poverty has grown at the fastest rate since the fall of the Soviet Union. In March 2017, truck drivers, not a particularly liberal group, staged a nationwide multiday strike. Mass anticorruption protests have been held not only in Moscow and St. Petersburg but also in 90 other cities across Russia's 11 time zones.

The United States would need to make its own moves toward common policy ground. Not as Trump at times has seemed inclined to do, way over on the Russian side of the divide, but also not by relegating Russia to second-class power status. Deter and coerce as needed while being open to compromises consistent with core U.S. interests. Seriously engage in what Henry Kissinger termed "a dialogue about the emerging world order" that has the goal of "develop[ing] a strategic concept for US-Russian relations within which the points of contention may be managed." Don't endorse Putin's strongman rule, but do face up to the reality driven home in the 2016 presidential election that two can play the game of trying to influence internal politics, and temper democracy promotion accordingly.

Within American politics the partisan nature of the Russia issue amid pro-Trump Russian election hacking and questionable associations of Trump aides and family with Russia, while raising major issues in their own right, could actually help support policy common ground. Traditional Republican hawkishness has been tempered by anti-Putin sentiment being equated with anti-Trump. Whereas only 10 percent of Democrats have a favorable view of Putin and only 28 percent support cooperation with Russia, 30 percent of Republicans view Putin favorably and 56 percent support cooperation with Russia. If Trump were to make a balanced effort at rapprochement, he'd have the Republican support that has eluded other presidents and peel off enough Democrats. Even if the effort is by a successor, including a Democrat, it would be hard for Republicans to so fully revert back to hawkishness as to be a major constraint. At the same time concerns about Trump being too soft on Putin have been sufficiently bipartisan that in July 2017 Congress toughened sanctions on Russia despite Trump's objections.

As to personal style, both Putin and Trump put a lot of weight on man-to-man interaction. There has been understandable concern about too much of a "bromance." Trump has an abiding admiration for authoritarians, which while not exclusively about Putin has seemed especially about him. At their first official meeting during the July 2017 G20 summit in Germany, Trump engaged Putin more than he did American allies. There is no expectation of either the depth of the Kissinger-Zhou relationship or the warmth of the Gorbachev-Reagan relationship. It is Putin the career operative and Trump the dealmaker. The optimistic scenario is that they can cut through considerations that might stand in the way of other leaders. The danger is that both have that combination of being thin-skinned and bullies, which can all too quickly blow a relationship apart.

U.S.-China

Even before Trump took office, a blue-ribbon commission warned that U.S.-China relations are "at a precarious crossroads." The ominous destined-for-war warning sees U.S.-China as the latest version of history's tense dance between an established power and an emerging one. By some counts 12 of the 16 such historical pairings, going back to Athens and Sparta in the Peloponnesian War through Britain and Germany in World War I, have ended in war. It's going to take statesmanship on both sides with a savvy mix of policy, politics, and the personal for U.S.-China to not become the thirteenth out of 17 global power transitions that ended in war.

"The Chinese Dream" is how President Xi Jinping conveys his overall policy approach. Its essence is greater prosperity at home and greater prominence internationally. By most every measure China has been increasing its power. Even a slightly slowed 6.7 percent 2016 GDP growth rate was well above most of the world. Its military has been expanding and modernizing. It plays a more extensive global diplomatic role. Its Asian Infrastructure Investment Bank (AIIB) seeks to rival the World Bank. It has been wielding increased soft power through more than 500 Confucius Institutes around the world teaching the Chinese language and promoting Chinese culture. Much of this greater power has been exercised in ways that can be considered standard competition among major powers. Some aspects, such as China's extensive sovereignty claims and military bases being built in the South China Sea, demonstrate a more aggressive nationalism. Xi Jinping's prioritization in his October 2017 Party Congress speech of greater investment in the military fed these and other concerns.

As with Russia, China may decide to pursue policies not conducive to improved relations with the United States. Here too my intent is less to predict than to make the case for another possible pathway. In that regard Xi also has seen how actions that raise concerns of China seeking its own Asian regional hegemony and broader global dominance have precipitated pushbacks not just from the United States but also from many other countries. This has been especially true in Asia. Also in Africa, China already has been encountering resistance from governments and societal groups that see its efforts to manipulate economic relations for political influence as the latest in a long line of exploitative imperialists. On the other hand, when China has been more collaborative in its diplomacy, its reputation has been enhanced and its interests have been better served. With Trump unsettling so many in the international community with his volatility and America First priorities, China has much to gain from policies that position it as the steadier one.

For its part the balance the United States needs to strike is in neither trying to maintain regional preponderance nor pulling out of Asia America First–style. Asian allies need reassurance that the United States will help check China from throwing its weight around too much. But many also are wary of getting caught in the middle of a U.S.-China tit-for-tat. They look to American military presence and diplomatic standing for deterrence and pressure when China becomes more assertive in the region, but also watch that the United States does not overplay its hand in ways that risk damaging their own interests in relations with China. Indeed, the greatest threats to America's standing in the region may well be self-inflicted, as with Trump's decision to back out of the Trans-Pacific Partnership, his penchant for insulting allies such as Australian Prime Minister Malcolm Turnbull, and his mistaking bombast for firmness against the North Korean nuclear weapons threat. Moreover, when the United States and China work together, as on the 2015 Iran nuclear nonproliferation and 2015 Paris climate change agreements (the latter being before Trump reneged on the U.S. commitment), the international community has been well served.

Both countries have political constraints to overcome. As part of his efforts to consolidate power Xi has cloaked himself in Chinese nationalism. He has been cracking down on even limited political freedoms at home. He repeatedly speaks of China reclaiming its historical greatness. This entails some riding the tiger in not letting things go as far as some would take them. Like People's Liberation Army Colonel Liu Mingfu says in his book, *The China Dream: Great Power Thinking and Strategic Posture in the Post-American Era*, with its message that America is standing in the way of China "becoming the strongest nation in the world" has gone through nine editions: We are not just rising, we will replace you as the major power. The Pacific was your lake, it is now ours. We again will be the Middle Kingdom, the center of the Earth, as we were centuries ago. In promoting the English translation, Amazon calls it "the definitive book for understanding the 'hawk' version of China's national destiny debate."

Counterpart American confrontationalism predates the Trump administration. In summer 2015, when Colonel Liu came to Washington to promote his book, he was hosted at a Georgetown dinner party with over 100 guests by Michael Pillsbury, a former Reagan administration defense official and author of *The Hundred-Year Marathon: China's Secret Strategy to Replace America as the Global Superpower*. The dinner party was less to fete Colonel Liu than to advertise his views in an I-told-you-so vein. While differing on who should come out on top, these hawks-of-a-feather share a view of where the U.S.-China relationship is going. Steve Bannon and others pushing aggressive economic nationalism, through Breitbart.com even without Bannon there and other mechanisms, take this even further, seeing us already at economic war with China and the true test of our times being what we do "to confront China on its rise to world domination."

Both publics have stayed in the middle. Whereas 52 percent of Chinese surveyed see the United States as intent on preventing China from becoming more powerful, the same poll showed a 54 percent to 40 percent margin of favorable views of the United States. Generationally the positive view was more characteristic of younger Chinese: 59 percent among 18–29-year-olds, 29 percent among those over 50. The American public shows a similar mix. It does have concerns about China: only 34 percent see China as dealing responsibly with world problems, and 56 percent see its role in Asia negatively. Yet on a list of 20 critical threats, both Chinese military power and its economic power were ranked in the bottom half. When U.S. policy choices were posed as containment versus engagement, 67 percent preferred engagement.

On the personal front, Trump and Xi got off to a better start than many had feared. Concern remains, though, that underneath the niceties of their direct encounters Xi and his team are wary of Trump's unpredictability. As an experienced China watcher reported amid the 2017 North Korea crisis, the Chinese greatly value *kaopu*, meaning reliability, yet Trump keeps showing himself to be *bu kaopu*, or unreliable. Xi and Trump have very different temperaments. Xi is deliberate, Trump is brash. Xi values respect shown for China's history and traditions, Trump exudes American boosterism and has little regard for history or any other cultures. It is worth reflecting back on the "what is your theory of history/here's mine" exchanges between Kissinger and Zhou and how such in-depth meetings provided broad understanding beyond issue-specific talking points and how valuable such meetings could be between leaders of the twenty-first century's two major powers.

———

I cannot but be wary about both these relationships. Some of my wariness relates to Putin and Xi, much to Trump. It may well be as *Financial Times* columnist Ed Luce speculates that "Trump is too narcissistic to change for the better." There are challenges. Some conditions are constraining, some conducive. The choices are there to be made. Whether Trump and his counterparts will make the right choices remains to be seen. What we do know is that constructive statesmanship by the leaders of the major powers is crucial to twenty-first-century global peace and security.

BUILDING INTERNATIONAL INSTITUTIONS

HISTORIAN PAUL KENNEDY CALLED IT "A DEVELOPMENT unique in the story of humankind," the initiative begun early in the twentieth century "to create international organizations to promote peace, curb aggression, regulate diplomatic affairs, devise an international code of law, encourage social development, and foster prosperity." Other than for the most starry-eyed world federalists, this effort would reduce but not eliminate the dynamics of major power geopolitics. The kinds of breakthroughs we discussed in the previous chapters still were essential for avoiding war. But so too there was a need, as political scientist Robert Keohane stressed, for "international institutions . . . [to] be components of any lasting peace." As important as so many of these international organizations are—by the end of the twentieth century there were over 6,000 such organizations—with its mandate "to save succeeding generations from the scourge of war . . . to maintain international peace and security," none is more central than the United Nations.

Imperfections aside, the UN has three unique strengths. It has global membership: 51 states at its founding in 1945, 193 today. It has a normative legitimacy that no other institution or major power can convey: the international community's ultimate "seals of approval and disapproval." Its mandate encompasses the full global peace and security agenda, from war prevention to conflict resolution, from human rights protection to sustainable development, and much in between. An effective UN thus is not sufficient for twenty-first-century global peace and security. But it is necessary.

Chapter 3 starts with **Woodrow Wilson** and the League of Nations, the UN predecessor that was to be the pillar on which the peace to end war was to be built. Wilson and his League, though, failed—and for reasons less about Americans blindly bent on retreating into isolationism after World War I than Wilson's own who-why-how-what that made for fundamental flaws in his design for the League and mismanagement of the U.S. domestic politics. **Franklin D. Roosevelt** succeeded where Wilson had failed. He led the way in creating the United Nations. He ensured that the United States would be a member. But his untimely death meant that he never got to play a direct role in bringing his ideas to fruition.

As things turned out, the first UN secretary-general, Trygve Lie, had such a difficult time in the position that he left calling it "the most impossible job in the world." Lie's successor, **Dag Hammarskjöld** (Chapter 4), proved differently. Far beyond any other secretary-general, Hammarskjöld made the position one of genuine leadership—a "secular Pope," as he and others called it—and showed what a strong, assertive, and determined secretary-general could contribute to global peace and security, and how essential that type of statesmanship is to making the United Nations what it needs to be in the twenty-first century.

3

Wilson and FDR:
Failure of the League of Nations,
Birth of the United Nations

WOODROW WILSON:
THE PEACE THAT DIDN'T END WAR, 1918–1919

WHO was Woodrow Wilson?

He was born Thomas Woodrow Wilson on December 28, 1856, in Staunton, Virginia. His father, Reverend Joseph Ruggles Wilson, was stern and demanding; his mother, Janet Woodrow Wilson, was the daughter of a Congregationalist minister. Religion was very much a part of the household. The family prayed twice a day, said grace before meals, and read the Bible at home. While worship-based religiosity would fade over the course of his life, Woodrow (he dropped Thomas as a young adult) carried forward a very strict sense of morality grounded in three core beliefs: "God judges man by standards of perfection, to which man must aspire; life is a constant struggle of good against evil; there is no room for compromise in that struggle."

The family also instilled a strong and lasting sense of Southern identity, cultural and racist. In 1859, the family moved from Staunton, Virginia, deeper into the South for his father's new position at the First Presbyterian Church of Augusta (Georgia). On January 6, 1861, a few months after Abraham Lincoln was elected president, Reverend Wilson preached on "Mutual Relations of Masters and Slaves as Taught in the Bible." When months later the Civil War started and the national Presbyterian Church equated secession with treason, calling on all ministers to affirm their allegiance to the federal government, Reverend Wilson became one of the organizers of the Presbyterian Church of the Confederate States of America.

While Woodrow would become the only American president to have been a university professor and the first to have been a university president,* as a child he didn't learn to read until about age 11. He progressed enough to get into Princeton, where he did everything from debate club to managing editor of *The Princetonian* newspaper to running the Baseball Association and the Football Association (but leaving the play on the field to others). After Princeton he was accepted for a political science Ph.D. at Johns Hopkins University seeking "to contribute to our literature what no American has ever contributed, studies in the philosophy of our institutions, not the abstract and occult, but the practical and suggestive, philosophy which is at the core of our governmental methods." Indeed his dissertation, published as the book *Congressional Government*, has remained a classic to this day. After various professorships, at 46 years old he was named Princeton president, the first person who was not a minister to hold the position. He took the role on with gusto, pushing curricular reform that became the model for modern liberal arts education. He embraced the role of public intellectual, traveling around the country and spreading these new educational ideals.

His fast track continued when in 1910 he was recruited by Democratic Party bosses to run for governor of New Jersey. As much as he had thrived on university life, he harbored ambitions to enter politics: "I do feel a very real regret that I have been shut out from my heart's *first*—primary—ambition and purpose, which was, to take an active, if possible a leading, part in public life, and strike out for

---

* Dwight Eisenhower was the other, having been president of Columbia University.

myself, if I had the ability, a *statesman's* career." He drew large crowds on the stump, showing how he could connect with average people well beyond what was expected from a pince-nez–wearing academic. On November 8, he was elected governor of New Jersey by a sizable margin of 54 percent to 43 percent.

Wilson characteristically stressed that while now in politics he was above it. "The future is not for parties 'playing politics,'" he declared, "but for measures conceived in the larger spirit, pushed by parties whose leaders are statesmen not demagogues, who love not their offices, but their duty and their opportunity for service." Such high-mindedness aside, in his first year in office he worked with the Democrat-majority legislature to pass more progressive legislation than any state in the country. Soon this less than one term governor, indeed someone with barely a year's experience in political office, was moving into a campaign for president of the United States. As both a Northerner by professional life and Southerner in his roots, Wilson's profile had considerable breadth of appeal. The convention was an epic political battle, with delegates split between Wilson, House Speaker "Champ" Clark of Missouri, and two other candidates. Among those helping Wilson in the mano-a-mano convention floor politics was a 30-year-old New York State senator named Franklin Delano Roosevelt, who got a local manufacturer to make 300 Wilson buttons to match those Clark supporters were wearing in their own floor demonstration. Finally, on the forty-sixth ballot Wilson got the nomination.

The general election was an unprecedented one. Republican incumbent William Howard Taft was running for reelection. But Theodore Roosevelt, Taft's predecessor and earlier patron, had formed his own Bull Moose Party. Eugene Debs was the Socialist Party candidate, as he had been in 1904 and 1908. Wilson held his own, by some accounts even doing better than Theodore Roosevelt, he of the bully pulpit, in speechifying. His New Freedom platform was no less progressive, including issues like trust-busting, where the esteemed lawyer Louis D. Brandeis was an advisor. On Election Day he won a 42 percent plurality in the popular vote, with Roosevelt (27.4 percent) and Taft (23.2 percent) splitting what could have been a Republican majority and Debs doubling his prior totals to 6 percent. In the Electoral College it was a Wilson landslide with 435 of the 531 electoral votes, more than any presidential candidate ever.

Wilson brought to his presidency a mix of personal strengths and weaknesses. He derived his personal capital from two main sources. One was his reputation as a man of ideas, having risen meteorically as a scholar and teacher and university president. He was an innovator, looking for new and better ways to be a professor, to run a university, or to govern a state with a long tradition of corruption. And he cast much of this in terms of virtue, positioning himself above politics even when in it. His first inaugural address had a strong moral element, railing against "the evil that has come with the good" and stressing the duty "to cleanse . . . to purify . . . a light that shines from the hearthfire of every man's conscience and vision of the right."

While his blend of the intellectual and the spiritual was inspiring at times, and one of Wilson's strong political skills was as an orator, it also fed a self-righteousness and arrogance that impeded a basic political skill, the art of compromise. When as Princeton president his plan for reforming student life was opposed by a faculty member whom he considered a close friend, he severed the friendship. As New Jersey governor he went on for three hours lecturing the legislature on the merits of an election reform bill in which they had little interest. "I may lose the battle over this bill," he pontificated, "but you cannot deprive me of power so long as I steadfastly stand for what I believe to be the interests and legitimate demands of the people themselves." When his presidential campaign manager asked what position he would receive in the new administration, Wilson rebuffed him, saying that "God ordained that I should be the next president of the United States. Neither you nor any other mortal could have prevented that." And as we'll see with the Versailles Treaty and League of Nations, with the added confidence of having guided the nation through war and having been hailed in the streets of one European city after another as the great savior of peace, he was more sure than ever of his own rightness and righteousness, an "arrogant denial of anybody's right to criticize him," as a leading figure of the day put it.

As often is the case with supreme self-confidence in one's own intellect and virtuousness, Wilson had an underlying insecurity. In his medical and psychobiography Edwin Weinstein brings out Wilson's tendency "to equate defeat with personal failure, and setbacks resulted in feelings of depression and a temporary doubting of his abilities." Wilson's own doctor, Cary Grayson, observed that when someone pushed Wilson to do something he seriously disagreed with, "he ceases to have any liking for that person." The few friends he had grew fewer, affecting not just his personal life but also limiting a valuable political resource.

His arrogance also contributed to his racism. On the causes of the Civil War he subscribed to the view that the Southern claim of states' rights on slavery was consistent with the Constitution. As president, Wilson did expand some parts of the civil service where Negroes would be employed on their side of the segregation divide. He also pushed back on some midlevel appointments that the most ardent segregationists opposed. But such actions were largely incidental to his administration's expansion of Jim Crow laws in the nation's capital, reversal of incipient efforts to integrate federal agencies such as the Postal Service, and the numerous Southern racists he appointed to his Cabinet. He had "never seen the colored people so discouraged and bitter as they are at the present time," Booker T. Washington commented after a trip to Washington. When the United States finally did enter World War I (1917), blacks enlisted but were kept in segregated units, mostly service units at that, the ones that dug the trenches, buried the bodies, and performed other menial tasks. "If the world is to be made 'safe for democracy,'" one black leader played off Wilson's declaration entering World War I, "that will mean us also."

In this and other ways Wilson truly was someone whose "rootage" powerfully shaped his "leafage."

WHY Wilsonianism?

Some presidents, such as Monroe, Truman, Nixon, Carter, Reagan, and Bush, had foreign policy doctrines named after them. Woodrow Wilson is the only president to have a full-scale "-ism" bearing his name. Wilsonianism has three main elements: an "exceptionalist" conception of America's global role; power in pursuit of principles; and peace through cooperation.

America's Global Role

When World War I broke out in 1914, Wilson made the case for U.S. neutrality in terms that echoed the "beware entangling alliances" warning George Washington left the young country with in his 1796 Farewell Address.

> Washington: "Europe has a set of primary interests which to us have none or a very remote relation."
> Wilson: "No nation should be forced to take sides in any quarrel in which its own honour and integrity and the fortunes of its own people are not involved."

But Wilson also evinced some of John Winthrop, the Massachusetts Bay Colony governor whose 1630 declaration that "wee shall be as a Citty upon a Hill, the eies of all peoples upon us" long has been cited as the essence of American exceptionalism and America's special role in the world. Wilson's support for the 1898 Spanish-American War was an early example, justifying the taking of the Philippines as a colony as having "only their welfare at heart," these "less civilized" people who needed to be guided along the path of self-government. As with many American exceptionalists, there is a mix of genuine sincerity, paternalism, and racism.

This mix comes through even more strongly in President Wilson's policies toward Latin America. He repeatedly intervened in Mexico during that country's revolution, sending the Navy and Marines into Veracruz in 1914 and 5,000 troops under the command of General John J. Pershing across the Rio Grande in 1916 pursuing the bandit-revolutionary Pancho Villa. He also sent U.S. military forces into Haiti in 1915, where they stayed until 1934; into the Dominican Republic in 1916, where they stayed until 1924; kept them in Nicaragua, where they stayed until 1933; and back into Cuba in 1917, where they stayed until 1922. "I am going to teach the South American Republics to elect good men!" he proclaimed in a classic Wilsonian mix of good governance liberalism and missionary zeal.

With regard to World War I, his inner George Washington remained prevalent even when in May 1915 the Germans sank the British cruise ship *Lusitania* with 128 Americans among the 1,198 people killed. He still saw the war as largely Europe's affair. But by 1917, with Germany now pursuing unrestricted submarine warfare and the "Zimmerman telegram" revelation of German efforts to enlist Mexico as an ally, Washington's isolation was proving less possible.* In his April 2, 1917, speech to Congress requesting a declaration of war, Wilson cited the American ships sunk and American lives lost and other actions of the imperial German government as constituting "nothing less than war against the government and people of the United States." But the thrust of this speech went beyond classical grounds for war, his inner John Winthrop defining the mission much more expansively:

> The challenge is to all mankind . . . The wrongs against which we now array ourselves are no common wrongs; they cut to the very roots of human life . . . Our motive will not be revenge or the victorious assertion of the physical might of the nation, but only the vindication of right, of human right.

---

* This was a secret message from Arthur Zimmerman, the German foreign minister, playing on Mexican anti-Americanism with the proposal of a German-Mexican alliance if the United States were to enter the war. It was British intelligence that intercepted and decoded it.

And the essence of what made America exceptional:

> To such a task we can dedicate our lives and our fortunes, every-
> thing that we are and everything that we have, with the pride of
> those who know that the day has come when America is priv-
> ileged to spend her blood and her might for the principles that
> gave her birth and happiness and the peace which she has trea-
> sured . . . We have no selfish ends. We desire no conquest, no
> dominion.

Among those greeting him as he stepped down from the podium
was Senator Henry Cabot Lodge, his soon-to-be nemesis over the Versailles Treaty and League of Nations, who shook his hand and said,
"Mr. President, you have expressed in the loftiest manner possible, the
sentiments of the American people." Walter Lippmann, the leading
international affairs journalist of the day, wrote: "Only a statesman
who will be called great could have made America's intervention mean
so much to the generous forces of the world, could have lifted the inevitable horror of war into a deed so full of meaning." Many later American presidents would speak in such sweeping terms about America's
global role; Wilson was the first.

Power in Pursuit of Principles

While Wilson didn't glorify military power the way Teddy Roosevelt
did, the notion of him as some professorial softie is way too stereo-
typic. True, he was reluctant to go to war. He reflected on his childhood memories of the Civil War and the destruction he had seen in
his native South. But all those military interventions and occupations
in Latin America were not exactly the work of a pacifist. When he did
take the nation into the Great War, it was more in the name of the
principles to be upheld than the power to be exercised: the duties of
virtue, not the virtue of war.

"The world must be made safe for democracy" is generally considered the iconic Wilsonian statement. What he actually meant by

this, though, was less universal than it sounded. "Every people has the right to choose the sovereignty under which they shall live," he stated in a speech leading up to U.S. entry into the war. In another he elaborated: "No right exists anywhere to hand peoples from sovereignty to sovereignty as if they were property." But this principle of self-determination was more for the European peoples of the now former Austro-Hungarian and Turkish-Ottoman empires. Outside Europe for the colonies held by Britain and France, Wilson qualifies the principle as needing to take into account "the interests of the populations concerned" but also giving "equal weight with the equitable claims of the government whose title is to be determined." While this in part reflects compromises forced by the British and French, Wilson's own racism comes through in statements such as only giving consideration to "well-defined national aspirations" and only to the extent that the actual exercise of self-determination would not feed into "elements of discord."

Peace Through Cooperation

Wilson's vision of peace was based on replacing classical balance of power stand-offs among big militaries with cooperation among nations. This was to be a seminal historical shift. The wars of ancient Greece between Athens and Sparta as chronicled by Thucydides were attributed to the breakdown of that era's balance of power. So too the centuries of European wars among Spain and Portugal, England and France, and all sorts of variants involving these and other European monarchies. Many trace World War I to the breakdown of the balance of power so carefully constructed by Prussian-German Chancellor Otto von Bismarck. Wilson, though, saw the occurrence of World War I as not simply another cyclical up-and-down but as demonstrating the inherent instability of balance of power strategies. He thus sought to forge "a community of power; not organized rivalries, but an organized common peace."

Wilson went partially public with these ideas during his 1916 reelection campaign, although casting them as a creed, not a program, so as to stay within his message of keeping the country out of war.

> Henceforth alliance must not be set up against alliance ... Only when the great nations of the world have reached some sort of agreement ... as to some feasible method of acting in concert when any nation or group of nations seeks to disturb those fundamental things, can we feel that civilization is at last in a way of justifying its existence and claiming to be finally established ... the nations of the world must in some way band themselves together to see that that right prevails as against any sort of selfish aggression.

That some way of banding together became the League of Nations as finalized at the June 1919 Paris Peace Conference and formalized in the Treaty of Versailles. For Wilson the League was the centerpiece for building the peace that was to end war, "an indispensable instrumentality ... the main object of the peace ... the hope of the world." Although he would win the Nobel Peace Prize for establishing the League, he would be unable to get his own country to join.

HOW did Wilson pursue peace?

Although it would not be until April 1917 that the United States entered the war, in his January State of the Union address, Wilson introduced the idea of a League for Peace. This developed further over the year into his Fourteen Points, one of which was for "a general association of nations ... formed under specific covenants for the purpose of affording mutual guarantees of political independence and territorial integrity to great and small states alike."

After the war ended with victory over Germany and its allies in November 1918, Wilson headed to the Paris Peace Conference. The key role the United States had played militarily and economically in the war gave him enormous prestige and leverage. Neither of his counterparts, British Prime Minister David Lloyd George and French Prime Minister Georges Clemenceau, was particularly enthusiastic about this League of Nations. Their national interests were more about restoring the old order than creating a new one, protecting their spheres of influence and gaining some new ones, as with the 1916 Sykes-Picot agreement divvying up the Middle East signed while the war was still raging and before the United States entered. Wilson's claim that he was representing the interests of humanity writ large, not just his own country, had Clemenceau at one point telling Colonel Edward House, Wilson's close confidant, "I can get on with you, you are practical . . . but talking to Wilson is something like talking to Jesus Christ!" Still Wilson had the leverage, and Clemenceau and Lloyd George went along with creating the League as part of the overall Versailles Treaty.

The key provision was Article X of the League Covenant:

> The Members of the League undertake to respect and preserve as against external aggression the territorial integrity and existing political independence of all Members of the League. In case of any such aggression or in the case of any threat or danger of such aggression the Council shall advise upon the means by which this obligation shall be filled.

This was to be a fundamentally new principle of "collective security" by which all member nations committed to come to each other's defense if any member nation was attacked—one for all, all for one, a single security system bringing all nations of the world together.

There was plenty to debate back home. Proponents saw the League as key to preventing another major war. The reassurance it provided would make disarmament possible, with attendant economic benefits. New institutions like the International Court of Justice would also contribute to peace. As the principal founder, the United States would be in a position to exert substantial influence in ways that would benefit U.S. interests. The principle of self-determination resonated with America's own democratic values. Some opposed it from a traditional isolationist standpoint, wanting to come back home and stay home now that the war was over. Others, so-called new nationalists, were more concerned about keeping newfound American global power unconstrained by any new international institution. Constitutional issues were raised as to whether the collective security commitment requiring League members to come to each other's defense violated the Constitution and basic principles of sovereignty.

Initially the American public was generally positive on approving the treaty and joining the League. A poll of newspaper editors from across the country found 52 percent fully in favor, 35 percent supportive with some limited changes, and only 12 percent completely opposed. Large-circulation city newspapers gave their readers a Yes-No poll, for which 76 percent said yes. Thirty-two state legislatures passed supportive resolutions. In the Senate most Democrats were inclined to hold the party line with their Democratic president. Republicans, who in the 1918 midterm election had gained a Senate majority, had some "irreconcilables," those firmly opposed whether as traditional isolationists or new nationalists. But more of the party members were "mild reservationists," open to support subject to some limited changes. The two-thirds' majority required for treaty ratification was there to be had.

Wilson grossly mishandled the politics. He had not included any senators in the delegation he took to the Paris Peace Conference. Nor any other Republicans, not even former President William Howard Taft, who was one of the founders of the supportive League to Enforce Peace. On his return he further slighted Congress, handing out drafts of the League covenant at a speech in Boston before he had shown them to the senators in Washington. As the debate developed, Wilson would brook no compromises. Some amendments, such as those pushed by Senate Foreign Relations Committee Chairman Henry

Cabot Lodge, were quite intentionally poison pills. Others were manageable without gutting the treaty. Even though as late as mid-August 1919 the vote count still had enough Republicans willing to join the Democrats for the two-thirds' ratification majority if Wilson would just make some compromises, he remained rigid in his purist position. One historian characterizes his formal presentation of the treaty to the Senate as "the schoolmaster incarnate . . . certainty that as he had dictated the laws and remade the map, the job must have been done right and that therefore these Senators must stamp, and quickly, their approval." Democratic Senate leaders urged him to work with them and moderate Republicans. No, Wilson countered, "anyone who opposes me . . . I'll crush! I shall consent to nothing. *The Senate must take its medicine.*"

Wilson decided to take things to the American people, who he felt surely would support him, even hail him. On September 2, he set out on a 22-day, 9,800-mile journey crisscrossing through the Great Plains, down into Texas, back up to the Rockies, and out to California, giving as many as ten speeches a day. He not only defended the particulars of the League but made his pitch at the deeper level of his vision, the "why." Wilson tried to tap America's sense of mission: "America is great because she has seen visions that other nations have not seen, and the one enterprise that does engage the steadfast loyalty and support of the United States is an enterprise for the liberty of mankind." It was America, he proclaimed, that "showed the way." Now "all the world believe[s] in America as it believes in no other nation organized in the modern world." All wasn't so high-minded, though. The Pueblo speech also accused opponents of the League of "disloyalty" and "deliberately falsifying" the facts.

A few days later Wilson suffered a massive stroke. He had had two strokes in his Princeton years, both when he was working especially hard. This one broke his health. His whole left side was paralyzed. His mental faculties were less damaged, at least initially, although it did make him even more intolerant of discord. When he got back to Washington, it was apparent that whatever resonance his speeches had had with the public, they had not spurred a political wave to move senators in his direction. The compromises still were there to be had. His illness made it even harder to engage. To the extent that he could, he made it clear that he would not budge. Those who were open to supporting the League but with caveats were not allotted the political space they needed. All this played into Senator Lodge's hands, making him seem the less unreasonable one. "We can always depend on Mr. Wilson," one opposing senator remarked. "He never has failed us. He has used all his powers to defeat the Treaty, because we would not ratify it in just the form in which he desired."

It was a moment when President Wilson would have done well to heed the advice Professor Wilson had offered to presidents in his book, *Constitutional Government*: "act in the true spirit of the Constitution and establish intimate relations of confidence with the Senate on his own initiative, not carrying his plans to completion and then laying them in final form before the Senate to be accepted or rejected." Instead on November 19, 1919, in one of the worst political defeats for a president in foreign policy, the Senate refused to ratify the Treaty of Versailles and bring the United States into the League of Nations.

WHAT: Balance Sheet

It took Wilson almost a month to respond publicly to the Senate defeat. On December 14, he issued a public statement, phrased in the third person, that "He has no compromise or concession of any kind in mind, but intends, so far as he is concerned, that the Republican

---

* His wife, Edith, his personal physician, Dr. Cary Grayson, and his closest political aide, Joseph Patrick Tumulty, tried to hide the seriousness of his medical condition from the public and press as it worsened. Over the last year of his presidency (1920), it wasn't at all clear how well and how much he was functioning and how much Edith Galt Wilson was playing a de facto presidential role.

leaders of the Senate shall continue to bear the undivided responsibility for the fate of the treaty and the present condition of the world
in consequence of that fate." In early 1920, some supporters got the
Senate to vote to reconsider. Wilson's attitude remained uncompro-
mising. "I would rather lead a fight for the League of Nations and
lose both my reputation and my life rather than to shirk a duty of
this kind."

For years I taught my foreign policy course as if Wilson had been
the victim of politically overpowering sentiment for retreat into traditional American isolationism. I am now convinced that the treaty
could have been ratified had Wilson not played the politics so self-
defeatingly. There he was with the country feeling the patriotism of
a great military victory and the pride of their president having been
hailed internationally. Opinion polls showed the American public as
well as newspaper editorial boards, albeit with some regional variation, to be favorably inclined. Senator Lodge had his personal as well
as political reasons for being unmovable, but Wilson could have gone
around Lodge with support from enough of the mild reservationists
to get to two-thirds. International law has sufficient flexibility and
generality to have come up with a formula that addressed legitimate
concerns about Article X without gutting it. It's not that Wilson tried
such a strategy but it didn't work. He didn't even try. The flaws in his
"how" traced back to his "who."

Even if the treaty had been ratified, as a blueprint for peace it had
structural weaknesses. French Prime Minister Clemenceau and British Prime Minister Lloyd George and their foreign ministers had
already drawn the now infamous Sykes-Picot lines rather haphazardly
dividing up the Middle East into states, the consequences of which are
still playing out a century later. The restriction of "self-determination"
largely only to conquered German and Turkish-Ottoman territories
reflected both Clemenceau's and Lloyd George's interest in preserving most of their own colonial empires and strands of Wilson's racism playing out in foreign affairs. When Indian, Chinese, Egyptian,
Vietnamese, and other anticolonial leaders came to Versailles with

claims for their own self-determination, Wilson joined Clemenceau and Lloyd George in turning them away, the Europeans as a matter of interests and for Wilson manifesting paternalism and racism.

Even more imminently explosive were the punitive economic terms imposed on Germany, what the young economist John Maynard Keynes wrote about in his farsighted book, *The Economic Consequences of the Peace*. Clemenceau was bent on "crush[ing] the economic life of his enemy" and Lloyd George "to do a deal and bring home something which would pass muster for a week." As to Wilson:

> The President had thought out nothing; when it came to prac-
> tice his ideas were nebulous and incomplete. He had no plan,
> no scheme, no constructive ideas whatever for clothing with the
> flesh of life the commandments which he had thundered from
> the White House. He could have preached a sermon on any of
> them or have addressed a stately prayer to the Almighty for their
> fulfillment; but he could not frame their concrete application to
> the actual state of Europe.

In these and other ways the Wilsonian vision was flawed. It had some analytic accuracy in diagnosing the balance of power's instability and some normative appeal in pursuing peace through cooperation. But the League of Nations design was prescriptively flawed. Here too there were elements of Wilson's arrogance. "Not just wrong but wicked" is how historian Margaret MacMillan characterizes his attitude toward opposition from his co-peacemakers. "God himself was content with ten commandments," Clemenceau remarked. "Wilson 'modestly' inflicted fourteen points on us." Even Wilson's own Secretary of State Robert Lansing, while generally supportive, had objected to some of the specifics of the League and the Versailles Treaty. Wilson shot Lansing's proposals down and Lansing resigned. As Professor Walter LaFeber, one of my own fabulous teachers, recounted the story in his Cornell diplomatic history course, Lansing was asked by a reporter what his view of the treaty was and what his own plans were. "I plan to go to the French Riviera and sadly watch the world fall apart." And Professor LaFeber's ending to the lecture: "He went, and it did."

This is not to blame Wilson for World War II. Principal responsibility lies with Adolf Hitler, Benito Mussolini, Francisco Franco, and Emperor Hirohito. Wilson deserves credit for seeking to be a peacemaker. Wilsonianism has had enduring impact, including the post–World War II United Nations designed largely by President Franklin D. Roosevelt, who had been Wilson's assistant secretary of the Navy and a League supporter. Nevertheless, the "who, why, and how" of Wilson's failure are instructive for our purposes.

FRANKLIN D. ROOSEVELT: FATHER OF THE UNITED NATIONS, 1945

He saw the United Nations as his most important legacy, *New York Times* journalist Anne O'Hare McCormick wrote of President Franklin Delano Roosevelt (FDR) based on an interview weeks before his death. It was "the crowning act of his career . . . the President who had succeeded where Woodrow Wilson failed in . . . getting an international security organization in motion." For the president who led the country out of the Great Depression and through World War II, this has a touch of hyperbole. Even so, that very history and track record underscores the importance FDR saw for the UN.

WHO was Franklin Delano Roosevelt?

He was born January 30, 1882. His parents both came from wealthy families with lineages tracing back to seventeenth-century Dutch settlers of Nieuw Amsterdam. James Roosevelt was a Wall Street lawyer with a family fortune from Manhattan real estate, West Indian sugar trade, and investments. Sara Delano's family was even wealthier from trade with China (tea in the 1840s, opium in the 1860s) and Hudson

Valley estates. Sara was James's second wife, 26 years younger. James was 54 when Franklin was born, had a heart attack when the boy was 10, and died when Franklin was 18, leaving Sara as the main parental influence. She was a domineering one, legendarily so.

The boy followed the aristocratic schooling route. He went to Groton, where he was a solid but not exceptional student, and as yet not much of a leader. Along with 16 of 18 classmates, he rode the Groton to Harvard conveyor belt. He began to emerge at Harvard, most notably as editor of *The Crimson* (he'd later quip to reporters about being a former newspaperman). He then went on to Columbia Law School.

This also was the period when his cousin Theodore was president (1901–1909). They were distant cousins who had had some interaction over the years and more now, including Uncle Theodore giving away his niece Eleanor as Franklin's bride in 1905. Franklin's political career began with his election to the New York State Senate in 1910. His political skills were evident in this very first race in a traditionally Republican district. He gave speeches in dairy barns and sat with folks on general store porches, shaking hands and flashing his radiant smile, a strikingly common touch for a country baron.

When Woodrow Wilson was elected president, Franklin garnered an appointment as assistant secretary of the Navy. This came in part through the campaigning he did for Wilson, in part from having some knowledge of the sea from his own sailing, and in large part from the sponsorship of Josephus Daniels, publisher of the *Raleigh News and Observer* who had taken to Franklin and who was named secretary of the Navy. Daniels proved a valued mentor, helping FDR learn "the folksy art of Washington politics." When FDR became president, one of his first appointments was of Daniels as ambassador to Mexico.

FDR served as assistant secretary of the Navy for the entire Wilson presidency. In December 1914, with World War I raging in Europe and concerns mounting about how long the United States could stay out, FDR sent a letter to British First Lord of the Admiralty Winston Churchill, proposing a visit to study their preparations and strategy. FDR made the trip but Churchill, piqued that this mere assistant secretary and not the protocol counterpart secretary had made the request, pushed the meetings to his aides. In December 1915, while getting ready to run for reelection on a platform of keeping the United States out of the war, Wilson initiated a naval readiness program that under the guidance of Daniels and FDR laid the basis for the Navy's fourfold expansion within six months of the April 1917 entry of the United States into World War I.

In 1920, FDR was chosen as the Democratic vice presidential candidate on the ticket headed by Ohio Governor James Cox. Although they lost the election, the campaign gave FDR national exposure at only 38 years old. But in 1921, while vacationing at the family cottage on Campobello Island off New Brunswick in Canada, FDR was stricken with polio. Plans to run for the Democratic nomination for U.S. Senator (New York) were shelved; any political future was highly uncertain. Helped by support from family and political associates, medical treatments that included his first trips to the mineral baths of Warm Springs, Georgia, and his own extraordinary will, FDR regained the strength and determination to restart his political career. The dramatic moment came with his presidential nominating speech for New York Governor Al Smith at the 1924 Democratic Convention in Chicago. His legs in braces and his arms guiding his crutches, he made his way to the podium and delivered the speech to rave reviews from the press.

Al Smith lost the race to Calvin Coolidge. When Smith was again nominated in 1928, he had to bow out of reelection for New York governor. FDR stepped in. Any doubts about his vigor were dispelled by his intense campaign. He delivered as many as 14 speeches a day, barnstorming all over the state. It was a tight election. Republican Herbert Hoover beat Smith in a landslide, including in New York. But FDR won the governorship.

Four years later, with President Hoover's political standing ravaged by the Great Depression, FDR ran for and won the presidency. He promised a "New Deal." He and Eleanor, the extraordinary First Lady, delivered it. Not that it was straight upward out of the Depression: full recovery didn't consolidate until the massive economic stimulus of World War II. Nor were his policies uncontroversial: while many saw FDR saving capitalism from itself, there were others who virulently opposed his "socialism." But FDR prevailed to the point that in 1940 he was elected to an unprecedented third term as president.

He then led the country through World War II: from the shock and fear of the devastating December 7, 1941, surprise attack on Pearl Harbor, to mobilization of the citizenry to grow the armed forces from 175,000 to 8,500,000 and harness the full economy to the war effort, and to a new global leadership role for the United States—which he then sought to continue through the United Nations.

FDR had enormous personal capital. Some of this came from the courage he demonstrated in his fight against polio. He and his political handlers minimized images and reports that made him look too handicapped. People had a sense for the strength of his struggle while limiting concerns about his actual physical fitness for the presidency. Even more fundamentally it was the adversity of polio that, as biographer Jean Edward Smith put it, was "how this Hudson River aristocrat . . . became the champion of the common man." As Rose McDermott states in her authoritative study on illness and presidents, the polio "lessened his tendency towards arrogance and produced a remarkable empathy." His recuperative trips to Warm Springs took this further. The old scratchy home movie footage of the empathic FDR with fellow polio patients highlights the common touch that few of such patrician lineage could exercise. "Franklin's disease gave him strength and courage he had not had before," Eleanor observed. "He had to think out the fundamentals of living and learn the greatest of all lessons: infinite patience and never-ending persistence." And in rural Georgia he witnessed poverty he rarely had seen, carrying that experience back into New Deal programs.

The eminent jurist and scholar Oliver Wendell Homes is said to have remarked that FDR had "a second-class intellect but a first-class temperament." One doesn't have to accept the former to agree with the latter. The smile, the voice on the fireside chats, the jaunty jaw and cigarette holder pointing upward: he exuded optimism in ways that reassured the American people. His steadiness in uncertain times helped others try to do the same. This kept people going through the Depression. It got people going in World War II. For me, even more than the biographies, this came through when, after my mother died in 2008, I found still in her papers a letter she received as a young teen-ager in Scranton, Pennsylvania, thanking her for tending her wartime "victory garden."

FDR also had quite adroit political skills. Along with his personal charm and persuasiveness, he had the cunning of *The Lion and the Fox*, as James MacGregor Burns titled his biography with the image going back to Machiavelli: "A prince must imitate the fox and the lion, for the lion cannot protect himself from traps, and the fox cannot defend himself from wolves. One must therefore be a fox to recognize traps, and a lion to frighten wolves. Those that wish to be only lions do not understand this." His management model of assigning the same task to more than one Cabinet official and aide is often cited for its effectiveness in generating policy initiatives. His capacity to coin the politically potent phrase—"the only thing to fear is fear itself" and "day of infamy"—is hard to match. While there were those who ardently hated him and his "socialism," his election victory margins were one landslide after another, including one for a fourth term.

As with other of our profiles, the attribution of personal capital is about statesmanship, not personal morality. FDR's affair with Lucy Mercer is well known. Eleanor discovered it in 1918, a year or so after it had begun. She considered divorcing him, he considered leaving her. By then they had five children. Mother Sara intervened, making clear to Franklin that a broken marriage would ruin his political career and, her own piece, call into question his inheritance. Eleanor gave Franklin an ultimatum to break off the affair. He did, for a while. But they kept contact. Lucy was with FDR at Warm Springs when he died.

WHY did FDR see the United Nations as central to postwar peace?

FDR's view of Wilson's League: right idea, done wrong. The pragmatist that he was, he saw the room for compromise. "I have read the draft of the League three times," he said in a June 1919 speech, "and always find something to object to in it, and that is the way with everybody." As the 1920 Democratic vice presidential candidate, FDR gave over 800 pro-League speeches, tacking away from Wilsonian idealism and pitching the League as a "practical necessity" to a public not fully persuaded that outright rejection had been wise. In his own 1932 presidential campaign, he was more critical of the League for its own failures and weaknesses. Meek responses to Japan's 1931 invasion of Manchuria, Italian fascist dictator Benito Mussolini's 1935 invasion of Ethiopia, and Hitler's aggression further convinced FDR that a new entity needed to be created.

Even before the December 7, 1941, attack on Pearl Harbor finally brought the United States into World War II, FDR's January 1941 "Four Freedoms" speech—freedom of speech, freedom of religion, freedom from want, freedom from fear, all to be pursued "everywhere in the world"—gave a glimpse of the peace he had in mind. The Atlantic Charter, signed months later (August 1941) with British Prime Minister Winston Churchill, spoke to principles "on which they base their hopes for a better future for the world," which included "establishment of a wider and permanent system of general security."

Despite the intensive mobilization required following the attack on Pearl Harbor, postwar strategizing for what would become the United Nations also got under way. Barely nine weeks after Pearl Harbor an Advisory Committee on Postwar Foreign Policy was set up based in the State Department. By March 1944, while FDR was also immersed in D-Day planning and the still uncertain war in the Pacific, a full draft for the postwar organization had been completed.

FDR tried to blend the liberal institutionalist belief that "no lasting peace was possible . . . unless an effective international organization were founded" with the realpolitik realization that "good intentions alone" were not enough against "the predatory animals of this world." This was especially evident in the role of the UN Security Council. The League of Nations architecture gave roughly equal powers and jurisdiction to the assembly of all member nations and the major powers council. Unanimity was required for major decisions. By contrast, the UN Security Council (UNSC) would have more power and greater jurisdiction than the General Assembly. Within the UNSC the major powers (United States, Soviet Union, Britain, China, and France) would be permanent members and each would have the veto; other countries would rotate on and off the Security Council with votes but not vetoes. More broadly, while Wilson saw most if not all international issues coming to the League, FDR recognized that major powers would continue to deal directly with each other outside the UN. The difference from nineteenth-century major power concerts like Metternich's Congress of Vienna or Bismarck's balance of power was that, after having endured two world wars within three decades, FDR calculated that at least when priority national interests were not involved, the major powers would work together to maintain peace.

Tensions with Soviet leader Joseph Stalin came close to derailing negotiations even before the Cold War broke out. Churchill also had ambivalences about the United Nations meddling with the British Empire and its colonies. FDR kept working these issues at the so-called Big Three summits. There was enough agreement that at the August 1944 Washington Conversation on International Peace and Security Organization (also known as the Dumbarton Oaks Conference) a declaration was issued that:

> there should be established an international organization under
> the title of The United Nations . . .
> To maintain international peace and security;
> And to that end to take effective collective measures for the
> prevention and removal of threats to the peace and the suppres-

sion of acts of aggression or other breaches of the peace, and
to bring about by peaceful means adjustment or settlement of
international disputes which may lead to a breach of the peace.

HOW did FDR succeed where Wilson had not?

For one thing, he strategized the domestic politics infinitely better.

From the start he made the effort joint with Congress and politically bipartisan. In August 1942, with his own internal planning
efforts still in their formative stages, he invited Wendell Willkie, his
Republican opponent in the 1940 presidential election but an ardent
internationalist, to be his unofficial global envoy on UN-related ideas.
One World, the book Willkie wrote the following year, became an
instant best seller. Other Republicans, not as locked into isolationism
as in the 1930s, signed on to a middle-ground party resolution calling
for "responsible participation by the US in a postwar cooperative organization among sovereign nations." This cautious embrace was picked
up on in the March 1944 State Department draft plan circulated to
congressional leaders posing the UN as "founded upon the principle of
cooperation freely agreed among sovereign peace-loving states" who
still "insist on retaining a large degree of freedom of action." "We
shall have to take responsibility for world collaboration," FDR urged
Congress in March 1945 in what would be his final speech, "or we
shall have to bear the responsibility for another world conflict." In a
classic FDR act of political outreach, he appointed a delegation to represent the United States at the June 1945 UN founding conference in
San Francisco* that included a number of Republicans, most notably
Senator Arthur Vandenberg (R-Michigan), the ranking member of

---

* San Francisco was chosen, as *New York Times* columnist Anne McCormick put it, for
the "youth in every line of its uplifted profile and the vigor in every breath of its brisk trade
winds . . . a sight for the sore eyes of delegates who come . . . [from] all the shattered cities
of the war zones. More than any other city, it is a sign of the promise of resurrection"
(Schlesinger, *Act of Creation*, 116).

the Senate Foreign Relations Committee and up until then an ardent isolationist.

To run the broader effort to mobilize public support, FDR recruited Archibald MacLeish, then the Librarian of Congress and later known as a leading writer and essayist, along with an aide by the name of Adlai Stevenson. One meeting, appropriately held at the Woodrow Wilson Library, included 40 citizen groups both liberal and conservative. Twitter and Facebook weren't around then, but an eight-page pro-UN pamphlet reached over 1.25 million people. Twenty-eight governors issued proclamations. Cities held town meetings. Churches held special prayer services. The League of Women Voters sent sound trucks around New York City and discussion guides to over 600 local chapters. Labor unions mobilized their members. The American Legion National Commander sent pro-UN letters to 12,000 posts around the country. The movie *Watchtower Over Tomorrow* was made. All told, on the eve of the San Francisco conference, polls showed that 94 percent of the public had heard of the UN and 80 percent supported it.

As to the international politics, there is more controversy over how well FDR managed. From the start as a matter of both strategic vision and national interests, FDR was a stronger believer in the UN than either Churchill or Stalin. Churchill was still trying to preserve the British colonial empire. Back in 1941, with Britain in desperate need of U.S. assistance against the Nazis, he had little choice but to go along with the Atlantic Charter provision on "the right of all peoples to choose the form of government under which they will live." As the war neared an end, Churchill resisted but FDR insisted this would apply not just to European countries taken over by Nazi Germany but to colonial peoples as well: "I can't believe that we can fight a war against fascist slavery, and at the same time not work to free people all over the world from a backward colonial policy."

Notwithstanding the joint Dumbarton Oaks declaration, U.S.-Soviet differences still remained. Stalin pushed for UN General Assembly votes for each of the 16 "republics" constituting the Union of

Soviet Socialist Republics, claiming justification as counterweight to U.S. de facto dominance of Latin American countries and their votes. At the February 1945 Yalta "Big Three" summit, FDR compromised on three General Assembly votes for the Soviet Union, with Ukraine and Byelorussia (Belarus) being granted their own voting rights membership. He also made concessions that played into Stalin's efforts to ensure communist control of postwar Poland and, as some historians see it, led to Soviet domination of most of Eastern Europe. The deal was flawed, FDR privately acknowledged, but ever confident in his ability to manage relationships, he felt that he could work things out with Stalin over time.

Even with its flaws and uncertainties, the Yalta agreement was greeted positively back in the United States. FDR received a standing ovation from a joint session of Congress at his post-Yalta speech. His theme was that with cooperation solidified for finalizing the defeat of the Nazis and moving closer to defeating Japan, as well as the agreement "to continue to build the foundation for an international accord that would bring order and security after the chaos of the war that would give some assurance of lasting peace among the Nations of the world," we have made "a good start on the road to a world of peace." He harked back to before World War I,

> twenty-five years ago [when] American fighting men looked to the statesmen of the world to finish the work of peace for which they fought and suffered. We failed them then. We cannot fail them again, and expect the world again to survive . . . We shall have to take the responsibility for world collaboration, or we shall have to bear the responsibility for another world conflict.

Toward that end, he announced April 25 as the date for the United Nations founding conference in San Francisco.

For the first time in his 13 years of addressing Congress, FDR did so sitting down. The Yalta trip was an exhausting one. *Time* may have titled its cover story "Eight Great Days on the Russian Riviera," but

Yalta in winter and stripped bare from years of Nazi occupation was not exactly in resort shape.* On top of the arduous travel by sea and plane, this was very much the type of trip about which FDR's doctors had grave concerns. Senators sitting close to the podium noticed the president was having trouble turning the pages with his left hand. He missed some words, misspoke others, especially on the left side of the pages, indeed on the left side of many words. The normally friendly press wrote that he had taken "his carefully prepared text for a buggy ride." Others noticed the expansion of a large pigmented lesion on the left side of his forehead—a sign of skin cancer that had begun to metastasize to the brain, which can lead to massive cerebral hemorrhages. Such a cerebral hemorrhage on April 12, 1945, while at Warm Springs preparing his keynote speech for the UN founding conference, killed Franklin Roosevelt at age 63.

WHAT: Balance Sheet

The San Francisco conference was to proceed "as President Roosevelt had directed," the new American President Harry Truman declared. Close to 300 delegates from 46 nations, another 3,500 staff and advisors, and more than 250 members of the press and other media of the day convened on the appointed date. Two months later on June 26, the Charter of the United Nations was signed. On July 28 the Senate ratified it by a resounding 89–2 margin. With the League of Nations, the United States had been one of the first to reject membership. With the United Nations, the United States was the first to fully approve its membership. The founding of the UN, President Truman affirmed, "owes its existence, in large part, to the vision and foresight and determination of Franklin Roosevelt."

Just as Wilson's who-why-how-what framework helped to explain his failures, so does FDR's help to explain his success. His leadership

---

* Churchill advised Harry Hopkins, a close FDR aide, that the only way to protect against the typhus and lice was to bring plenty of whiskey.

qualities flowed so much from his persona and its blend of personal capital and those lion-and-fox political skills. The American people trusted him enough to give him the unprecedented third presidential term, and then a fourth. "He lifted himself from a wheelchair," as Jean Edward Smith put it in the epigram starting his 858-page biography, "to lift the nation from its knees." Along with this personal credibility, FDR articulated the vision for why the United States should join— indeed, take the lead on—a postwar international organization. He masterfully managed the domestic politics. Notwithstanding some problematic compromises, he did marshal the Big Three agreements needed to get the UN established.

While designing an international institution is its own act of statesmanship, FDR's untimely death meant that he never got to play a direct role in bringing it to fruition. Eleanor Roosevelt very much left her mark as a member of the U.S. delegation to the UN from 1945 to 1952 and, in particular, her role as chair of the UN Human Rights Commission and her leadership on the 1948 Universal Declaration of Human Rights. Some historians believe that the Cold War, which among other things impeded the role the UN could play, might have been avoided or at least significantly tempered had FDR been there to provide the shrewd diplomacy needed to navigate the risks and opportunities in relations with Stalin and the Soviet Union.

Another we'll-never-know is whether FDR's musing about resigning the presidency and taking on leadership of the UN would have come to pass. His cousin Margaret "Daisy" Suckley, with whom he was very close, said he had confided such an interest to her a number of times. "The P. would like to be that person [head of the UN] if he could," she noted in her diary. Benjamin Cohen, part of his New Deal "Brain Trust," sent him a memo expressing concern that his health was worrisome for a full fourth term, and with bipartisan support for the UN still not assured, why not propose to Congress that he would become "the Chief Executive Officer of the new international organization to maintain the peace." FDR's response was "a tremendously interesting analysis—and I think a very just one," but he felt he had to see the end of the war through as president. Of course, even if he had decided to resign once the war was over and to take on the UN leadership, whether Stalin or even Churchill would have agreed is highly uncertain. Still it is an interesting speculation.

While the UN Charter did give the UN secretary-general a broader remit than the League of Nations had given its secretary-general, it still was more circumscribed than FDR's own view of someone who, as historian Evan Luard put it, "would play an active role on the world's stage, perhaps indeed be the dominant figure of world politics." As if channeling FDR, Luard goes on: "If the world organization was itself to become a powerful force in the world, then its chief executive too must become a more powerful figure, able to inject an international viewpoint into the bickerings of national governments; to arouse the conscience of the world when international action was urgently needed; and to act as a watchdog always on the alert for situations where the peace could be threatened." On this, though, FDR didn't carry the day. Instead the first UN secretary-general, Trygve Lie, would leave the position calling it "the most impossible job in the world."

Lie's successor, Dag Hammarskjöld, proved differently. Even within the formal limits of the position, Hammarskjöld showed how to make the secretary-general a powerful player and in turn make the UN the institution that FDR had hoped it would be.

4

UN Secretary-General Dag Hammarskjöld: The "Secular Pope," 1953–1961

In his passing the community of nations has lost one of the greatest servants it ever had—a brilliant mind, a brave and compassionate spirit. I doubt if any living man has done more to further the search for a world in which men solve their problems by peaceful means and not by force than this gallant friend of us all . . . this memory will always be with us as a reminder of the best that the United Nations can be and of the qualities which it demanded of us all.

—*Adlai Stevenson, U.S. ambassador to the UN*

I inherited a belief that no life was more satisfactory than one of selfless service to your country—or humanity.

—*Dag Hammarskjöld*

WHO was Dag Hammarskjöld?

Dag Hammarskjöld was born in 1905, the youngest of four sons in a prominent Swedish family. His father, Hjalmar, served in numerous high-ranking Swedish government positions, including governor of Uppsala and prime minister during World War I. This sense of service was further intensified by a view of Christian charity and sacrifice that came from his mother, Agnes, whose family included clergymen.

Dag was a brilliant student. He completed his first undergraduate degree in two years, a second in another two years, a law degree in another two years, and a Ph.D. in economics in four years. At 31, he became undersecretary in the Ministry of Finance and simulta-

neously chaired the Board of Governors of the Bank of Sweden. At
43 he was appointed undersecretary in the Foreign Office. By 44 he
was secretary-general of the Foreign Office. After the war he moved
up to deputy foreign minister. He also was vice-chair of the Swedish
delegation to the 1951 UN General Assembly meeting in Paris, and
the following year he was acting delegation chair for the meeting in
New York.

For all his accomplishments within Sweden, there still was the "who
is this guy?" question and "just your average bureaucrat" assessment
when on April 1, 1953, the Security Council (SC) voted 10 yea with one
abstention to name Dag Hammarskjöld the second secretary-general
of the United Nations.

For a position like secretary-general, which for all its prestige carries
limited actual power and authority, personal capital is crucial. While
Hammarskjöld's professional stature coming into office was impressive but short of stellar, he brought substantial moral capital and added
to it over the course of his secretary-generalship. In an interview with
Edward R. Murrow shortly after he was appointed secretary-general,
he spoke of his "belief that no life was more satisfactory than one
of selfless service to your country—or humanity." And that, among
other things, required "the courage to stand up unflinchingly for your
convictions," as his father had done as Sweden's prime minister during
World War I with his strict insistence on neutrality, even though that
prompted his whole Cabinet to resign. Dag would show comparable
conviction in being a statesman of the UN Charter even when that
meant taking on the United States, Soviet Union, or other Security
Council permanent members. In *Markings*, the posthumous collection
of his journal writings, we get the sense of an underlying spirituality of someone who believed in faith but not necessarily a particular
faith, who read the Bible but also had books in his personal library by
the great humanist Albert Schweitzer. In the midst of the 1960–1961
Congo crisis, he was working on a Swedish translation of Jewish philosopher Martin Buber's *I and Thou*. He was, as his 1961 Nobel Peace
Prize biographical sketch put it, a Renaissance man.

His political skills were not the sharpest. His conflicts with the Security Council permanent members could have been more adeptly handled even while pursuing the same strategic goals. He also could be less than diplomatic with other officials. "When a delegate begged off a meeting due to fatigue," recounts executive assistant Andrew Cordier, "Hammarskjöld's response was to stamp up and down the corridor outside his office repeating, 'Sissy, sissy. The man has to sleep!'" Even Brian Urquhart, also a close aide who went on to be a distinguished UN diplomat in his own right, temporarily abandons his rosy portrayal to recognize how Hammarskjöld "did not suffer slowness of mind gladly . . . Mutual resentments often resulted."

At the core he was a very inner-oriented personality. The poems, literary reflections, and diary entries in *Markings* chronicled his struggles to understand the human condition and the nature of his solitude. Some convey quite a bit of anguish, a persistent melancholia. Urquhart contended that Hammarskjöld's "lack of close personal obligations and ties was a great advantage in carrying out the crushing duties of the Secretary-Generalship." Unconstrained by family life and its demands, Hammarskjöld was "free to work and think at all hours, and to leave for anywhere at any time and at a moment's notice."

WHY the bold vision of the UN?

Hammarskjöld didn't overestimate the role the UN could have. He was never a World Federalist. But he also did not believe the world could afford to underestimate the UN's role. The UN was crucial for preventing crises and managing them when they occurred. Its role was to do "the quiet work of preparing the ground, of accommodation of interest and viewpoint, of conciliation and mediation, all that goes into the winning of consent to agreed solutions and common programmes."

While the P5 (permanent members: at that time the United States, Soviet Union, Britain, France, and Republic of China-Taiwan) did get to choose the secretary-general, once selected, Hammarskjöld saw his primary responsibility as serving the organization through its Charter. To the extent that the principles of the Charter and the preferences of the P5 were in sync, there was no issue. But when Charter principles and P5 preferences varied, in Hammarskjöld's vision the former took precedence. The secretary-general would make his own determination of when there was commonality and when not, true to the UN being "a universal organization neutral in the big power struggles over ideology and influence in the world." The secretary-general had a "right of initiative," discretionary authority to act even without Security Council or General Assembly authorization as long as they had not explicitly prohibited such action.

Hammarskjöld operated according to a nuanced conception of neutrality. In work with political implications the secretary-general must be neutral in the sense of being "wholly uninfluenced by national or group interests or ideologies." But neutrality did not mean never taking a position: "if the demand for neutrality is made . . . with the intent that the [Secretary-General] should not be permitted to take a stand on political issues in response to requests of the General Assembly or the Security Council, then the demand is in conflict with the Charter itself." Impartiality required not being biased to one or another party to a conflict, but to the extent that one party was the greater violator of UN Charter principles and provisions, to remain neutral would be to betray those principles and provisions.

Upon his 1957 reelection to a second term, Hammarskjöld was even more explicit that while most of what the secretary-general does is with the guidance of the Security Council, "I believe it in keeping with the philosophy of the Charter that the secretary-general should be expected to act also without such guidance, should this appear to him necessary in order to help in filling any vacuum that may appear in the systems which the Charter and traditional diplomacy provide for the safeguarding of peace and security." This made all the more crucial the secretary-general's own personal capital as well as political skills. Without these qualities the secretary-generalship can be "little more than an empty shell of high-sounding aims and principles and of good but largely unfulfilled intentions."

Hammarskjöld was particularly attuned to the moral dimension of leading the world's principal international institution. "Vous êtes mon homologue laique," Pope Pius told him when they met at the Vatican. "You are my lay counterpart." Hammarskjöld once remarked to his friend the poet W. H. Auden that the secretary-general position was like being a "secular Pope," the United Nations a "secular church of ideas." Within his own persona such spiritually infused secularism traces back to his mother, Agnes.

But this wasn't simply about him or the secretary-general position. Hammarskjöld envisioned an international civil service that, as he defined it in a lecture at Oxford, would be "a dedicated professional service responsible only to the Organization [UN] in the performance of its duties and protected insofar as possible from the inevitable pressures of national governments." Among other things this meant confronting the long tentacles of America's McCarthyism. In the waning days of Trygve Lie's secretary-generalship, a U.S. federal grand jury had alleged that the UN was infiltrated by American staff with communist sympathies if not affiliations. While the grand jury didn't name names, the Senate Judiciary Committee did, accusing 38 Americans who worked in the UN Secretariat of being communists. In one of his last executive orders before leaving office, President Harry Truman authorized loyalty investigations of all Americans working for international organizations. Lie had complied, allowing the FBI to actually set up shop in the UN's New York building. Conscious of the risks of making himself a McCarthyite target if he was too confrontational, yet also knowing how antithetical this was in spirit and precedent to his vision of an international civil service, Hammarskjöld maneuvered firmly but deftly to end the FBI presence.

Two cases especially bristled. Ralph Bunche—winner of the 1950 Nobel Peace Prize for his role as lead UN negotiator of armistice agreements ending the 1948 Arab-Israeli war, also formerly a U.S. State Department diplomat, and among the foremost African-

Americans of his time—was being harassed by McCarthyites. While in his past Bunche had some limited associations with groups and individuals later deemed communist fronts, there was no evidence that Bunche was in any way disloyal himself. The witnesses who testified against him to the Senate investigative committee were later convicted of perjury. Hammarskjöld made his views quite clear: he promoted Bunche to UN undersecretary for special political affairs.

With her husband Gunnar, fellow Swede Alma Myrdal had written *An American Dilemma: The Negro Problem and Modern Democracy*, a searing study of race relations full of evidence of discrimination and worse against Negroes.* Alma, now director of the United Nations Education, Scientific and Cultural Organization (UNESCO) Department of Social Sciences, had her visa denied unless she signed the equivalent of a parole agreement requiring her to report her movements within the United States and making her subject at any time to summons by immigration authorities. "Alma's troubles made me see red, so utterly unreasonable and humiliating as it is," Dag wrote to Gunnar. Working with U.S. Ambassador to the UN Henry Cabot Lodge, Jr., a moderate Republican, Dag got the visa restrictions lifted as well as an official statement that none of what had transpired should be construed as reflecting on her integrity.

This combination of big ideas of what the UN and the secretary-general could and needed to be and the practical and particular steps to actualize it through its people shows Hammarskjöld as visionary but not utopian, pragmatic but with ambitions for doing better. What was needed was a combination of "perseverance and patience, a firm grip on realities, careful but imaginative planning, a clear awareness of the *dangers but also of the fact that fate is what we make it*." He had a sense of what he wanted that fate to be. He soon had his first opportunity to provide the statesmanship for achieving that.

---

* The Carnegie Foundation for the Advancement of Teaching, which funded the study, intentionally turned to non-Americans, convinced that only non-Americans would provide an unbiased analysis.

HOW Hammarskjöld strengthened the office (Secretary-General) and institution (UN)

Three major issues demonstrate Hammarskjöld's statesmanship: preventing a crisis over American prisoners of the Korean War held by China, 1954–1955; resolving the 1956 Suez crisis; and seeking to resolve the 1960–1961 Congo crisis.

Crisis Prevention: The Peking Formula, 1954–1955

In the latter months of the Korean War a U.S. B-29 dropping leaflets over Manchuria was shot down by the People's Republic of China (PRC) and 11 airmen were taken prisoner. By the terms of the July 1953 Korean Armistice Agreement, prisoners of war were to be repatriated to their respective countries. But on November 24, 1954, with the war over and talks ongoing over prisoners of war held by both sides, a Chinese military tribunal convicted these airmen along with two other Americans of espionage, imposing prison sentences ranging from four years to life. U.S.-PRC tensions already were running high amid a crisis in the Taiwan Strait and the U.S.-Republic of China (Taiwan) mutual defense treaty.

This still untested secretary-general stepped up. Within weeks Hammarskjöld engineered passage of a resolution by the UN General Assembly condemning the PRC and calling on the secretary-general to undertake "continuing and unremitting efforts" to "act in the name of the United Nations" to free the prisoners. He was to do so "by the means most appropriate in his judgment," discretionary language that Hammarskjöld insisted on. Still, for the secretary-general of an organization that had denied the PRC membership, to get it to reverse a decision it already made dealing with a country it considered its enemy was a particularly difficult mission. That it succeeded was in large part due to Hammarskjöld's statesmanship.

Hammarskjöld's initial cable sent to PRC Premier Zhou Enlai was extraordinarily well crafted. It actually played down the General Assembly resolution since the United States had loaded it up with anti–Red China rhetoric. Instead he again grounded his strategy in the principles of the UN Charter mandating the secretary-general to reduce international tensions anywhere in the world, even on issues with nonmembers, and to do so in a fair manner. From the text of the cable itself: "I would appreciate the opportunity to take this matter up with you personally. For that reason I would ask you whether you could receive me in Peking." The communication was immediate, it was personal, and it was in a respectful tone. Within a week, while noting that he deemed the General Assembly resolution "absurd," Premier Zhou invited Hammarskjöld to Peking "in the interest of peace and relaxation of international tension." This would be the first time a UN secretary-general had gone to any national capital to negotiate, let alone to that of a nonmember.

The press pushed hard for comments in the days leading up to this historic trip. "I hope you'll excuse me if I do not go into anything that will happen," Hammarskjöld said at a press conference, "and I will not speculate in any way on what might happen."

QUESTION: [D]o you not feel that the head of the world Organization is now going to Peking to kneel somehow before Mr. Zhou Enlai for the release of the thirteen Americans?
HAMMARSKJÖLD: I do not get your point.
QUESTION: I mean do you not feel there is a kind of humiliation for the United Nations . . . to go to China to beg them or ask them to release the thirteen Americans?
HAMMARSKJÖLD: I am not going anywhere to beg anybody for anything. I am going to bring up a situation which in my view calls for mutual consideration with the background to which I can refer in the General Assembly resolution.

Hammarskjöld arrived in Peking on January 5. Zhou was a tough negotiator with a strong sense of his country's interests, as we saw in Chapter 1. He made his assertions about espionage. Hammarskjöld made his case for why the Americans should be treated as standard prisoners of war. Even as they agreed to disagree on the facts, he suggested, in the interest of the peace and relaxation of international tension as was cited in Zhou's invitation, would China still act "in a spirit of justice and fairness—before [its] own conscience?" The official joint statement at the end of the negotiating round six days later seemed on the surface standard bromides for no progress. Underlying that, though, was incipient agreement on what became known as "the Peking formula" by which Zhou could save face and have arm's length from the U.S. demands by responding in the spirit of peace and to Hammarskjöld as custodian of that peace. Moreover, the two men had struck a chord of personal rapport: Urquhart wrote of "mutual respect and understanding," while biographer Roger Lipsey described "good chemistry."

The United States was not being particularly helpful. Political criticisms raged. Secretary of State John Foster Dulles felt no one should be talking to those Red Chinese. Even more damaging was the April 11 assassination attempt against Zhou Enlai by the Taiwanese secret service with CIA assistance. But Hammarskjöld kept at it. As he set off for a vacation with friends on the Swedish coast to celebrate his fiftieth birthday (July 29), he got a message from the Chinese embassy in Stockholm wishing him a happy birthday and asking what gift he might like to receive. Release of the American prisoners, he responded sincerely even if a tad facetiously. Three days later, a cable arrived from the Swedish ambassador to China transmitting a message from Zhou Enlai:

> The Chinese Government has decided to release the imprisoned U.S. fliers. This release from serving their full term takes place in order to maintain friendship with Hammarskjöld and has no connection to the UN resolution. Zhou Enlai expresses hope that Hammarskjöld will take note of this point.
>
> Zhou Enlai congratulates Hammarskjöld on his 50th birthday.

The combination of the shrewd statecraft of the Peking Formula and leader-to-leader personal rapport had worked. A dangerous

situation had been defused. This allegedly inconsequential international bureaucrat showed himself to be quite consequential. "The
whole episode has given the organization and my position notice-
ably greater weight," Dag reflected in a letter to his brother Bo. He
meant both parts of the statement. "To rejoice at a success is not the
same as taking credit for it," he wrote in his diary. "To deny oneself
the first is to be a hypocrite and a denier of life; to permit oneself
the second is a childish indulgence which will prevent one from ever
growing up."

Crisis Resolution: Suez, 1956

What made the Suez crisis the most serious the world had faced since
the end of World War II was how a secret attack against Egypt by
Britain, France, and Israel fed into three dangerous dynamics: the
Arab-Israeli conflict, Third World nationalism/anti-imperialism, and
the Cold War.

In May 1948, in one of its first major actions, the UN had approved
a two-state partition creating the State of Israel and intending to create the State of Palestine. This, though, led to war, not peace. The UN
worked out a series of armistice agreements starting with Israel-Egypt
(February 1949) and in the months that followed between Israel and
Lebanon, Jordan, and Syria. The United States, Britain, and France
pledged in the Tripartite Declaration of 1950 to prevent violations of
the armistice agreements. Still the situation was tenuous at best, with
recurring clashes and casualties from Arab *fedayeen* raids and Israeli
counterstrikes. In late 1955 the Security Council dispatched Hammarskjöld to try to tamp things down. He made some progress but could
see that with its deep historical roots and antagonisms the Arab-Israeli
conflict was going to be a major challenge.

While Egypt had been officially independent since 1922, it was only
with the 1952 revolution led by Colonel Gamal Abdel Nasser that British influence in the country was seriously challenged. Nasser's nation-
alization of the Suez Canal in July 1956 was hailed by many in the
colonial and ex-colonial world as a blow against European imperial-

ism. For Britain Suez was a crown jewel of empire, an engineering feat when built in 1858–1869 and crucial to commerce ever since. There also was great concern over how such an act of defiance might reverberate through an empire already strained. For France the direct costs were less but the symbolism equally concerning.

The United States had its own Cold War issues with Nasser. Along with other Third World leaders, Nasser was at the forefront of the Non-Aligned Movement. Worse, he was tilting to the Soviet bloc. In late 1955, Egypt had signed an arms deal with Moscow (funneled through Czechoslovakia). In May 1956, Nasser established relations with Mao's China. The Soviet Navy paid a port visit to Alexandria. In retaliation, the Eisenhower administration withdrew U.S. funding and blocked further World Bank funding for the Aswan High Dam, Nasser's signature project then under construction.

The Egyptians were showing Hammarskjöld some flexibility, but the British and French were feigning interest in a negotiated settlement. They already had decided to invade and were meeting secretly with the Israelis. On October 29 Israel launched the attack. Its forces moved quickly to within 20 miles of the Suez Canal. As planned, Britain and France issued an ultimatum demanding a cease-fire and offering forces that would "temporarily" occupy the Canal Zone to separate the belligerents and keep shipping lanes open. Also as planned, Israel agreed to the proposal. As expected, Egypt rejected it. British bombers stationed on Cyprus were at the ready. Naval flotillas set out with troops aboard.

The United States, thinking very much in Cold War terms, was now concerned about the Soviet Union positioning itself as the friend of Arab nationalism. On October 30, UN Ambassador Henry Cabot Lodge, Jr., introduced a Security Council resolution calling for an immediate cease-fire and noninterference by outside powers, only to have it vetoed by Britain and France. The next day the British and French began bombing Cairo and landing troops along the Suez Canal.

Hammarskjöld was outraged. Here were two permanent Security

Council members attacking another member state. They did so in violation of the agreement they had signed as guarantors of regional peace (the 1950 Tripartite Declaration). They had directly deceived him. They never really were interested in a compromise resolution of the Suez Canal issue. "I want him [Nasser] destroyed," British Prime Minister Anthony Eden reportedly had said. "And I don't give a damn if there's anarchy and chaos in Egypt." Hammarskjöld never before publicly criticized member states; he did so this time and in the principled terms he held dear:

> As a servant of the Organization, the Secretary-General has the duty to maintain his usefulness by avoiding public stands on conflicts between Member nations unless . . . such an action might help to resolve the conflict. He must also be a servant of the principles of the Charter, and its aims must ultimately determine what for him is right and wrong.

As with the Peking Formula, Hammarskjöld again demonstrated shrewd statecraft. On November 1 he engineered the very first Emergency Special Session of the General Assembly under a precedent called "uniting for peace," which empowered the General Assembly to act if the Security Council was paralyzed and to do so without being subject to Security Council permanent members' veto. By a vote of 64 to 5 with 6 abstentions, a resolution passed calling for an immediate cease-fire, the withdrawal of all foreign troops, and empowering the secretary-general to take further actions.

Amid all this came a crisis in Hungary, one of the Eastern European states the Soviets had made a Cold War satellite. Political unrest had been building in recent weeks. The reformist Imre Nagy, deposed once by the Soviets, had been brought back to power after a wave of popular protests. On November 1, he announced Hungary's withdrawal from the Warsaw Pact. On November 4, the Soviet Red Army invaded. Talk about overloading the circuits, here's what the Security Council schedule looked like:

Sunday, October 28, 4:00–9:50 P.M., Security Council meeting on
  Hungary
Tuesday, October 30, Suez, 11:00 A.M.–1:10 P.M., 4:00–7:55 P.M.,
  9:00–11:05 P.M.
Wednesday, October 31, Suez, 3:00–7:20 P.M.
Thursday/Friday, November 1–2, Suez, 9:50 P.M.–4:20 A.M.
Friday, November 2, Hungary, 5:00–8:50 P.M.
Saturday, November 3, Hungary, 3:00–6:50 P.M.
Saturday/Sunday, November 3–4, Suez, 8:00 P.M.–3:00 A.M.
Sunday, November 4, Hungary, 3:00–5:25 A.M., 4:00–8:10 P.M.
Monday, November 5, Suez, 8:00–10:25 P.M.

On November 4, Israel and Egypt agreed to a cease-fire. Britain
and France continued their military operations. The Soviet opportun-
ism the Eisenhower administration had feared manifested in an offer
to send Russian air and naval forces to Egypt ostensibly to help restore
peace. Washington put its own pressure on London and Paris, including a partial oil embargo and financial sanctions. By November 6 the
combination of UN diplomatic pressure and U.S. economic coercion
got the British and French to sign on to the cease-fire.

Given the checkered history of Middle East cease-fires, though,
there needed to be some mechanism for enforcement and political stability. Working closely with Canadian Foreign Minister–UN Ambassador Lester (Mike) Pearson, and in consultation with a number of
member countries other than Security Council permanent members,
Hammarskjöld developed a plan for a United Nations Emergency
Force (UNEF). The UNEF was the very first UN peacekeeping operation. The idea was one thing; getting a peacekeeping force to Egypt
quickly and making it effective were quite another. How would a force
be put together quickly and with an acceptable composition? How to
allay Egyptian concerns about sovereignty?

On the composition of the force, Hammarskjöld and Pearson
insisted that the troops be drawn from countries that were not permanent members of the Security Council. It was a brilliant move that

demonstrated an understanding of fostering legitimacy through context. It was greeted with widespread support. Offers for troops came from 24 countries. The troops were drawn from 10: Brazil, Canada, Colombia, Denmark, Finland, India, Indonesia, Norway, Sweden, and Yugoslavia. Some countries were said to be offended that they were left out! Recognizing that only the United States had the logistical capabilities to get the forces to Egypt expeditiously, an arm's-length arrangement was struck whereby U.S. airlifts moved UNEF troops to a staging area outside Egypt.

Another matter was uniforms. Having a distinctive insignia would both help with safety by making UN peacekeeping troops recognizable and would be good for morale and esprit de corps. Thus was conceived the idea of the UN blue helmets/blue berets. Because there wasn't time to place a large manufacturing order, U.S. Army surplus helmets were acquired and painted blue.

On November 13, Egyptian Foreign Minister Mahmoud Fawzi expressed unwillingness to accept Canadian forces in the UNEF because of Canada's membership in the British Commonwealth. In Hammarskjöld's view, the Egyptian objection was outrageous. The Canadians had worked with him on creating UNEF and had even threatened to leave the Commonwealth if Britain refused to accept the cease-fire. As with the Peking Formula, Hammarskjöld devised a creative formulation that both acknowledged Egypt's sovereign rights to decide whether or not a peacekeeping force could enter its country, and asserted the UN's right to comprise the force. His persistence and framing of the argument succeeded. As the first UNEF contingent headed out, inclusive of Canadian troops, Hammarskjöld was with them.

Still, the issue remained of who would decide when the mission had ended and when UNEF had to leave. Nasser argued that the decision should be entirely up to Egypt. Hammarskjöld preferred the decision to be made by the UN. Nasser would not agree. Hammarskjöld countered with an understanding by which the UN recognized Egypt's right to request UNEF withdrawal but that Egypt would agree to make any such request contingent on the completion of UNEF's mission.

Having successfully completed the negotiations and created a more stable partnership with the Egyptians, Hammarskjöld returned to the UN a hero. President Eisenhower affirmed his support: "The last thing we must do is to disturb any of the delicate negotiations now going on under the leadership of Secretary-General Dag Hammarskjöld. We must do nothing that could possibly delay his operations, impede them, or hurt them in any way." The following year Hammarskjöld was unanimously reelected to a second term as UN secretary-general. The General Assembly hailed him as "our supreme International Civil Servant, a 'self-effacing man' of 'scrupulous objectivity.' "

Crisis Unresolved and Worse: Congo, 1960–1961

While some African countries had moved from colonialism to independence without violence, the Belgian Congo had not. Within a week of the country's formal independence on June 30, 1960, political instability flared. The country was soon engulfed in a multisided war among Congolese factions as well as Belgian troops and Western mercenaries, with the United States and the Soviet Union drawn in Cold War style with their own proxies.

Belgium, late to the African colonial game, acquired the Congo in 1885. Even by fellow monarch colonist "standards," King Leopold II was extraordinarily exploitative. Early on the Belgian Congo became the focal point for international protests led by the crusading journalist E. D. Morel and including the likes of Mark Twain and Arthur Conan Doyle. It was the basis for Joseph Conrad's searing novel *Heart of Darkness*. A portrait of Conrad hung in Hammarskjöld's apartment.

Belgium did little to prepare Congo for independence. The British and French at least had created some political institutions that provided initial foundations for their former colonies. When Congo became independent, the country did not have a single doctor of its own, no engineers, no army officers, and but one lawyer—in a country nearly five times the size of France.

Joseph Kasavubu and Patrice Lumumba, two very different leaders of the independence movement, split the vote in the first free Congolese election. Kasavubu was more traditional. Educated by Roman Catholic missionaries, he hailed from the Bakongo, one of the largest ethnic groups, and held the "highest" position Congolese could achieve in the Belgian colonial civil service. Lumumba was a more fervent independence leader, arrested at least twice by the Belgians, whose Congolese National Movement brought together various ethnic and tribal groups. Since neither man could form a parliamentary coalition, Kasavubu became president and Lumumba became prime minister. Rivalry and distrust, though, remained. "If Kasavubu claimed to be the father of the nation," as one UN official put it, "Lumumba regarded himself as the messiah of his people."

On top of these tensions the army's enlisted forces mutinied against the central government's decision to not immediately promote Congolese in the officer corps. Reports spread of killings, rapes, and other violence against whites. Belgium responded with troop deployments. Masses of Europeans fled; these were the teachers, judges, doctors, engineers, air traffic controllers, and other professionals needed to keep the country running.

On July 11, the Congolese province of Katanga announced its decision to secede. This was Congo's key economic province, rich for mining and accounting for 50 percent of annual revenues and 75 percent of foreign exchange. Leading the secession was Moise Tshombe. He was well connected to Belgian and other Western business interests, so much so that *Time* magazine called him "the solemn black defender of white capitalism in middle Africa, a rarity."

On July 12, Kasavubu and Lumumba jointly requested UN assistance to reverse the Katanga secession and stop Belgian aggression. Conscious of the need to move quickly, Hammarskjöld invoked Article 99 of the UN Charter: "The Secretary-General may bring to the attention of the Security Council any matter which in his opinion may threaten the maintenance of international peace and security." In other words, the UN's agenda did not depend solely on what the Security Council may tell the secretary-general to pay attention to; directives may be issued by the secretary-general as well.

Hammarskjöld pushed for a peacekeeping force. This was different from the Suez crisis, which had been an *inter*-state issue concerning countries that had invaded another nation. As an *intra*-state intervention, Congo raised knotty issues of sovereignty and political neutrality. It also raised Cold War tensions as both the Soviet Union and the United States already were picking their favorite Congolese leaders. In an all-night session Hammarskjöld secured a Security Council resolution establishing the United Nations Operation in Congo ("Opération des Nations Unies au Congo," ONUC in French) with three objectives: ensure withdrawal of the Belgian troops, help the elected government restore and maintain order, and assist the government in providing services until the country could do so on its own.

The Security Council adjourned at 3:25a.m. Hammarskjöld kept working through the night. He sent troop requests to Ghana, Guinea, Mali, Morocco, Tunisia, and Ethiopia: he wanted the operation to show African support and solidarity. He then contacted the Americans and the Soviets and requested them to coordinate an airlift of the international force. By July 18, the first 3,500 ONUC peacekeeping troops were in the Congo.

Tshombe, though, refused to let ONUC into Katanga. The Belgian forces supporting him resorted to the circular argument that they wouldn't withdraw until order was established, but given its limited mandate ONUC couldn't enter Katanga until the Belgians indicated they would allow them in peacefully. In early August Hammarskjöld went back to the Security Council for another resolution, toughening the demands for Belgian withdrawal and clearly stating that ONUC had the right to enter Katanga. He then took off for the Congo to meet directly with the leaders. He hammered out an agreement with Tshombe for ONUC forces to arrive August 15. By September 9, the Belgians had withdrawn from Katanga.

Lumumba, though, objected that while the agreement covered Belgian withdrawal it did not end the Katanga secession. He attacked Hammarskjöld personally. When Lumumba rebuffed Hammarskjöld's request for a meeting, the secretary-general returned to New York to consult further with the Security Council. In Hammarskjöldian style this was as much a statement to, as a consultation with, the Council:

> I have been forced to act with great firmness in relation to many
> parties. One of them has been the central government itself. I
> do not believe I have ever failed in courtesy. On the other hand,
> I do not excuse myself for having stated clearly the principles of
> the Charter and for having acted independently on their basis,
> mindful of the dignity of the Organization—and to have done so
> whether it suited all those we are trying to help or not.

It was around this time that Lumumba first turned to the Soviets for military aid. He also ordered his personal guards to harass UN security officers, even sending Congolese troops to arrest Canadian soldiers aboard a UN plane. The Red Cross reported Lumumba's orders to slaughter civilians that, Hammarskjöld relayed to the Security Council, are "a most flagrant violation of elementary human rights and have the characteristics of a genocide since they appear to be directed toward the extermination of a specific ethnic group." The secretary-general came back to the dilemma of neutrality: "Should it be supposed that the duty of the United Nations to observe strict neutrality in the domestic conflicts and to assist the central government means that the United Nations cannot take action in such cases?" For Hammarskjöld this was about Congo; for our generation it has been about Bosnia, Rwanda, Syria, and Congo again.

With Lumumba's actions as both cause and pretense, and with CIA covert support, President Kasavubu dismissed Prime Minister Lumumba. Even before Lumumba had turned to the Soviets for aid, the United States had tagged him, as CIA head Allen Dulles put it, "a person who was Castro or worse." This was less based on evidence than an assessment of his background such that Dulles deemed it "safe to go on the assumption that L [Lumumba] has been bought by the Communists." Larry Devlin, the CIA station chief, later recounted in his memoirs how he drafted a how-to paper for Kasavubu "outlining step-by-step the actions he should take before dismissing Lumumba and what he should do in the aftermath."

Lumumba retaliated by calling for the Congolese army to revolt. All this further complicated the UN role. Hammarskjöld knew that any UN action appearing to favor one side would destroy ONUC's claim to impartiality. At the same time he recognized that amid the threat of large-scale violence, they must try to maintain order.

In yet another twist, on September 14, Congolese Colonel Joseph Mobutu launched his own military coup. He'd cleared his plans with the CIA. His vehement anti-Soviet views hit the sweet spot. "The more I considered Mobutu's plan," Devlin wrote, "the better it sounded." He would stay in power, Mobutu assured Devlin, "only so long as necessary to get the Soviets out of the Congo and to create a democratic regime." Mobutu would rule Congo (later renamed Zaire) for over three decades with extraordinary brutality and corruption.

While it was the United States doing the interfering, it was the UN that bore the brunt of the criticism. International perceptions of UN impartiality were fading. The Soviets especially led this charge. As the calendar would have it, the opening of the annual General Assembly session was the next week with many heads of state in attendance, including Soviet Premier Nikita Khrushchev. "While granting independence in form," Khrushchev declared, "colonialists do their utmost to maintain colonial oppression." He went directly after Hammarskjöld: "They have been doing this unseemly work through the UN Secretary-General, Mr. Hammarskjöld, and his staff." The attack was quite strident, threatening, and personal:

If the Secretary-General cannot muster the courage to resign in, let us say a chivalrous way, we shall . . . ensure the Secretary-

General shall be taken and conveyed in a cart, wearing nothing but a shirt, holding a torch of burning wax weighing two
pounds; then taken, in the said cart, to the Trusteeship Council, where, on a scaffold that will be erected there, the flesh will
be torn from his breasts, arms, thighs and calves with red-hot
pincers, burnt with sulphur, and [a few more tortures thrown
into the mix] . . . reduced to ashes and his ashes thrown to the
winds.

Khrushchev further proposed that the position of secretary-general be
abolished and replaced with a "troika," an executive body consisting
of three individuals representing the East, West, and nonaligned countries. The goal here went beyond Congo to weakening Hammarskjöld
and the secretary-generalship on an ongoing basis.

Hammarskjöld was determined to resist. It wasn't just the personal aspect; we've seen how Hammarskjöld's predominant focus
since assuming the office of secretary-general had been to strengthen
the institution of the Secretariat and preserve its independence. He
refused to even entertain Khrushchev's proposal and argued passionately that member states needed to consider the deleterious practical
effects of the troika system. He delivered a bold and full-throated
defense of his conduct as secretary-general and his vision of the UN:

I regret that the intervention to which I have found it necessary
to reply has again tended to personalize an issue which, as I
have said, in my view is not a question of a man but of an institution . . . It is not the Soviet Union or, indeed, any other big
powers who need the United Nations for their protection; it is
all the others. In this sense the Organization is first of all their
Organization, and I deeply believe in the wisdom with which
they will be able to use it and guide it. I shall remain in my post
during the term of my office as a servant of the Organization in
the interest of all those other nations, as long as they wish me
to do so.

Hammarskjöld's speech was met with thunderous applause and a standing ovation that lasted several minutes.

In early December Lumumba was captured by Mobutu. On January 17 he was brutally murdered. Mobutu and Tshombe both reportedly were on the scene. Belgian members of the Katangan gendarmes were part of the firing squad. While the CIA was not directly involved in the actual act of assassination, it had a hand in the planning. UN forces that had been trying to protect Lumumba were targeted by Mobutu's forces with a shoot-to-kill order if they interfered. Still, the UN and Hammarskjöld personally were the ones blamed. The Soviets called for his resignation. African and Third World leaders attacked him. A riot in the Security Council public gallery turned violent, with protesters abusing UN guards while trying to make their way toward Hammarskjöld. These confrontations were not spontaneous but were staged with support from a number of delegations, which in themselves made the point. Hammarskjöld received piles of hate mail. For the first time in his life he had become an "object of hatred among a small minority."

Even amid this cacophony, Hammarskjöld managed to get the Security Council to pass a resolution toughening up ONUC's mandate. Resolution 161, passed February 21, 1961, called for "all appropriate measures to prevent the occurrence of civil war in the Congo, including arrangements for cease-fires, the halting of all military operations, the prevention of clashes, and *the use of force, if necessary, in the last resort*" (emphasis added). Even qualified as a last resort, this authorization of the use of force was a major step in what UN peacekeeping forces could do. On this basis as well as another provision calling for the withdrawal of mercenaries, in August ONUC launched Operation Rumpunch in Katanga. But ONUC forces were outgunned and outmaneuvered by Tshombe's forces and CIA-supported mercenaries.

At this point Hammarskjöld decided he needed to negotiate directly with Tshombe. Having been successful with Zhou Enlai in 1954–1955 and Nasser in 1956, he was confident he could do the same with the

Congolese leader. They agreed to meet in Ndola, a town in neighboring Rhodesia. Preparations were made for Hammarskjöld to arrive on September 18, 1961.

He never arrived. His plane, a Transair DC-6 named the Albertina, crashed eight miles from the Ndola airport. Hammarskjöld was dead.

It was an accident, pilot error, according to the official story. The UN's own investigation was less conclusive, leaving open that sabotage prior to the plane taking off or an attack on it in flight "cannot be excluded." That was where it was left. Revelations over the years have intensified doubts. In 1992, two former UN officials sent a letter to the British newspaper the *Guardian*, claiming that mercenaries in the pay of a Belgian mining firm were responsible. In 2011, British researcher Susan Williams presented extensive evidence for the plausibility of assassination as published in *Who Killed Hammarskjöld? The UN, the Cold War and White Supremacy in Africa*. This spurred creation of the Hammarskjöld Commission, composed of distinguished international jurists, to address the question: "Does significant new evidence about Dag Hammarskjöld's death exist?" Its answer: "Undoubtedly it does." It made numerous requests for declassification of U.S. documents under the Freedom of Information Act. The requests were denied. The commission recommended that the UN reopen its inquiry as a matter "both of history and of justice." In 2013, the General Assembly voted to do so. The 2015 report from the panel "concluded, among other things, that there was significant new information with sufficient probative value to further pursue aerial attack or other interference as a hypothesis of the possible cause of the crash." In December 2016, in one of his final acts as secretary-general, Ban Ki-moon got the General Assembly to authorize further investigation. While still short of definitive, the investigative commission report released in September 2017 deemed "it plausible that an external attack or threat was a cause of the crash." The commission cited the continued unwillingness of the United States and other governments to release potentially vital information and called on them "to allow us to fill the remaining gaps in the narrative so the whole truth can finally be known. It remains to be seen whether it ever will.

WHAT: Balance Sheet

The "General Assembly meets today in the shadow of an immense tragedy," its president spoke to and on behalf of those assembled. "By giving life and dynamism to the Secretary-General's office, he [Hammarskjöld] gave life and impetus to the Organization itself." The eulogies followed one after the other. Even Nikita Khrushchev paying a condolence call at the Swedish embassy in Moscow conceded that while "our relations were somewhat 'special' . . . Hammarskjöld was a great man." Especially moving was this statement from a senior security officer at UN headquarters: "People were crying openly in every office, on every staircase. I had never seen so much sadness . . . disbelief . . . sheer grief." I was in fifth grade at the time in suburban New York. I didn't write this, but another fifth-grader from a nearby school did: "Dag Hammarskjöld I think was a great man because he wanted peace. He was indeed a brave man. Dag Hammarskjöld went on a trip a week ago. People told him not to go but he went and was killed."

In his eulogy U.S. Ambassador to the UN Adlai Stevenson lamented how "in his passing the community of nations has lost one of the greatest servants it ever had—a brilliant mind, a brave and compassionate spirit . . . This memory will always be with us as a reminder of the best that the United Nations can be and of the qualities which it demanded of us all." In a meeting a few months later with Sture Linnér, one of Hammarskjöld's closest Swedish friends and colleagues, President John F. Kennedy remarked that "in comparison to him, I am a small man. He was the greatest statesman of our century." Given all the CIA did in Congo to undermine Hammarskjöld's work, and perhaps some U.S. involvement in his death, these statements rankle. Stevenson appears not to have known what was going on. It's not clear whether President Kennedy did: Linnér's account of the meeting carries intriguing hints:

> The meeting . . . started with Kennedy explaining the background to his actions . . . He had, for his own political survival, felt obliged to heed the deep aversion towards communism or extreme left views in general, which even long after McCarthy's hysterical heyday played an important role in domestic American politics. He had gradually come to realize how unjustified it was to oppose the UN Congo policy for that reason, and since it was now too late to express his apology to Dag Hammarskjöld, he wanted to do so to me.

While some of the praise ascends into hagiography, Dag Hammarskjöld most assuredly was an extraordinary statesman. The Peking Formula prevented a potential crisis between the United States and the People's Republic of China. The Suez crisis entailed taking on two permanent members of the Security Council (Britain and France), balancing the Cold War interests of two others (United States and Soviet Union), navigating the dynamics of Third World nationalism, and at least somewhat modulating the Arab-Israeli conflict. The Congo crisis was not resolved but less because of what Hammarskjöld didn't achieve than what other parties did to undermine his efforts.* Nor was his statesmanship record limited to the three crises on which we have focused. In 1958 amid instability in Lebanon, he strengthened the UN Observation Group there and established a new UN office in

---

* After Hammarskjöld's death the situation grew even worse. Fighting continued, factionalism deepened. In 1965, with U.S. support, Mobutu staged his second coup. He ruled for over three decades repressing all political opposition, cultivating a personality cult (including changing his name to Mobutu Sese Seko and the country's name to Zaire), and creating a kleptocracy that left his people impoverished. When Mobutu finally was deposed in 1997, his legacy left the country so devastated that it (now renamed Democratic Republic of Congo) descended into internal war that continues to this day, despite UN diplomacy and peacekeeping forces, with a death toll over five million people.

Jordan to address tensions with Syria and other issues. In 1959 he sent a mediator to deal with the Thailand-Cambodia border dispute and a personal representative to deal with tensions between Laos and North Vietnam. In 1960 he went to South Africa following the Sharpeville massacre to pressure the apartheid government. At a time when international travel was neither quick nor easy, especially to Africa and Asia, Hammarskjöld undertook 76 international missions over the eight and a half years he was secretary-general.

He did have his failures and his limits. His offer to mediate the 1956 Hungarian crisis was flatly rejected by Moscow. This was too much a core Cold War issue for even a strong and assertive secretary-general to penetrate. In Congo he ran up against the inherent difficulties intra-state conflicts pose for the UN. The sovereignty-based sensitivity to international intervention, the whims and weaknesses of competing domestic leaders, and other dilemmas of nation- and state-building that have become all too familiar over the last few decades were being manifested then in Congo. His emphasis on impartiality over neutrality—no inherent bias for or against any party to the conflict but willing to take action if one side is the far more egregious aggressor—sought that elusive balance between fairness and effectiveness.

As a leader Hammarskjöld exemplified qualities central to our "who" framework. His prior record of service and the sincerity of his commitment to the UN as an institution gave him immense personal capital. His courage was clear and evident. He of course had ambition; we saw that from the early stages of his career, although as secretary-general it was more about the office than himself. To the extent that he had charisma it was more about capability than color, more about determination than dynamism. His sharp political skills were quite the surprise for those who initially saw him as a standard bureaucrat. He was self-confident enough to engage in negotiations with formidable counterparts and skilled and savvy enough to keep coming up with political formulas and legal bases for mutually agreeable diplomatic resolutions.

He also had his rough edges, as noted earlier: demanding, with a touch of arrogance, engendering some resentment. Whether in spite of or because of such imperfections, he was a truly extraordinary secretary-general. He "combined sound, hard realism with an extraordinary imagination," his close aide Andrew Cordier reflected. In the "hubbub" of the pressures of a crisis, as Brian Urquhart observed, "his quiet but commanding personality was very effective . . . In such circumstances only firm and unquestioned leadership can provide the impetus required to keep all the various participants moving in relative harmony and in the same direction."

A few months before his death Hammarskjöld composed a poem for his diary:

> Tired
> And lonely,
> So tired
> The heart aches
> . . .
> It is now,
> Now, that you must not give in.

In never giving in he proved wrong the impossible-job lamentation of his predecessor.

A HAMMARSKJÖLDIAN SECRETARY-GENERAL

While speaking to Hammarskjöld's high SARL, it is a cruel irony that there have been no Hammarskjöldians among successor secretary-generals. As we've seen, even amid the exigencies of crises, Hammarskjöld was conscious of not just dealing ad hoc with the issues at hand but also of establishing practices, processes, and precedents seeking to institutionalize the secretary-general role and the UN. The superpowers drew from his tenure a never-again lesson ensuring that only compliant candidates would be considered for secretary-general. Successor secretary-generals for their part learned the lesson of being less assertive and independent. One was derided as not having much more of a role in key issues of the day than a "head waiter," another as having so little political weight that if he fell out of a boat there wouldn't even be much of a splash. "SG" became short for scapegoat as major powers passed the buck of blame to the UN, deflecting from their own shares of responsibility.

Kofi Annan came the closest to the Hammarskjöld model. He was the only other secretary-general to win the Nobel Peace Prize (2001). He provided crucial leadership on many issues. His overall persona exuded moral authority in ways that, à la Hammarskjöld, exceeded his bureaucratic background as a mid- to low-level UN official and diplomat. New York society pages buzzed with his celebrity status. His secretary-generalship, though, was among the casualties of the 2003 Iraq war. In the period between the Al Qaeda attacks on September 11, 2001, on the United States and the Bush administration's launching of the war in Iraq on March 20, 2003, Annan worked to find enough common ground by which either war would be averted or sufficient consensus would allow the Security Council to authorize military action. But he tried to do so largely quietly, behind the scenes, tactically. He did not draw nearly enough on the enormous prestige he had built. When the Bush administration launched its war, he didn't say much more than "this is a sad day for the United Nations and the international community."

No question that taking on the United States at the height of its unipolarity and against such a fervently self-righteous administration was not only a formidable task but also a potentially transformational moment. To have asserted the authority of the United Nations on such a sweeping issue of international peace and security even when challenged by the sole superpower of the day—indeed, precisely when challenged by the sole superpower of the day—could have strengthened the UN in ways well beyond the Iraq issue. To be sure, Secretary-General Annan was hardly the only one who didn't step up against a war so ill-conceived. But as much as any one individual and more than most, he could have made a difference.

Ban Ki-moon, Annan's successor, reverted to the nondescript secretary-general mold; the *Economist* graded him 3 out of 10 on speaking truth to power. When he joined with the head of the Red Cross in what was widely advertised as "an unprecedented joint warning" for states to end conflicts, respect international law, and aid refugees—"enough is enough," Ban declared—it barely got any media coverage. Especially telling was the back-and-forth of the January 2014 UN-sponsored Geneva peace conference on Syria. Contending that no agreement was possible unless all major parties to the conflict were participating, Ban invited Iran. The United States objected. Ban was forced to disinvite the Iranians. While there are all too many others who bear much more responsibility for the Syrian tragedy, the point here is to note the dynamics of a UN-sponsored peace conference for which the UN secretary-general issues an invitation only to have to then rescind it because of American pressure—quite the contrast to Hammarskjöld's determination to take on the major powers in the Suez crisis.

The agenda for UN reform runs long and cuts deep. A 2016 report by a commission chaired by former Australian Prime Minister Kevin Rudd delineated 10 principles of change along with specific recommendations in 15 issue areas. Others have come up with their own agendas. While all are important, as with any large complex organization—be it a government, large corporation, university, or the like—unless there is strong and inspiring leadership at the top, little is likely to happen.

Some UN-watchers are hopeful about the new secretary-general, António Guterres. For his to become a Hammarskjöldian secretary-generalship, four elements are key:

- Statesman of the Charter

This was Hammarskjöld's core operating principle. Of course, the secretary-general has to be sensitive to the interests of member states. Especially the powerful ones: the P5 members are the ones that hire and fire you. Much of the responsibility is as the agent of the Security Council as well as the General Assembly. But the secretary-general does need to be independent and assertive as warranted by the demands of international peace and security. Article 99 of the UN Charter confers on the secretary-general authority to take the initiative "to bring to the attention of the Security Council any matter which *in his opinion* may threaten the maintenance of international peace and security" (italics added), as Hammarskjöld did in the 1960–1961 Congo case. Beyond that, he didn't just bring matters to the attention of the Security Council for its action but took the initiative for his own action, citing Article 100's mandate to member nations "to respect the exclusively international character of the responsibilities of the Secretary-General and staff and not to seek to influence them in the discharge of these responsibilities." The authority to take the initiative . . . exclusively international character of the responsibilities—this authority and these responsibilities are the essence of the uniqueness of the secretary-general as leader of the world's principal international institution.

- Soft Power as "Secular Pope"

"In no other hall, from no other platform can a world leader speak to all humanity." This was the introduction Ban Ki-moon gave to Pope Francis for his September 2015 UN speech. With prime access to the same hall and same platform, the UN secretary-general needs again to be the "secular Pope," arousing the conscience of the world and inspiring with a vision, realistic but ambitious, of what it truly means to be an international

community, and in particular what the UN can and needs to do
to help get us there.

• Prioritize Peacekeeping Reform

No issue is more crucial to the UN's credibility than peacekeeping. The $7 billion budget for peacekeeping is close to 30 percent
larger than the core UN budget. About 92,000 personnel are
deployed in 15 current "blue helmet" peacekeeping operations
globally. Yet the prominent story lines are about sexual abuse by
peacekeepers in the Central African Republic, the failure to stop
mass atrocities in Sri Lanka, peacekeepers being overrun by an
Al Qaeda affiliate in the Golan Heights, the cover-up of Suda-
nese attacks against civilians in Darfur, the heavy casualties in
Mali and Congo, and complicity in bringing cholera to Haiti. A
2015 internal commission made 140 proposals for reform. Plenty
more have come from think tanks, scholars, and nongovernmental organizations (NGOs). While reform involves many players,
the fact that "DPKO" (Department of Peace-Keeping Operations) falls within the Secretariat gives the secretary-general
both responsibility and opportunity for having strong impact.

• Reinvigorate the International Civil Service

In the Oxford speech that was his last, Hammarskjöld spoke
of "a dedicated professional service . . . recruited primarily for
efficiency, competence and integrity . . . on a wide geographic
basis . . . responsible only to the Organization [UN] in the performance of its duties and protected insofar as possible from
the inevitable pressures of national governments." As needed as
this was in the mid-twentieth century, it is even more so now
given the scope and complexity of the early twenty-first-century
global agenda. The balance needs to be reconfigured for fewer
political plums and more merit-based opportunities, cultivating a

new generation of experts, globally representative and with skills across the full range of the UN's portfolio.

The supply is there. Just ask any admissions officer or career placement staff at one of the universities that is part of the Association of Professional Schools of International Affairs (APSIA). But the international careers market is a competitive one. Young professionals also have opportunities with home governments, other international institutions, the private sector, and NGOs. For the UN to compete it has to shed its staid, bureaucratic, overly political image. A more dynamic secretary-general, inspiring young people and convincing them that they can make a difference, would be enormously motivating.

———

Nice ideas, but why would the major powers allow all this to happen? The United States bristles at encroachments on its prerogatives—and not just anti-UN conservatives and Trumpian America Firsters but also, to an extent, liberal multilateralists. Russia nods toward the UN when useful for criticizing and constraining the United States but goes its own way when it decides to do things like annex Crimea and assist Bashar Assad with atrocities in Syria. China won't even let the secretary-general and other UN officials do a ceremonial meet-and-greet with the Dalai Lama. Smaller member nations have been defiant in their own right.

If politics as usual prevails and preservation of prerogatives remains the priority, none of this will happen. The UN will continue to be largely ineffectual. There will be more deadly conflicts like Syria in which it is unable to play a significant role. More peacekeeping missions that fail to keep the peace. More global health pandemics like Ebola in which too little is done too late and too poorly. UN credibility will be further undermined, its brand further damaged. Yet trading off some prerogatives for a UN that is more effective at what only the UN can do is a net positive even for the major powers: actually, given the global scope of their interests, *especially* for the major powers. So too it is for less powerful countries that have less capacity of their own and less other recourse globally. "A more independent U.N. leader . . . may be an occasional irritant," as one of the more astute UN-watchers put it, "but also more useful when it really matters."

With a new secretary-general only recently in place, it is an opportunity to change the profile to what it once was—and can be and needs to be again.

RECONCILING THE POLITICS OF IDENTITY

Two households, both alike in dignity,
In fair Verona, where we lay our scene,
From ancient grudge break to new mutiny,
Where civil blood makes civil hands unclean.
—William Shakespeare, *Romeo and Juliet*, Prologue, 1–41

EVOLUTIONARY BIOLOGISTS AND ANTHROPOLOGISTS TRACE conflicts over identity—who I am, who you are, and what the differences are between us—back to long-ago tribal societies. Whether defined by race, religion, nationality, ethnicity, culture, or caste, history is replete with such "politics of identity." As tragic as Shakespeare's star-crossed lovers driven to suicide were, the toll has been far greater from the modern world's genocides, ethnic cleansings, and other mass atrocities committed in the name of identity.

This is not to buy into any "ancient hatreds" thinking about historical inevitability. History shapes. It does not determine. It does not just get played out. It gets played on, all too often by leaders who, when it serves their own agendas, purposefully activate and intensify historically rooted tensions. As a Bosnian schoolteacher put it amid the ethnic cleansing of the early 1990s incited by Slobodan Milosevic and other Serb demagogues, "We never, until the war, thought of ourselves as Muslims. We were Yugoslavs. But when we began to be murdered because we are Muslims things changed. The definition of who we are today has been determined by our killing."

Some leaders foment. Others, the peacemakers, pursue reconciliation. Here we highlight three such cases.

Nelson Mandela (Chapter 5) and his leadership in ending the racist apartheid system and leading South Africa's peaceful transition to democracy is the iconic case. The dignity with which he endured nearly three decades as a political prisoner inspired many people around the world as well as in his own country. His moral capacity to differentiate between hatred of the system and hatred of whites presented a very different model from those seeking retribution and revenge.

Yitzhak Rabin (Chapter 6) is the epitome of the soldier turned peacemaker. The top Israeli military commander in the 1967 war conquering the West Bank and other Arab territories, he became the prime minister who in 1993 shook hands with Palestine Liberation Organization leader Yasir Arafat and signed a series of peace agreements—only to be assassinated by a fellow Israeli. True, the pieces of peace he laid were partial. But without them there would be even less chance of ever getting to a full Arab-Israeli peace.

I also include **Betty Williams and Mairead Corrigan** (Chapter 7), everyday people who, as founders of the Northern Ireland Women for Peace, played key roles in decreasing the 1970s' Catholic-Protestant violence of "The Troubles." Motivated by what the Nobel Peace Prize Committee called "a passionate desire to make a stand against all violence and terror," they made a crucial breakthrough that paved the way for the 1998 Good Friday peace agreement.

When demagogic political leaders intentionally fuel identity-based tensions, hatreds become all the more visceral, the killing wanton and massive. When statesmen like Mandela and Rabin and everyday people like Corrigan and Williams provide more positive leadership, reconciliation is possible. We draw lessons for our era's identity-based conflicts.

5

Nelson Mandela:
Iconic Statesman of
Reconciliation, 1956–1999

WHO was Nelson Mandela?

He was born Rolihlahla (colloquially it means "troublemaker") Dalibhunga Mandela on July 18, 1918. His family was of the Thembu clan in the Transkei province of Eastern Cape, part of the Xhosa people. His father, Gadla Henry, was the grandson of tribal royalty and, through that lineage, a village headman. Mandela's mother, Nosekeni Nkedama, was the third of Gadla's four wives. A converted Methodist, she had Rolihlahla baptized. At seven years old the boy was sent to a mission school. All entering children were given a Christian name. His teacher Miss Mdingane named him "Nelson."

Gadla died when Nelson was nine. The family moved to Mqhekezweni, the Thembuland provincial capital, at the invitation of Chief Jongintaba Dalindyebo, who agreed to become Nelson's guardian. As per tribal custom the child was accepted into the Great Palace as if he was Jongintaba's own. This made Nelson an Xhosa aristocrat. It also put him in a position to be sent to some of the best schools open to Africans, culminating in 1939 at the South African Native College at Fort Hare.

Johannesburg, where he went after Fort Hare, was a very different environment than he had experienced previously. Apartheid, the total separation of the races with the black African majority brutally repressed and economically subjugated, had not yet been codified—that would come in 1948—but racism and discrimination were everywhere. Here he first came into contact with the African National Congress (ANC), black Africans' liberation movement, and leaders such as Walter Sisulu, who would be Mandela's most politically influential colleague. By this time Mandela aspired to be a lawyer. With Sisulu providing the introduction, Lazar Sidelsky, a Jewish lawyer who had black clients as well as white, hired Mandela as a clerk. Mandela considered Sidelsky "the first white man to treat me as a human being," the man who "trained me to serve our country."

But he didn't take Sidelsky's advice to stick to the law and stay out of politics. The ANC needed reinvigoration. Mandela rose through the ANC ranks and in 1952 was made national volunteer-in-chief of the civil disobedience Defiance Campaign. The apartheid government arrested and convicted him under the loosely interpreted Suppression of Communism Act, but his sentence was suspended. It also was in 1952 that he finished a diploma in law that, while not a full degree, allowed him to practice. With Oliver Tambo, whom he had known at Fort Hare and who would be another close political ally in the struggle against apartheid, Mandela & Tambo opened as the first black African law firm.

For his continued ANC activism Mandela was arrested in December 1956 with 155 others for "high treason." As principal strategist and spokesman for the group over the four years that their trial dragged out, he got much of the credit when they finally were acquitted. Still the apartheid regime's repression intensified, outlawing the ANC. Mandela, forced underground, nevertheless got a statement out through the ANC office in London. "No power on earth can stop an oppressed people determined to win their freedom," he declared in words that resonated internationally as well as in South Africa. "The struggle is my life," he said, affirming his own commitment. "I will continue fighting for freedom until the end of my days." When in 1962 his refuge was discovered and he was put back on trial, his fame was such that the government resorted to prohibiting even peaceful protests outside the courthouse. This trial, in which he delivered his "Black Man in a White Court" testimony and closing "Statement from the Dock," further enhanced his role and image as the embodiment of the anti-apartheid movement. No wonder the regime convicted him with a life sentence to be served on Robben Island, a prison off the coast of Cape Town, close enough to be in sight as a tease for the prisoners.

Over the next 27 years and 6 months of imprisonment, Nelson Mandela endured enormous physical and emotional hardship. Prisoners were roused at 5:30 a.m. They spent all morning sitting in the courtyard, cross-legged in four rows, forbidden to talk, crushing piles of stones into fine gravel with five-pound hammers. They could not rest until lunch, after which they worked again until 4 p.m. By 8 p.m. the night warder ordered everyone to go to sleep. During weekends, prisoners were kept inside their cells all day except for half an hour of exercise. Political prisoners were given the fewest privileges. They could only have one visitor every six months. They could write and receive only one letter in that same time. Even that was heavily censored. While good behavior was held out as a way to get at least some privileges, Mandela was resolute. He refused to address warders as *baas* (boss). He became a spokesman for prisoner interests, polite but firm, taking on the wrath of warders but gaining the respect of fellow prisoners. He showed little emotion, hiding anger, bitterness, doubt, and despair. He rarely if ever showed weakness. He was exceptionally self-disciplined. He exercised every morning in his cell. After years of asking, he finally received permission to start a small garden in the prison courtyard.

His hardest moments in prison occurred while alone, particularly in times of solitary confinement. "The worst part of imprisonment is being locked up by yourself," he wrote. "You come face to face with time and there is nothing more terrifying than to be alone with sheer time. . . . Was your sacrifice worth the trouble? What would your life have been like if you hadn't got involved?" While not particularly religious or spiritual, he found faith a source of strength. Every Sunday, he attended church services no matter which denomination had been chosen for the day. He took Holy Communion regularly, saying it gave him a sense of inner quiet and calm.

By the early 1980s, Free Mandela had become the rallying cry of the global anti-apartheid movement. It was heard at the United Nations where the Security Council, which had been calling for the release of South African political prisoners for many years, now made specific mention of Mandela. It spurred the most extensive foreign policy protest movements in the United States since the Vietnam War. The Freedom at 70 concert held in London in July 1988 to commemorate Mandela's seventieth birthday drew 72,000 and was broadcast by BBC to 200 million viewers in 60 countries. "Apart from the birthday of the Lord Jesus," a fellow political prisoner mused with a touch of hyperbole, "no birthday has ever been as widely celebrated as Nelson's 70th."

On February 11, 1990, following negotiations with South African President F. W. de Klerk, Nelson Mandela was released from prison. On May 10, 1994, Nelson Mandela was inaugurated as the president of South Africa. Before getting into the "why, how, and what" and the rest of the story, there are two points to make about the "who" at the center of this story.

Mandela's personal capital was second to none. There couldn't be a better fit with our conception of moral capital as authenticity of commitment rooted in the leader's personal traits. He combined a heritage deeply rooted in tribal tradition with having worked his way up through the ANC. There he was in his 1962 trial, dressed in a traditional Xhosa leopard-skin cape while masterfully defending himself and his fellow prisoners, embodying the traditional and the modern. Once out of prison he would be greeted at rallies in the townships as Madiba, his clan name representing the intimacy of kinship and respect of ascribed status, and then change into a tailored suit to go negotiate with the Afrikaner government.

He repeatedly showed courage in putting himself on the front lines of the struggle, manifesting that commitment to "an ideal for which I am prepared to die." While hiding underground and evading police, he gained a reputation for daring. On Robben Island, where upon arrival he was told by a guard "this is an island, and this is where you'll die," he remained defiant as he felt the cause warranted it.

Early in his career he struggled to control his temper and ego. The 1962 and 1964 trials appear to have been tempering. As biographer Anthony Sampson put it, "he had emerged from his two trials with more strength and depth than even some close friends had imagined possible . . . the showmanship expressed in different roles had contracted into a single clear commitment . . . he seemed . . . at peace with himself." Mandela grew increasingly adept at not letting bitterness or defeat show either to adversaries who could exploit it or supporters who depended on his strength and steadiness.

His political skills were adroit. His early exposure to Chief Jongintaba's leadership style of command and openness in tribal meetings showed him how to listen but also lead. Mandela's combination of legal training and political experience gave him enormous self-confidence in his powers of persuasion. The verdicts in his trials were foregone conclusions, but he saw how the courtroom could be political theater. His jailers had the keys but he could still make his own political points during talks over his release. As a campaigner he masterfully blended a touch of the regal from his clan roots with the politician's techniques of meet-and-greet-and-connect. To gain trust among whites he showed much less of the frown of bitterness than the smile of reconciliation—and it was a smile that was "like the sun coming out on a cloudy day." His embrace of the Springboks, the Afrikaners' favorite rugby team, was packed with symbolism and emotional connectivity. "You don't address their brains," he explained. "You address their hearts." Meanwhile, he was a tough negotiator with Afrikaner President de Klerk.

He was, as Oliver Tambo observed, "the born mass leader . . . He is commanding with a tall, handsome bearing . . . dedicated and fearless . . . He cannot help magnetizing a crowd." And from his successor Thabo Mbeki, "We all saw ourselves reflected in his glory, . . . a glory that arises in his humility, his sense of forgiveness." When U.S. President Bill Clinton made his first visit to South Africa, and President Mandela used the occasion to deliver a speech highly critical of U.S. foreign policy on issues like Cuba and Iran, Clinton let it go in order to, as a *Washington Post* reporter put it, bask in the "aura of moral authority that had made Mandela so revered."

But as extraordinary as his public leadership skills were, he had many failings in his private life. His marriage to his first wife, Evelyn, failed. The demands of his political work were partly to blame: at one point his five-year-old son Thembi asked Evelyn if his father lived somewhere else. Also to blame was Nelson's infidelity, particularly with a 22-year-old social worker named Winnie Madikizela, whom he married in 1958. They would stay married until 1996, but this too was a rocky relationship. It was only three years into their marriage that Nelson had to go underground, and then came his years of imprisonment. While Winnie played her own leadership role in the anti-apartheid movement, over time she became increasingly involved in corruption and crime. They were divorced in 1996.*

Mandela's relations with his children also were problematic. "My greatest regret, and the most painful aspect of the choice I made," Mandela acknowledged, was his family life. "To be the father of a nation is a great honor; but to be the father of a family is a greater joy. But it was a joy I had too little of." We've stressed throughout this book that leaders are not perfect people. That actually reinforces the point about the possibilities of leadership. Imperfect people may apply and can succeed. The personal, though, often is a cost when, as with Mandela, "the struggle is my life."

WHY reconciliation over retribution?

In opting for reconciliation rather than retribution, Mandela demonstrated true statesmanship.

---

* In 1998 he married Graca Machel, widow of the revolutionary leader and president of Mozambique. They remained married until Mandela's death on December 5, 2013.

The ANC Youth League's 1948 Basic Policy Document, of which
Mandela was a primary author, while issued in the name "of an
oppressed people . . . waging a long, bitter and unrelenting struggle
for its national freedom," also acknowledged "the concrete situation in
South Africa, and realize that the different racial groups have come to
stay." The Congress of the People the ANC convened in August 1953
was multiracial: whites supportive of the African nationalist cause,
the Indian Congress, and the Coloured People's Congress as well as
the ANC. The Freedom Charter, formally adopted two years later,
begins with the declaration "that South Africa belongs to all who live
in it, black and white." It continues: "We, the people of South Africa,
black and white together as equals, countrymen and brothers adopt
this Freedom Charter; and we pledge ourselves to strive together, spar-
ing neither strength nor courage, until the democratic changes here
set out have been won."

The government's response was his 1956 arrest for high treason. A
few years later, on March 21, 1960, came the Sharpeville massacre
where 69 anti-apartheid protesters were killed and 186 wounded. Still
Mandela stressed nonviolent civil disobedience. Yes, "we felt that the
Government will not hesitate to massacre hundreds of Africans . . .
but as far as we were concerned we took the precautions to ensure
that violence will not come from our side." Once released from prison
he tried again, writing a letter to Prime Minister Hendrik Verwoerd
calling for a constitutional convention to create a multiracial democracy. The government instead cracked down further.

It was in this context that Mandela turned to violence. "If the government reaction is to crush by naked force our non-violent struggle,"
he told local and foreign journalists brought to meet with him in a
safe house, "we will have to reconsider our tactics. In my mind we are
closing a chapter on this question of a non-violent policy." *Umkhonto we
Sizwe* (MK), "Spear of the Nation," was created as the armed offshoot
of the ANC, with Mandela as chairman and Joe Slovo, a leader of the
South African Communist Party, second in command. December 16,
the date when in 1838 the Afrikaners defeated the Zulus at the Battle

of the Blood River, was chosen for the first attacks. "The time comes in the life of any nation," leaflets read, "when there remain only two choices: submit or fight." Violent revolutions around the same time in China, Cuba, Algeria, and elsewhere provided some sense that this was the way for South Africa to go.

Mandela had very little training or expertise with sabotage or guerrilla action. He tried reading up: Clausewitz, Mao, Menachem Begin on the Irgun in Israel, even a classic work about South Africa's own Boer War. In January 1962 he sneaked out of the country to build support for MK. He attended the Conference on the Pan-African Freedom Movement for Central, East and Southern Africa. He took military training in Ethiopia. "First lesson in demolition" was one of his daily diary entries. Photos show him dressed in military fatigues, pistol in his belt. Amnesty International, then a newly formed human rights group committed to nonviolence, refused to adopt him as a prisoner of conscience.

On August 5, 1962, shortly after reentering South Africa, Mandela was captured. This was his "Black Man in a White Court" confession to the crimes but defense of the justness of disobeying unjust laws. He argued that the case was not only about him, but also that it was "a trial of the aspirations of the African people. [You say I broke the laws, but] we as Africans [not just me] are neither morally nor legally bound to obey laws which we have not made, nor can we be expected to have confidence in courts which enforce such laws." His initial conviction was only for inciting strikes and unlawful exit and entry, but with further evidence of his role in the MK (including from an informant labeled "Mr. X"), Mandela was put back on trial. For over four hours in his even more famous "Statement from the Dock," he proceeded to go through the history of the ANC from its founding in 1912. He went through the injustices of apartheid—poverty, malnutrition, disease, illiteracy, menial jobs, the pass laws with their restrictions on living and movement, and "the lack of human dignity."

> Whites tend to regard Africans as a separate breed. They do not
> look upon them as people with families of their own; they do

not realize that they have emotions—that they fall in love like
white people do; that they want to be with their wives and children like white people want to be with theirs; that they want to
earn enough money to support their families properly, to feed and
clothe them and send them to school . . . Africans want to be part
of the general population, and not confined to living within their
own ghettoes . . . Africans want to be allowed out after eleven
o'clock at night and not to be confined to their rooms like little
children.

He acknowledged being a leader of MK. After trying for decades to
pursue nonviolence, "when this form was legislated against, and then
the Government resorted to a show of force to crush opposition to its
policies, only then did we decide to answer violence with violence."
And he ended: "I have cherished the ideal of a democratic and free
society in which all persons live together in harmony and with equal
opportunities. It is an ideal which I hope to live for and to achieve. But
if needs be, it is an ideal for which I am prepared to die." Yet even then
he separated his version of African nationalism from those that sought
to "drive the White man into the sea." He was never viscerally anti-
white. His own life experiences included whites who had helped him.
The system and the "race maniacs who govern our beloved country"
were one thing, as he had differentiated back in 1961, but the Cauca-
sian race was another.

In the early 1970s a new generation of black activists arose as the
Black Consciousness movement led by Steve Biko, a medical student
at the University of Natal. Black Consciousness spread among the
youth, drawing upon the Africanist tradition of black politics that
incorporated a sense of black assertiveness and a view of their parents'
generation as having failed at the task of liberation. No more ANC-
style multiracial coalitions; blacks needed to escape the paternalism
of white liberals. The government retaliated with a new law requiring
Afrikaner as the official language of instruction in schools. Massive
student protests ensued: while English was not indigenously African,

Afrikaner was the language of the oppressor. In June 1976 an estimated 20,000 high school students living in Soweto, a black ghetto in Johannesburg, went on strike, only to be brutalized by the police. An estimated 700 protesters died and thousands were arrested. Soon after, Steve Biko was arrested, tortured, and killed.

While Mandela smuggled out from prison a statement in support of the Soweto revolt, he had his doubts about the Black Consciousness movement. Some of this was leadership rivalry. He and other ANC leaders had not anticipated how wide the generation gap had become. In his fiery leadership while alive and in his martyrdom, Biko was a competitor for the anti-apartheid mantle. The Soweto riots spurred the most substantive United Nations action to that point, an arms embargo imposed by the Security Council against South Africa. The movie *Cry Freedom,* based on Biko's life, with the same director, Richard Attenborough, who had made *Gandhi,* was a global hit.

Mandela also was concerned about the rejection of multiracialism. Mandela felt Black Consciousness was making the same mistakes as the Black Panthers in the United States of developing their own version of racism. The emphasis on blacks developing in their own distinct way, however paradoxically, reinforced principles of apartheid. The youthful idealism was admirable in its spirit but not sufficiently disciplined or strategic.

Mandela also knew that unity was necessary to end apartheid. With many Black Consciousness leaders incarcerated on Robben Island, he invited them to present their ideas to the older prisoners and vice versa. This wasn't easy or straightforward. One Black Consciousness leader who sought Mandela out and was persuaded by his multiracial strategy was beaten up by his comrades as a sellout. But he stuck to his views and over time was joined by others. Mandela also used sports as a vehicle for unity, integrating the prison soccer/football teams rather than having them ANC versus BC.

Most of all Mandela's vision of reconciliation was rooted in the traditional African concept of *ubuntu.* Ubuntu is best characterized as an African version of humanism stressing the interconnectedness of all peoples in society. "I always knew that deep down in every human heart, there is mercy and generosity," Mandela wrote. "No one is born hating another person because of the color of his skin, or his background, or his religion. People must learn to hate, and if they can learn to hate, they can be taught to love, for love comes more naturally to the human heart than its opposite." For all the arguments about justifiable retribution for a system as evil as apartheid, ubuntu taught that retribution hurt everyone. Mandela's message was both to the whites—"a better life for *all*," as the tag line for his 1994 presidential candidacy read—and to his fellow blacks—to be the ones taking the lead in building "a society of which all humanity will be proud," as he urged in his inaugural address as president.

HOW was apartheid ended?

Mandela's Walk to Freedom

In January 1985, South African President P. W. Botha thought he'd come up with a clever strategy. With the international Free Mandela movement and other anti-apartheid pressure increasing, he'd offer Mandela release from prison on the condition that he renounce violence as a political instrument. If Mandela refused, then the world would see that Mandela was the problem. "The choice is his," Botha told the parliament. "All that is required of him now is that he should unconditionally reject violence as a political instrument, a norm which is respected in all civilized countries of the world."

Mandela refused. And he yet again reversed the accusation. In what would be his first statement heard publicly since his 1964 imprisonment, he got a message smuggled out to be read at a Soweto rally celebrating the Nobel Peace Prize recently awarded to Bishop Desmond Tutu. "Only free men can negotiate. Prisoners cannot enter into contracts . . . I cannot and will not give any undertaking at a time when I and you, the people, are not free . . . Let Botha renounce violence. Let him say that he will dismantle apartheid. Let him unban the people's organization, the African National Congress . . . Let him guarantee free political activity so that people may decide who will govern them."

Principled, yes, and also a shrewd negotiating strategy. International pressure mounted, including from the United States. Despite President Ronald Reagan's continued belief that Mandela and the ANC were the problem, the anti-apartheid movement had become the most politically potent foreign policy protest movement since the Vietnam War. With members of Congress, civil rights leaders, mayors, religious leaders, Hollywood celebrities, and other prominent citizens peacefully and dramatically chaining themselves to the fence around the South African embassy in Washington and submitting themselves to arrest, the movement struck a chord. The contrast with the footage being beamed into American living rooms of police crackdowns in the townships and streets of South Africa was striking (that is, until the apartheid government imposed stricter censorship). Economic sanctions had so much bipartisan support in Congress that President Reagan's veto was overridden by whopping 313–83 and 78–21 margins. States and cities divested stocks in their public pension funds from companies trading with and investing in South Africa. The economic burden was mounting. The sense of cultural isolation was arguably even more powerful: South African teams were banned from some international sports, South African citizens restricted from travel to certain parts of the world, and even when able to travel they often were made to feel like pariahs.

Botha doubled down. He imposed a state of emergency in cities and townships across the country. Mass arrests were made. The death toll reached more than three people a day. He would not lead his country to "suicide." He blamed "communist agitators" and the foreign media. But the economic crisis worsened. The rand, South Africa's currency, plunged. The Johannesburg stock exchange had to be shut down for days at a time. When a group of South African businessmen set up their own meeting with Oliver Tambo outside the country, Botha denounced them as traitors.

And Mandela was ill. In November 1985 he had surgery for an

enlarged prostate. The operation was successful, but this was a 67-year-old man who had spent nearly a quarter century living in prison conditions. Whatever else Botha and others thought about him, they knew that were Mandela to die in prison the reaction would be even more explosive than anything thus far.

Kobie Coetsee, the minister of justice and a former deputy minister of defense and intelligence, was designated to pay Mandela a surprise visit. Not much of substance was discussed, but the meeting was cordial, literally and figuratively. Coetsee offered Mandela a glass of sherry, his first drink in 24 years. But President Botha kept ratcheting up the repression. In June 1986 he extended the state of emergency nationwide. The month before he'd ordered air strikes on neighboring capitals Harare (Zimbabwe), Lusaka (Zambia), and Gaborone (Botswana), claiming they were harboring ANC bases.

For his part Mandela was concerned about the toll that the intensifying violence was taking on already meager livelihoods in the townships. In March 1989 he sent President Botha a 10-page memorandum.

> The deepening political crisis in our country has been a matter of grave concern to me for quite some time, and I now consider it necessary in the national interest for the African National Congress and the government to meet urgently to negotiate an effective political settlement.

The agenda needed to be both transition to majority rule and to address "the concern of white South Africa . . . that majority rule will not mean domination of the white minority by blacks." He ended with an appeal to Botha to "seize it [the moment] without delay."

> I believe the overwhelming majority of South Africans, black and white, hope to see the ANC and the government working closely together to lay the foundations for a new era in our country in which racial discrimination and prejudice, coercion and confrontation, death and destruction will be forgotten.

Botha finally agreed to meet with Mandela. The meeting was set for July 5. It amounted to little more than general talk. Mandela proposed that political prisoners be released. Botha said no. No progress was made on the other issues Mandela had raised. When word of the meeting leaked out, Botha's office called it simply "a courtesy call."

Six weeks later, Botha resigned the presidency. The new president, Frederik Willem de Klerk, was chosen because of his solid pro-apartheid credentials. He hailed from a politically prominent Afrikaner family. As minister of education he'd opposed proposals to integrate universities and supported funding cuts to universities that allowed students to conduct even peaceful anti-apartheid demonstrations. In the 11 years he had been in the Cabinet he had not supported a single proposal for reform of apartheid. But he also could see that the country was in trouble and that unrest at home and ostracism abroad had reached the point where some new strategies needed to be considered.

President de Klerk's initial inclination was toward less unequal but still separate arrangements whereby blacks had more voice and rights but only within their own political and societal institutions. Mandela and other ANC leaders held the line. Meanwhile, de Klerk's own National Party was being squeezed by extremists even further to the right and liberals on the left. A group of prominent Afrikaners holding secret meetings with Oliver Tambo and other ANC leaders in England reported back that there was a basis for negotiations.

In October 1989, Walter Sisulu and five others serving life sentences from the 1964 Rivonia trial were released. But not Mandela. On December 12, de Klerk finally met with Mandela. De Klerk pushed his idea of group rights. Mandela rejected this as maintaining white domination. He again stressed that he would not agree to his own release unless the ban was taken off the ANC and other political groups. De Klerk didn't concede, but he did listen. When the time came on February 2, 1990, for the president's speech opening the annual session of parliament, de Klerk announced a whole series of reforms: lifting the ban on the ANC as well as the South African Communist Party, releasing many political prisoners, easing the state of emergency, suspending capital punishment, and permitting exiles to return. Other reforms included the writing of a new constitution. Blacks would be allowed to vote. There would be equality under the law. And then because he "could play an important part" in this process and noting "that he has declared himself to be willing to make a constructive contribution to the peaceful political process in South Africa," Nelson Mandela was to be released from prison.

I recall sitting at home nine days later, a snowy day in Washington, DC, a sunny one in South Africa, watching live coverage of Nelson Mandela's walk to freedom. He waved to the crowds waiting outside the prison gates, smiling, some hugs for longtime supporters. Then into a car headed to Cape Town city hall where 50,000 people had gathered. And the whole world was tuned in to what for me remains one of my most moving moments of television watching.

Negotiating the Breakthrough

A peaceful transition to black majority democracy and a multiracial society beginning with Mandela's release from prison was by no means a given.

Afrikaners were wary at best. A poll showed 86.9 percent believed black majority rule would decrease white prosperity, 84.6 percent believed that it would decrease white safety, and 78.2 percent believed that it would not guarantee white minority rights. The untenability of apartheid was sinking in, but the favored option among Afrikaners was a federal state with power sharing (55.6 percent), not a unitary state even with minority rights protected (15.6 percent). And after years of state propaganda about how dangerous, evil, and white-hating he was, Nelson Mandela was feared more than trusted. Groups of army officers and policemen were financing white vigilante groups, aiding and abetting attacks on the ANC, and even training assassins. The Afrikaner Resistance Movement, clad with Nazi-like insignias, pursued secession to carve out an Afrikaner *volkstaat*.

Their hero now in their midst, ANC supporters were at once joyful and tense. While Mandela had shown loyalty by not accepting his own release without his comrades also being freed and the ban on the ANC being lifted, he had conducted the negotiations largely on his own. Some within the ANC criticized him for an ostensibly too cordial relationship with de Klerk. Mandela responded with a mix of accepting criticism while asserting leadership. Yes, leaders must not lose sight of "the principle that they are servants of the people," but those criticizing his degree of secrecy in dealing with de Klerk "do not understand the nature of negotiations." Comrades would have to trust him.

The first formal round of negotiations between the government and the ANC was convened May 2, 1990. Both sides found out "nobody in the room had horns," as one delegate put it. They also had some sense of shared interest, of being in the same boat with "sharks to the left and right," as another put it. The government pushed the ANC to fully renounce violence. The ANC offered a cease-fire but not a renunciation, at least not until the government ceased its state-sponsored violence and cracked down on white vigilantes and sufficient progress had been made on the overall agenda to end apartheid.

There also was the problem of Chief Mangosuthu Buthelezi, Zulu tribal leader and head of the KwaZulu Bantustan, the most populous of the apartheid-era homelands (areas designated just for blacks with some limited self-rule). Buthelezi and his Inkatha Freedom Party (IFP) aspired to be the alternative to Mandela and the ANC nationally. But rather than engage in the emerging political process, he and his party precipitated more political violence than either the ANC or the whites. Press stories at the time uncovered extensive de Klerk government collusion with Buthelezi, providing financial support, training, and in some instances operational help in attacks on ANC supporters in the townships. Later investigations by the Truth and Reconciliation Commission would reveal even more than was reported at the time.

In February 1992 de Klerk's National Party was defeated in a parliamentary by-election by the Conservative Party running on a platform opposing negotiations. In one of his bolder steps de Klerk called a referendum the next month on whether to proceed with negotiations for a new constitution. With an 86 percent turnout and 68 percent support, he got the vote of confidence he needed.

But the violence continued. On June 17, armed Inkatha supporters joined by white men with blackened faces and with colluding local police attacked the Boipatong township, killing 45, including women and children. This was the fourth mass killing in a black area near Johannesburg within a week. When Mandela came, he was confronted with posters urging "Mandela Give Us Guns." "Self-Defense Units" (SDUs) were being set up outside the ANC and with links to crime gangs. Mandela broke off negotiations with de Klerk and demanded justice. But at the same time he had Cyril Ramaphosa, chair of the ANC negotiating team, meet with a government representative in quiet talks to keep the process alive. On another track he channeled the discontent among the masses into the biggest general strike in the country's history, with over four million workers participating.

When Mandela met again with de Klerk in September 1992, he pushed hard on the need to start making significant progress if they were to have any chance of containing the violence. He finally got de Klerk to agree on calling a constitutional convention and moving toward elections. Still the haggling continued on what, when, who, and how. And the violence continued. In March 1993, twenty people including six schoolchildren were massacred near Table Mountain, a prominent landmark rising above Cape Town. With indications that the ANC bore some responsibility along with Inkatha and the government, Mandela was unsparing in his condemnation, stressing that the truth must be found even if it involved the ANC.

An even more explosive incident followed. On April 10 Chris Hani, second only to Mandela in popularity as an ANC leader and with a huge following among black youth, was assassinated. An Afrikaner woman who happened to see the license plate number of the escape car told the police. They captured the culprit, a far-right white Polish immigrant, and found evidence of the Conservative Party's complicity. De Klerk asked Mandela for help calming the situation. Rather than be strictly accusatory, Mandela struck a powerfully reconciliatory chord:

> A white man, full of prejudice and hate, came to our country and
> committed a deed so foul that our whole nation now teeters on
> the brink of disaster. A white woman, of Afrikaner origin, risked
> her life so that we may know, and bring to justice this assassin . . .
> Tonight I am reaching out to every single South African, black
> and white, from the very depths of my being . . . With all the
> authority at my command, I appeal to all our people to remain
> calm and to honor the memory of Chris Hani by remaining a
> disciplined force for peace.

Mandela's speech ran on TV and radio that evening at 7:00, at 8:00,
at 11:00. His leadership was widely credited for the rioting being much
more limited than feared. Whites were coming around to seeing Mandela as crucial, not antithetical, to order and stability. He just might
be a man of peace.

In late June Mandela went so far as to secretly meet with General
Constand Viljoen and other leaders of the *volkstaat* secessionist movement. Despite their military strength, Mandela warned secessionist
leaders that if they chose to go this route "it will be a long and bitter struggle, many people will die and the country will be reduced to
ashes. [So think about a couple things:] You cannot win because of
our numbers; you cannot kill us all. And you cannot win because of
the international community. They will rally to our support and they
will stand with us."

Yet again showing his shrewd negotiating skills, Mandela used the
Hani assassination to get de Klerk to commit to a date for elections.
The date was set for April 27, 1994. Momentum also picked up in the
constitutional negotiations. By November 1993 negotiators had agreed
on many provisions. Majority rule remained a sticking point. De Klerk
kept pushing for provisions such as a two-thirds' majority requirement
on major policies. Mandela stayed firm on the standard 50 percent.

Here too he prevailed. On November 18 the new constitution for the new South Africa was approved by the full plenary.

The campaign for the first presidency of postapartheid South Africa kicked off: Mandela versus de Klerk. Mandela's campaign slogan, "A Better Life for All," embodied his effort to consolidate support among blacks while seeking at least some support among whites. You could see it in his sartorial selections: elegant suits when meeting with white businessmen, patterned silk shirts in traditional colors when going into the townships. While no politician always tells people what they need to hear, not just what they want to hear, Mandela resisted pandering. In one instance when challenged by a white audience about ANC radicals, he scolded back that as Christians they should be ashamed for all those years of having concocted religious justifications for apartheid. When some ANC groups turned to violence, he pushed back: "We must accept that responsibility for ending violence is not just the government's, the police's, the army's. It is also our responsibility . . . We should put our own house in order." When some in the crowd jeered back, Mandela laid down the challenge. "Do you want me as your leader?" "Yes," the crowd now responded more supportively. "Well as long as I am your leader, I will tell you always when you are wrong."

Buthelezi remained a problem. It wasn't until eight days before the election that he finally called off the Inkatha violence and agreed to accept the new political system with the compromise that there would be a role for the Zulu monarchy. On March 10, a little more than a month before the election, the leader of the Afrikaner Resistance Movement issued a mobilization call via a right-wing radio station. Hundreds turned out, well armed. While some official military and police joined in, the army put the rebellion down.

The campaign culminated in a Mandela–de Klerk televised debate. In many of the exchanges de Klerk got the best of Mandela. But Mandela hit the mark with his closing statement about the beloved country becoming "a shining example to the entire world of people drawn from different racial groups who have a common loyalty, a common love, to their common country." In a move strategized with a political consultant who had worked for Bill Clinton, he surprised de Klerk, walking across the stage with his hand extended—"a masterful stroke," de Klerk would later concede.

Election Day came. In cities, townships, and rural areas, people came out to vote. They waited in long lines. Some walked miles. When the full vote count was tallied, the ANC had garnered 62.6 percent of the votes. This gave the ANC 252 of the 400 seats in the National Assembly and control of seven of nine provincial legislatures. Some in the ANC had hoped for two-thirds' majority in the National Assembly, which would have allowed the party to control the drafting of the constitution and much else. Mandela saw the value of the solid but smaller margin, the better to encourage consultation and buy-in. On May 9 the National Assembly formalized the election results. Nelson Mandela was president of South Africa.

Guests from close to 170 countries turned out for President Mandela's inauguration. A billion people watched on TV. Two national anthems played, the old Afrikaner one and "God Bless Africa," the ANC anthem. Three of Mandela's prison guards were there as his guests. "We enter into a covenant," the new president said in his inaugural speech, "that we shall build the society in which all South Africans, both black and white will be able to walk tall, without any fear in their hearts, assured of the inalienable right to human dignity—a rainbow nation at peace with itself and the world."

President Mandela

The incoming president's agenda was full. Economic sanctions and global recession had weakened the overall economy. Within that was an 8:1 ratio of white to black economic inequality. Close to half the black population was below the poverty line and without electricity, basic sanitation, clean water, or decent housing. An interim constitution was in place and a Government of National Unity had been established with de Klerk as a deputy president and some Cabinet posts allocated to his National Party. A permanent constitution was needed, as was an overhaul of the political system. Expectations among blacks were sky high. Trepidations among whites were up there as well.

An initial goal of one million new housing facilities wasn't met, but 700,000 units were built. Free health care was expanded for women and children. Not all those living in urban shantytowns and poor rural areas got clean water, electricity, and better schools—but many did. Jobs were created, not as many as targeted but more than before. Political killings decreased dramatically, from 3,794 in 1993 to 470 in 1997. Crime, though, sharply increased.

Doing better than this would have been hard for any president, let alone one who had never served in political office before, and who was 76 years old and had endured what Mandela had. Still Mandela was not much of a policy president. This was a very different role for him than anything before, requiring some skill sets that were not his strength. All along and then especially after the constitution was approved in 1996, he delegated much to Deputy President Thabo Mbeki.

The Winnie saga continued. Despite everything, he appointed her deputy minister for arts, culture, science and technology. Yet she added new scandals to the old ones with kickbacks, embezzlement, and other corruption. When he finally fired her, she fought back. Their divorce came to a head in 1996. Here was the president of the country testifying in open court hearings about how once he was out of jail, his wife refused to even share a bedroom with him, while carrying on with various lovers. His confession of personal hurt and loneliness did less to arouse sympathy than make him look weak and misdirected.

His judgment also failed him in some high-level appointments. Anti-apartheid activist Reverend Allen Boesak, named ambassador to the United Nations, was immersed in scandals including allegations that his foundation had embezzled over $800,000 donated by singer Paul Simon from his tour and from Danish and Norwegian foreign aid. Mandela gave in to the pressure to withdraw the appointment but did so while defending Boesak. While Mandela lived frugally, many nouveau powerfuls did not. "The government stopped the gravy train," Bishop Tutu admonished, "only long enough to get on it." Mandela criticized Tutu for going public with the issue. Tutu in turn called him just "an ordinary politician."

Mandela's presidency ultimately was less about policy particulars than the politics of reconciliation. The multiracial democracy that he had pursued most of his life, on which inroads had been made in the 1990–1994 transition, now needed to be consolidated and institutionalized. "Heal the divisions of the past," the preamble to the 1996 Constitution reads, "build a united and democratic South Africa." Some of this was done through formal mechanisms like the new Bill of Rights and Constitutional Court. But Mandela knew how important a personal touch was for reassuring whites. When asked to name a personal hero, he cited Kobie Coetsee, the government official who started the dialogue with him. He named Coetsee president of the Senate. He continued developing the relationship with General Viljoen, leader of the right-wing extremists, to the point that the general spoke of "the great mutual trust and regard" he and Mandela had. He attended worship in an historic Afrikaner church in Pretoria. He hosted a reconciliation lunch for the wives and widows of former apartheid leaders and black activists, including the widows of apartheid architect Prime Minister John Vorster and the assassinated Steve Biko. The invitation list for his 1998 wedding to Graca Machel, widow of former revolutionary leader and president of Mozambique Samora Machel, included one of his former jailers (who was now manager of the souvenir shop on Robben Island). "I used to do it for the money," a long-serving Afrikaner presidential bodyguard stated, "now it's for him [Mandela]. I'd take a bullet for him."

Especially powerful was his support for the Springboks rugby team.* Rugby was a largely all-white sport. The Springboks were the whitest, the most Afrikaner of the teams. While on Robben Island, Mandela would support any team but the Springboks. After many years banned from world competition because of apartheid, South

---

* Notwithstanding Hollywood hype, the Matt Damon–Morgan Freeman movie *Invictus* (2009) got the gist of this.

Africa was hosting the 1995 Rugby World Cup. The opportunity was
as rich in symbolism as U.S.-China Ping-Pong diplomacy. In the run-
up to the tournament President Mandela met publicly with Francois
Pienaar, the Springboks captain. At 6 feet 4 inches, 240 pounds, he
was the Afrikaner Adonis. At the final match against the renowned
New Zealand All-Blacks (named for their team uniforms) Pienaar led
the team in singing a mix of "Nkosi Sikelele iAfrika," an old Xhosa
liberation song, and a traditional Afrikaner anthem, with President
Mandela standing alongside in a Pienaar jersey and Springboks team
cap, the proverbial picture worth thousands of political messages.
When the Springboks won in overtime and claimed the world title, all
of South Africa celebrated together.

Mandela's support among whites, 1 percent before the election, soon
went over 50 percent. That was a mixed blessing within the ANC.
Some factions still held to the liberation mind-set, not convinced that
reconciliation was better than retribution. "The small minority in our
midst which wears the mask of anarchy," Mandela pushed back in
his 1995 state of the nation address, "will meet its match in the government we lead." Other dissent came from dashed expectations for
social change and economic progress. The gap between promise and
performance was, as we've noted, a real one. While pledging to keep
pushing for progress, Mandela also spoke to the need to "rid ourselves
of the culture of entitlement which leads to the expectation that the
government must promptly deliver whatever it is that we demand."

The country could not go fully forward unless it figured out what
to do about the past. In July 1995, the Truth and Reconciliation Commission (TRC) was established with the mandate to "forgive but not
forget." Bishop Tutu was made chairman, with an Afrikaner Methodist minister as his deputy. Perpetrators of political crimes during
apartheid (1960–1994 was the defined period), whether government
officials, right-wing vigilantes, ANC, Inkatha, or others, could apply
for amnesty. Determinations would be made on an individual basis.
The hearings were open for public attendance and televised live. They
were as much bearing witness as testifying. Victims told some hor-

rific stories. Government documents calling for indiscriminate killings were uncovered; the Biko assassination was described in gruesome detail. Botha, de Klerk, and other prime ministers were all implicated. It was amid these allegations that de Klerk, already disillusioned by having less of a role than he wanted, resigned from his position of deputy president.

The TRC issued its report in 1998. Some 8,000 amnesty applications had been filed. Many were granted. Some were denied, for example, the four police officers who killed Biko. The report was 3,500 pages long. Some Afrikaners criticized it for being too harsh on them, while some ANC said it was too lenient on Afrikaners. Mandela could have stayed at arm's length, leaving Bishop Tutu and the TRC to take the heat. He didn't. He commended the TRC for having done "a remarkable job." While the report wasn't perfect, "I approve of everything they did."

One step remained for President Mandela: to not serve a second term as president. He had announced this as his intent back in July 1996. The new constitution had been ratified. The TRC was up and running. On a continent where one liberation leader after another once in office stayed there, Mandela was determined that the democracy he had struggled his whole life to realize would not repeat the mistakes of so many neighbors. He was following in the footsteps of George Washington rather than Robert Mugabe (Zimbabwe), Jomo Kenyatta (Kenya), Kwame Nkrumah (Ghana), Sekou Toure (Guinea), and so many others. True, he was now 80 years old, but as we know he lived to 95. When elections were held on June 2, 1999, Nelson Mandela was not on the ballot. On June 16 Thabo Mbeki, who had been Mandela's deputy, was sworn in as president. Nelson Mandela was retired, at least officially.

WHAT: Balance Sheet

Considering what was transpiring in other countries faced with their own politics of identity, the Republic of South Africa is an even more powerful story. Rhodesia-Zimbabwe, where guerrilla warfare led to white flight and a liberation-movement-turned-brutal-dictatorship, was right next door. The Israeli-Palestinian conflict was entering its latest vicious phase, the *intifada* (uprising, insurrection). First rumblings were heard from what would become ethnic cleansing in Bosnia. After more than 40 years of apartheid and the fuller history of 350 years of white minority domination and black African subjugation, there were plenty of reasons for thinking that South Africa would also travel a violent route.

It is exceedingly hard to imagine South Africa's very different course of events would have happened without Nelson Mandela.

Mandela's "long walk to freedom" was not a straight or pure path. Early on he was so associated with violent tactics as commander in chief of Spear of the Nation that Amnesty International refused to recognize him as a prisoner of conscience. Throughout he was a skilled politician. His personal life had two failed marriages and problematic relations with his own children. But the dignity with which Mandela endured his nearly three decades as a political prisoner inspired so many people at home and globally. His commitment to reconciliation presented the world with a very different model from those seeking retribution and revenge. His moral capacity to differentiate between hatred of the system and hatred of whites was a sharp contrast to demagogic leaders in so many other parts of the world fomenting identity-based mass killings. U.S. Ambassador James Joseph's assessment, cited earlier, bears repeating that "once I got to know him [Mandela], I felt that he even exceeded the myth—which is rare about a human being."

Mandela exemplified personal capital. His tribal chieftain roots endowed him with some from the start. The courage he demonstrated in so many instances—as head of the 1952 Defiance Campaign, as spokesman for fellow prisoners in the 1956–1961 treason and 1964 Rivonia trials, and on Robben Island all those years—showed that he was of, not above, his people. The tolerance and deep commitment to reconciliation that he embodied convinced whites of his sincerity. To again quote Ambassador Joseph: "I can't think of anybody as a head of state who has demonstrated the spirit of forgiveness, the capacity for reconciliation better than he has. I mean, you talk about Gandhi, you talk about Martin Luther King, Jr., but they were not also heads of state, who had to deal with politics rather than just moral values." All this amounted to a robust personal capital account on which to draw during the transition and his presidency, to counter those—ANC and Inkatha and Afrikaner—who sought to disrupt and destroy what he was building.

Some high personal capital leaders don't have the requisite political skills. Mandela did. We've seen this in him turning his trials into platforms for putting the system itself on symbolic trial, organizing Robben Island prisoners, maneuvering intra-ANC politics, and negotiating his prison release and then the political transition. His support for reconciliation was both moral belief and political strategy, a way of disarming and dividing the opposition as well as a genuine vision of what South African society should be.

For all our caveats about charisma often being overestimated, Mandela really was the paragon case. His persona even more than his policies legitimized reconciliation: the grace in his smile, the embraces, the openness and responsiveness even while holding his ground, the outreached hand even while scolding an opponent or a crowd. His personification of his country helped South Africa transform from global pariah to darling of the international community. He could one day be "an old-fashioned aristocrat, another as an impassioned revolutionary, and the third as a world statesman . . . [yet] unlike so many leaders in the age of television there was little artifice about his guises." This makes it even more significant that he didn't cultivate a personality cult; for example, he said no to proposals to rename the Krugerrand currency the Mandelarand.

While his ANC mentor Walter Sisulu and ANC colleague Oliver Tambo, Bishop Tutu, Steve Biko, and, yes, Winnie all played their own crucial roles, only Madiba was the actor indispensable. It is exceedingly hard to argue that someone else could have done what he did, which places him in the high end of our SARL rankings.

What about de Klerk? He did free Mandela. His predecessor, Botha, had opened the door a crack but was unwilling to swing it open. De Klerk did so soon after becoming prime minister. He took the further gamble of calling a referendum two years into the transition and amid substantial Afrikaner discontent. He won that electoral test. When he agreed to the new interim constitution with majority rule and only limited power sharing, he endured attacks that he'd given the country away. When he and his party lost the 1994 elections to Mandela and the ANC, he was gracious in his election night concession, "I hold out my hand to Mr. Mandela in friendship and cooperation." Mandela later expressed gratitude for de Klerk's role in avoiding civil war. "Apartheid was wrong," de Klerk acknowledged in testimony to the Truth and Reconciliation Commission. It is on the basis of actions and statements like these that many credit his role.

Two arguments can be made on the other side. One counters the positives of what de Klerk contributed with negatives. He was duplicitous. From the beginning he sought a constitution and electoral system with sufficient power sharing for whites to have substantial autonomy and a fallback veto. His other compliments of de Klerk notwithstanding, Mandela saw through the effort to drag out negotiations "to allow time for me to fall flat on my face and show that the former prisoner hailed as a savior was a highly fallible man who had lost touch with the present situation." This is to an extent not that different than any party going into a negotiation with a hard-line initial position and trying to weaken an opponent. But in ramping up state-sponsored violence in collusion with Afrikaner extremists and Inkatha, de Klerk and his government went beyond trying for a solution favorable to their interests to being part of the problem. Some of this was known at the time; much came out later in the TRC hearings in what, despite de Klerk's denials, Chairman Bishop Tutu called an "avalanche of information" about de Klerk's direct complicity. These charges as well as his more general decrying of the TRC as nothing more than a "witch hunt" cast some doubt on the sincerity of his "apartheid was wrong" apology.

The core question for SARL rankings is uniqueness, whether

another leader would have made the same choices and if so whether the leader in question possessed particular qualities crucial to the break-through. Given South Africa's dire situation—the economy suffering from sanctions and a loss of international investor confidence, the world sports boycott eliciting a siege mentality, the security situation at home growing riskier for whites, and the possibility of that mythic aging political prisoner dying while still in custody—it's not hard to postulate another leader making the same choices de Klerk did.

For all the problems South Africa still has, the progress that has been made would not have been possible if not for Mandela's extraor-dinary statesmanship. It came back to "ubuntu," as President Barack Obama eulogized following Mandela's death on December 5, 2013, "a word that captures Mandela's greatest gift: his recognition that we are all bound together in ways that are invisible to the eye; that there is a oneness to humanity; that we achieve ourselves by sharing ourselves with others, and caring for those around us."

———

As celebratory of life as Mandela's funeral was, that of Israeli Prime Minister Yitzhak Rabin, assassinated amid his own pursuit of peace and reconciliation, was profoundly somber.

6

Yitzhak Rabin:
Soldier as Peacemaker, 1992–1995

WHO was Yitzhak Rabin?

He was born March 1, 1922, to Nehemiah Rubtizov (Rabin) and Rosa Cohen, both recent arrivals to Palestine, he from the United States (where he'd originally immigrated as a young boy fleeing pogroms in Ukraine), she from Russia.* Yitzhak was part of the first *sabra* generation, Jews born in Palestine, who showed both what could be achieved—making the desert bloom, creating governing structures, establishing schools and other services—and what the challenges were for two peoples, Jews and Arabs, with antagonistic identities and competing claims to the same land.

Both his parents, as Yitzhak put it in his memoirs, were "active participants in the Jewish people's struggle for national rebirth." Rosa became head of the Haganah defense unit for Haifa while the family lived there (Haganah was an army that Palestine Jews were forming separate from the British one). In Tel Aviv she was elected to the city council. Her health long precarious, she died from heart disease and

---

* When Nehemiah had first tried to enlist in the Jewish Legion, organized by Britain during World War I to help evict the Turks from Palestine, he was rejected (a bad leg). He reapplied to a different recruiting office with a changed last name—now Rabin—and got in.

cancer in 1937. Nehemiah, who had been active in the Jewish Tailors' Union back in the United States, became a member of the Tel Aviv Labor Council. He would live to 85, dying in 1971 while his son was ambassador to the United States.

Though a city boy, Yitzhak developed strong interest in agriculture and the land. He was accepted into the prestigious Kadouri Agricultural School in the northern Galilee region. Within a year Arab-Jewish clashes spread to Kadouri, requiring Rabin and other students to learn guard duty and weapons handling. The instructor was Yigal Allon, a Kadouri alumnus who while only a few years older was renowned for his military prowess. Allon took to Rabin, inviting him to join the Palmach, the newly formed elite fighting force of the Haganah. Around the same time the budding agriculturalist was offered a scholarship to study water and irrigation engineering at the University of California, Berkeley. With World War II raging, Nazi armies in North Africa, and the Vichy French collaborator government in Lebanon, Yitzhak chose the more immediate and pressing service to his homeland in the Palmach.

Yitzhak stayed in the Palmach through the war, resisting temptations to join the British army "with its shiny boots and smart beret," instead remaining "the Palmachnik in his careless, shabby outfit— one part farmer, one part soldier, and one part underground agent sworn to maintain secrecy even before his friends." After the war, as the British commitment to an independent Jewish state became increasingly in doubt, the Haganah and Palmach mounted operations against the British. On October 10, 1945, with Rabin as deputy commander, the Palmach attacked a British detention camp from which 200 Jews, Holocaust survivors who had made it to Palestine, were about to be deported. As Rabin's first direct encounter with Holocaust survivors, it left a powerful impression. The following June on what came to be known as Black Sabbath, the British set out to break up the Haganah and Palmach, arresting Rabin and other key officers.

His release came a few months before the United Nations General

Assembly approved a partition creating two independent states, Israel and Palestine. That, though, was not to be. For all the joy of May 14, 1948, the day on which the State of Israel was proclaimed, the very next day the armies of five Arab states—Egypt, Jordan, Lebanon, Syria, and Iraq—invaded Israel. Rabin served in a number of capacities: initially deputy commander of the Palmach, then a deputy to Allon on the southern front, and in April 1948 commander of the Harel brigade breaking the siege of Jerusalem.

Once a truce was signed, Yitzhak attended to some personal business: marrying Leah Schlossberg. She had come to Palestine in 1933, her family fleeing Germany as Hitler rose. They'd met in Tel Aviv. For a while she served in the Palmach, even getting into a battalion of which he was deputy commander. She was the extrovert to his introvert, the outgoing and more demonstrably warm one, and his fierce defender against critics. They would have two children, Dalia and Yuval; their marriage lasted 47 years, ended only by his assassination.

Arab armies were not the only challenge to the new Israeli state. In June 1948 the Irgun, a right-wing paramilitary-terrorist group led by Menachem Begin, brought in a huge cache of arms aboard the ship *Altalena* without authorization from Prime Minister David Ben-Gurion. At minimum this was an effort to undermine the authority of the government and the official military Israel Defense Force (IDF); some within the Irgun were planning to use the arms to pull off a coup. Under orders from Allon and Ben-Gurion, with Rabin part of the command from the Tel Aviv beaches, the *Altalena* was attacked. Just a few years after the Holocaust, and barely a month after having achieved their own state, Jews were killing Jews. While emotionally torn, Rabin held to the view that "there is only one army, and that is the Israel Defense Forces."

Rabin continued to rise in the IDF, becoming chief of staff in January 1964. He was in that position when in early June 1967, with Egyptian, Syrian, Lebanese, and Jordanian forces mobilizing along Israel's borders for a surprise attack, Israel launched its own preemptive strikes. The Six-Day War proved to be Israel's greatest military victory. Some controversy surrounded Rabin's role. In the days leading up to the war amid the stress of the situation, along with too much nicotine (he was a chain smoker) and too little food, exhaustion sidelined him for about a day. He returned to command and, along with Defense Minister Moshe Dayan and Brigadier General Ariel Sharon, was one of the heroes of the war.

After close to 30 years in the military, Rabin stepped down as chief of staff. In 1968 he became ambassador to the United States and served in Washington for the next five years. He returned to Israel with the intent of going into politics as a Labor Party candidate for the Knesset (national legislature). Less than a year later, when the controversies over Israel's unpreparedness for the October 1973 Yom Kippur War toppled the government of Prime Minister Golda Meir, Rabin was chosen as Labor Party leader and the new prime minister. This was the period of Secretary of State Henry Kissinger's shuttle diplomacy, in which partial peace agreements were reached between Israel and Egypt, Syria, and Jordan. Rabin and Kissinger, who had forged a close relationship during the years Rabin was in Washington, also sealed agreements for substantially increased American aid.

A financial scandal involving his wife, Leah, caused him to resign as prime minister in April 1977. The ensuing election was won by Menachem Begin, the former Irgun-*Altalena* leader, and his right-wing Likud Party. The next few years were a real low point for Rabin. He stayed in the Knesset but lost the Labor Party leadership to longtime rival Shimon Peres. Long held in high regard by the Israeli public, while still respected for his military career, he was seen as just another flawed politician.

Amid the outcry over the 1982 Israeli invasion of Lebanon in which Israeli forces were complicit in massacres by their Lebanese Christian allies in Beirut refugee camps, Begin's successor, Prime Minister Yitzhak Shamir, formed a national unity government including Rabin as defense minister. Rabin was in this position in 1987 when the first Palestinian intifada ("uprising"), the most extensive violence in the West Bank and Gaza in the 20 years of Israeli occupation, broke out.

While his initial response was to crack down even more—"break their bones" was how his orders were characterized—he came to see that unrest among Palestinians ran too deep for the occupation to be maintained indefinitely. Thus began his transformation from tough defense minister and career soldier to the prime minister who in 1993 led the way to key breakthroughs toward peace.

Before we get into the why and how of that, we should take stock of the qualities that defined who Rabin was as a leader.

Rabin was rich in personal and moral capital. He had the authenticity of being a prominent part of the founding generation, in fact the first prime minister to have been born in the land of Israel. Accounts of his courage are legion. He was there on the battlefields for the founding of the state. As IDF chief of staff he led the victory of the 1967 Six-Day War. He was the one turned to as prime minister after the controversies of the 1973 Yom Kippur War and as defense minister during the *intifada* in the 1980s. He was dubbed "Mr. Security" when running for prime minister in the 1992 election. And his pursuit of peace with the Palestinians was "the peace of the brave," as Bill Clinton put it. As an officer throughout his career, as both his sister Rachel and daughter Dalia stressed to me, he took personally every loss of life by a soldier under his command. His standing by his wife during the 1970s' financial scandal, while incurring a steep political price in the moment, over time added further to the sense of the quality of his character.

He also exemplified how it can be less a matter of charisma making for leadership than charisma arising out of leadership. He was gruff, not polished, with a speaking style more suited for military command settings than television audiences, a persona more comfortable hammering out policy details than kissing babies. After he was assassinated in November 1995, I was moved but not surprised by the grief among Israeli friends and colleagues of my generation and line of work. But what really struck me were the guitar-playing and candle-lighting teenagers I saw paying their homage at the makeshift memorial in the square where Rabin had been assassinated. For all his rough edges and un-coolness, Rabin had connected with Israeli youth. His granddaughter Noa spoke in her eulogy for so many in her generation: "You were the column of fire that went ahead of the camp, and now we are left only with the camp, alone, and we are so cold and sad . . . we lived in the light of your values, always. You never forsook anyone, and now they have forsaken you . . . The ground has slipped away from under our feet, and we are trying somehow to sit in this empty space that has been left behind."

Rabin's political skills were more mixed. He gets much praise for his decision-making skills, anchored as they were in core beliefs about the centrality of Israeli security while pragmatic about how best to achieve that. Aides speak of how analytic he was, devouring as much information as they provided, probing to get at hidden premises, taking into account immediate pressing factors while also thinking strategically. His "analytical brilliance in cutting to the core of a problem," in the view of Henry Kissinger, "was awesome." He was less adept at the pulls and tugs of politics. He let political rivalry with Shimon Peres get to him. It was distracting and distorting at times, a two-way street, of course. His greatest political failing, tragically so, was in violating the leadership dictum to "keep the opposition close, control the temperature," as his pursuit of peace with the Palestinians grew ever more contentious within Israeli politics.

WHY make peace with the PLO?

It was one thing for Israel to have signed a peace treaty with Egypt and its charismatic President Anwar Sadat, even to have agreed to truces and cease-fires brokered by the United States with Syria and its dictator Hafez Assad—but to negotiate with the arch-terrorist Yasir Arafat and his Palestine Liberation Organization (PLO)? Why would Mr. Security allow his team to secretly go to Oslo, Norway, and meet with Arafat's aides and then himself go to Washington, DC, and at a special ceremony on the lawn of the White House sign on to the agreements reached (the Oslo Accords)?

Yitzhak Rabin had come to the view that, while peace would not guarantee Israeli security, Israel could never be secure without peace.

As a military man Rabin had a keen sense of what Israeli military power could and could not achieve. Israel's earlier wars—the 1948–1949 war of independence, the 1967 Six-Day War, and the 1973 Yom Kippur War—had been about having the military might to defeat surrounding Arab states on the battlefield: army versus army (actually, armies), air force versus air force(s), military force for military objectives. In recent years, though, for Israel as for much of the world, war was becoming "politics by other means" in ways that even Clausewitz may not have had in mind. The 1987 intifada really drove the point home. More than ever before this was a grassroots Palestinian uprising, not one orchestrated by Arafat and the PLO. It reflected both deep despair and genuine national aspirations, the repression of which was harder, more uncertain, and more costly. Some 2,000 Palestinians were killed, another 18,000 injured, and 120,000 imprisoned or detained—yet the unrest continued. This was "a problem like none in our previous experience," Rabin stated on Israeli television. "It is far easier to solve classic military problems. It is far more difficult to contend with 1.4 million Palestinians . . . who are employing . . . systematic violence without weapons, and who do not want our rule." For all of Israel's military might he came to see that "the solution can only be a political one."

The overarching global geopolitical context was shifting in ways that created a mix of opportunities and uncertainties. The end of the Cold War meant that Arafat and the PLO could no longer count on Soviet aid and protection: opportunity. But it took with it some of the regional containment rationale for U.S. support for Israel: uncertainty. Moreover, U.S.-Israeli relations had been sharply strained in 1990–1991 by a dispute between the Bush (George H. W.) administration and Prime Minister Yitzhak Shamir over Israeli settlements in the occupied territories. Shamir's truculence reached the point where Secretary of State James Baker told the Israelis, in effect, here's our phone number, "when you're serious about peace, call us." Rabin knew how integral relations with the United States were to Israel. As ambassador he had played a key role in deepening these ties. Getting them back on strong footing was essential. The U.S.-Israeli "special relationship is invaluable," the 1991 Labor Party platform affirmed. While Israel should resist any American "dictates" on crucial issues, "differences of opinion should be ironed out by means of talks, and every effort should be made to avoid situations of loss of confidence." On his first trip to the United States after defeating Shamir in the 1992 election, he gave a "blistering dressing-down" to the American Israel Public Affairs Committee (AIPAC) for what he considered more harm than good in its lobbying on U.S.-Israeli relations.

Favorable shifts in the regional balance of power also were a factor. The end of the Cold War meant enemies like Syria could no longer count on Soviet backing. Iraq was weakened by its defeat in the Gulf War. The PLO's support for Saddam Hussein had angered Saudi Arabia and other aid-providing Arab states. For its part, Israel was gaining strength from the 500,000 Soviet and Eastern European Jews who were now free to emigrate. While there still were those seeking to destroy Israel, the situation was about as propitious as any Israel had ever had for taking risks for peace.

At the same time the occupation was taking an increasing toll on Israel itself. It was strengthening the right wing in ways that both hurt Rabin politically and personally tapped deep distrust extending back to the 1948 *Altalena* clash. The expansion of settlements was further empowering the *haredim* ("those who tremble at the word of God") and other ultra-Orthodox in ways that not only hurt the prospects for peace but also, for a secular nationalist such as Rabin, raised concerns about the fabric of Israeli society. To Rabin groups such as Gush Emunim, with their militant advocacy of Jewish settlements in the West Bank, were a "cancer in the body of Israeli democracy."

Meanwhile the IDF, the institution in which Rabin so deeply believed, was having its ethical fortitude compromised and its morale undermined in suppressing the intifada. And its own death toll was rising: as many soldiers were killed in 1992 as in the first four years of the intifada combined, and then an even higher number in the eight months of 1993 prior to the signing of the Oslo Accords. In his speech right after the 1967 Six-Day War upon receiving a Hebrew University honorary degree, Rabin spoke of the "supreme mission" IDF soldiers knew they were entrusted with "to maintain, even at the cost of their lives, the right of the Jewish people to live its life in our state, free, independent and in peace and tranquility." Yet even at that moment of triumph he empathized both with his soldiers for "their comrades fallen beside them," and for "the terrible price paid by our enemies [that] also touched the hearts of many of our men." Pushing back against those who would get too accustomed to "the triumph of conquest and victory," he cautioned that "we go forth to war when we are forced to, when there is no other choice. We fight for survival, only when the other side makes war absolutely necessary."

In these and other ways Rabin believed that peace would make Israel stronger. Pursuing peace and ensuring security were not an either/or choice. "Peace you don't make with friends," he acknowledged, "but with very unsympathetic enemies." "I will fight terror as if there were no peace talks," was one leg of a favorite Rabin axiom, "and I will pursue peace as if there were no terror."

HOW did Rabin seek peace with the Palestinians?

Initially Rabin felt he had a better chance of achieving peace with Syria than with the Palestinians. Just as Israel gave back to Egypt land captured during the 1967 war (the Sinai Peninsula) as part of their 1979 peace treaty, it would return the land captured in that same war (Golan Heights) to Syria as part of their peace treaty. Like the Sinai, the Golan would be demilitarized; and like the Sinai (a large desert) its topography (heights) provided sufficient separation for Israel to be reasonably confident of protection against a surprise attack. As brutal a dictator as Syrian President Hafez Assad was, he had negotiated the 1974 disengagement agreement the prior time Rabin was prime minister. Just as Secretary of State Henry Kissinger had been the intermediary for the 1974 agreement, Clinton administration Secretary of State Warren Christopher carried Rabin's proposal to Assad. But Assad was unwilling to make the deal.

Meanwhile, at a secluded estate outside Oslo, Norway, at what ostensibly was an academic conference, secret talks had begun between Israelis and PLO officials. The Israelis were lawyers and academics, but they were coordinating with Yossi Beilin, key aide to Foreign Minister Shimon Peres. Various efforts to engage the PLO had been made over the years by Israeli "doves." Little had come of them. This time, though, there seemed to be some traction. In February 1993, when Peres first briefed Rabin on the Oslo talks, Rabin was reluctant: "skeptical," Peres characterized him, "sometimes he wholly disbelieved in them." But Rabin agreed to let them continue. In May he agreed to upgrade the talks to the official level under Peres's guidance. It wasn't until August that Rabin began to believe that there could be a viable deal. "On four or five major issues, they agreed to [things] I had doubted they would agree to," Rabin later told an Israeli journalist. He and Arafat exchanged messages through an intermediary to clarify key details, which also gave Rabin more of a sense of whether Arafat, not just his negotiators in Oslo, was committed to a deal.

On the morning of September 9, 1993, while I was working in the State Department, I got a call from my boss, Ambassador Samuel Lewis, director of the Policy Planning Staff. "Come to my office." Sam was among the most distinguished diplomats of his generation, having served as U.S. ambassador to Israel under Presidents Carter and Reagan for both the 1978–1979 Camp David Egypt-Israel Peace Agreement and the 1982 Israeli invasion of Lebanon. When I got to his office, he handed me two sheets hot off the fax machine. "We handle lots of paper every day, much of it less important than folks think in the moment. These two sheets, these two letters, are truly historic. Take a look."

The first was a letter from Yasir Arafat, chairman of the Palestine Liberation Organization (PLO), whose charter called for Israel's destruction.

> The PLO recognizes the right of the State of Israel to exist in peace and security ... The PLO commits itself to the Middle East peace process, and to a peaceful resolution of the conflict ... The PLO renounces the use of terrorism and other acts of violence.

The second letter was from Israeli Prime Minister Yitzhak Rabin, who had been fighting the PLO for decades.

> The Government of Israel has decided to recognize the PLO as the representative of the Palestinian people and commence negotiations with the PLO within the Middle East peace process.

This exchange of letters accompanied the Oslo Accords, the Declaration of Principles (DOP) that after many months of negotiations had been reached, in which the government of Israel and the PLO committed to "an end to decades of confrontation and conflict, recognize their mutual legitimate and political rights, and strive to live in peaceful coexistence and mutual dignity and security and achieve a just, lasting and comprehensive peace settlement and historic reconciliation."

Norway had worked well for the quiet negotiations, secluded from the media's klieg lights. But Washington was the venue of choice for the signing ceremony. Plans were quickly made for a mega-event on the White House lawn a few days later, September 13. As much as he was committed to pursuing peace, Rabin was leery about standing with Arafat on the world stage and being beamed back to Israel where, while the majority was supportive, the opposition was already boisterous and visceral. You need to come, President Bill Clinton stressed. And you'll need to shake hands with Yasir Arafat. No traditional kisses, Rabin drew the line, and Arafat can't wear his usual holster and revolver. The handshake was not the warmest in history.

But it happened. "This signing of the Israeli-Palestinian Declaration of Principles here today, is not so easy neither for myself, as a soldier in Israel's wars, nor for the people of Israel," Prime Minister

Rabin explained. "We have come to try and put an end to the hostili-
ties, so that our children, our children's children, will no longer experience the painful cost of war, violence and terror . . . Let me say to you,
the Palestinians: We are destined to live together on the same soil, in
the same land . . . Enough of blood and tears. Enough. We harbor no
hatred to you . . . We are today giving peace a chance." He ended with
the last stanza of the Jewish Mourner's Kaddish: "He maketh peace
on His high places. He shall make peace for us all and for all of Israel.
And they shall say: Amen."

The Oslo Accord Declaration of Principles laid out both first steps
and an ongoing negotiation process. Palestinians would begin to gain
some self-government under a newly established Palestinian Authority
with the understanding that Arafat would return from exile in Tunisia.
Israel would first withdraw its forces from the Gaza Strip and the city
of Jericho. Negotiations then would start on permanent status and
such issues as refugees, settlements, borders, security arrangements,
and Jerusalem. Meanwhile the two sides would build cooperation on
economic development, trade, water, the environment, and related
policy areas. A five- to six-year time line was set for the full transition.

Many in Israel hailed Rabin as a hero. Some fumed that he was a
heretic. Even before delving into the details of the agreement, opponents attacked the very idea of Arafat and the PLO as partners. Still,
polls showed over 60 percent support. The Knesset approved the deal
by a comfortable margin; indeed, three members of Likud defied their
new party leader, Benjamin Netanyahu, and abstained rather than
vote against. Negotiations pressed ahead. On May 4, 1994, the "Gaza-
Jericho first" follow-on agreement was signed. On October 26 a full
peace treaty was signed with Jordan. For years, Jordanian King Hussein had been secretly coordinating and cooperating with Israel on
some issues, including a series of secret meetings with Rabin during
Rabin's first prime ministership. But a formal peace treaty could not
have happened without the Oslo process.

Other Arab countries also broke some of their ice with Israel. Liaison offices were exchanged with Morocco. An agreement to do the

same with Tunisia was reached in principle. Qatar hosted an Israeli delegation as part of regional multilateral talks on arms control and regional security,* Bahrain the same for talks on regional environmental issues. Israel had some dealings with Oman, even very quietly with Saudi Arabia. The six-nation Gulf Cooperation Council suspended parts of their anti-Israel trade sanctions.

Israel was also reaping other benefits. The Tel Aviv stock market jumped more than 80 percent in the first six months after the Oslo Accords were signed. The economy grew by 20 percent, per capita income reached $17,000, twentieth highest in the world. Foreign direct investment in Israel went from $180 million per year to close to $6 billion. Tourism almost doubled.The United States increased arms sales, military aid, and technology transfers to ensure Israel's military edge. Over 50 countries, many in the Third World with affinity to the Palestinian cause, now saw fit to finally establish diplomatic relations with Israel. Others that already had official relations now stepped them up. When Rabin came to the UN, a forum at which denunciations of Israel had become routine, some 80 heads of state sought to meet with him.

But terrorism persisted. In the first six months following the Oslo signing, there were 22 Palestinian terrorist attacks, killing 28. Then came a spate of suicide bus bombings: Afula, April 6, 1994, killing eight; Hadera, a week later, killing five; Tel Aviv, October 19, killing 22; Beit Lid, January 22, 1995, killing 18 soldiers and one civilian waiting at a bus junction; in Gaza, April 9, killing eight, including one American; Tel Aviv, July 24, killing six; and over 40 other smaller-scale terrorist attacks. These were almost all carried out by Hamas and Islamic Jihad, more extremist than the PLO now was, but some did come from PLO-controlled territory. It was another example of a "spoilers" strategy: derail a peace process that you don't want to succeed, especially when the "peace train" has actually left the station.

* While working in the State Department, I was a member of the U.S. delegation to the Arms Control and Regional Security (ACRS) talks in Doha, Qatar, in May 1994.

On the same day (October 14, 1994) that Rabin, Peres, and Arafat were announced as joint winners of the Nobel Peace Prize, an Israeli soldier named Nachshon Wachsman who had been kidnapped by Hamas turned up dead.

Spoilers resorting to terrorism were not limited to the Palestinian side. The first major terrorist attack post-Oslo was committed in February 1994 by Baruch Goldstein, a Brooklyn-born Israeli religious extremist, who opened fire on Palestinian worshippers in the Cave of the Patriarchs in Hebron, killing 29 and wounding another 125. Shin Bet, the internal Israeli security agency counterpart to Mossad, suspected that Goldstein had "received at least tacit approval" from ultra-Orthodox rabbis who claimed biblical writ giving these lands to the Jewish people as a higher authority than what any earthly government such as Rabin's might claim. Among the others who held this view was a then unknown 23-year-old named Yigal Amir.

Some decline in the Israeli public's support for the Oslo strategy was understandable given the spate of terrorism. Even though Hamas and Islamic Jihad and not the Palestinian Authority (PA) were the principal perpetrators, the PA had agreed to do much more than it had been doing to prevent terrorism. Even some Oslo supporters pointed out flaws in the terms. But there was a fundamental difference between such specific criticisms and the fixed rejection from the start by the religio-ideological Israeli right wing.

Rabin's political advisors encouraged him to make his case to the settler movement. While prime minister back in the 1970s, Rabin had supported settlements that had a security rationale. But even then he opposed settlements based on Judea-Samaria biblical claims. "What do you think? That the government is going to follow every folly of every 100 guys?" Once Menachem Begin became prime minister in 1977, and continuing in the 1980s with Likud and National Unity governments, the brakes were off. By the time of Oslo the settler population had grown to 120,000, with many of the sites quite intentionally in and near Palestinian population centers.

The Oslo Declaration of Principles left the settlements issue for final status negotiations. Rabin froze any new settlements while allowing some growth in existing ones. Still the settlers' attacks on him were vicious. One settler leader told him that if the IDF came to evict them "they will be resisted as if they are soldiers of the Third Reich." Another wrote Rabin a letter accusing him of not "identify[ing] with the suffering of the Jews." Some ultra-Orthodox rabbis went so far as to claim certain Talmudic teachings applied to Rabin including "din moser," justifying the killing of someone who delivered Jews to a hostile power, and "din rodef," permitting the killing of an aggressor in order to save an innocent victim.

On September 28, 1995, Rabin and Arafat signed the follow-on Oslo II. This divided the West Bank into three zones: Area A, major towns and cities such as Ramallah, Jenin, and Bethlehem where Israeli forces would be fully withdrawn and the Palestinian Authority would have full control; Area B, in which the PA would have control over civilian matters while Israel retained control over security with reduced but not fully withdrawn forces; and Area C, in which Israeli forces would remain until a permanent status agreement was reached. Israel would retain control of all borders. Provisions were laid out for the Palestinians to conduct elections in both the West Bank and Gaza. These transitions were to be implemented within six months. Permanent status negotiations were to start as soon as possible but no later than May 4, 1996, and would end no later than May 4, 1999.

The number of Israelis killed by Palestinians, which had spiked from 30 in 1993 to 73 in 1994, fell to 53 in 1995. Rabin gave Arafat and the PA some credit. They "have taken a series of measures that have foiled attacks." But "they can do more, much more." Still he kept to his overriding message: "We did not return to an empty land. There were Palestinians here who struggled against us for a hundred wild bloody years . . . Today . . . we rule more than two million Palestinians through the IDF, and run their lives by a Civil Administration. That is not a peaceful solution."

At the same time the Knesset was debating Oslo II, a protest rally was held in Jerusalem's Zion Square. Protesters carried posters of

Rabin in a Nazi uniform with a Hitler mustache. Yitzhak Rabin, Israel's war hero, its prime minister, was portrayed as the German fascist who exterminated 6,000,000 Jews. Among the speakers at the rally was Likud leader Benjamin Netanyahu, excoriating Rabin in terms that approached "traitor." A former general who was a member of Rabin's Cabinet, driving to the Knesset, got caught in the mob; he would later tell friends he felt more in danger than in his most threatening moments in battle. As the crowd started heading for the Knesset building, reinforcement emergency security forces had to be called in. After virtually every legislator had his turn at the microphone, a bare 61–59 majority approved Oslo II.

Shabak, Israel's top internal security service, grew increasingly concerned about threats to Rabin. Rabin's official car had been a basic sedan, a Chevrolet Caprice. In March 1995, Shabak head Carmi Gillon told Rabin he needed to switch to an armored car. When Rabin demurred, he was told the main concern was not Hamas but his Israeli opponents. While he conceded on the car, he would not agree to wear a bulletproof vest. "Are you out of your mind? I'll never wear a bulletproof vest in my own country," Rabin protested. "I could understand his position," Gillon would later write in his memoirs. "He was this Palmach soldier who fought in Israel's wars for thirty years, who commanded the Army in the victorious Six-Day War . . . and he's supposed to suffer this humiliation?"

The pro-peace movement planned its own demonstration for the night of November 4. It was a Friday, Erev Shabbat. Over 100,000 people showed up in the plaza near Kings of Israel Square in Tel Aviv. There was music. There was poetry. Shimon Peres spoke. And then Rabin: "Peace entails difficulties," he acknowledged, "even pain. Israel knows no path devoid of pain."

But the path of peace is preferable to the path of war. I say this to you as someone who was a military man and minister of defense, and who saw the pain of the families of I.D.F. [Israel Defense Forces] soldiers. It is for their sake, and for the sake of

our children and grandchildren, that I want this government to
exert every effort, exhaust every opportunity, to promote and to
reach a comprehensive peace.

And he warned: "Violence is undermining the very foundations of
Israeli democracy. It must be condemned, denounced, and isolated."

Back in the United States I was visiting my sister and cousins in
Philadelphia, having a family dinner in a Chinese restaurant, when
I noticed pictures of Yitzhak Rabin on the television above the bar.
Seemed odd, it wasn't a news time slot. The photos stayed up there and
had that austere look. I walked up to the bar, asked for the audio to be
turned up, and heard the tragic news. Rabin had been shot. The prime
minister of Israel had been killed by a fellow Israeli. Assassinated. It
was *din rodef*, the religious extremist assassin Yigal Amir readily told
the police. "God decided Rabin would die," was how his brother and
co-conspirator Hagai put it.

November 4, 1995, proved to be a much more fateful evening than
I, or anyone else, could have imagined.

WHAT: Balance Sheet

Three questions to be addressed in assessing what Rabin's statesmanship achieved:

- How much credit does Rabin get for what was achieved?
- Would there have been peace had Rabin not been assassinated?
- Given that the conflict has gotten so much worse, was this really
  a breakthrough?

How much credit does Rabin get for what was achieved?

A great deal. Another very high SARL ranking.

Others get credit, too. Shimon Peres, for one. Despite their long-
standing political rivalry, on this issue their differences were complementary. Peres the visionary saw the full transformational possibilities,

while Rabin the analyst assessed the details. But Peres did not have the personal capital to lead the breakthrough. It was Rabin who was Mr. Security. Even critics acknowledge that as terrorism increased and opposition to Oslo mounted, Rabin's persona was what saved Knesset approval of Oslo II. While we'll never know whether Rabin would have been reelected in 1996, we do know that Peres lost to Benjamin Netanyahu. Peres was valuable, Rabin was indispensable. He wasn't a soldier who had left that role and become a peacemaker. He was the soldier *as* peacemaker.

And Arafat? He did share in that Nobel Peace Prize. But he played his role at best ambivalently. He did take some steps to restrain terrorism and start building Palestinian self-governance. But while his concern about maintaining legitimacy with his people amid sellout charges from Hamas and Islamic Jihad had some credence, it didn't explain away the failure to crack down on terrorism or justify the corruption and other abuses of power. In Chapter 1 we had the Kissinger-Zhou equal statesmanship partnership, in Chapter 2 Gorbachev warranting principal credit and Reagan some. The Rabin-Arafat case, like Mandela-de Klerk (Chapter 5), falls further down the spectrum with some, but even less, of the credit shared.

Mention also must be made of key supporting actors, starting with the Norwegians who, tapping their contacts on both sides and their soft power reputation, incubated the process. The baton-passing from Norway to the United States reflected the power and position needed going forward. President Bill Clinton made a huge investment in the issue and assembled a diplomatic team to work the issue virtually 24/7. His "Shalom, chaver" (goodbye, friend) was among the most poignant tributes to the assassinated Rabin. While much of this bore Clinton's unique touch, it's likely that some other American president could have played a similar role. Moreover, while Clinton continued to try to work the Israeli-Palestinian issue for the rest of his time in office, little progress was made once Rabin was gone.

Rabin's main failing was in underestimating the political opposition—even when his own security forces warned him, urged him, to wear that bulletproof vest. One is reminded of what Abraham Lincoln's aides John Hay and John Nicolay remarked. Lincoln surely "was too intelligent not to know he was in danger. But he had himself so sane a mind and a heart so kindly, even to his enemies, that it was hard for him to believe in a political hatred so deadly as to lead to murder."

Would there have been peace had Rabin not been assassinated?

More likely than not.

I make that assessment keeping in mind two caveats. One is the inherent uncertainty of counterfactuals. But it's possible to make credible claims of plausibility and even probability based on what we do know and what we can extrapolate based on the evidence we have. The second caveat is that the Oslo process had flaws. Contrary to the claims of right-wing critics that it was too much too quickly, it actually was too little too slowly. The logic of going step by step with interim arrangements was that Israelis needed reassurance that peace would bring security and Palestinians needed time and assistance to lay the foundations for self-governance. But it also meant, as American negotiator Aaron Miller put it, that "even while they negotiated as friends, partners, and equals, the sides were forced to play their respective roles as occupied and occupier." Along the same lines, it allowed spoilers to perpetrate violence "showing" that Oslo wasn't working before it had time to show that it was working. To an extent this was to be expected, spoilers doing as they do in such situations, the more progress, the more effort to spoil.

No question that Rabin was dismayed and at times infuriated by Arafat's combination of inability and unwillingness to stop the terrorism. Arafat did respond to the pressure Rabin brought in the October 1994 Hamas kidnapping of the Israeli soldier Nachshon Wachsman, rounding up hundreds of Hamas members and working with Israel in trying to find Wachsman. When Wachsman was found it was too late—he had been killed. Still even the head of Shabak acknowledged that "Arafat earned many points" for his cooperation once pressed. By

1995 the terrorism death toll had started to fall. The greatest increases, and the ones that started again to directly involve the PLO and PA, not just Hamas and Islamic Jihad, came *after* Rabin's assassination.

Was Arafat truly committed to peace? "Of all the hands in the world," Rabin said after the White House handshake, "this was the one I never wanted or dreamed of touching." In negotiations Arafat showed little flexibility, holding to minimum and maximum positions as one and the same, staying more inclined to parry Israeli and American proposals than to initiate his own. Outside of negotiations he kept reverting to inflammatory rhetoric. He ruled within the Palestinian Authority with much more concern about preserving his own power than being of, by, and for his own people. In these and other ways he fit the pattern of revolutionary leaders who have difficulty transitioning to governing.

Yet Rabin and Arafat did begin to develop a relationship. Arafat wasn't doing everything Rabin wanted, but then again Israel wasn't doing everything the PA wanted. This was a negotiation, a process. Leah Rabin later wrote in her own memoirs that as frustrating and angering as working with Arafat could be, Yitzhak did gain some respect for him. On at least one occasion, the White House signing of Oslo II, there even was some playfulness, with Arafat remarking that Jews and Arabs were long-lost cousins and now even closer as peace partners, and Rabin responding, "It seems to me, Mr. Chairman, that you might be a little Jewish."

Arafat appears to have come to hold Rabin in quite high regard. Journalist Dan Ephron, whose account of this period is among the richest available, writes that "Arafat seemed to revere Rabin's military bearing and fear his temper." In Bill Clinton's judgment, despite differences past and present, their relationship worked because of "Arafat's regard for Rabin and the Israeli leader's uncanny ability to understand how Arafat's mind worked." When U.S. Consul-General Edward Abington broke the news of Rabin's assassination to him, Arafat cried: "'I've lost my partner.'" Abington recalled, "He showed tremendous shock and grief. He was devastated." Security considerations precluded Arafat from being invited to the funeral. A few days later during the mourning period, secretly brought into Israel, Arafat made a *shiva* visit to Leah and family.

Would Rabin have been able to prevent Arafat from turning back to obstructionism and terrorism as he did in ensuing years? Was Arafat's rejection of the Clinton administration's 2000 peace plan (at Camp David and then at Taba, Egypt) and fomenting of the second intifada decisive evidence that he was not able or willing to fully make that transition from revolutionary leader to head of government? Or were his policies more the reaction to Israeli turns against Oslo under Prime Ministers Benjamin Netanyahu (1996–1998) and Ariel Sharon (2001–2006)?

Debate continues on these questions. Aaron Miller's assessment that, even if Rabin had lived, "the crisis triggered by Oslo's flaws would still have come, but it would probably have been less severe" is well-balanced. I once asked Dalia Rabin, Yitzhak's daughter and a former member of the Knesset and deputy defense minister, whether she thought peace would have been achieved had her father lived. She paused. He was becoming quite frustrated with Arafat, she said. But he also saw the progress they had made. While wary about whether Arafat would genuinely follow through enough to get to a peace conducive to Israeli security, he felt it could be done. And she reminded me of that core precept of his: "I'll fight terrorism as if there are no negotiations, and negotiate as if there is no terror."

Although Rabin stuck to the position that there would not be an independent Palestinian state while the Oslo process proceeded, this may have been a case where public statements are not revelatory. It would make no political or negotiating sense to indicate intent to go further sooner than necessary. In his Knesset speech on Oslo II he used the wording, "We would like this to be an entity which is less than a state." Not we insist. We would like. Key aides believed that Rabin had come to realize that there could be no final peace agreement short of this. This likely would not have been a full return to the borders existing before the 1967 war. Mr. Security kept a keen focus on the need for some forward security along the Jordan River. On Jerusalem, the settlements he had continued to permit were mostly in the surrounding environs. And he had his own deep personal attachment to the city where he was born, on which he had broken the siege in the 1948 war, where he was so uncharacteristically emotional at the Western Wall when his forces had captured the Old City in the 1967 war. In mid-1994 he issued an "unequivocal" statement that "Jerusalem must be united, under Israeli sovereignty and the capital of Israel." He later showed some interest in the "dual addresses" configuration by which Jerusalem would be Israel's capital and the surrounding village of Abu Dis and possibly some of East Jerusalem the Palestinian capital.

What we do know is that substantial progress was made in Rabin's two years and less than two months of the Oslo process. After decades of being enemies sworn to each other's destruction, Israel and the PLO had come together in a peace process. They granted each other mutual recognition. They signed the initial Declaration of Principles (DOP). They built on it with two other main agreements, Gaza-Jericho (May 1994) and Oslo II (September 1995), as well as numerous working-level ones on issues such as economic cooperation, financial matters, education, and security cooperation. They set in place the Areas A-B-C as the beginning of Palestinian self-rule and Israeli withdrawal. The way was cleared for Israel to sign a peace treaty with Jordan. As many as 15 Arab governments engaged in multilateral talks with Israel on issues such as arms control and regional security, water, regional economic development, the environment, and refugees. Concrete steps were taken, such as joint naval exercises for search-and-rescue operations and incidents at sea. In May 1994 a draft "Multilateral Declaration of Principles on Middle East Arms Control and Regional Security" was negotiated with American and Russian assistance. Israel began establishing bilateral relations with a number of these Arab countries and improving its relations globally with countries for which the Palestinian issue had been an obstacle.

Rabin's funeral, in its own tragic way, spoke to how much the world saw him as a peacemaker. More heads of state attended than had ever before gathered anywhere in the Middle East. "He was a man of courage, a man of vision," King Hussein eulogized. "I grieve the loss of a brother, a colleague, and a friend." Egyptian President Hosni Mubarak mourned him as "a fallen hero of peace." Despite all the uncertainties, Bill Clinton is firm on the overall Rabin-and-peace question: "[H]ad he not lost his life on that terrible November night, within three years we would have had a comprehensive agreement for peace in the Middle East." Israeli journalist Ari Shavit, despite some tough criticisms of Oslo, is certain as well: "To this day I am convinced that if Rabin had not been assassinated, peace would not have been assassinated." Indeed that was precisely what Yigal Amir had in mind: kill Rabin and kill peace.

Given that the conflict has gotten so much worse, was this really a breakthrough?

It is hard to hold out much hope these days for Israeli-Palestinian peace. But never, of course, say never. We saw that with Nelson Mandela and the peaceful transition of apartheid to democracy. We saw it with the peaceful end of the Cold War after decades on the nuclear brink and one global confrontation after another. Israeli novelist Amos Oz said it well when he called what Rabin had achieved "an emotional breakthrough," and how "the cognitive block fell away. In spite of everything, we now face the Palestinians, nation to nation, to discuss the division of the land. That is no small feat. Peace is an experiment that has not yet failed." Many would dearly want to be able to say more. But were it not for the statesmanship of Yitzhak Rabin, we would be saying even less.

Mairead Corrigan and Betty Williams: Northern Ireland Women for Peace, 1972–1977

M any winners of the Nobel Peace Prize have come from civil society and NGOs, including Mairead Corrigan and Betty Williams, founders of Northern Ireland Women for Peace, who made a major breakthrough in the Catholic-Protestant conflict that was tearing Northern Ireland apart. While their roles were not of the magnitude of Nelson Mandela's and Yitzhak Rabin's, we see in this brief profile how through a combination of conducive conditions and choices made, ordinary people can do extraordinary things.

WHO are Mairead Corrigan and Betty Williams?

When Ireland finally wrested its independence from Great Britain in 1921, after three years of open war and struggles that went back much further, the six counties that were mostly Protestant stayed within the United Kingdom (known as Ulster, or Northern Ireland) while the 26 mostly Catholic counties became the Irish Free Republic (in 1949, the Republic of Ireland). The Protestant minority left in the Irish Free Republic was only about 8 percent of the population, many of whom emigrated in ensuing years. The Catholic minority in Northern Ireland was much larger, about 35 percent, feeding into sectarian violence pitting the now Catholic-dominated Irish Republican Army (IRA) against the British government and Protestant militias. The Catholics were known as the Unionists pursuing a single Ireland, and the Protestants were known as the Loyalists to the British Crown.

By 1976 Northern Ireland was in its sixth year of "The Troubles," a period in which killings and other violence between Catholics and Protestants were rapidly escalating. On the one side the Provisional IRA, a breakaway group from the long-standing IRA, had turned to bombings and other urban guerrilla tactics. On the other British troops were now deployed in larger numbers and with more firepower, along with Protestant militia groups such as the Ulster Volunteer Force. On January 30, 1972, "Bloody Sunday," British troops shot and killed 14 Catholic protesters, the largest number killed in a single incident up to that point. The death toll, only 16 in 1969, reached 479 just in 1972 and stayed at high levels for each of the next four years. Bombings increased almost 30 percent, to 473 incidents in 1976.

On August 10, 1976, a British patrol in pursuit of an IRA getaway car through West Belfast shot the driver dead. Passing by on the sidewalk was Mrs. Anne Maguire with her four children. The dead driver's car swerved, crashing into the railings around St. John the Baptist school. The baby in the pram, the two-and-a-half-year-old walking with his mom, and the eight-and-a-half-year-old riding her bike were all killed. Anne was seriously injured. The 7-year-old walking ahead a few yards survived.

Mairead Corrigan, Anne's sister, rushed to the hospital. On the way out the BBC interviewed her. "It's not violence people want," she said, sobbing. This wasn't just the fault of one or the other. The British patrols did the killing, but the IRA member shouldn't have been moving so openly and speeding through a heavily populated neighborhood. "Only one percent of this province wants this slaughter." The BBC reporter, his years of experience notwithstanding, was visibly moved while still on camera. The interview ran and reran on local TV and was picked up by channels in Britain and around the world.

Betty Williams had been driving with her four-year-old daughter when she came upon the emergency crews on the scene of the Maguires' accident. That evening she saw Mairead Corrigan's interview on television. "The death of the Maguire children," she later reflected, "burst a dam inside me." The next day she canvassed friends and neighbors. "Do you want to have peace? Do you want to be able to live without having to be afraid of having your husbands and children killed by bombs and bullets?" She drew up petitions. News spread to other parts of Belfast. Two days later Betty was interviewed by the BBC about the signatures on the petitions from over 6,000 Protestant and Catholic women alike. Betty and Mairead met at the funeral for the Maguire children. From there they launched Northern Ireland Women for Peace, which over the next months would organize numerous marches and demonstrations on a scale not seen since The Troubles had started, and which received huge national and international media attention.

When all this happened, Mairead Corrrigan was 32 years old, single, and a secretary at a Guinness brewery. She'd grown up in The Falls, a poor Catholic ghetto in Belfast, in a devout family. Since her girlhood she'd been part of the Legion of Mary, a lay Catholic welfare organization doing voluntary social work in Catholic neighborhoods throughout Belfast. She was sympathetic to the cause of liberation from British control and Protestant dominance. On two different occasions she had encountered British soldiers inappropriately stopping and searching young Catholic women, only to be beaten when she protested. She once had considered joining the IRA but objected to its excessive violence.

Betty Williams was 33, married since she was 19, and had two children. Although she was Catholic, her husband was Protestant, and three of her four grandparents were non-Catholic (two Protestant, one Jewish). She too had run-ins with the British, having been arrested and interrogated late one night in a case of mistaken identity. On the other hand, when she'd stopped to kneel in prayer for a young British soldier who had been shot, she was castigated by Catholic passers-by for caring about the enemy. She'd had one cousin killed on his doorstep by Protestant militias and another cousin killed while driving by an

IRA-planted bomb. She was working two jobs as a night waitress and an office receptionist.

This everywoman quality and the sincerity and conviction Corrigan and Williams conveyed gave them their own version of personal capital. They also showed tremendous courage. When a 13-year-old Catholic boy was killed by a British soldier on October 10, they were attacked by a mob bent on retaliation, not nonviolence. Corrigan was pelted with eggs at a rally in Belfast. Police told Williams to take out the lightbulbs in the front hall of her home for protection. "The threats will not stop me," Corrigan said. "The peace campaign will go on, and nothing will stop us."

The other side of their everywoman-ness was political inexperience. They partially compensated for their own limited political skills by bringing in an experienced peace activist, Ciaran McKeown, to help run the organization (relabeled Peace People), but, as we'll see, problems still developed.

WHY did these two ordinary women become leaders of a peace movement?

The crash that killed the Maguire children was more than another statistic. It was personal. For Mairead Corrigan it was her niece and nephews. For Betty Williams, living only a few blocks away, it could have been her own children. Corrigan asked the BBC reporter to interview her, although it's doubtful she had a sense of the extent to which her sadness and outrage would resonate. Williams, the dam bursting within her, made the decision to get out there with petitions, although she too likely didn't foresee that this would go well beyond her neighbors and friends.

There also was some pent-up frustration over the limited role of women in Irish politics and society. The men on both sides needed to stop the violence. "These people do not know what sort of women they are taking on," was how Betty Williams responded to threats made against them. While there isn't any evidence that they thought in these terms or took it in this direction, their actions carried on a long tradition going back to Aristophanes' *Lysistrata*, in which Greek women withheld sex from their men as pressure to end war and make peace. "The point of our campaign," they did say, "was to get all *men* of violence to lay down their arms" (italics added).

Their vision of nonviolence was central to the First Declaration of the Peace People, the organization they formed along with Ciaran McKeown:

> We have a simple message to the world from this movement for Peace.
> We want to live and love and build a just and peaceful society.
> We want for our children, as we want for ourselves, our lives at home, at work, and at play to be lives of joy and Peace . . .
> We recognize that there are many problems in our society which are a source of conflict and violence . . .
> We reject the use of the bomb and the bullet and all the techniques of violence.
> We dedicate ourselves to working with our neighbours, near and far, day in and day out, to build that peaceful society in which the tragedies we have known are a bad memory and a continuing warning.

They didn't get much past this when it came to concrete proposals. They pushed some ideas for integrating social institutions such as schools and recreation centers. When a German reporter asked if their goal was power-sharing, Williams fell back on "Sorry, we never talk politics." Yet for the IRA the conflict wasn't just about stopping the violence; it was also about retributional justice with ends that in its view justified the means. For the Protestant Loyalists it was about preserving their power and position, their version of ends justifying the means of violence. Between these positions, the nonviolence/no politics alternative was the one being squeezed. Its vision was too inchoate, without enough of a "how to get there" or even what "there" was, which became a major limitation.

HOW did they pursue their goals of nonviolence and reconciliation?

The rallies took off with unprecedented speed and growth. The first was held on August 12, two days after the Maguire children were killed. It drew about 1,000 people. The rally two days later drew 10,000. A week later 20,000. Another week later 25,000. For the first time since The Troubles began, large numbers of Catholics and Protestants were joining together, as in the double-march in Derry/Londonderry, with Catholic women marching on one side of the River Foyle and Protestant women on the other, then meeting on the Craigavon Bridge. Especially symbolic was a December 5 rally on the banks of the Boyne River, where in 1690 Protestant William of Orange defeated Catholic King James II, and now groups from Northern Ireland and the Republic of Ireland joined forces.

The movement also spread internationally. A huge rally was held in London, starting in Hyde Park, going to Westminster Abbey, and culminating in Trafalgar Square with the archbishop of Canterbury preaching, Joan Baez singing, and Corrigan and Williams among the speakers. The Women's Association of West Germany presented a petition of support with six million signatures. Corrigan and Williams also made a trip to the United States to build support and in particular to urge Irish-American supporters to cut off money and arms they had been providing to the IRA.

Spontaneity was great, but sustainability required structuring an organization. In April 1977 Peace People convened a convention. On the one hand, there was interest in maintaining a highly decentralized organization with autonomous local committees. On the other hand, if Peace People were to make an impact at high levels, the leaders needed to be visible and have the necessary control over message and strategy with an infrastructure sufficiently bankrolled and at least semi-professionalized.

They also were finding out that being above or outside politics in a conflict that was politically driven wasn't viable. In May 1977, they boldly called for demilitarization, giving the militias on both sides three months to turn in their weapons. The deadline was not met. Few weapons were turned in. Demilitarization is exceedingly difficult to achieve even when a conflict is resolved, let alone while it is still raging.

Another issue involved Queen Elizabeth II's visit to Northern Ireland in August 1977 as part of her silver jubilee (25 years since her coronation). Corrigan and Williams were among those invited to a dinner aboard the royal yacht, *Britannia*. The dominant sentiment in the Catholic community hostile to the monarchy was to not attend, especially since the date was the anniversary of the deaths of the Maguire children. Not to accept, though, would seem like they were taking the full Unionist position and would risk losing the support of Protestants. They went, and it did further damage their support among Catholics.

Even if Corrigan and Williams had been more politically skilled, it would have been tough going. The backlash was severe. The Provisional IRA and Catholic supporters treated them as infidels in their own church. A Catholic-controlled newspaper called them "'vultures' who wanted another 50 years of Protestant supremacy." The Protestant Loyalist militias kept up their side of the bombings, assassinations, and other attacks. The British government manipulated them, as two Irish authors put it, "as an ideological weapon against the Provisionals."

Still, the violence did come down. Deaths fell from 295 in 1976 to 111 in 1977 and 82 in 1978. The 1971–1976 total was 1,752 deaths. Over the 22 years from then until 1998 when the Good Friday Agreement was signed, the total was 1,689. On October 10, 1977, Mairead Corrigan and Betty Williams were named recipients of the Nobel Peace Prize. "They refused to bow to bleak skepticism, they simply acted," the Nobel citation read, "a courageous, unselfish act that proved an inspiration to thousands, that lit a light in the darkness, and that gave fresh hope to people who believed that all hope was gone . . . what we all hope may prove to be the first dawn of a new day bringing lasting peace to the sorely tried people of Ulster."

The Nobel Prize was double-edged. It affirmed what Corrigan and Williams had achieved. But their decision to personally keep part of the funds after having said the award would go to Peace People, while defensible as reimbursement for costs incurred (allowable under the terms of the award), severely tarnished their personal capital based on commitment to the cause. Other differences also opened up between them, within the organization, and in the support base they had started to mobilize. Within a year of receiving the Nobel, Corrigan and Williams had stepped down from leadership of the Peace People. In 1980, Williams resigned fully. The following year Corrigan did as well.* The organization continued, although with a much less central role in the pursuit of peace and reconciliation that, finally in 1998, with American negotiator George Mitchell playing a key role along with Northern Ireland political party leaders John Hume and David Trimble, culminated in the Good Friday Agreement that established peace, albeit a fragile one, in Northern Ireland.

WHAT: Balance Sheet

"Religion," one student said, is a red herring.
I said if so, it was a red herring about the size of a whale.
—*Conor Cruise O'Brien, noted Irish intellectual and diplomat*

The Northern Ireland conflict went well beyond different beliefs in God. It was cultural, historical, and about social boundaries, eco-

---

* Williams left for the United States, where in 1996 she founded the World Centers for Compassion for Children, working with children afflicted by war in numerous countries. In 2004, she emigrated "back" to the Republic of Ireland. After a few years Corrigan got involved again with Peace People and became its honorary president. In 2006, Williams, along with fellow women Nobel Peace Prize laureates Jody Williams, Shirin Ebadi, Wangari Maathai, and Rigoberta Menchú Tum, established the Nobel Women's Initiative.

nomic position, and political power: Identity. Who I am, who you are, and what the differences are between us. And such differences: "The Protestants," as one journalist captured it, "are convinced that the Catholics are dirty, lazy, 'Republicans' who do nothing except make babies. Catholics believe that Protestants are heartless and stingy, hate all Catholics, and salute the queen, morning and night, in their living rooms."

Such deeply divisive politics of identity provide context both for both the scope and limits of what Mairead Corrigan and Betty Williams set in motion. At that moment in 1976 the future looked bleak. While there never is only one factor, the Northern Ireland Women for Peace/Peace People get a great deal of the credit for the steep decline in the death toll of The Troubles. They inspired people to speak up, stand up, and turn out against the violence. They catalyzed outrage from the people in whose name the violence was being perpetrated, yet who were paying the price. To be sure, it was never going to be just a "month's time" in which an exhilarated Mairead Corrigan mused that "there's not going to be a bombing or a hijacking, or a shooting. There's going to be peace." But the death toll never again reached pre-1977 levels: not a full resolution, but a seminal breakthrough.

The limits of what they achieved were in part self-inflicted. The controversy over the Nobel Prize award money left them open to charges of personal aggrandizement and was especially damaging to the personal capital they derived from their everywoman-ness. Spontaneity was valuable in getting things started, but organizational skills and structure were needed for sustaining the movement. While they were right in trying to avoid being political in the sectarian-partisan sense, being purely apolitical in a conflict so deeply political doesn't work.

Yet while they reached their limits, they also warrant credit for how their breakthrough opened the way for others. The Committee on the Administration of Justice was established in 1981 and went on to become Northern Ireland's leading human rights NGO. They set a precedent for women in a leadership role in a resistant political culture. Susan McHugh, who had a similar everywoman profile to Corrigan and Williams, mobilized her "Peace '93" at a point when things were teetering after the IRA had stepped up its terrorism in England. The Northern Ireland Women's Coalition was formed in 1996 by two women, one Catholic and one Protestant, to try to ensure women were well represented as delegates to the peace talks then beginning. George Mitchell would later write the foreword for a book about Corrigan and Williams, recognizing their contribution to what ultimately became the Good Friday Agreement.

The SARL assessment here is less clear than in the Mandela and Rabin profiles. Would someone else hit personally by The Troubles have reacted similarly to Mairead Corrigan? Would the "dam burst" for someone else living amid all this deadly conflict as it did for Betty Williams? We can't know for sure; there aren't as many unique qualities as in our other profiles. And over time other groups and individuals moved the process along; David Trimble and John Hume received their own Nobel Peace Prizes in 1999. Still, motivated by their heartfelt desire to take a stand against violence and terror with that sense of "now, for heaven's sake, something must be done," they made the initial breakthrough on which others built. While even after the Good Friday Agreement Northern Ireland's politics of identity have continued to be contentious and at times violent, conflicts have stayed well short of what they were back in the days of The Troubles.

Corrigan and Williams and their Northern Ireland Women for Peace/Peace People demonstrate the statesmanship role that individuals, civil society, and NGOs can play in our sense of impact felt, not just position held—something we continue to see, and need, in seeking reconciliation amid the politics of identity underlying much of the most severe violence in today's world.

POLITICS OF IDENTITY'S
ALTERNATIVE PLOTLINE

It is so much easier to foment the politics of identity than to reconcile them. The dynamic of who I am, who you are, and the differences between us—whether racial, religious, ethnic, sectarian, or tribal—drives many of the deadliest twenty-first-century conflicts and lurks within other potential ones. We see this in the Middle East: Sunni-Shia, Israeli-Palestinian, Kurds; in Africa, where ethnic and tribal conflicts rage across the continent; in Asia, within countries like Burma and Indonesia and the historically rooted, competing nationalisms of China and Japan; and in the nativism, racism, and other aspects of identity politics intensifying in the United States and much of Europe.

The script is a common one: Remind one's in-group of past sins and current injustices at the hands of the Other. Stir up fear that They are getting what We deserve, and at the extreme They are coming after Us. Invoke religious or other higher-order precepts, selectively interpreted as need be, eye-for-an-eye and self-defense. Interests can be negotiated. The edge can be taken off ideology. But identity when exploited by demagogic leaders can be much more absolutist. Exploited is the operative word. It is true, as William Faulkner once said, "the past is never dead, it's not even past." History continues to play out—but not deterministically. It gets played on most insidiously by those who, when it serves their own agendas, purposefully activate and intensify historically rooted tensions.

But as we've seen, another plotline is possible.

How much better off South Africa is today, even with the problems it does have, than if Nelson Mandela had not provided the statesmanship for a peaceful political transition. The transition that Mandela led the country through has not broken down. While polls show that 69.7 percent say that progress still needs to be made on national reconciliation, 59.2 percent acknowledge the progress that has been made and 64.6 percent continue to believe "one united South African nation" remains possible. Mandela's impact also reached well beyond South Africa—a global icon that, even if not fully replicable, was a touchstone for other leaders and societies pursuing the statesmanship of reconciliation over retribution.

How much better off Israel would be if Yitzhak Rabin had not been assassinated and had the opportunity to further develop the breakthrough with the Palestinians. The November 2015 twentieth anniversary of his assassination spurred much reflection on where Israel is today and where it could have been. Assassin Yigal Amir's belief that he was doing God's work was virulently reembraced by the Israeli right wing. Others stressed the progress made in the 1993–1995 period, how Israeli interests were strengthened in so many ways, and the opportunities missed for putting Israel in so much of a better position at home and internationally than it is in today. Even with the terrorism that has continued and the threats from Iran, Lebanon's Hizbollah, and others, groups such as Commanders for Israel's Security composed of over 200 retired Mossad, military, and other security officials "with some 8000 years of cumulative service in Israel's security forces," support a two-state solution and peace with the Palestinians.

How much better off Northern Ireland is, even with some violence and the political transition still not consolidated, with the spiraling killings of The Troubles stanched by the social movement catalyzed by the Northern Ireland Women for Peace. Having tarnished their own personal capital and reached the limit of their political skills, Betty Williams and Mairead Corrigan largely faded from the scene. The baton was handed to more experienced political leaders such as John Hume and David Trimble, as well as mediating diplomats such as George Mitchell. But in their moment Williams and Corrigan showed how critical spurs for transformational statesmanship could come from civil society and NGOs.

Today's politics of identity urgently require comparable statesmanship. First and foremost, it needs to come from parties to the conflict. Leaders who share group identity (be it national, ethnic, religious, or racial) are most able to have the personal capital to make the case for reconciliation, not retribution. When one of Us says we should seek to work with Them, the message carries an authenticity that cannot be programmed in. The particular origin varies case to case: Mandela's was from embodying the anti-apartheid struggle, Rabin's as Mr. Security, Williams and Corrigan as everyday people enduring the pain of The Troubles. Shrewd political skills also are needed to turn message and messenger into an effective strategy. For Mandela this meant savvy balancing, on the one hand restraining more radical elements and leadership challengers within the ANC while maintaining his own credibility, and on the other being tough enough with the Afrikaner leadership to get concessions while tempering the demonic view much of the Afrikaner population held of him. Rabin was less successful in the political balancing he faced. His own sense of the compelling strategic logic of pursuing peace with the Palestinians on top of his long-held antipathy for the Israeli right wing left him tragically unable or unwilling to abide by the keep-the-opposition-close, control-the-temperature stratagems. Political skills are where Williams and Corrigan ran into their limits, and it was left to others to build on their breakthrough.

Reinforcing support needs to come from leaders in the international community. Sanctions can be imposed, as they were against apartheid. Incentives can be offered, as with the economic assistance provided to the postapartheid Mandela government and to both the Israelis and the Palestinians. Diplomatic sponsorship and intermediation can be provided, as with both the Israeli-Palestinian and Northern Ireland Catholic-Protestant talks. Some of this reinforcement must come from leaders of major nations, whether American presidents or other countries' leaders as may fit the situation. Some must come from global leaders like the "secular Pope" of an invigorated UN secretary-general bringing to bear the imprimatur and resources of the United Nations. NGOs, more disposed as they often are than

governments to principled advocacy and with experience and expertise at the grassroots work crucial for cultivating popular acceptance
if not support for reconciliation, also can play a vital role.

Along with these instrumental types of support, we need inspira-
tional voices for the ultimate oneness of humanity. This is what leadership theorist Howard Gardner calls "enlarging the sense of 'we.'" With
religion so much a part of the politics of identity, religious leaders have
crucial roles to play—like Pope Francis, for example, with his capacity to bring people together in the spirit of the generic definition of
"catholic" ("broad in sympathies, tastes or interests; all-embracing").
So, too, those who are embodiments of mixed identities—like London Mayor Sadiq Khan and his self-depiction: "I am the West, I am a
Londoner, I'm British, I'm of Islamic faith, Asian origin, Pakistan heritage." The philosopher and economist Amartya Sen speaks of "plural
identities," recognizing that while even in a globalized world deep-
seated identities remain core, people can have other broader senses of
affiliation and commonality layered on in addition to, not instead of.
The more voices speaking to humanity's commonality and the more
actions demonstrating it in practice, the more possible it will be for the
Mandela-Rabin-Williams/Corrigan plotline to prevail.

ADVANCING FREEDOM AND PROTECTING HUMAN RIGHTS

THE TWENTIETH-CENTURY "FREEDOM AGENDA" HAD THREE main elements: decolonization and independence for vast swaths of Africa, the Middle East, and Asia; democratization of countries from both communist rule and military regimes; and protection of human rights wherever and by whomever they were being repressed. Our profiles in this section focus on leaders who are representative of all three types of struggles:

- **Mahatma Gandhi,** for the anticolonialism and pacifism that not only shaped India but also resonated globally (Chapter 8);
- **Lech Walesa,** who made Poland the first big democratizing crack in the Soviet bloc (Chapter 9);
- **Aung San Suu Kyi,** for her defiance of the Burma-Myanmar military dictatorship, while also taking into account her much criticized role in the 2017–18 Rohingya crisis (Chapter 10);
- **Peter Benenson,** founder of Amnesty International, for spurring the global movement of human rights NGOs (Chapter 11).

For all that has been achieved, according to the think tank–advocacy organization Freedom House, the last year in which more countries had gains in freedom than declines was 2005. The *Economist*'s Democracy Index has fallen to 5.5 (on a scale of 1 to 10). "Things are unquestionably getting worse," the founder of the Oslo-based Freedom Forum (the Davos for dissidents, according to the BBC) reflected on the state of human rights, "and that is not embellishment or melodrama." Amnesty International warns of the spread of "Orwellian" technologies of repression, including in ostensible democracies.

Some transformational forces will continue to be bottom-up, with civil society activists and people power movements hitting the streets, networking through Twitter and Facebook, and building like-minded transnational coalitions. But without bold and dynamic leadership, popular movements run greater risks of being crushed or losing their way. The 2011 Arab Spring, so inspiring in the moment but lacking the leadership needed to guide it, is a case in point. The twenty-first century needs its own peacemakers if further breakthroughs are to be made in advancing democracy and protecting human rights.

Gandhi: Exemplar of Anticolonialism, Apostle of Nonviolence, 1914–1948

Generations to come, it may be, will scarce believe such a one as this
ever in flesh and blood walked upon this earth.
—*Albert Einstein*

Reflecting on his influence on the course of the nationalist movement in India
and the wider fate of European imperialism as it teetered to its fall, it is not
hard to see his life as a telling illustration of the power of the individual to
affect the course of history.
—*Biographer David Arnold*

The more I read about Gandhi, the more he is a bizarre guy.
—*One of my student research assistants*

WHO was Mahatma Gandhi?

He was born Mohandas Karamchand Gandhi on October 2, 1869, the youngest of four children. His family was Viashya, the third highest of the four castes in the Hindu system. Though his ancestors were grocers, his father and other male relatives held prominent positions in local government within the British colonial system. His mother, who was quite religious, instilled in Gandhi Hinduism within the *bhakti* tradition, which is based more on individual devotion than formal ritual. She also taught him to have a meticulous regard for cleanliness and neatness.

In 1888 he went to London to study law. At first he adopted the trappings of a young English gentleman, dressing accordingly, even signing up for lessons in dancing and elocution. His vegetarianism tempered this, being more unusual in London than in India and exposing him to more unconventional types who also were involved in a range of controversial political and social issues. He finished his studies and in 1891 headed back to India. Once home, though, he did not make the headway he expected given his training and his family standing. So when in 1893 the opportunity arose to represent a company with business interests in South Africa, he decided to go there.

Even his experience with British colonial rule back in India did not prepare him for the discrimination he encountered in South Africa. Indians were treated almost as badly as blacks, even worse in some ways since they had no claim to indigenous roots. The commissioner of native affairs in Transvaal, near where Gandhi was living, called for "the lower castes who form the mass [of the Indian immigrants] . . . filthy in habit and a menace to the public health" to be separated out "to reside for sanitary reasons in places set apart." Nor was it just the lower castes. Indian merchants were semibarbarous, a leading newspaper editorialized. Gandhi had his own degrading experiences, as when ordered by a judge to remove his turban while in court and being kicked off a train despite having purchased a first-class ticket because only whites were allowed to travel in that luxury.

He turned his law practice to combating social injustice. He worked against the tax on Indians who wanted to stay in South Africa after their period of indentured labor expired, against immigration restrictions requiring every Indian eight years and older to obtain a new certificate of registration, and against Supreme Court invalidation of Hindu marriages. He became more political, leading the "Great March" with 50,000 striking workers. He made repeated trips back to London to lobby but to no avail.* And he became more spiritual

* South Africa was a dominion within the British Empire, with higher status and greater relative autonomy than a colony like India but still subject to policies set in London.

and philosophical, beginning to develop his doctrines of *satyagraha*, Sanskrit for the struggle for truth, and *ahimsa*, or nonviolence. It was in these years that he also wrote *Hind Swaraj*, literally translated as "Indian Self-Rule," which showed that his home country was very much on his mind. On July 8, 1914, now 44 years old, he left South Africa to return to India.

While he had been somewhat involved in the Indian National Congress (INC), the leading anticolonial party, he was not much known. His rapid rise came less from playing the inside game among the refined elites than from the outside as a leader of the poor and as a voice and symbol of the spiritual. "He did not descend from the top," wrote Jawaharlal Nehru, who would become a close ally and himself the first prime minister of independent India. "He seemed to emerge from the millions of India, speaking their language and incessantly drawing attention to them and their appalling conditions." He would continue to embody this role through the civil disobedience movements he organized in the 1920s and 1930s, through the achievement of independence in 1947, up to his assassination on January 30, 1948, and his enduring legacy.

Gandhi epitomized the moral dimension of personal capital. By 1921 he was widely referred to as "Mahatma," a holy person and sage. He was revered for a wisdom that was more populist than priestly, more Jesus-like than Pope-like. The Hindu epics have tales of *avatars*, descendants of God who come to earth to aid mankind. The 70-year-old paralytic man who claimed wearing Gandhi's photograph around his neck and "uttering Gandhi's name" cured him "when all remedies failed" was one example of Gandhi as avatar. In a broader cultural sense Gandhi had an authenticity that tapped precolonial Indian pride. Ideas such as *satyagraha* were contemporary applications of centuries-old Hindu traditions. The spinning wheel that became one of his symbols exemplified village self-reliance, as handspun *khadi* cloth became the uniform for independence activists. Business suits were replaced by shawl, loincloth, and sandals. Gandhi's ascetic lifestyle linked personal self-control and improvement to the broader national cause. Yet for all his spirituality, to again quote Nehru, "his smile is delightful, his laughter infectious, and he radiates light-heartedness." He was able to galvanize millions of people in ways that Nehru and other nationalists could not.

His self-sacrifice was there to be seen on a daily basis. The fasts he frequently undertook—by one count, 14—as political pressure also served as the personal purification that he believed necessary to be a worthy leader. He endured numerous arrests, two of which left him close to death. He repeatedly thrust himself into communities torn by Hindu-Muslim violence, seeking conciliation.

In some respects he was strikingly politically inept. He was not much of a public speaker: his voice high-pitched, his manner not commanding of crowds. After having mobilized the 1930 "Salt March" against British taxes on this village food staple, he didn't play his hand very well for concessions from the colonial authorities. Even Nehru often was frustrated with Gandhi's unwillingness or inability to be practical about what was required to create a modern nation-state. On occasion he did show himself savvy for political maneuvering against rivals and opponents. When in 1938 Nehru lost the presidency of the Indian National Congress to the more radical Subhas Chandra Bose, Gandhi worked the party politics to get Nehru back in power the following year. And he managed to repeatedly get under Winston Churchill's skin who suggested that Gandhi "ought to be lain bound hand and foot at the gates of Delhi and then trampled on by an enormous elephant with the new Viceroy seated on its back," labeled him a "malignant subversive fanatic," and pushed for keeping him in jail despite his life-threatening fast so that "we should be rid of a bad man and an enemy of the Empire if he died."

Gandhi also had some less admirable qualities. His views on some of the era's other major conflicts were not exactly of the high *satyagraha* morality. There was his 1940 "Dear Friend" letter to Adolf Hitler acknowledging that "many of your actions are monstrous and unbecoming of human dignity, especially in the estimation of men like me who believe in universal friendliness," but also going pretty far in trying to reach out to him saying that "we have no doubt about your bravery or devotion to your fatherland, nor do we believe that you are the monster described by your opponents." Gandhi affirmed "my sympathies are all with the Jews . . . They have been the untouchables of Christianity . . . If there ever could be a justifiable war in the name of and for humanity, a war against Germany to prevent the wanton persecution of a whole race, would be completely justified." Still, "I do not believe in any war."

More personally, without getting too Freudian, Gandhi had a peculiar and sometimes troubling attitude toward sex. As was traditional, he married in 1883 at age 13. His child bride, Kasturbai Kapadia, came from the same caste, a year older, illiterate. They stayed married until her death in 1944, but by his own admission he was quite cruel to his wife. Between 1888 and 1900 they had four children (all sons), whom he also treated poorly. In 1906 he adopted *brachmacharya*, a vow of celibacy, as part of his practice of self-control. Biographers see this somewhat paradoxically as a manifestation of a preoccupation with sex. Throughout his life he would sleep with naked women ostensibly to test that self-control, including a grandniece and the wife of a grandnephew.

Gandhi the man was not all that Gandhi the image held him to be. But that is the point. Imperfections and all, he still had extraordinary impact on events in his own country and beyond, very much a telling illustration of the power of the individual to affect the course of history.

WHY: Gandhi's anticolonialism

Books on Gandhi's thinking fill whole library sections. Our focus is on the four aspects that most bear on his anticolonialism (and even these are in summary form).

Civilizational: He who saw England as the "center of civilization" when he set out for London as a young law student came through life experience to see British rule as culturally alien to his India. Yes, colonialism was politically repressive and economically exploitative. Worst was how the overlay of the British way of life was suffocating the very essence of Indian society. The rationale for self-rule in *Hind Swaraj* was revitalizing India's internal sense of itself or "freedom would be empty of real meaning." "What is *Swaraj*?" the "Reader" (the questioner) asks the "Editor" (representing himself) in a dialogue evocative of the debate between Krishna and Arjuna in the Hindu classic *Bhagavad Gita*. Unless society itself is changed to reconnect with India's own history, traditions, and culture, all we will have is "English rule without the Englishman . . . it will be called not Hindustan but Englishstan. This is not the *Swaraj* I want."

The spinning wheel and khadi exemplified the destructive "thread" colonialism "wove." Even more than the economics of the English textile trade displacing village production, Gandhi focused on the cultural clash with the "incredibly heartless and inhuman processes" of faraway industrialization. Nor was it only on this issue that Gandhi overly glorified simpler times. He saw limited value in the structures of a modern state, even that of an independent India, or a modern economy, even one run by Indians. "Every village will be a republic or *panchayat* having full powers . . . self-sustained and capable of managing its affairs." For many fellow anticolonialists in the Congress Party, such views were unrealistic for the mid-twentieth century.

Nonviolence: Satyagraha, the struggle for truth, had to be pursued in a manner consistent with *ahimsa*, nonviolence. For Gandhi, unlike some anticolonial leaders in other parts of the world, independence was not an end justifying guerrilla warfare or other such means. The means had to be consistent with the ends: "The pursuit of truth did not admit of violence being inflicted on one's opponent but that he must be weaned from error by patience and compassion." Indeed, the path of nonviolence would bring one closer to truth or other virtues sought: "And patience means self-suffering. So the doctrine came to mean vindication of truth, not by infliction of suffering on the opponent, but on one's self."

This, though, was not pure Thoreauvian civil disobedience of an individual safeguarding one's own values and conscience. It was intended as communal collective action for changing, not just resisting, unjust laws and practices. Nor was Gandhi's nonviolence absolute. He opposed Subhas Chandra Bose's formation of a military force to fight the British. But in 1942 at a point when the independence struggle seemed to be falling apart, he joined other Congress Party leaders in calling on Indians to "do or die." "I might be ready to embrace a snake," he wrote, "but if one comes to bite you, I should kill it and protect you." These, though, were exceptions to an overall vision that led Lord Mountbatten, the last British governor-general of India, to acknowledge what "all India owes to Mahatma Gandhi—the architect of her freedom through non-violence."

Social Justice: Gandhi also pushed for abolishing the caste system's untouchability. In one of his earliest speeches he called it "an ineffaceable blot that Hinduism today carries with it." This was another aspect of the purification from within, without which political independence would have only limited value and even less virtue. "Shall we not have the vision to see that in suppressing a sixth (or whatever the number) of ourselves, we have depressed ourselves? No man takes another down a pit without descending into it himself and sinning in the bargain." They were not *dalits*, the derogatory term for the untouchables; they were *harijam*, children of God. He welcomed them into his ashram.

The Congress Party, its leadership drawn extensively from upper castes, balked at Gandhi's openness. The socialist left derogated such cultural constructs as distracting from the "true" struggle of class conflict. Yet *dalit* activists deemed Gandhi's approach too gradualist. Even so, a provision of the 1948 Indian constitution, passed amid cries of "Mahatma Gandhi *ki jai* (hail)," bans untouchability. While the ban proved more formal than actual, this was another way Gandhi's ideas inspired further efforts at social justice in India and globally.

Hindu-Muslim Unity: "India cannot cease to be one nation because people belonging to different religions live in it." Hindus and Muslims were one within the Indian nation, a divided family but still a family. Going back to his Constructive Program of the early 1920s, Gandhi sought to cultivate greater Hindu-Muslim unity through joint national schools and colleges and other bottom-up initiatives. His 1931 Resolution on Fundamental Rights and Economic Changes, written with Nehru, called for religious neutrality in an independent unified state. He was convinced that Hindu-Muslim tensions were being fed by British divide-and-rule ploys and that they would subside once independence was achieved. However true the former was, independence caused tensions to intensify, not to subside. Political competition and distrust grew among leaders, including between Gandhi and Muslim League leader Muhammad Ali Jinnah. Somewhat paradoxically for all his efforts at unity, Gandhi's very embodiment as a Hindu sage, as exploited by Jinnah and other Muslim leaders, added to Muslims' sense of the need for their own independent state. That Gandhi was eventually assassinated by an ultranationalist Hindu extremist accusing him of having been too sympathetic to Muslims is a tragic irony.

Gandhi's HOW

Gandhi's return to India came within months of World War I breaking out. Britain's requirement that India commit troops (over one million soldiers and thousands of noncombatants) and resources (a war tax and other measures amounting to over £150 million) to the Motherland's fight accentuated India's rising demands for a greater voice in its own affairs. Instead the British used wartime as rationale for tightening control and then in vicious cycle dynamics met the rising political protests by extending restrictions beyond the end of the war. The affirmation of self-determination in Woodrow Wilson's Fourteen Points initially raised Indian nationalist hopes. Gandhi was among those the Indian National Congress had chosen to represent them in Versailles, only to have the British colonial government replace the INC designees with its own hand-picked Indians.

Gandhi called for a nationwide *satyagraha* mobilization of civil disobedience and worker strikes. On April 13, 1919, in the northern city
of Amritsar, the British opened fire on protesters. Close to 400 were
killed and over 1,500 wounded. Historians see the Amritsar massacre
as a turning point, laying bare "the intrinsic violence of British rule, a
savage indifference to Indian life, and an utter contempt for nationalist feeling and peaceful protest."

The Non-Cooperation and Civil Disobedience Movement of 1920–
1922 that Gandhi organized in the wake of Amritsar had three main
aspects. One was boycotting the British system in its various manifes-
tations: their goods, their schools, the limited elections they allowed,
the taxes they imposed, and defiance of various laws. Particularly
dramatic were the July 31, 1921, bonfire burnings of foreign cloth all
over the country. Gandhi personally torched the massive one-mile-
diameter pile in Bombay. The second aspect of the movement was his
Constructive Program of building up the traditional Indian civilizational side of khadi production, basic education, alcohol temperance,
reforming the caste system, and Hindu-Muslim unity. The third was
working with Nehru and others in the Congress Party on explicitly
political measures.

On January 26, 1930, the INC issued a declaration of independence:
"We believe that it is the inalienable right of the Indian people, as
of any other people, to have freedom . . . The British government in
India has not only deprived the Indian people of their freedom but
has . . . ruined India economically, politically, culturally and spiritually." Gandhi's influence was especially evident in this latter phras-
ing. He followed up with a petition to Lord Irwin, the British viceroy,
with 11 grievances including the release of political prisoners and the
abolition of the tax on salt and the government's monopoly on its production and sale. Focusing on salt, a basic household staple, had a
symbolism in India akin to the American colonies' Boston Tea Party.
On March 12, Gandhi set out with a group of followers (including
Muslims, a Christian, and some untouchables) on a 200-mile walk to
the sea. Many others joined along the way, including local and foreign

journalists. After 25 days he reached the coast on April 6, waded into the sea, and lifted a pinch of salt. "With this, I am shaking the foundations of the British Empire," he declared. Salt protests spread across the country, spurring tens of thousands of people, with an estimated 60,000 Indians arrested for their defiance. Gandhi, of course, was among them.

When World War II broke out in September 1939, the Congress Party initially made its support contingent on a British pledge for Indian independence. Prime Minister Winston Churchill, he of the "malignant subversive fanatic view" of Gandhi, refused. On August 8, 1942, Gandhi and the Congress Party passed the "Quit India" resolution citing "India's inalienable right to freedom and independence" and demanding that the British leave. Nonviolence was to be the mode of struggle, drawing on "all the non-violent strength . . . gathered during the last 22 years of peaceful struggle . . . they [the people] must remember that non-violence is the basis of the movement." When the British retaliated by outlawing the Congress Party and arresting Gandhi and other leaders, nonviolence was overtaken by a wave of attacks on police stations, post and telegraph offices, and other official sites. An estimated 2,500 Indians were killed or injured and over 100,000 Indians were imprisoned, many kept in jail until the end of the war. The British considered shipping Gandhi and other Congress Party leaders off to South Africa or Yemen. Realizing this would exacerbate the situation, they backed off.

After the war, with Churchill crushingly defeated for reelection and the new Labour government less committed to the burdens of empire, independence became imminent. The main question was whether the Raj (quasi-colonial name the British used) would be partitioned into two countries, India and Pakistan. Interestingly, demands for an independent Pakistan only began in the early 1930s. In 1916, as leader of the All-India Muslim League, Jinnah had signed the Lucknow Pact with Congress Party leaders setting out guarantees of Muslim minority political rights within the Raj and the to-be-independent India. Over time, though, Jinnah and other Muslim leaders had reason to grow

skeptical of such guarantees. In 1940 Jinnah led passage of the "Pakistan Resolution," declaring, "Muslims are a nation according to any
definition of a nation, and they must have their homelands, their territory and their State."* Gandhi and Jinnah conducted extensive talks
in 1944 but failed to come to a common approach. Gandhi continued
making his one-civilization argument that Muslims could be granted
sufficient autonomy in their majority regions to assure their interests
and traditions. He even proposed a coalition national government with
Jinnah as prime minister. Jinnah saw the differences as too deep to be
bridged within a single country. Given the tensions in their own relationship, he doubted whether Gandhi's assurances were sincere—and
even if they were, whether they could withstand the animosities of
Hindu extremists. He also had his own political ambitions. So too for
their part Nehru and other Congress Party leaders were less ready to
concede their own interests in India's top positions.

While continuing to push for Hindu-Muslim unity and nonviolence, Gandhi made his own missteps. In 1946, when negotiations for
a single federated India with limited central government and strong
provincial governments were getting some traction, Gandhi called on
the British to leave immediately with an Indian national government
taking charge and a constitutional assembly deferred until after independence. He meant this sincerely, believing that single-state unity
could be worked out by Hindus and Muslims themselves. But it played
into the Muslims' fears. It also caught other Congress Party leaders off
guard. From that point on they largely cut Gandhi out of the formal
negotiations.

He put his principal efforts into trying to stop the intensifying violence. In October 1946 in East Bengal, what would become East Pakistan and eventually Bangladesh, several hundred Hindus were killed

---

* The very word "Pakstan" (without the *i*), derived from the initials of the Raj's five
northern provinces: **P**unjab, **A**fghan Province (North-West Frontier Province), **K**ashmir,
Sind, and Baluchi**stan**, was not coined until 1933, and even then as a name for the region
within the single state of India.

by Muslims. Gandhi spent the next four months in the region going village to village, meeting with both Hindus and Muslims. In March 1947 he did the same in Bihar, where the attacks had been Hindu on Muslim. His hopes that such efforts might strengthen the case against partition were to no avail. On August 14–15, 1947, the British declared two independent states, India and Pakistan, with Pakistan split into West and East areas on the two sides of India. If the rationale for partition was to avoid mass violence, the split had the opposite effect. The two countries went to war. Extremists on both sides were unleashed, and an estimated 500,000 people were killed. Another 14 million became refugees.

Gandhi went to Calcutta, which had been experiencing some of the worst communal violence, including the "Great Calcutta Killing" in which an estimated 4,000 were slaughtered and 11,000 injured. Both sides had unleashed "goondas" (thugs). Riots were widespread. "A recital of man's barbarism," Gandhi called it at a prayer meeting when he arrived in August 1947. His initial efforts produced only a brief respite in the violence. Even he was forced to muse that "what was regarded as the 'Calcutta Miracle' has proved to be a nine days' wonder." He turned to a fast pledging "to end only if and when sanity returns to Calcutta." By the third day doctors warned that he was risking death. But the fast was having its effect. A band of goondas came to confess. The governor sent a note that the city had become strikingly calm. A joint Hindu-Muslim group of local leaders came to him with a pledge: "We the undersigned promise to Gandhiji that . . . we shall never allow communal strife in the city and shall strive unto death to prevent it." At least during the partition period, there was no more major communal violence in Calcutta.

He next went to Delhi, where local Hindu authorities had been complicit in pushing 60,000 Muslims into internal refugee camps. He visited the camps and pressured local authorities to provide better treatment—"shamed" them into it, as one historian puts it. On January 13, 1948, he launched a fast seeking "a reunion of hearts of all communities." In response, 100,000 government employees signed pledges to work for intercommunal peace. Muslim leaders invited him to speak at one of their shrines.

This micro-level violence prevention strategy had limits. Geography among other forces worked against its sustainability. One such force proved all too imminent. On January 30 a Hindu extremist, Nathuran Godse, assassinated Gandhi. "How can I, who am a Hindu by birth, a Hindu by creed and a Hindu of Hindus in my way of living be an 'enemy' of Hindus?" Gandhi had responded when Hindus accused him of being pro-Muslim. The line of argument had worked with some, but not with Godse and his co-conspirators. "My shots were fired at the person . . . unfairly favorable to the Muslims," Godse would proclaim in court, "whose policy and action had brought rack and ruin and destruction to millions of Hindus."

WHAT: Balance Sheet

As with every other breakthrough in our book, Indian independence was not the result of one person's effort. Jawaharlal Nehru was the first prime minister and remained in that position until his death in 1964. With all due respect to Nehru, one can picture someone else politically astute and policy oriented filling his role. Gandhi was, as Nehru put it, the soul of India. This spirituality combined with his own version of political savvy that allowed Gandhi to connect with and activate people from all strata of Indian society and that denuded British claims to legitimacy was both unique and crucial to defeating colonialism: very much a high SARL ranking.

Being that "most truly bright and precious jewel in the crown of the King," as Churchill called India, its loss reverberated throughout the Empire. Inspiration was felt and validation cited by anticolonial movements across Asia, Africa, the Middle East, and Latin America. While each country had its own dynamics, India was the vanguard for the end of a centuries-long denial to so much of the world of political independence. "For large numbers of people in countries which had been colonized by Europeans, or who were tyrannized by authoritarian or racist rulers," as historian David Hardiman put it, "Gandhi became a figure who symbolized and stood for the assertion of the oppressed."

Some of these movements went the way of violence, guerrilla warfare, and the like. Others were sufficiently heartened by Gandhian nonviolence to stick largely to peaceful means. One award-winning study covering 323 cases spanning the 1900–2006 period shows a higher success rate in nonviolent political resistance than violent cases in terms both of achieving immediate objectives and bringing about more durable peace and freedom. We saw this in Chapter 5 with Nelson Mandela's anti-apartheid movement. Indeed for Mandela there was the added factor that Gandhi's anticolonialism had started while he was in South Africa, something Mandela "never forgot."

So too with the American civil rights movement, a different context but also powerfully connected, for which Gandhi was "the guiding light of our technique of nonviolent social change," in the words of Dr. Martin Luther King, Jr. Going back even before Dr. King, civil rights leaders were reading Gandhi's works. In 1936, a delegation of prominent African-American Christian leaders went to India to meet with him. King spent a month in India in 1959. His sermons link Gandhi and Jesus. The Montgomery bus boycott was a direct application of nonviolence, as were most of King's modes of political action. The essence of the movement was about social justice, although without Gandhi's *Swaraj* glorification of the past.

Had Gandhi lived, it's not clear what his role would have been in a newly independent India. He was a mobilizer and inspirer far more than a practitioner of governing, as Nehru had observed earlier on. Indeed, this pattern of greater adeptness at the poetry of political change than the prose of governing is one we'll see throughout this section of the book.

The arena of Hindu-Muslim relations was where Gandhi fell furthest short of his own aspirations. On the one hand, his respect for religion in a generic sense, his belief in an Indian Hindu-Muslim "joint family," and his commitment to nonviolence conveyed to many

Muslims that he had their interests at heart and sought justice for
them. Even with all that has transpired, we still see Muslim commem-
orations of Gandhi, as in Bangladesh in 2009 on the 140th anniversary of his birth.

> Verses from the Koran were read, followed by a passage from the
> Bhagavad Gita, then Buddhist and Christian prayers, making the
> event as self-consciously inclusive as Gandhi's own prayer meet-
> ings. Five Muslims and three Hindus spoke—against religious
> extremism and for harmony, the rule of law, clean politics, rural
> development, social equality . . . The fact is that such a man of
> flesh was born on our subcontinent and we are his descendants,
> said a woman introduced as a human rights advocate. "I feel his
> necessity in every moment."

On the other hand, the centrality Gandhi gave to Hinduism as the
organizing principle for society and as the basis for the political system fed fears that even if unintended his approach could be hijacked
and radicalized by Hindu fundamentalists. As well on the Muslim-
Pakistani side, there have been all too many purveyors of unbridge-
able animosity and fomenters of antagonism. It is they, on both sides,
who bear the bulk of responsibility for the horrors of partition and the
decades of war and other India-Pakistan tensions that have ensued.

9

Lech Walesa: From Communism to Democracy, 1980–1990

WHO is Lech Walesa?

Lech Walesa was born September 27, 1943, during the Nazi occupation of Poland. His father, Bolek, had been dragged off to a labor camp before the baby's birth. He survived but died soon after returning home. It was from his mother, Feliksa, and her family with its strong religious tradition—at least one priest or nun in every generation—that Lech got his Catholic grounding.

He grew up with Poland under Soviet domination and communist rule. His schooling was vocational. Not much in those years that bears on our focus other than perhaps one schoolmaster singling him out as a "troublemaker" (and smoker). He was drafted into the army and made corporal but went no higher. He had a series of jobs as an electrician, notably one starting in May 1967 at the massive Lenin Shipyard in the city of Gdansk. He soon met Danuta Golos, and they married in November 1969.

Walesa's first significant experience in opposition politics came in 1968. Authorities closed down a production of *Forefather's Eve*, an 1830s' play about that era's struggles under Russian occupation. The ensuing protests were met by brutal government crackdowns, including an incident in December 1970 in which Polish security forces shot and killed 45 striking workers. This was a major turning point for

Walesa. "My worst fears had been realized," he later wrote. "Poles had fired against Poles." He began moving into the leadership of those pushing for labor unions independent of government control and for more solidarity across the spectrum of the opposition: workers, the Church, intellectuals, students.

On the eve of May Day 1978, Walesa was among those who established the Founding Committee for Free Trade Unions of the Coast. In December 1979 he was the main organizer of an unofficial memorial service outside the Lenin Shipyard honoring the December 1970 martyrs. The police couldn't prevent the service. Over 7.000 people turned out, bringing stones to build a memorial. Walesa was fired for his organizing role, which was why he was outside the Lenin Shipyard when the August 1980 strike broke out. After dramatically scaling the 12-foot perimeter fence to get in, he was enthusiastically embraced by fellow workers. A month later he was elected chairman of the National Coordinating Commission of the Independent Autonomous Trade Union, better known as Solidarity.

In little more than a year Solidarity had over 10 million members. When in December 1981 the Polish government, spurred by the Soviet Kremlin, imposed martial law, Walesa was imprisoned. He was freed 11 months later and continued the struggle throughout the 1980s. In February 1989 the Polish regime finally agreed to "Round Table Talks" with Solidarity on political reform. Solidarity was legalized and allowed to compete in elections set for that June. Even with rules that while more open than before still heavily tilted to the Communists, Solidarity scored such a huge victory that the gradual and partial opening the regime had intended gave way over the next 18 months to the first postcommunist democratic government in the Soviet bloc, with Lech Walesa as president of Poland.

Walesa derived the personal capital crucial to his leadership from four main sources: the Catholic Church, the authenticity of being a worker himself, the personal sacrifices he endured and courage shown for the cause, and the international acclaim he received.

Over 95 percent of Poland's population is Roman Catholic. Notwithstanding virulent anti-Semitism and other sordid elements of its past, in the communist era the Church had developed a social philosophy embracing the workers' cause. "It's painful that workers have to struggle for their basic rights under a workers' government," Cardinal Stefan Wyszynski, archbishop of Warsaw, sermonized amid strikes in 1976. As fate would have it, when Pope John Paul I died in September 1978, the white smoke in the Vatican signaled the selection of the Polish Cardinal Karol Jozef Wojtyla as the new Pope (taking the name John Paul II). Walesa was among those the Pope met with in his historic June 1979 visit to Poland. They met again in January 1981 at the Vatican. It was not just the link to the Pope: omnipresent on Walesa's lapel was a pin depicting the "Black Madonna of Czestochowa," a four-foot-high icon to which the Polish faithful had been making pilgrimages for centuries. In one speech after another he stressed the complementarity in which the Church tends to "the spirit of man" and Solidarity "sees to the body."

Walesa's like us/not above us quality generated personal credibility with workers. "You and I, we eat the same bread," he told a room packed with steelworkers. He mangled his grammar just as they did. His strength as a speaker was in simplifying without making simplistic, talking with his audience, not to them or down at them. "Sometimes he doesn't even make any sense," a Polish journalist remarked. "But he is always reassuring. He energizes people." At the same time Walesa the worker had to keep key opposition movement intellectuals convinced that even though "he isn't capable of abstract thought," as one complained, he deserved to be the leader. He was the common man as hero, knowing well the grinding realities of daily life while embodying hopes for a better future. When the regime put out a doctored video showing Walesa allegedly disrespecting the Church, it was seen for what it was.

People also knew the sacrifices Walesa had endured and the courage he had shown. He was repeatedly fired from jobs for union activism (portions of 1976, 1978–1979, 1980). He was arrested multiple times. With the Soviets allegedly having tried to assassinate Pope John Paul II. Walesa had ample concern for his own life. In a 1983 interview he spoke of at least three such plots against his life just in 1981 (one in Rome, one in Geneva, and one in Poland). All along there had been another path available to him, going back to 1972 when his mother asked him to join her in emigrating to the United States. He had declined.

The international community focused on Walesa more than any Eastern European leader. He was *Time* magazine's 1981 Man of the Year. He won the 1983 Nobel Peace Prize. Many a diplomatic demarche from Western governments was issued in his defense. These accolades were both affirmation of the leadership he was showing and in turn accentuation of that role by dint of the global attention. While he had his internal critics and rivals, for much of the world the Polish revolution was Walesa and Walesa was the Polish revolution.

Walesa's political skills were a mix of the carnal and the crafty. For all their mangled grammar and seeming incoherence, his speeches drove home points "stabbing the air with his hands for emphasis, making all the right gestures with almost flawless timing." His craftiness was in holding a diverse opposition together. He had to navigate being not so radical as to play into the government's rationale for an even more repressive crackdown, including a Soviet invasion, while not being seen by more assertive elements of Solidarity and the broader opposition as too compromising. He also used this moderation and international standing as leverage against the government: if you don't make a deal with me, you'll have to deal with the more radical elements.

Ego and vanity at times got the better of his judgment. Some thought the adulation went to his head. The government gave him a new six-room apartment in a fashionable Gdansk district. With an element of compliment but mostly as criticism, one author called him a "consummate, even outrageous manipulator." There were times when he pushed to get his way just to get his way. At one point when he was reelected chair of Solidarity but by a closer margin than he wanted, he scarcely showed up on the convention floor after the vote, instead watching the proceedings on a television monitor in a well-guarded room nearby. He lashed out at some opponents as potentially even more totalitarian than the government. Yet many of his own decisions were made arbitrarily without much consultation within Solidarity or with its coalition partners. One book about him was titled *Walesa: Democrat or Dictator.* After having recommended Solidarity ally Tadeusz Mazowiecki in 1989 as prime minister in the first postcommunist government, he ran against him in the 1990 presidential contest. And there have been charges of having been a government informer for a period during the communist years, which he has vociferously denied.

All told, he was the principal leader guiding Poland through the 1980s' decade of freedom and democratization. His charisma had more of a Rabin than Mandela quality, an earthy authenticity. "With his bushy moustache, ever-present pipe, and unfashionable clothes," as one journalist put it, he was hardly "a Hollywood type. Yet . . . men, women, and children in all walks of life were eager to reach out to touch him—the slightest touch was sufficient—if only to feel that, by touching, they were now part of the man who was leading Poland to a new beginning."

WHY: Walesa's vision

Four main ideas motivated Walesa: pro-workers, anti-Russia, pro-Church, and pro-democracy.

Workers had long been the leading edge of Polish political unrest in the communist era. With Soviet-led central planning stressing rapid industrialization, industrial workers increased from 8.4 percent (1950) to 14.7 percent (1980) of Poland's total population. Industry's share of GDP more than doubled in that same period, from 24.3 percent to 50.9 percent. Workers led the 1956 "bread and freedom" strikes and protests that brought down party leader Edward Ochab, as well as the more extensive 1970 strikes and protests that brought down Ochab's successor, Wladyslaw Gomulka. The 1976 strikes and protests shook the regime of Gomulka's successor, Edward Gierek. And the 1980 strikes and protests that birthed Solidarity brought Gierek down and ultimately led to the fall of communism.

In his 1983 Nobel Peace Prize speech Walesa stressed "my belief in the justness of the working people's demands and aspirations." These would never be achieved by state-controlled unions with their party-selected leaders. Independent trade unions were essential. In September 1979, the Committee for Free Trade Unions that Walesa had helped found the year before issued a Charter of Workers' Rights: "Only independent trade unions, which have the backing of the workers whom they represent, have a chance of challenging the authorities; only they can represent a power the authorities will have to take into account and with whom they will have to deal on equal terms." The pledge to allow independent unions that the 1970 strikes had extracted from the regime had gone unfulfilled. Solidarity was determined not to let that happen again.

The anti-Russia element of Polish nationalism ran deep. Russia was among the countries that had carved up Poland in the late eighteenth century, essentially taking it off the map of Europe as an independent state until it was reconstituted by the post–World War I Treaty of Versailles. The newly created Soviet Union lost little time in trying to take much of Poland back in the Polish-Soviet war of 1919–1921. While they failed then, the 1939 Nazi-Soviet Non-Aggression Pact set up the coordinated invasions of Poland that ignited World War II. As horrific as the Nazis were, it was Stalin's Red Army that had carried out the Katyn Forest massacre of over 4,000 Polish officers. Stalin's postwar promises of "liberation" and "free elections" became Soviet occupation and installation of one Moscow-controlled communist government after another. Warsaw was chosen as the locale for the euphemistically named Treaty of Friendship, Cooperation and Mutual Assistance—the Warsaw Pact—through which the Soviets maintained Cold War control of Eastern Europe, including two Red Army divisions stationed on Polish soil. And while shrouded in denials, the Kremlin-KGB hand almost certainly had a hand in the 1981 attempted assassination of Pope John Paul II. Just as the Polish communist regime's internal control had depended on Soviet Russian external support, so the struggle for freedom within Poland could not succeed without breaking Moscow's hold.

In October 1984 Father Jerzy Popieluszko, a leading Solidarity ally, was beaten to death. His body, laden with rocks, was dropped into the Vistula River reservoir. Addressing the 250,000 people who turned out for Father Popieluszko's funeral, Walesa spoke of the regime having "killed not only a man, not only a Pole, not only a priest. Someone wanted to kill the hope that it is possible to avoid violence in Polish political life." And the link: "Solidarity lives because Popieluszko shed his blood for it."

The pro-democracy element developed over time. Groups like the Workers' Defense Committee (KOR, its Polish acronym), formed by dissident intellectuals during the 1976 strikes, were key allies providing legal aid and financial assistance to arrested workers as well as working more broadly on freedom and human rights (including support from Amnesty International). Jacek Kuron, Adam Michnik, and other intellectuals published books and magazines (e.g., a Polish translation of George Orwell's *Animal Farm*, with its thinly disguised satirical critique of communist totalitarianism), held forums, and engaged in other more directly political dissent. It was in consultation with KOR that Solidarity included freedom of speech, greater media freedom, and the release of political prisoners in its original 1980 demands. Martial law and the party's effort to destroy both Solidarity and KOR erased any doubt that worker demands and broader political transformation must be achieved together. Walesa's 1985 report "Poland Five Years After August 1980" posed Solidarity as not just a union but a liberation movement as well. Workers opposing a state claiming to be a workers' state could get at the heart of its claim to legitimacy and be the vanguard of broader political transformation.

HOW did Walesa pursue political transformation?

As vast as the Soviet Union was, with much of its northern coast along the Arctic Ocean, it relied heavily on Polish ports such as Gdansk on the more navigable Baltic Sea coast. The huge Lenin Shipyard, built in the 1950s, was both workhorse and showpiece. It also had been the principal location of the 1970 and 1976 labor activism. And so it was again in the summer of 1980.

The previous year the Polish economy, while never a star performer, was in such bad shape as to have had its first GDP decline since 1947. When in July 1980 the Polish government imposed steep price increases for meat and other staples, the 20,000 Lenin Shipyard workers were among those who went on strike to demand a pay hike and other benefits. On August 14, in a moment made for television but relatively spontaneous, Lech Walesa scaled the 12-foot fence into the Lenin Shipyard and took charge of the strike committee. The government tried to buy off Walesa and the Lenin Shipyard workers by giving him his old job back and granting pay raises just for them. In refusing to accept these terms and merging demands with other strikers from all over Poland, the Gdansk strike became more than a local affair and as Walesa would later reflect, "Solidarity was born."

On August 23, negotiations commenced with Deputy Prime Minister Mieczyslaw Jagielski. Jagielski wanted to meet privately. In a shrewd move Walesa insisted on meeting in a glass-walled room that allowed workers to watch from the corridors and with loudspeakers blaring the audio of the negotiations into the courtyard. On August 31, the Gdansk Agreement was signed. It granted not only economic benefits like pay raises and price controls on food and other staples but also political provisions including recognition of workers' right to form independent trade unions, the right to strike, and freedom of the press and speech. On September 15, a charter was issued for the Independent Self-Governing Trade Union: "Solidarity." On September 17, Lech Walesa was elected chairman.

On December 16, a year after Walesa's call to workers to bring stones to build it themselves, with 150,000 people in attendance and other Solidarity leaders, Catholic bishops, party officials, and military officers standing with Walesa, the Monument to the Fallen Shipyard Workers was unveiled. The monument included three steel crosses hung with anchors, symbolizing the crushed rebellions of 1956, 1970, and 1976. It was the first monument honoring victims of communist oppression built in a communist country. In January 1981 Walesa had his meeting at the Vatican with Pope John Paul II. "I wish to assure you," the Pope said to Walesa in public remarks after their meeting, "that during your difficulties I have been with you in a special way, above all through prayer." Photos of Walesa kneeling and kissing the Pope's ring circulated internationally and back in Poland.

None of this sat well with the Soviets. These are "counterrevolutionary elements," Kremlin leader Leonid Brezhnev warned: Solidarity and its allies were pushing for "bourgeois-type elections" and doing so "in cahoots" with that Polish Pope and with help from the West. "The enemy would not have been raising his hand menacingly," Brezhnev reprimanded the Polish regime, "if the party had shown more firmness . . . It is now high time that the leadership of the 'Solidarity' trade union was put in their proper place. On February 11, 1981, General Wojciech Jaruzelski, who as Polish defense minister in 1968 had commanded Warsaw Pact troops in the Soviet-led invasion of Czechoslovakia dousing the Prague Spring, was named chairman of the Council of Ministers.

With the economy still in the doldrums, strikes continued throughout 1981. The police responded with increasing violence. Tensions peaked in early December when Jaruzelski, now also first secretary of the party, accused Solidarity of seeking to overthrow the government. Martial law was declared. Solidarity was made illegal. Walesa, KOR leaders, and some 10,000 others were arrested. Underground activists kept the resistance movement alive. Poles revised the words of the national anthem to show support for Walesa. "Lead us, Walesa, from the sea-coast to Silesia," they sang, "Solidarity will rise again and be victorious."

The government tried to play the divide-the-opposition gambit, offering to release Solidarity leaders but not KOR ones. Walesa countered with the threat of another strike. In November 1982, he and all but 60 prisoners were released. In July 1983, martial law was suspended but not abolished. Solidarity was still deemed illegal. Public meetings were prohibited without a permit. But football/soccer games were still allowed. On September 28, 1983, with the Lechia Gdansk team playing the heralded Italian Juventus and the match nationally televised, Solidarity saw the opportunity to show its strength. They sneaked Walesa in. At halftime they got cameramen to pan to him in the crowd. The shouts went up, "Solidarnosc! Solidarnosc! Solidarnosc!" The Lechia manager said the team heard it in the dressing room and "it sent shivers down our spine." State television put the game's second half on six-minute delayed transmission and without sound. It wasn't quite the potency of Mandela and the Invictus rugby match, but sports again helped make a powerful political statement.

The following month Walesa was named Nobel Peace Prize laureate. The international recognition and media attention that followed raised the risks for the authorities of throwing him back in jail, or worse. Walesa tested this at the November 1984 funeral for the assassinated Father Popieluszko, the first time he had spoken at a public event since his imprisonment. He went further with the release in September 1985 of the 500-page "Poland Five Years After August 1980" report laying out in great detail the case for independent unions and for broad political transformation. The government condemned it. Western reporters and diplomats thought otherwise.

In November Walesa called for a boycott of yet another party-ratifying election. His agenda here also was to balance out pressure within Solidarity for a tougher line. A younger generation of workers was rallying around its own leaders, calling strikes without consulting Walesa and the established Solidarity leadership and with more inclination to use violence. Protecting his own position and assuaging his own ego was part of the motivation. Part also was the political pragmatism of moderation. Pope John Paul II had made clear that his continued support depended on the movement remaining nonviolent.

Another price hike in April 1988 set off another round of strikes. By August the strikes were even more widespread and more driven by local activists. Finally, Jaruzelski agreed to "Round Table" talks with Solidarity and others in the opposition. These talks ran from February 6 to April 5, 1989. Solidarity was finally relegalized. Elections were set for June with guarantees of some, albeit limited, competitiveness. All the seats in the reconstituted Senate would be competitive, but only 35 percent of the seats in the Sejm (lower house) would be. The party and its satellite mini-parties would retain the others. Another 35 seats, called the National List, were reserved for the party with the only stipulation that candidates needed to get 50 percent of the vote; Solidarity and other parties could be on the ballot and get votes, they just couldn't win. Media censorship was reduced enough for Solidarity to get some press coverage and put political ads on television and radio, although much less than the party reserved for itself. The calculation echoed de Klerk's strategy of opening the system enough for Mandela and the African National Congress to compete but not so much that the Afrikaners would lose power.

Like de Klerk, Jaruzelski and the party had grossly misread the people. Solidarity won 99 of the 100 seats in the Senate, and 160 of 161 seats for which it was allowed to compete in the Sejm. Of the 35 candidates on the National List, only three registered the requisite 50 percent. But the built-in guarantees still gave the party 65 percent of the Sejm. Jaruzelski was named to the newly created presidency. He in turn designated another general, Czeslaw Kiszczak, as prime minister. The next day Jaruzelski called in Walesa and proposed a grand coalition with Solidarity joining the Communists in the government, albeit as a junior partner. Walesa had learned a thing or two about political maneuvering. Invoking the will of the people along with some political horse-trading, he and other Solidarity leaders convinced enough of the satellite parties to support their counterproposal of a co-equal coalition government. Jaruzelski looked to Moscow. The signal from Mikhail Gorbachev was very different than that from Leonid Brezhnev back in 1981. With China's Tiananmen Square massacre on June 4 having just shown the risks of blocking peaceful political change and political rumblings over much of Eastern Europe, Gorbachev was even more committed to nonintervention. On August 24, with his options limited by Gorbachev, President Jaruzelski named Tadeusz Mazowiecki, a Solidarity ally supported by Walesa, as the first non-communist prime minister anywhere in the Soviet bloc.

Why did Walesa propose Mazowiecki and not himself? In his own account he appears concerned that putting himself forward would be going too far, too fast. This fits the caution and pragmatism he frequently showed along the way. A less kind interpretation, and one that squares with his excesses of ego, was that he foresaw how difficult the immediate agenda was going to be and the prospects for popular disappointment. He may have envisioned an Italy-style quick rise and fall of governments, with power still anchored at party headquarters (in Gdansk, of course).

Whatever the calculation, Walesa quickly regretted it. Mazowiecki excluded Walesa's closest allies from his Cabinet. By the spring of 1990 the Mazowiecki-Walesa rivalry had escalated. Walesa positioned himself as advocate for workers opposed to the "shock therapy" the Jaruzelski-Mazowiecki government was using to transition to a market-based economy. He also was reacting to Poland losing its postcommunist uniqueness in the eyes of the world as the Berlin Wall came down; Vaclav Havel led Czechoslovakia's "velvet revolution," and much of the rest of the Soviet bloc was moving in that direction.

By July 1990 Walesa was pushing for direct election for the presidency. The presidency needed to be strengthened as an institution and the occupant chosen directly by the people. "It wasn't that I wanted to run for president," he told journalists disingenuously, "but that I had to." Six candidates ran in the November 1990 first round. Walesa finished first but his 40 percent was less than the required 50 percent, requiring a second round. Mazowiecki finished third (18.7 percent),

with second place going to the Polish-Canadian businessman Stanis-
law Tyminski, who campaigned on vague promises to make everyone
rich. Walesa won the runoff decisively with 74 percent of the vote.

Walesa's presidency got mixed reviews. He negotiated final withdrawal of Soviet troops from Poland. He supported Polish membership
in NATO and the European Union, although both were finalized later
(in 1999 and 2004, respectively). Domestically, though, politics were
more contentious. The economy performed well short of expectations.
More than one million workers joined protests against social spending cuts. Walesa tried pushing blame to others in his government,
appointing and dismissing four prime ministers. So popular as leader
of the revolution, he was defeated for reelection in 1995 by Alexander
Kwasniewski, a former Communist.

WHAT: Balance Sheet

No one person wrote the Polish script. Pope John Paul II provided
inspiration, guidance, and cover. KOR and other civil society activists
helped shape some of the driving ideas. But Lech Walesa was the one
doing the most to make things happen, keeping things going from the
August 1980 Lenin Shipyard strike through the repression of martial law to the 1989 and 1990 elections of the first postcommunist
government in the Soviet bloc. He was a man of the workers yet also
politically shrewd. Despite his flaws, it's hard to conceive of Poland's
struggle for freedom succeeding without him.

And it was Poland's struggle that stirred the broader Eastern European transformation. Within months of the August 1989 formation
of the Polish coalition government, Hungary had adopted a new constitution for multiparty democracy, Vaclav Havel's "velvet revolution"
ended Czechoslovak Communism, Bulgarian Communist leader
Todor Zhivkov was forced to resign, Romania's Nicolae Ceausescu
was executed, and the Berlin Wall had come down. While each of
these countries had its own leaders, the example of Walesa and Poland
was an important part of the dynamic.

Doesn't this, though, bring us back to Gorbachev (Chapter 2)? He could have given General Jaruzelski license to crack down. True, but a main reason Gorbachev came to see the Eastern European bloc countries as more a burden than an asset was the persistence and potency that Solidarity demonstrated throughout the 1980s despite the varying strategies for containing and destroying it. So it was a mutually interactive shaping: Gorbachev's choices shaped the choices Walesa had, and he in turn shaped the choices facing Gorbachev.

That Walesa was not as successful as president as he had been as revolutionary leader shows how the leadership qualities that governing requires do not always carry over from the qualities needed to effectively lead a revolution. The "who" of his personal biography, the "why" of his vision, and the "how" of his political skill set fit well the challenges of transformation from communism to democracy but less so the more transactional nature of governing. There are cases when the same profiles work well for both. And there have been cases in which revolutionary leaders prove horrific once in power. While Walesa surely avoided the latter, he fell short of the former.

10

Aung San Suu Kyi: A Cautionary Tale, 1988–

"Soon the world will witness a remarkable sight," *New York Times* Pulitzer Prize–winning columnist Nicholas Kristof wrote in January 2016 with reference to Aung San Suu Kyi, a "beloved Nobel Peace Prize winner presiding over 21st-century concentration camps." The atrocities being committed against the Rohingya, a Burma-Myanmar Muslim minority, have been of such magnitude that world leaders, including United Nations Secretary-General Antonio Guterres and U.S. Secretary of State Rex Tillerson, labeled them ethnic cleansing. True, the Myanmar military, which retained extensive autonomy even with the return to democracy, are the main perpetrators. Aung San Suu Kyi's position as state counselor carries substantial power but very little over the military. Even so, while not condoning the atrocities, she has said and done so little to end them that she has been widely condemned as complicit.

Does this annul all that she did in the 1988–2015 period to lead the restoration of democracy in Myanmar? How can she be included in a book about peacemakers? These are tough questions, heartfelt concerns. I've wrestled with them. As with other profiles, lessons need to be drawn from what was and wasn't worthy in the leader's record as well as what was and wasn't achieved. With contrasts as stark as these, the Aung San Suu Kyi profile serves as an especially cautionary tale.

WHO is Aung San Suu Kyi?

She was born on June 19, 1945. Her father, General Aung San, was a leading figure as both soldier and statesman in the Burmese independence movement. "Vigorous, magnetic," as a leading scholar of Burma put it, he was to be the prime minister. But on July 19, 1947, he was assassinated by a political rival. He died a martyr, seen by many as the Father of the Nation.

Daw Khin Kyi, Aung San Suu Kyi's mother, also was a prominent figure. A strong proponent of women's rights, she served as director of the National Women and Children's Welfare Board, in 1953 becoming Burma's first minister of social welfare. In 1960 she was named ambassador to India, the first Burmese woman to hold ambassadorial rank.

Aung San Suu Kyi spent her teenage years in India, attending a girls' school in New Delhi while her mother was ambassador. She then went to England to St. Hugh's College at Oxford, where she studied philosophy, politics, and economics. It was at Oxford that she met Michael Aris, a British student studying Himalayan and Tibetan culture. For a few years they went their own ways, he to the kingdom of Bhutan as a tutor to the children of the royal family and she to New York for a staff position at the United Nations. They stayed in touch and were married January 1, 1972. Over the next 16 years they lived in Bhutan, England, Japan, and India, pursuing their respective studies.

In March 1988, with her mother quite ill, Aung San Suu Kyi returned to Burma. By then Burma* had been under military dictatorship for 26 years, since the 1962 coup led by General Ne Win. The country was in

---

* In 1989, claiming that Burma was an imposed colonial name, the military regime changed the country's name to Myanmar. Most saw this as a ploy to claim nationalism while distracting from its repressive rule. Some scholars disputed it on the ground that both "Burmah" and Myanmar trace back long before colonization. Since the return to democracy, both terms are being used.

economic crisis, the "Burmese way to Socialism" having been largely
a road to ruin. Political unrest had been increasing, led by university
students and others calling for a return to democracy. Ne Win, forced
to resign in favor of another general, warned the demonstrators that
"when the army shoots, it shoots to hit." That it did when on August
8, 1988, general strikes (the "8-8-88 uprising," a numerologically aus-
picious date) were held in the capital city of Rangoon and in cities
around the country. Death toll estimates by some accounts went as
high as 10,000.

With the daughter of the Father of the Nation back in Burma, protesters turned to her. She initially moved cautiously. She sought counsel from some of her father's old friends. She met with activists. She
tried writing an open letter to the military junta proposing a commission that would plan for open multiparty elections. On August 24,
while participating in a memorial rally at Rangoon General Hospital,
Aung San Suu Kyi was persuaded to make brief remarks. Two days
later she took the bigger step of being a featured speaker at a mass rally
of over 500,000 people at the holy Buddhist Shwedagon Pagoda. "The
sincerity in her voice and the power of her message hooked the crowd
immediately," one activist later wrote. Thus began the political leadership role she would play for the next three decades: through house
arrests, hunger strikes, separation from her husband even in his dying
days, and death threats.

Her family identity provided an initial endowment of personal capital. To tap this, though, she had to overcome public doubts about
her authenticity from having lived her adult life outside of Burma and
being married to a foreigner, especially a Briton, given the colonial legacy of wives taken and children sired only to be abandoned. Rumors
were that she didn't even speak very fluent Burmese. The Shwedagon
Pagoda speech, delivered in fluid Burmese and in the same simple, elegant, and powerful manner her father was known for, dispelled the language issue. That she had lived overseas and had a mixed-nationality
family, she affirmed, had not lessened her love of her country and its
people. "I could not, as my father's daughter, remain indifferent to all

that is going on. The national crisis could, in fact, be called the second struggle for independence."

Her announcement a few weeks later that she would lead a new political party, the National League of Democracy (NLD), showed that she was in Burma to stay. Her first period of house arrest began July 20, 1989, when she awoke to a street barricaded with barbed wire and a wall of trucks. When news reached her about how brutally colleagues were being treated in prison, she went on a hunger strike in solidarity. This was when Amnesty International first designated her as a prisoner of conscience. In 1991, cited as "one of the most extraordinary examples of civil courage" and as a symbol "for the many people throughout the world who are striving to attain democracy, human rights, and ethnic conciliation," she was awarded the Nobel Peace Prize. It would not be until 2012 that she could go to Oslo and accept the prize and deliver her laureate lecture. Many times in the intervening years she referred to the Nobel Prize as her life insurance policy; the international acclaim and visibility made it harder for the military to eliminate her.

Even when she was freed from house arrest in 1995, the regime persistently harassed her, preventing her from going to meetings and not allowing her to leave the country without risking being denied reentry. This became especially cruel when in 1997 her husband, Michael, developed prostate cancer. The junta smeared her in the press as a bad wife who wouldn't go take care of her dying husband. She'd already been cut off from him and their two sons back in England for close to 10 years. Michael passed away on March 27, 1999.

Her courage was also tested by threats to her own life. In an incident a few months before her July 1989 house arrest, she and her team were out in Burma's southwestern delta region. Their convoy was stopped by a line of soldiers kneeling in the firing position. With only one other colleague, Aung San Suu Kyi walked ahead. Only at the last moment did an officer order a stand-down. Another encounter came in 1998, when her convoy was blocked on a bridge from leaving Rangoon. A 13-day standoff ensued, Aung San Suu Kyi refusing to retreat until dehydration and illness forced her to. And in May 2003, a year after her release from house arrest, she was granted permission to travel to Depiyan and other towns in northern Burma to open a series of NLD offices and new youth groups. It was a setup. Two "monks" stopped her convoy, buying time for hundreds of men armed with guns, iron rods, bamboo sticks, and bricks to swarm down and attack. At least 80 people were killed in the melee. Aung San Suu Kyi was injured by a rock hurled through her rear car window. Still she beseeched her followers to adhere to Gandhian resistance. She was sent to Insein Prison, a place notorious for unsanitary conditions, disease, meager food portions, and even torture. Yet another brief interval of freedom had ended.

The legitimacy conferred by the *sangha*, the Buddhist monks, added to her moral authority. Right after her 1995 release from house arrest, she traveled to meet with Burma's most respected monk, one known for his opposition to the regime and his humanitarian work. Her Nobel Peace laureate speech was replete with references to Buddhism and spiritual-political synergy. On September 22, 2007, in the "Saffron Revolution" (named for the traditional golden-yellow color of Buddhist monks' robes) thousands of monks joined in a pilgrimage to Aung San Suu Kyi's house. She had not been seen since she had been rearrested in 2003. "This was our leader to get democracy," one of the monks said. "We all felt deep compassion for her."

Her charisma also resonated with the masses. Many personally revered her, conferring the honorific "Daw," copying her dress, praying for her safety, even claiming her as a *bodhisattva*, an enlightened one able to reach nirvana but who postpones doing so to help save those suffering. Internationally she was an icon. In 1993, a delegation of Nobel Peace laureates sought to come to Burma to see her, only to be rebuffed by the regime. "The aura surrounding her is still an extraordinary thing to witness," a seasoned BBC correspondent reported. "When she turns her attention to you, her charm and charisma can be overpowering."

As to political skills, she masterfully tapped symbols: for example, the Shwedagon Pagoda was not only a holy Buddhist site but also the very spot where her father had called for independence in 1946. Early on she set out to rebuild the NLD, recruiting from a wide range of societal sectors and the younger generation, not just the "uncles" who hailed back to the years before military rule. She found ways to stay close to the people even while confined by house arrest, as with her over-the-fence speeches, standing on a table in the garden with loudspeakers attached to trees to address the crowds. As word spread in November 2010 of her imminent release, huge crowds gathered, calling "Mother! Mother!" while chanting the national anthem.

Like others of our profiles with their admirable qualities, she also had her personal flaws. She could be "moody, temperamental, difficult," as a journalist who spent extensive time with her put it. She could lose her cool. She imposed profound sacrifices on her family, her husband as well as her sons. Once she was out of house arrest, and less an icon than an aspiring political leader, other issues—most especially the mass atrocities against the Rohingya—arose that would tarnish her moral capital and test the political skills that she accrued in rising to be the singular leader of the movement to restore Burma to democracy.

WHY did Aung San Suu Kyi lead Burma's struggle for democracy?

Aung San Suu Kyi's vision had two core components: a political commitment to democracy and human rights, and a cultural-religious grounding in Buddhism. On a third element, the rights of ethnic minorities, she long was more equivocal.

Burma's political repression was among the worst in the world. Telling jokes about the junta could land you in prison. So could writing poems about democracy, holding any gathering of more than five people without a permit, speaking to journalists or human rights groups, protesting high gas prices, or providing medical care for AIDS victims without approval. Despite the country's rich resources, without mechanisms of accountability the military had been unchecked in pursuing its economically disastrous policies. Most of all, as Aung San Suu Kyi put it in one of her most famous speeches, the Burmese people needed a "freedom from fear."

Only with democracy could this freedom be achieved. Only with democracy could the economy be rebuilt. Only with democracy, she wrote in an open letter to the UN Commission on Human Rights, could there be "a peaceful, stable and progressive society where human rights, as outlined in the Universal Declaration of Human Rights, are protected by the rule of law." Having studied Gandhi during her time in India, Aung San Suu Kyi stressed nonviolence as the means for achieving these goals. Within that her conception of national reconciliation very much included the military. She aspired to again see it as the honorable institution her father had started to build, genuinely serving the nation and the people. In this sense her conception of reconciliation was similar to Mandela's, she with regard to the military and he to the white minority.

She understood the need for reassurance that democracy and human rights were not foreign ideas, that these ideas were compatible with Buddhist and other culturally traditional values. She honed the interrelationship as "spiritual renewal + political renewal = freedom." The regime was the one not living up to Buddhist precepts. They exemplified the teaching that one of the four causes of societal decline and decay is leadership positions gained by men lacking in morality and learning. She spoke of her house arrest and other hardships as having helped her grow spiritually.

But this grounding of majority political rights in traditional Buddhist culture was not particularly inclusive of ethnic minority rights. The ethnic minorities issue had been a problem throughout Burma's history. As in so much of the world, the statehood lines drawn by the colonial power (Britain) bunched together various ethnic and religious groups with long, tense histories. Non-Burman and/or non-Buddhist minorities comprise about one-third of the population. The 1947 Panglong Agreement, negotiated by Aung San Suu Kyi's father, General Aung San, set terms with some of these groups for a federal state with significant local autonomy. Ultranationalists among the military and some Buddhist sects opposed even this degree of openness and diversity. Some saw it as a factor in Aung San's assassination. Successor leaders ignored the Panglong Agreement. Insurgencies and repression followed over the ensuing years, interrupted by various temporary cease-fires, taking a toll of over one million people killed.

The group that has faced the most repression has been the Rohingya, a people of mixed ethnic heritage (Bengali, Turk, Moghul, and Persian) and of the Muslim religion concentrated in the coastal state of Rakhine, partially bordering Bangladesh. While they were not included in the Panglong Agreement, they initially were granted citizenship. In 1982, the military regime promulgated a citizenship law which acknowledged 135 ethnic groups as eligible for citizenship but excluded the Rohingya, in effect leaving them stateless. They lost the few social and economic benefits they had been recieving, had their land ownership rights further circumscribed, their travel restricted, and ethnic cleansing operations like Operation Pyi Thaya ("Clean and Beautiful Nation") in the 1990s launched against them.

While leader of the opposition, minority group rights were not as much a part of Aung San Suu Kyi's vision as majority political rights. In some respects this was understandable given the struggle against the military regimes. Even so, some saw in speeches such as the 1989 "Need for Solidarity among Ethnic Groups," addressed to the Kachins, a mixed ethnicity and mostly Christian group fighting for independence or at least greater autonomy, emphasis at least as much on telling minority groups not to be divisive as pledging to be integrative. With regard to the Rohingya, she was at best standoffish, not engaging in vilification like the military and Buddhist extremists but also not raising her voice in support.

HOW did she lead the breakthrough for democracy?

From the start the junta worried about Aung San Suu Kyi's potential for leadership. She had returned to Burma just as political unrest began raging and the military was cracking down brutally. The day of her coming-out Shwedagon Pagoda speech, they tried to keep the crowd down by spreading word that it had been moved to a different site. They removed all those pictures of Aung San they'd hung all over the country in their own effort to claim a link to his legacy. They took him off the paper currency. She was not to be called by her name, referred to only as "the lady." Within a year she was put under house arrest.

Even with Aung San Suu Kyi confined and martial law in force, pressure mounted. The Burmese people were further energized by neighboring "people power" movements in the Philippines, which in 1986 overthrew longtime dictator Ferdinand Marcos, and in South Korea in 1987 forced a return to democracy after a period of military rule that had lasted longer than that in Burma. The junta, now calling itself the State Law and Order Restoration Council (SLORC), gambled on allowing multiparty legislative elections for 1990. The response was extraordinary. Some 92 political parties competed. Turnout was 72 percent, the highest in history. With Aung San Suu Kyi providing leadership despite her confinement, the National League for Democracy won in a landslide, with 59 percent of the vote and 392 of 492 contested legislative seats. The SLORC annulled the results. It arrested many of the winners.

Aung San Suu Kyi used her cachet as a Nobel Peace laureate to increase pressure on the regime. In 1993, the Clinton administration withdrew the American ambassador. In 1997, it imposed a first round of economic sanctions. The Bush administration ratcheted the sanctions up further. The European Union imposed its own sanctions. The UN Security Council issued a statement calling for the release of political prisoners, although it couldn't get a formal resolution past Russian and Chinese vetoes.

Aung San Suu Kyi was in and out of house arrest during these years. Even when not confined, she was harassed in her movements around the country and prevented from going abroad. Meanwhile the economy continued its steep decline. Fleeing protests and the prying eyes of journalists and bloggers, the junta took on the outsized expense of moving the capital to the remote inland city of Naypidaw. It rebranded itself the State Peace and Development Council (SPDC). Social services deteriorated to the point where the only country with worse public health services was Sierra Leone. Repression was intensified. A leaked video of the lavish wedding of SPDC head Than Shwe's daughter, wearing rows of diamonds like a shawl, drove home the luxury in which the military cabal reveled.

By August–September 2007 the most extensive protests since 1988 broke out. The quintupling of fuel prices and skyrocketing inflation exacerbated the public's already bleak economic situation. And for all its self-cloaking in Buddhism, the regime was unleashing attacks on dissident monks, even raiding monasteries—thus the "Saffron Revolution" dramatic pilgrimage of thousands of monks to Aung San Suu Kyi's house, turning to her as "our leader to get democracy." With such scenes beamed by satellite television and posted on the Internet, both in Burma and internationally, the repression could no longer be kept quiet. Even the regional multilateral organization ASEAN (Association of Southeast Asian Nations), typically unwilling to criticize member countries' domestic policies, expressed its "revulsion" at the wanton violence.

Under pressure, the regime in April 2008 issued a proposed new constitution that it claimed provided a road map back to democracy. While the proposed constitution called for elections with multiparty competition, it built in a guarantee of at least one-fourth of the seats in the national legislature and one-third in regional and state legislatures for the military's Union Solidarity and Development Party (USDP). The military would also maintain control of the ministries of defense and home affairs (which among other things licenses civil society and international NGOs). The constitution also had Clause 59F, which barred anyone who had or had had family with foreign citizenship from being president—quite an unusual provision for a national constitution, directed at one person in particular, namely Aung San Suu Kyi. The accompanying election laws prohibited any political party if it had members who are "convicts."

Whatever chance the military had of gaining goodwill was negated by its handling of Cyclone Nargis, the devastating storm that hit Myanmar on May 2. Nargis killed 85,000 people, left another

54,000 missing, and wreaked damage equal to 27 percent of GDP. The government first failed to provide strong enough warnings. It then offered little in the way of emergency assistance. It rebuffed international humanitarian aid offers, calling them regime change in disguise. Whatever legitimacy the regime had left was squandered. Still, when the election was finally held on November 7, 2010, the USDP claimed to have won close to 80 percent of the national legislative seats and General Thein Sein was declared president. The United Nations, United States, and European Union all rejected the elections as neither free nor fair.

Thein Sein turned out to be the de Klerk to Aung San Suu Kyi's Mandela. He saw the unsustainability of the system. International isolation had to be ended to make any headway on the decrepit economy. That would not happen without freeing Burma's most internationally renowned political prisoner. Rumors circulated as government cars went in and out of her complex. People gathered by the thousands. On the evening of November 13, 2010, Aung San Suu Kyi was released from house arrest. The crowd sang "Kaba Ma Kyei," the national anthem.

International support and reengagement came quickly. Within weeks Secretary of State Hillary Clinton came and met with both Aung San Suu Kyi and President Thein Sein. The following month it was British Foreign Minister William Hague. Aung San Suu Kyi went to Europe and delivered her two-decade postponed Nobel Peace Prize speech in Oslo, received an honorary degree at Oxford, and an award from Amnesty International in Dublin. Her September 2012 visit to the United States included an address to a joint session of Congress. President Obama received her at the White House and then came to Burma that November. U.S. and EU sanctions were cut back. Within the region Burma was made the 2014 chair of ASEAN.

At home, though, just as de Klerk did not equate freeing Mandela with conceding the political transition, so Thein Sein opened the system but sought to stay in control. Some political prisoners were released, but new arrests were made. The BBC was allowed back in, but reporters writing critical stories still were harassed. Election laws were changed sufficiently for Aung San Suu Kyi to be eligible to run for parliament in the 2012 by-elections filling open seats and for the NLD as a party to participate. But she and other NLD candidates found their posters defaced and their permits for rallies at soccer stadiums turned down. Nevertheless, she won. Indeed, the NLD swept 43 of the 45 seats.

For her part, Aung San Suu Kyi faced a transition from symbolic inspiration to political leadership. Balancing calls for retribution against the military with the pragmatic need for reconciliation was particularly challenging. Her vision, as we saw, distinguished between opposing the particular policies of the juntas from valuing the military as an institution. You in the military and we in the democratic opposition have more in common with each other than did blacks and whites in South Africa, she drew the comparison, and they achieved peaceful transition. In 2013, she accepted the invitation to join the military on the reviewing stand for the annual Army Day parade commemorating the World War II resistance against Japanese occupation. There she was sitting with the very generals who had kept her under house arrest all those years and had imprisoned and tortured so many. Her intent was to convey that she, like Mandela, was committed to reconciliation, not retribution. Not all in her NLD party or the broader opposition shared her reconciliatory approach. "It's truly very risky," said one. "The people and party members are asking many questions about her strategy."

Concerns also were being expressed about her views on the Rohingya. We noted earlier how Aung San Suu Kyi's motivating vision gave more emphasis to pro-democracy political prisoners than to repressed ethnic-religious minorities. In June 2012, riots broke out, with both Rohingya Muslims and Rakhine Buddhists burning the other community's houses, mounting attacks and other violence. President Thein Sein imposed martial law and posed the choices as either resettling the Rohingya to neighboring Bangladesh and other Muslim countries or keeping them in refugee camps. Aung San Suu Kyi's response, calling on the government to ensure safety while noting that violence had been committed on all sides, was more politically pragmatic than human rights–principled. She was cautious about going too far, too fast so as not to alienate the military regime still in power and prospective Buddhist voters. For activists and international human rights groups this was too little, too slow.

In May 2015, six months before the crucial November transfer-of-power elections, the military-controlled parliament passed a law authorizing regional authorities to require mothers to space their children three years apart—ostensibly promulgated out of general concern for infant and maternal health, but blatantly pushed by the hard-line Buddhist Ma Ba Tha (Association for the Protection of Race and Religion) to keep Muslim birth rates down. While Aung San Suu Kyi criticized the law, her overall caution about not alienating Buddhist voters was evident in the NLD, which in the past had included Muslims on its legislative candidate list, having none for the 2015 elections. Nevertheless, Ma Ba Tha smeared her as a Muslim sympathizer, posting doctored pictures of her in a hijab.

Even with these and other questions in the air, Aung San Suu Kyi's popularity and the thirst for democracy spurred an NLD landslide: 77 percent of the vote and 887 seats, compared to 10 percent and 117 seats for the USDP. President Thein Sein congratulated Aung San Suu Kyi—on his Facebook page—pledging to "respect and obey the election results and transfer power peacefully." But this did not include revoking Clause 59F. The NLD would get to name the new president, but it could not be Aung San Suu Kyi. The work-around was to install Htin Kyaw, a loyal aide, as president while parliament created the new above-the-president position of state counselor for Aung San Suu Kyi, including foreign minister, coordinator of all cabinet ministries, and other powers. The military vehemently opposed. All those green uniforms got up and dramatically walked out of parliament. But since this wasn't a constitutional change, they couldn't block it.

On February 1, 2016, the NLD-dominated parliament met for the first time. On March 30, President Htin Kyaw was inaugurated. On April 1, the bill creating the position of state counselor was passed. On April 7, Aung San Suu Kyi was named to this position.

WHAT: Balance Sheet

After 54 years under military dictatorship, Burma was again a democracy. It wasn't a full democracy. The military retained significant political control. Still, overcoming 53 years of full military rule (1962–2015) was quite a breakthrough.

There is no question about Aung San Suu Kyi's high SARL ranking in this regard. She had the lineage to her father, Father of the Nation. She brought her own extraordinary courage and character. There was the propitiously fateful woman-and-moment timing of 1988 when her mother became severely ill and when the anti-regime movement boiled over. All told, she faced plenty of constraints under conditions that were at best only partially conducive.

Questions remain, though.

Will the democratic transition last?

The military has not fully returned to the barracks. They retain blocs of seats in the national parliament, as well as regional and state legislatures, and can block constitutional changes. They maintain control of the very ministries that affect them the most (Defense and Border Affairs) and that in the past have been the basis for internal repression (Home Affairs). They also control the General Administrative Department (GAD) that has extensive power at the state and regional levels on such matters as tax collection and land management, including terms of compensation for state seizures, the arbitrariness of which has frequently set off rural protests. With most of the country's judges carrying over from appointments made during military rule, and the judiciary reporting to the Home Affairs Ministry, the men in green have substantial influence in that branch as well. Their economic stakes are in sectors such as mining, telecommunications, and ports most attractive to foreign investment. Reporters Without Borders ranks Burma 131st out of 180 countries on press freedom. Other countries' democratic transitions have ended up undermined by the deep state. How far will the military be willing to let Burma go?

Indeed there already is speculation that military chief General Min Aung Hlaing, his popularity rising among many precisely because of the military's campaign against the Rohingya, may run for president in 2020.

Transitional justice poses a major test. Every country coming out of dictatorship has had to find its path between pursuing justice for past abuses and sufficient reassurance for present political stability. Burma's military dictatorship killed thousands, unjustly jailed tens of thousands, and violated the human rights of millions. Working out the terms of transitional justice so that they are neither deemed too vindictive by the military nor too appeasing by the broader Burmese people is a delicate balancing act—one for which Aung San Suu Kyi will get principal credit or blame.

Even if these and other politics go well, Burma still faces formidable socioeconomic challenges. Recent economic growth has been encouraging, achieving the highest GDP growth rate in Southeast Asia. But with Southeast Asia's second lowest GDP per capita (only Cambodia is lower), Burma has a long way to go. McKinsey Consulting Group estimates that $650 billion in investment is needed by 2030. Among other societal problems are low life expectancy and poor education. While these issues are much less strictly in Aung San Suu Kyi's portfolio, the ultimate goal of the institutionalization of democracy depends, as it has in so many other countries, on sufficient socioeconomic progress that people feel the new political system is having material impact on their lives.

Will Aung San Suu Kyi use power as well as she challenged it?

It wasn't only the military that questioned Aung San Suu Kyi's creation of her above-the-president position. Was it a power grab? The original formulation was so sweeping, including the ministries of education, energy, and electric power as well as minister of the Office of the President and minister of foreign affairs, that she was forced to drop the three domestic ministries. Even then she largely had control of the executive branch and some oversight of the legislature. Or was it Clause 59F, barring the will of the people to have her as their leader, that was unjustified? We've seen many other leaders of revolutionary and political reform movements reach well beyond the democratic principles they'd espoused in their accumulation and use of political power. While Aung San Suu Kyi's path to power was more consistent with democratic principles, power once achieved poses its own test.

The poetry-prose distinction between the political skills it takes to bring about political reform—convey a motivating narrative, invoke symbols, show the courage of resistance—and the operational mindset and other policy-making skills needed to govern is another concern. Aung San Suu Kyi has no prior experience in governing. Nor do most members of her party. The younger generation had its professional growth stunted. While these are legacies of the prior regime, they impact the new regime's capacity to achieve the objectives for which it now is held responsible.

How much will she be discredited by the Rohingya crisis?

Even before the 2017 crisis exploded, Aung San Suu Kyi was showing what at best could be called disregard for the plight of the Rohingya. The call by the UN's Special Rapporteur for Human Rights in Myanmar on her government to improve Rohingya living conditions within its first 100 days was not met. In May 2016, she reprimanded the American ambassador for referring to these people as "Rohingya" rather than the government-preferred "Bengali." Violence ratcheted up starting in late 2016, with Rohingya militants attacking an army post and the army retaliating by burning villages, forcing thousands more to flee to Bangladesh or be pushed into internment camps and, according to a National Public Radio report, committing "systematic rape." Aung San Suu Kyi did appoint an international advisory commission chaired by former UN Secretary-General Kofi Annan. But its report, calling for "concerted action . . . to prevent violence, maintain peace, foster reconciliation and offer a sense of hope," was largely ignored.

While Aung San Suu Kyi had appointed the Annan Commission, her response to its report was largely rationalization ("we are a young and fragile country facing many problems . . . we cannot just concentrate on the few") and deflection (the government needed time to find out "what the real problems are"). Anticipating severe criticism, she canceled her trip to the United Nations General Assembly, the same forum at which she had been hailed on prior visits.

Yet what had been a serious issue before was becoming a major humanitarian crisis. NGOs such as Human Rights Watch and Fortify Rights provided satellite imagery documenting the atrocities. A *New York Times* reporter with 20 years' experience covering one humanitarian disaster after another wrote that this was the worst he had ever seen. Seven of Aung San Suu Kyi's fellow Nobel Peace laureates issued a statement calling the plight of the Rohingya "a textbook case of genocide." UN Secretary-General Guterres and U.S. Secretary of State Tillerson made the ethnic cleansing statements cited earlier. Others went even futher, calling it a genocide.

Not pushing the Rohingya issue during the election campaign and transition for fear that the military would seize on it and not follow through with the transfer of power, while not pure, may have been necessarily pragmatic. Even once in power there was an argument for initially moving carefully, given the deep state power the military still maintained and the polarization posed by Buddhist extremist groups such as Ma Ba Tha. And radicalized Muslim groups such as the Arakan Rohingya Salvation Army had perpetrated attacks on government sites. But the military's responsibility for the escalation of the violence and brutality inflicted on the civilian population far exceeded any fault-on-both-sides equivalence.

"Did the world get Aung San Suu Kyi wrong?" as reporters Amanda Taub and Max Fisher posed the question. There surely had been some idolization of The Lady. And there are ample grounds for outrage over her unwillingness to draw more on the moral authority she built up over the years and the political authority her position does provide. Perhaps she may still prove to be, as columnist and seasoned international correspondent Roger Cohen leaves open, "the best hope of completing the task [of] completing an unfinished nation, clawing it from the military that has devastated it." Time will tell. Either way, we can learn the most by drawing insights and lessons from her full story, the cautionary tale that it is.

Peter Benenson, Amnesty International and the Global Human Rights Movement, 1961–1967

On May 28, 1961, an appeal was launched by the British lawyer Peter Benenson on behalf of the world's "prisoners of conscience." The appeal was so successful that it rapidly developed into a permanent international nongovernmental organization (NGO): Amnesty International. The contemporary global human rights movement was launched.

WHO was Peter Benenson?

Peter James Henry Solomon was born in 1921 in London. His father, Harold Solomon, hailed from a Jewish-British financier family. A brigadier-general in World War I, he died when Peter was nine. Peter's mother, Flora (nee) Benenson, was a Russian Jewish émigré, daughter of a gold tycoon and related to the Rothschilds. Peter took the surname Benenson later in life.

With her mix of upper-class noblesse oblige and liberal idealism, Flora was a social and political activist. In the 1930s she helped resettle refugee children fleeing the Spanish civil war and Hitler. During

World War II, she organized food distribution for the British government, for which she was awarded the OBE (Order of the British Empire). She was a close friend of Chaim Weizmann and supporter of the Zionist cause. She had an affair with Alexander Kerensky in his exile, the Russian revolutionary leader who overthrew the czar only to be overthrown by Lenin.

For her young son's tutor she hired a recent Oxford graduate, Wystan Hugh (W. H.) Auden, whom she summarily fired for being "off-hand, ill-kempt and a chain-smoker . . . with an upper-class accent so grotesque as to make for near-incomprehensibility." Benenson got his formal schooling at Eton and Oxford (Balliol College). Manifesting some of his mother's activism, and having read Arthur Koestler's *Spanish Testament* about the brutalities of Generalissimo Francisco Franco and his forces in the Spanish civil war, Benenson established a Spanish relief committee, prompting the Eton headmaster to raise concerns about the boy's "revolutionary tendencies." His next campaign was aimed at the plight of Jews who had fled from Hitler's Germany, getting school friends and their families to raise £4,000 to bring young German Jews to Britain. His time at Oxford was interrupted by World War II, when he was assigned to Bletchley Park and the Ultra code-breaking team. After the war he returned to Oxford and finished his law studies.

He joined the Labour Party and tried electoral politics, running four times for the House of Commons, all unsuccessful. In the early 1950s, as an observer for the Trade Unions Congress of political trials in Franco's Spain, he witnessed union members and other dissidents denied fair trials and thrown into horrid prison conditions. With political trials also going on in Hungary and South Africa (the young Nelson Mandela was one of the defendants), he helped start a new organization, called Justice. This was to transcend British partisan lines, an all-party organization, sending observers to political trials irrespective of the political complexion of the regime: a precursor of the model adopted by Amnesty International.

In 1959 Benenson contracted a serious illness and went to Italy for

an extended period of convalescence. The year before he had converted to Catholicism and this period became one of sustained self-
reflection. It's not clear why he rejected his Judaism. In her memoirs
Flora only says that she saw in it his determination to help others and
that while "I do not share his religious faith ... my satisfactions too
have come in seeking to help people; and if this doesn't sound too prig-
gish, it has brought its own reward." While in Italy he showed great
interest in the work of Danilo Dolci, a Christian idealist known for
his Gandhian emphasis on collective self-help and civil disobedience.

In November 1960, now back in England, Benenson was struck by
a story in the press about two Portuguese students sentenced to prison
by dictator Antonio Salazar for making a toast to freedom in a Lisbon
café. As yet another case in which formal legal efforts were having
little impact, Benenson began to conceive a strategy of wider pressure. With a few colleagues, including prominent Quaker Eric Baker
and international lawyer Louis Blom-Cooper, they launched "Appeal
for Amnesty" as a campaign to free political prisoners—"prisoners
of conscience" (POCs)—all over the world. Through Blom-Cooper's
friendship with the publisher of the *Observer*, Benenson's article "The
Forgotten Prisoners" was prominently featured in the May 28, 1961,
Sunday paper. They also got *Le Monde*, the *New York Herald-Tribune*,
and other newspapers around the world (even one in Barcelona, defy-
ing Franco) to publish it. It may well have been among the most successful op-eds in the history of such articles. Donations flowed in,
as did information about various POCs and offers to help. Amnesty
International (AI) was born.

Benenson's political skills worked well for Amnesty's founding.[*]
He catalyzed the movement, traveled extensively in promotion of the
cause, recruited members, and took on major POC cases. His keen
sense for the power of symbols and images was evident in the now

---

[*] Since this profile moves from Benenson as an individual to Amnesty International as
an organization and ultimately the broader human rights movement, it fits best to talk
about moral capital later in the "What" section.

iconic Amnesty insignia, a candle with barbed wire partially around it, with the Chinese proverb "Better to light a candle than curse the darkness." He had worked with the prominent Irish diplomat Sean MacBride and brought him in as AI's international chairman. The scores of lawyers he knew from his years as a barrister and the fore-runner NGO Justice also helped. His energy and leadership, in a certain sense his charisma, were key to AI's rapid growth.

But he also was impulsive, capable of poor judgment, didn't always see projects through to full fruition, and resisted accountability to any-one but himself. Some of this was tempered by shifting from general secretary to the less managerial role of president—but only some. Ben-enson balked at coordinating his role with the new general secretary, Robert Swann, even though Swann was a fellow Etonian whom he had chosen. He still viewed himself as AI and AI as him. Internal ten-sions culminated in cross-accusations between Benenson and others within AI of misuse of funds and alleged infiltration by British intel-ligence. Benenson resigned as president. He then changed his mind and withdrew his resignation to fight it out with Swann and others he deemed enemies within the organization. A story then broke that linked Benenson himself to questionable cooperation with the Brit-ish government in a case involving Rhodesia and controversies over its white-minority government resisting transition to black African majority rule.

In March 1967 Amnesty's executive committee called an emergency meeting. Benenson refused to attend. Chairman MacBride attributed the organization's crisis to Benenson's "erratic actions" and "wild and wide-ranging charges and some unilateral initiatives." Benenson was forced to resign. He would never again be active in the organization. He died at 84 years old in 2005.

WHY: AI and the human rights vision

Drawing from his own religiosity, Benenson sought to "re-kindle a fire in the minds of men . . . to give him who feels cut off from God a sense of belonging to something greater than himself, of being a small part of the entire human race." This wasn't a renunciation of traditional religions. The *Observer* "Forgotten Prisoners" article quite intentionally was published on Trinity Sunday. Catholic and Protestant church officials were included in the launching conferences held in London and Paris, as was the Grand Rabbi of England; Benenson also had his team search for a representative Buddhist. Indeed, one of AI's goals was to support freedom of religion; many of the POCs had been arrested for their religious observances. The organization was to be a moral authority, religiously infused but not formally linked to any particular denomination, to be deployed against politically motivated human suffering—that is, for human rights. When such rights are egregiously violated, Benenson wrote in the very first Amnesty International newsletter, "We shall strive to mobilize world opinion to the point where it can no longer be flouted by the abusers of political and religious liberty."

A sense of the failures of the political world to address human rights also was a factor. Back in 1948, amid the clamor about there now being an international community and having learned the lessons of the Nazi Holocaust, the United Nations issued the Universal Declaration of Human Rights (UDHR). "What matters," though, Benenson wrote, "is not the rights that exist on paper, but whether they can be exercised and enforced in practice." In the ensuing years the UN fell well short of fulfilling the expectations its UDHR had articulated. Some other entity was needed if human rights were going to be protected. Amnesty International was to be that other entity. Benenson linked 1961, the year of AI's founding, to the centennial of the emancipation of the serfs in Russia and the outbreak of the American Civil War. If 1861 marked the freedom of the body from bondage, 1961 would mark the freedom of the mind. AI would do this in ways that transcended global political divisions, appealing to those "who are tired of the polarized thinking which is the result of the Cold War and similar conflicts but who are deeply concerned with those who are suffering simply because they are suffering."

HOW was Amnesty International established and built into a leading human rights NGO?

It's helpful to look at Amnesty International's development in three phases: launch and consolidation (1961–1970), rise to prominence (1970s–1980s), and partially ceding to the movement it seeded (1990s on).

Launch and Consolidation (1961–1970): In "The Forgotten Prisoner" Benenson had defined a prisoner of conscience as "any person who is physically restrained (by imprisonment or otherwise) from expressing (in any form of words or symbols) any opinion which he honestly holds and which does not advocate or condone personal violence. We also exclude those people who have conspired with a foreign government to overthrow their own." Four interconnected objectives were laid out: work for the release of POCs from prison; ensure fair trials for those accused yet not imprisoned; broaden rights of asylum for political refugees; and work internationally for greater freedom of opinion.

These were to be achieved through a political version of bearing witness. POCs were "adopted" by local groups formed in communities, schools, places of worship, and the like. Any particular POC could be adopted by more than one local group in more than one country. Letter-writing was a main tactic: letters to the prisoners, to their families, to the repressive governments, to the local groups' own governments, to newspapers and other opinion shapers, as well as to the UN and related bodies. Vigils and protests were organized for more macro-level publicity. In some cases legal help was provided.

Groups had three other parameters. "Rule of three": As a show of impartiality during the Cold War, each group was to adopt three POCs—one from the West, one from the communist bloc, and one from the Third World. Human rights were to be advocated irrespective of the political system doing the abusing. "No WOOC" (work on own country) was a second parameter. While a key element of the overall campaigns was to activate and support antirepression forces within offender countries, the adopter groups formally affiliated with

Amnesty had to work on cases outside their own domestic politics. And, third, groups must also adhere to the nonviolence proviso that POCs "have neither used nor advocated violence."

It was Nelson Mandela whose case provided an early test of the nonviolence parameter. Mandela had been adopted as a prisoner of conscience in 1962 when he was jailed on charges of trying to organize a strike of African workers and attempting to leave the country without a passport. Amnesty advocated his case, tried to free him from jail, and sent books to help him study in prison for his LL.B. law degree. But when in 1964 he was convicted for his leadership role in the militant guerrilla Spear of the Nation, Amnesty members voted to stick to the nonviolence condition and drop Mandela as a POC. They would still advocate for humane treatment and his right to a fair trial, but he would no longer be a focus of letter-writing and other campaigns.

By 1965 Amnesty had grown from 12 to 400 grassroots adopter groups. By 1970 this more than doubled, to 832. Consultative status, which provided observer privileges and access to official documents and diplomatic offices, had been achieved with UN entities such as the Human Rights Commission and also the Council of Europe. Working relations had been established with the International Red Cross and the International Commission of Jurists as well as with various trade unions, student organizations, churches, war veterans, and other like-minded groups.

The growth was both a sign of Amnesty's success and an organizational challenge. Part of that challenge was Benenson's own role, a version of founder's syndrome in which the qualities crucial to launching a new venture do not carry over to the next stages of organizational development. Part also was how to balance the grassroots activism with the need for a larger and more professionalized central office that greater prominence requires. Incidents such as a local group adopting an East German prisoner who turned out to be a criminal endangered Amnesty's brand credibility. In 1968 the post-Benenson leadership vested designation of all POCs in the International Secretariat (IS). The IS staff issued a handbook of do's and don'ts for local groups. The biannual international assembly that elected a council, set priorities, and reviewed policy still provided a channel for member input.

Global Prominence (1970s–1980s): Its Campaign for the Abolition of Torture (CAT), initiated in 1972, really put Amnesty International on the map. AI convened expert conferences and other meetings to bring together officials, activists, and legal experts to develop strategies for protecting individuals facing or under arrest. It added an "urgent action" mechanism for rapid response. Through these and other initiatives AI played a role at every stage of the CAT: getting torture onto the UN General Assembly agenda, having substantial input into provisions of the UN agreement, and building sufficient support among global publics for the convention to be ratified by enough states to enter into force in 1986. "It was Amnesty International, with its combination of attention to detail and zeal of purpose," one expert concludes, "that carried the day. Without that degree of energy the Convention against Torture (adopted in 1984) would never have seen the light of day."

While this of course did not fully end torture, it did have real impact in a number of cases. Chile and the dictator General Augusto Pinochet provide a particularly salient example. Amnesty's pressure on Pinochet began soon after his 1973 coup. One report concluded that torture had taken place on a large scale; another documented over 3,000 people having been executed or disappeared and tens of thousands who were tortured. Once Pinochet was finally forced from office in 1988, the Convention on Torture provided basis for his arrest in England and threatened extradition to Spain and house arrest in Chile.

Amnesty also kept its letter-writing strategy going. An example of its success involved a worldwide appeal on behalf of Julio de Pena Valdez, a Dominican Republic trade union leader, subjected to torture by the dictatorship. After his release, de Pena Valdez reflected: "When the two hundred letters came the guards gave me back my clothes. Then the next two hundred letters came and the prison director came to see me. When the next pile of letters arrived, the director got in touch with his superior. The letters kept coming and coming: three thousand of them. The President was informed. The letters still kept arriving and the President called the prison and told them to let me go."

Other major successes followed. In 1979 Amnesty exposed the massacre of at least 100 children in the Central African Republic. It helped free South Korean POC Kim Dae-jung, whom the military dictatorships had repeatedly imprisoned and who went on to be elected his country's president. And it grew at astounding rates: between 1970 and 1980, the number of local-level groups went from 832 to 2,200; International Secretariat staff grew from 19 to 150; and the budget of approximately $70,000 increased to over $4 million.

Some cases were more problematic. In Guatemala, where for decades the military dictatorship had been oppressive and murderous, Amnesty documented abuses but it took many years for the situation to even start to change for the better. While its violence had precluded POC status for the West German urban terrorist Baader-Meinhof gang when some members were first arrested, AI did support their hunger strike protesting prison conditions. But right when Amnesty was defending the hunger strikers, other gang members hijacked a Lufthansa plane and flew it to Somalia.

Ceding to the Movement It Seeded (1990s on): British human rights scholar Stephen Hopgood cites the 1994 Rwanda genocide as "when the torch passed" from Amnesty International to other NGOs, such as Human Rights Watch (HRW), whose strategy and structure were more conducive to a changed human rights agenda. The situation demanded quicker action than Amnesty's organization of local groups could muster and more direct engagement than its letter-writing campaigns and vigils could provide. Human Rights Watch was equipped to send investigators right out into the field. With offices in a number of major capitals, including non-Western countries such as Brazil, India, and South Africa, HRW was better positioned to lobby governments.

There were other dynamics as well. The human rights agenda had expanded to a wider range of issues, such as ethnic conflicts, civilian protection, child soldiers, human trafficking, and refugees. These were not the issues on which Amnesty had developed its capacity for action. They entailed different strategies than individual prisoners of conscience. There still were plenty of POC cases, but they were now more part of, than close to all of, the human rights agenda.

The traditional prohibition on working within one's country ("no WOOC"), while useful for navigating impartiality during the Cold War, increasingly impeded AI's attractiveness to those in the global South who were most concerned with human rights issues within their own country. You ended up "with the least politically exciting people in the country" joining Amnesty, as one disillusioned member put it. "Anybody who cared about Zambia was going to be fighting for democracy in Zambia. They weren't going to join an organization that told them why you can't fight for democracy in Zambia." Or, as an African staff member put it more harshly, the no WOOC rule "is utterly rubbish . . . It's bullshit . . . it is a misunderstanding of what human rights is. Human rights in the south is domestic. Human rights in the north is foreign policy. You gotta decide where you're going to be. If you're going to be a real human rights organization, it's gotta be domestic issues."

Meanwhile the field of global human rights NGOs was growing highly competitive. Others in addition to Human Rights Watch, with home bases in the United States or Europe but with more extensive engagement in the global South and core missions more geared to the emerging agenda, included Médecins Sans Frontières (Doctors Without Borders), International Rescue Committee, Lawyers Committee for Human Rights, and the Open Society Institute. More and more indigenous human rights NGOs also came on the scene: for example, the Human Rights Institute of South Africa, South Asia Forum for Human Rights, Latin American Association for Human Rights, and ALTSEAN-Burma. Google "international human rights NGOs" and you get hundreds more in both categories.

This is not to say Amnesty disappeared or became stagnant. It has continued to grow, with membership now over seven million. It has opened offices in South Africa, Brazil, India, and elsewhere in the global South. Its website now lists a wider range of areas of activity including armed conflict, corporate accountability, indigenous peoples, living in dignity, and sexual and reproductive rights. It still has high brand recognition. To the extent it has ceded its lead position, it did so to the movement that it seeded.

WHAT: Balance Sheet

Amnesty International was, as Professor Wendy Wong of the University of Toronto put it, "the NGO that made human rights important." Human rights principles, of course, trace back deep into human history: in the core ethics of major world religions, in the international humanitarian law underpinnings in the philosophies of Grotius and Kant, in such foundational political documents as the Magna Carta, the French Declaration on the Rights of Man, and the American Declaration of Independence and Bill of Rights. History also has had prior human rights activists: the early nineteenth-century British Anti-Slavery Society, the mid-nineteenth-century International Committee of the Red Cross, and Oskar Schindler and Raoul Wallenberg saving Jews during the Holocaust, to name a few. But never before was there an international human rights movement as extensive and impactful as there was in the last few decades of the twentieth century and as there is today. Amnesty International blazed the trail.

It did so through an organizational version of the moral capital and political skills we have highlighted in individual leader profiles. Especially in the context of the ideologically driven Cold War, Amnesty's founding principle of opposing political repression "regardless of where it occurs, who is responsible or what are the ideas suppressed" gave it a powerful claim to moral authority. The "rule of three" by which each grassroots group adopted one prisoner of conscience from the Soviet bloc, one from the West, and one from the Third World staked out impartiality within global geopolitics. As such it both drew on the existing lineage of human rights norms and strengthened those norms going forward.

Information has been AI's main political resource in having this impact. AI built itself into a credible alternative source of information on human rights abuses: credible because of the impartiality it was known for that official government sources could not be counted on to have and because of the accuracy and thoroughness that its country reports and other studies consistently demonstrated. It shrewdly deployed the information, sometimes flooding it out, other times narrowly targeting it. Other means used were formal presentations as well as the orchestration of symbolic actions and events. As such AI exemplified the "information power" strategy through which NGOs can exert substantial political influence.

To be sure, human rights abuses have by no means been eliminated. But government policies have been changed, individual lives profoundly affected, and other political realities shaped. Direct causality cannot always be demonstrated. But credible claims are made for Amnesty's impact both in specific cases and more generally, as with the Convention on Torture. Citing its belief "that the defence of human dignity against torture, violence, and degradation constitutes a very real contribution to the peace of this world," the Nobel Committee awarded Amnesty International the 1977 Nobel Peace Prize as co-recipient with the Northern Ireland Women for Peace.

Amnesty has had its critics and problems, as we've seen. Its leadership of the human rights movement today is less than it once was. Indeed, not just for Amnesty but for all concerned with human rights, much remains to be done. Repression persists and by some measures is growing. Those who prioritize and affirm human rights debate whether the principles as well as the practice are overly Western-centric for the twenty-first-century world. Nevertheless, the very fact that there is a global human rights movement with thousands of NGOs working on a wide range of issues with a bevy of strategies is in no small part due to the norms strengthened and policy impact demonstrated by Amnesty International since Peter Benenson founded it more than half a century ago in 1961.

BACKLASH AND BACKSLIDING, OR RENEWED BREAKTHROUGHS

Much was achieved, as these cases exemplify. After centuries of colonialism, colonies no longer exist anywhere in the world. Communism lingers in just a few countries and even there it is not as repressive as it once was. Many fewer military governments exist. Human rights NGOs are active almost everywhere.

Yet as we look around our twenty-first-century world, we see more backsliding and backlash than breakthroughs. We earlier cited Freedom House's assessment of 2005 as the last year in which more countries had gains in freedom than declines. The *Economist*'s Democracy Index has gone down to 5.5 out of 10 despite the foreboding warnings of human rights activists.

Why these negative trends? Four dynamics are at work.

Difficulties of democratic consolidation: Many new democracies have been having difficulties consolidating initial breakthroughs into strong political institutions. In Walesa's Poland, while elections have continued, steps taken by the ruling Law and Justice Party since its victory in late 2016, as assessed by Freedom House, "threaten the constitutional order" and constitute "a coordinated assault on the rule of law." Aung San Suu Kyi's Burma has the precarious balance with the military's continuing power. So too has democratic consolidation been proving problematic in other cases we haven't included: for example, Ukraine, which was suffering from its own democracy-sapping corruption even before the 2014 Russian intervention; the Philippines, where President Rodrigo Duterte has killed over 7,000 people in the name of a war on drugs; Turkey, where President Recep Tayyip Erdogan has grabbed power far beyond his democratic mandate; and Brazil, where corruption charges caused a sitting president to be impeached, her successor to come close to the same fate, and her predecessor to be convicted and sentenced to prison.

Failure of democratizing movements such as the Arab Spring: Recall the hope and excitement emanating from the Arab world in those few months from late 2010 to early 2011. The self-immolation of a Tunisian produce vendor protesting petty bribes sparked the overthrow of a dictator in power for over 20 years. Young Egyptians mobilizing through Twitter and Facebook took over Cairo's Tahrir Square and brought down President Hosni Mubarak after close to 30 years in power. Politically hopeful stirrings surfaced in Yemen, Bahrain, and Syria. Yet other than Tunisia, where democracy has managed to hold on, massive repression, civil wars, and the rise of the Islamic State (ISIS) turned the Arab Spring into Arab Winter.

Crisis of Western democracies: Even with historical perspective tempering what at times feels like woe-is-me-ism, the internal strains that Western democracies currently are going through are profoundly dangerous. The *Economist* downgraded the United States from a full to a flawed democracy in its index. Freedom House also lowered its ranking of the U.S. Both did the same for a number of Western European countries. For all the fomenting by demagogues like Donald Trump and issue campaigns like Brexit, the sources of discontent run deeper than just a particular individual, issue, or election cycle. While there are differences between the United States and Western Europe in personalities and other particulars, three disruptive societal forces—economic discontent from widening income inequality and narrowing economic opportunity, cultural anxiety from immigration and long-festering racial and ethnic tensions, and personal insecurity from terrorism in their own cities—are mixing together in a potent "witch's brew" that threatens the fundamental bases of our democracies. A Harvard study showing only 30 percent of American Millennials saying it is "essential" to live in a democracy compared to 72 percent among those born before World War II, and comparable patterns in Western Europe, point to a worrisome generational trend. "Western liberal democracy is not yet dead," *Financial Times* columnist Edward Luce writes, "but it is far closer to collapse than we may wish to believe."

Strengthened forces of repression: Chalk up autocrats being "on the run" as another bout of wishful thinking. They have increased repression as necessary to try to hold on to power. They have done so with techniques old and new, the brutality of political prisons as well as their own manipulation of new technologies initially hailed as liberating and liberalizing. As Russian hacking into the U.S. 2016 presidential election dramatically demonstrated, they can go on the offensive and do so with quite the mastery of social media.

Clearly the twenty-first century needs its own committed, courageous, and dynamic leadership if freedom and human rights are to advance. Some lessons drawn from our profiles follow.

Moral capital remains crucial for the "who" of this kind of leadership. It can be derived from different sources: Gandhi from his spirituality, Walesa from his earthiness, Aung San Suu Kyi from her lineage to her father, Benenson from the virtue of his cause. The claims can't be contrived. They have to have authenticity in the eyes of those who would be led. The courage shown and costs borne—jail time, fasts, lost jobs, threats to life, even assassination in Gandhi's case—manifested commitment to the cause. Comparable authenticity and courage are essential for future leaders. What is not required, though, is being a perfect person: there are no saints among our profiles insofar as their personal lives.

The guiding visions need to continue to blend the universal and the particular, values and practices that hold true for all peoples and ones rooted in different nations' history and culture. Gandhi's anticolonialism combined a more general opposition to imperial rule with elements like *satyagraha* broadly rooted in India's historical culture and Hindu spirituality. Walesa and Aung San Suu Kyi drew on their respective religious traditions, the Catholic Church in Poland and Buddhism in Myanmar, for validation, along with their shared goal of democracy. The "rule of three" that Benenson established as the basis for Amnesty International advocacy (one prisoner of conscience from the West, one from the communist bloc, and one nonaligned) sought to get beyond global politics to the transcendent human rights at stake. Today, with questions such as the optimal balance between individual rights and societal responsibility and how best to achieve a just society less answerable by a set ideology, the challenge is, as Canadian scholar Michael Ignatieff put it, blending "local ethics in a globalized world."

Along with this "why," the "how" also remains critical. All our profiles had the political skills, some similar and some more specific to their particular political cultures, to be effective rather than merely earnest. Yet all were more effective in political transformation from the old order than in political institutionalization of a new order. Gandhi had a much better sense of why India should be independent than how to run the independent state. Walesa's presidency was short-lived and very mixed. The Rohingya crisis has raised profound concerns about whether Aung San Suu Kyi will be as committed to democracy and human rights in power as when challenging it. Benenson was forced out of the organization he created for the good of the organization. As we look ahead we should bear this pattern in mind.

The international community needs to play a strongly supportive role, providing assistance, amplification, and insurance: assistance in overcoming local authorities' repressive efforts; amplification to facilitate international media exposure countering efforts to muffle the messages; insurance—to be more precise, life insurance—in the international approbation and potential retaliation and reprisals that authorities risk if movement leaders are killed or die in custody.

In this regard I have concerns about both the United States and the United Nations. While we Americans often laud our country for the values that infuse our foreign policy, the record is more mixed than often acknowledged. Yes, the United States has supported democracy and human rights more often and in more places than any other major power. The cases of Poland and Burma are part of that. But the overall pattern has been of the United States supporting democratic principles when it has been reinforcing of its geopolitical interests but not doing so when there was a strategic choice between power and principles.

Backing Walesa fit well with overall Cold War strategy, as did supporting Aung San Suu Kyi with regional competition with China. But in the bulk of other cases over the course of the Cold War, the United States opted for the "he may be an SOB but he's our SOB" calculus and the "ABC" (Anybody But Communists) designation of who was a democrat. In today's age of terrorism one has to be concerned about comparable SOB and "ABT" (Anybody But Terrorists) calculations again pushing democracy and human rights to the side. Public pressure may mount in some high-profile cases, but while 87 percent of Americans acknowledged that human rights were important, when asked to rank human rights compared to other foreign policy goals, in a list of 11 goals it came out tenth.

The UN's Human Rights Council, ostensibly reformed back in 2009, remains rife with hypocrisy. The International Criminal Court (ICC) has had some but limited impact. UN "blue-helmet" peacekeepers have too often turned out to be human rights violators themselves. Were our earlier recommendations for a stronger Hammarskjöldian secretary-general to be adopted, then the UN could play more of a leadership role both with its unique global bully pulpit and in internal reforms for more programmatic effectiveness.

Much will fall to global NGOs. True, NGOs are not as pure as sometimes depicted: they have their own organizational imperatives (like pleasing their funders) and their own NGO-NGO rivalries. But advancing freedom and protecting human rights are their raison d'être. They don't have the power to impose policy change, but they can catalyze governments and international institutions to act. They wield quite substantial "information power," as Margaret Keck and Kathryn Sikkink put it in their award-winning book *Activists Beyond Borders*. Indeed, technological advances made in the 20 years since the Keck-Sikkink book have added to NGO information power. We have seen this in Burma with NGOs like Fortify Rights and Human Rights Watch using their own access to satellite technology to publicize photos of Rohingya villages being burned. Other examples include the Satellite Sentinel Project monitoring Sudan and South Sudan and the

Commission for International Justice and Accountability playing a lead role in gathering evidence of war crimes in Syria.

Some transformational forces will continue to be bottom-up, civil society activists and people power movements hitting the streets, creatively tapping technology and other aspects of what Anne-Marie Slaughter calls the "networked age." But without bold and dynamic leadership—like India had from Gandhi, Poland from Walesa, and Burma had for a least a period from Aung San Suu Kyi—popular movements run greater risks of being crushed or losing their way. The twenty-first century needs its own profiles in statesmanship if further backlash and backsliding are to be averted and renewed breakthroughs are to be made in advancing democracy and protecting human rights.

FOSTERING GLOBAL SUSTAINABILITY

"HOW COULD A SOCIETY FAIL TO HAVE SEEN THE DANGERS that seem so clear in retrospect?" This stark question posed by Jared Diamond in his aptly titled *Collapse: How Societies Choose to Fail or Succeed* has stayed with me. Diamond recounts the histories of Easter Island, Norse Greenland, and other flourishing societies gone extinct whose tragic fates could have been prevented. "Choose" is the operative word. Sure, at least once in history a giant asteroid may have hit the Earth out of the blue and destroyed the civilization of the day (dinosaurs?). But most of the time societies fail or succeed based on choices the societies have made. "Globalization," Diamond sharpens the point for our twenty-first-century world, "makes it impossible for modern societies to collapse in isolation."

It was only in the late twentieth century that global sustainability finally started to be recognized as a priority. **Gro Harlem Brundtland** (Chapter 12), three-time prime minister of Norway, played a key role as chairwoman of the United Nations–sponsored World Commission on Environment and Development (WCED) in the 1980s and director-general of the World Health Organization (WHO) from 1998 to 2003. The Brundtland Commission prioritized sustainable development, defined in its most basic terms as "meeting the needs and aspirations of the present generation without compromising the ability of future generations to meet their own needs." As WHO director-general, Brundtland made health an integral component of the overall global antipoverty agenda. With a vision of the modern world as "a single microbial sea washing over all humankind," she also pushed for greater focus on pandemic prevention. While policy in both areas has fallen short, Gro Brundtland's statesmanship was crucial in the initial strides that were made and in putting sustainability on the global agenda in an enduring way.

When the Rockefeller Foundation was established in the early twentieth century, one of its principal emphases was on global health, fighting yellow fever, malaria, hookworm, and other widespread diseases plaguing poor parts of the world. In our twenty-first-century world the Bill and Melinda Gates Foundation plays an even more extensive role. Its $44 billion endowment makes it the largest philanthropic foundation ever. Global development and global health are top priorities. Its global health funding is so substantial that a few days before a WHO meeting in Geneva, a Swiss newspaper ran the headline, "The Health of the World Depends More on Bill Gates Than on the WHO." Though an exaggeration, it made a point about the role of the **Gates Foundation** (Chapter 13) and more broadly about philanthropy statesmanship.

We long have been greatly concerned with "WMD," weapons of mass destruction. We also now confront two other "MD" threats: "EMD," environmental mass destruction, with climate change here and now, not just down some distant road; and "DMD," diseases of mass destruction, global pandemics for which deaths can run into the millions and economic costs into the billions. Avoiding EMD and preventing DMD are not just nice-to-have considerations to be tacked on once more immediate factors are calculated, be they quarterly profit margins or voter preferences or interest group pressures. Sustainability is one of the twenty-first century's crucial challenges for the ultimate security of survival.

12

Gro Harlem Brundtland:
Our Common Future, 1987–2003

WHO is Gro Harlem Brundtland?

Gro Harlem was born April 20, 1939, in Oslo to two politically involved parents. Her father, Gudmund, became personal physician to the Norwegian prime minister, and later minister of social affairs and minister of defense in Labor Party governments. Her mother worked for the parliamentary group of the Labor Party. "I was lucky," Gro reflected later in life, "to be brought up in a family of strong convictions, deeply held values of solidarity, justice and equality."

Gro's leadership and political interests were already evident in secondary school. She was elected school president. With a group of "radical students," as she self-characterizes in her memoirs, she founded *We Students* as the official magazine of the School Socialist Society. She studied medicine at the University of Oslo, graduating in 1963. Later that year her husband, Arne Olav Brundtland, received a visiting scholar fellowship at the Harvard Center for International Affairs where he worked with, among others, Professor Henry Kissinger. Gro enrolled in the Harvard School of Public Health, where she earned a master's degree in public health. She traces her interest in the relationship between public health and the environment to these studies.

Her first major political appointment was in 1974 as minister for environmental affairs. In 1981, with the Labor government losing popularity during bad economic times, the sitting prime minister resigned and Gro was named in his place. She was the youngest person (age 41) and the first woman to hold the office in Norway. But popular discontent with Labor couldn't be stanched, and the Conservative Party won the elections later that year. She remained party leader in opposition. When Labor regained control, she served twice more as prime minister (1986–1989 and 1990–1996).

Her international involvement began in that interregnum between her first and second prime ministerships when in 1983 the United Nations created the World Commission on Environment and Development (WCED) and chose Brundtland to chair it. She guided the WCED, or as it came to be known, the Brundtland Commission, through its own troubled political waters and pathbreaking work on "sustainable development," culminating in its 1987 report, *Our Common Future*. In 1998, after her final term as Norway's prime minister and with the World Health Organization (WHO) rocked by major scandals, the international community again turned to Brundtland to provide crucial leadership as WHO director-general.

It was both her personal capital and political skills that situated Brundtland for the statesmanship needed in both instances. With international development such a divisive global North-South issue, the WCED chairmanship was normatively loaded. If it were someone from a developing country, the work risked being written off by the developed countries. The flip-side concern was that a chair from the global North could undermine the commission's standing in the global South. The combination of Norway's reputation as an advocate of global justice and Brundtland's own record on social issues sufficiently countered such concerns, which she then built on once chair. At the WHO her standing as a doctor and work outside of politics on public health issues added further to the personal capital she brought to the position.

One example of her prior political skill was her handling of a massive North Sea oil spill while minister of the environment. The 1969 discovery of North Sea oil had been a huge boon to the Norwegian economy. But in April 1977 a massive blowout hit the Bravo drilling platform. Environment Minister Brundtland was thrust into the limelight. She came out of it having shown adroitness both in coordinating emergency action to control the spill and in dealing with the press. Over the rest of her term she earned environmentalist kudos for establishing the sprawling Hardangervidda national park while on other issues balancing environmental goals with Norway's social democratic commitment to full employment, showing herself to be "a skilled and accomplished practitioner of the art of the possible."

Being the first woman prime minister posed particular political challenges. One of her aides commented on how she rose in the party despite or perhaps precisely because of "her straight talk and complete lack of veneration for 'the older wise gentlemen.'" She recounts the bias-infused question from a reporter: "Is it only men who describe you as rock-hard, strong-willed, and obstinate?" Her response was rebuffing: "I seldom see rock-hard used to describe male politicians"—and affirming—"I wouldn't have won any [political battles] if I had not been what you call obstinate."

WHY sustainable development?

The first major protest demonstration I went to in college was Earth Day 1970. The modern environmental movement was taking shape. E. F. Schumacher's *Small Is Beautiful*, excoriating consumerism for its dehumanizing effects as well as environmental damage, was being passed around the dorm. In an economics class the professor had us read *Limits to Growth*, a study by a group called the Club of Rome drawing on an MIT computer model showing how "the earth's interlocking resources—the global system of nature in which we all live—probably cannot support present rates of economic and population growth much beyond the year 2100, if that long, even with advanced technology." Concern for the environment also was spreading internationally. The first UN-sponsored conference on the environment was held in Stockholm in 1972. The conference called on all "Governments and peoples to exert common efforts for the preservation and improvement of the human environment, for the benefit of all the people and for their posterity."

Developing countries, though, while sharing concerns about the environment, were concerned that limits to their growth would keep them mired in poverty. For decades the United States had pushed a conception of modernization based on ratcheting up economic growth to that take-off point that would launch developing countries out of poverty. In 1974, the UN General Assembly approved the "Declaration of a New International Economic Order" blaming the rich countries of the North for a system that made it "impossible to achieve an even and balanced development of the international community" and the consequent ever-widening gap between developed and developing countries. By the early 1980s, with the United States and Europe mired in their own recessions, and conservative leaders like Ronald Reagan and Margaret Thatcher in ascendance, there was not much receptivity to castigating the rich or to heeding pro-environment pleas.

This was the context in which Gro Harlem Brundtland was asked by UN Secretary-General Javier Perez de Cuellar to lead this new World Commission on Environment and Development. It was clear to her that without ideas that would both bridge North-South divides and integrate economic and environmental concerns, this effort would end up as another divisive or at best ho-hum report. That was the fate of the 1980 report by an independent multilateral commission convened by Willy Brandt, former West German chancellor and leader of the Socialist International, which had a strident North versus South tone. The 1982 Independent Commission on Disarmament and Security Issues, chaired by former Swedish Prime Minister Olof Palme, of which Brundtland was a member, met a similar fate.

Sustainable development, "meeting the needs and aspirations of the present generation without compromising the ability of future generations to meet their own needs," was that bridging and integrating concept. "The 'environment,'" as Chairwoman Brundtland wrote in the foreword to the final report, "is where we all live; and 'development' is what we all do in attempting to improve our lot within that abode. *The two are inseparable*." It was "Our Common Future," as the commission's report was titled: common in the present tense, the fate of North and South as one world, and in the future sense of sustainability over time with the next generations in mind.

Of course, there was much for all to support under the sustainable development umbrella. Who was against saving the world and safeguarding it for our children and grandchildren? But there were plenty of conflicts over how best to do that: clashing views of priorities among the over 300 recommendations, competing interests on which trade-offs to make, and differing assessments of optimal strategies even when objectives were agreed upon. Even if politics could have been set aside, working out all these elements posed formidable policy challenges. But politics couldn't be set aside in the work of the commission, let alone in what would follow.

HOW did Brundtland advance sustainable development?

The politics inside the commission were problematic from the start. The head of the UN Environmental Programme turf-consciously tried to block the WCED from being created. Failing that, he got a confidant appointed as the vice chair who repeatedly tried to go around Brundtland. He "considered me a relatively young and inexperienced woman and clearly believed that it would be easy to wrest control from me. He would be disappointed."

The membership was drawn from 23 countries, broken down geographically as six countries from Europe, three from North America, four from South America, four from Asia, and six from Africa and the Middle East. Politically and economically the membership included seven countries from the industrial developed North, four from communist countries, seven from low-income countries, and five from better-off developing countries. While in keeping with this as an independent commission, created by but not beholden to the UN, members did not have to strictly represent their home countries.

Still, those interests and perspectives were part of the mix. This multilateral diversity was crucial for credibility and legitimacy. It also made consensus-building quite challenging. After the first meeting, one commissioner expressed doubt that they could reach shared and workable conclusions on any one of the issues, let alone all of them.

And not a lot of resources were provided. Although governments such as Canada, Norway, Sweden, Denmark, and Japan were supportive, the United States was not; the Reagan administration rebuffed pleas for funding. The commission began with barely half its budget committed.

Right away Brundtland showed she was serious about this being a working commission. The Secretariat provided real expertise in conducting research and developing working papers, some of which were published on an interim basis to road test key ideas. Commissioners met seven times in their four years, in cities around the world, each meeting lasting between six and twelve days. One feature that was innovative at the time and is now well established was opening some sessions to NGO and civil society representatives. This helped broaden the range of ideas and enhanced the commission's legitimacy. It also created some dicey political situations. As part of the meetings in São Paulo, Brazil, the commissioners made a field trip into Amazonia to visit an experimental forest project run by the NGO World Wildlife Federation. When he heard they were coming, the governor of the state, a strident anti-environmentalist, insisted they come to a dinner in their "honor." Brundtland felt they couldn't refuse. So she prepared her own after-dinner speech affirming the commission's position "in polite but unambiguous terms." The governor got wind of what was to come and left during dessert.

Global North commissioners pushing for environmental protection were in a do-as-we-say-not-as-we're-still-doing mode given Reagan-Thatcher policies. Broader debate over unfair terms of trade also played in. Sugar was one case cited, in which the global South sugar-exporting countries had to produce 32 times as much sugar as they had 15 to 20 years earlier to pay for the same amount of industrial exports.

International Monetary Fund structural adjustment policies still were prioritizing export-oriented but environmentally damaging production such as palm oil in Indonesia. Some global South commissioners had trouble getting beyond the standard colonialism-imperialism critique. Other issues like nuclear energy didn't break out in North-South terms but had their own sharp differences. Still others carried national redlines; for instance, the U.S. commissioner was opposed to a carbon tax and any increases in gasoline taxes.

Brundtland knew that she needed enough compromises to achieve consensus but not so many that the report got too watered down and lost its policy edge. The report also needed to be comprehensive but avoid devolving into a potpourri with no central organizing concept. With the final report fully drafted, the commissioners met in Tokyo. Much had been worked out, but the differences remaining were enough that it took an all-nighter to get the final report approved. In that session and throughout the process, as the commission executive director put it, "It was Dr. Gro Harlem Brundtland's stature and skill as Chairman that was critical in guiding the Commission through many difficult moments, holding them together and achieving our ultimate consensus." *Our Common Future*, with its core concept of sustainable development and over 300 recommendations, was released at a press conference the next day.

Brundtland had been reelected Norway's prime minister the year before. She doubled up to see the commission through. She was especially focused on building support and promoting policy changes by governments along the lines of the report's recommendations. In 1989 her party was voted out, only to be reelected in 1990. She served again as prime minister until resigning in 1997. In 1998, she returned to international leadership on the sustainability agenda as director-general of the World Health Organization (WHO).

The WHO was then in crisis. "WHO: Change or Die" was how a 1995 editorial in the *British Medical Journal* put it. Its longtime director-general, Dr. Hiroshi Nakajima, had been mired in corruption scandals including crony contracts. The agency was demoralized:

"bureaucratic and hamstrung by internal politicking," as a BBC report put it. The well-respected head of its anti-AIDS policy had resigned, citing major disagreements with Nakajima. All this was happening at a time when AIDS was raging, longtime diseases like malaria and tuberculosis were continuing to take an immense toll, nearly 30 new diseases had emerged, and 20 diseases believed to have been wiped out had reemerged.

On her first day on the job Brundtland issued new ethical guidelines for the organization. She reformed the management structure with a new leadership team, which included five women and four men, akin to a cabinet in a parliamentary system. She initiated the World Health Survey coordinated with national health authorities and established an extensive database on child and maternal health, infectious diseases, communicable diseases, and health services capacity and access. She also began forging links to private health organizations, to the business world more broadly, and to NGOs. In these and other ways she sought to reestablish the WHO's reputation as the lead agency in global public health.

Three examples: One was the WHO's role in passing the Framework Convention on Tobacco Control (formal name for the global anti-tobacco treaty). As the leading cause of preventable deaths worldwide, tobacco use is very much a public health issue. Efforts had been under way for a number of years to globally limit the sale, production, and use of tobacco products. So while she didn't initiate the effort, Brundtland provided the political skills and other leadership to bring the treaty to fruition. Clearly it hasn't fully resolved the tobacco issue. The tobacco industry has continued to seek, in the WHO's own words, "to undermine or subvert tobacco control." It is no surprise that the United States has refused to join the effort. But 180 countries have signed on. And the precedent of the first global treaty worked out under WHO auspices was set.

In a second example, Brundtland and the WHO played a key role in the creation of the public-private partnership Global Alliance for Vaccines and Immunization (GAVI). By the late 1990s progress on immunizing children in poor countries against the six major child-hood diseases—tuberculosis, diphtheria, tetanus, pertussis, measles, and polio—had fallen off. Working with the World Bank, Brundtland called a summit including industry leaders, NGOs, medical researchers, and practitioners. GAVI was formed as a new coalition with the WHO providing technical expertise and Brundtland serving as the partnership chair. It was formally launched at the 2000 Davos World Economic Forum with a $750 million start-up grant provided by the Bill and Melinda Gates Foundation. By 2002 GAVI had helped to dramatically decrease drug prices, including an 80–90 percent price drop for some HIV/AIDS antiretrovirals, which helped to slow the rate of spread of new HIV/AIDS cases, as well as a 33 percent drop for tuberculosis medicines.

In a third example, in November 2002 a farmer in rural China was diagnosed with a rare infectious incurable disease, severe acute respiratory syndrome, or SARS. Over the next few months more cases were reported in China and Hong Kong and by global travelers in Toronto, San Francisco, and Frankfurt. For reasons of pride and economics (fear of losing trade and tourism), China initially was reticent about sharing information and cooperating in other ways. But with SARS potentially becoming a global pandemic, quick and decisive action was needed. Brundtland used her political skills to lean on China in ways that allowed face-saving but got cooperation. On March 12, 2003, she issued a global alert. Working with the U.S. Centers for Disease Control and Prevention (CDC), the WHO got 60 medical teams on the ground. The media was engaged to spread public awareness, but carefully, to avoid sowing panic. National governments needed to be convinced to cooperate. Brundtland's leadership was crucial in overcoming these obstacles. By April–May the spread of SARS had peaked. The last reported case was in 2004.

Beyond strengthening the WHO itself, Brundtland made global public health not just its own domain but also put it "at the core of the development agenda . . . as the key to poverty reduction"—that is, as very much a part of sustainable development. She created a Commis-

sion on Macroeconomics and Health to document how greater investment in health had broader economic benefits for developing countries
both in reducing costs by more disease prevention and increasing benefits from workers not losing productivity to illness and death. The
Roll Back Malaria campaign, launched in partnership with the World
Bank, the UN Development Programme, and UNICEF, was an initiative along these lines. In sub-Saharan Africa alone estimates were of
300 million people afflicted with malaria, with a million deaths a year.
Malaria care accounted for as much as 40 percent of public health
budgets, 30–50 percent of inpatient admissions, and 50 percent of
outpatient visits, with an estimated cost of $12 billion. While funding
shortfalls and other factors slowed progress, the WHO's leadership
catalyzed NGOs such as the Malaria Consortium, Against Malaria
Foundation, and Nothing but Nets (insecticide-coated mosquito nets,
a low-cost, highly effective protection), which raised supplemental
funds and provided additional expertise. By 2016 the 50 percent target reduction in malaria deaths had been exceeded at 62 percent.

When the Millennium Development Goals were established at the
UN new-century 2000 summit as the basis for "a new global partnership to reduce extreme poverty," three of the eight goals—to reduce
child mortality; improve maternal health; and combat HIV/AIDS,
malaria, and other diseases—were explicitly about health. Two others
partially involved health (i.e., reducing childhood malnutrition as part
of fighting hunger and access to clean water as part of environmental
sustainability). Health affected development. Development affected
health. These goals exemplified the overarching framework of sustainable development.

WHAT: Balance Sheet

The case for Brundtland's role as transformational statesmanship is
strong although not as seminal as some of our other profiles. While
others also played substantial roles in the sustainability movement,
her SARL ranking is well warranted. The personal capital and

political skills she brought were a special, even if not unique, combination. While the world is not where it needs to be, without Brundtland's role in it we would be even more dangerously short of achieving
those goals.

As the most widely read UN report in history, and with a Google
hit count over 97 million, the Brundtland Report was the one that
branded sustainable development, fleshing it out intellectually as well
as building broad political support and giving it policy applications.
The formulation of "meeting the needs and aspirations of the present
generation without compromising the ability of future generations to
meet their own needs" had a clarity of message while encompassing a
complex array of policy domains. It squared the quality-quantity circle
of environmental and other quality of life considerations with more
economic growth. It quite usefully framed an overall multifaceted
effort and provided a context and some initial criteria for making policy choices. It was a prime example of how international commissions
can exert what scholars call "the power of ideas . . . reinforced and
legitimized by the very institutions, conferences, government agencies
and development initiatives that adopt it as a guiding principle."

It also helped work through the North-South global divide that
had deepened and intensified over the prior decade. It made the case
for, as in the report title, "our common future." Northern developed–
Southern developing country tensions were there throughout the process. Even though commissioners were officially independent, they
still had at least tacit accountability to their home governments—and
none were tabula rasa; all had the perspectives that came with their
lineage and their work. Oil companies and other interest groups also
kept a hand in. But unlike the previous Brandt Commission and much
of the back and forth within the UN, compromises were hammered
out. Some solutions did water things down too much, but many balanced political consensus with policy coherence. Commissioners later
interviewed were unanimous that Brundtland's "skills at moderating
discussions, encouraging both debate and compromise, were essential

to the success of the Commission." One went so far as to say it was "really a joyful experience to work with her."

The same year that the Brundtland Report was issued, the Montreal Protocol on Substances That Deplete the Ozone Layer, one of the most far-reaching global environmental treaties, was signed. In working out the terms for North-South collective action to close the dangerous hole that had been opening up in the Earth's atmosphere, the Montreal Protocol established the principle of "common but differentiated responsibility." Since the industrial countries were the principal producers and consumers of the chlorofluorocarbons (CFCs) that were causing the ozone hole, they bore more of the responsibility (costs, production cutbacks) for ameliorating the problem. But developing countries had to bear some of the responsibility since any further CFC production and use would make the problem worse. The problem was a common one, the responsibility differentiated—a tangible embodiment of the Brundtland Report's conceptions of our common future, one world, and sustainable development.

The following year the UN created the Intergovernmental Panel on Climate Change (IPCC) with leading scientists from around the world. Its first report stressing the importance of stepped-up multilateral cooperation helped lay the basis for the 1992 Earth Summit, held in Rio de Janeiro, whose formal name, the UN Conference on Environment and Development, tracked with the Brundtland Commission's formal name ("UN" substituted for "World," "Conference" for "Commission"). The Rio treaty (Framework Convention on Climate Change, or UN FCCC in the alphabet soup) makes repeated references to sustainable development in acknowledging the need for more development in environmentally conscious ways ("enable economic development to proceed in a sustainable manner").

On global health we see a similar mix of major accomplishments by Brundtland's WHO director-generalship yet still with a long way to go. She righted the WHO ship when amid internal disarray and poor policy performance it was way off course. Remember that "change or die" warning. Under her direction, the WHO not only achieved some immediate global health objectives, but it also established global health as a crucial component of sustainable development. Poverty would never be alleviated, no matter how sophisticated the economic formulations, if diseases like HIV/AIDS and malaria kept decimating populations. Global health thus became integrated into the Millennium Development Goals. Although short of the targets set for the 2000–2015 period, significant progress was made (e.g., child mortality rates in developing countries were reduced by more than half, albeit not by the full two-thirds' target).

The SARS crisis prompted passage in 2005 of the International Health Regulations, requiring countries to report disease outbreaks that risk spreading beyond their national borders and empowering the WHO to declare a global health emergency with travel and other restrictions. While legally binding, there has been limited compliance and little in the way of enforcement against noncompliant countries even in the face of pandemics like the 2009 swine flu outbreak, which killed over 200,000 people globally. The hit on the WHO budget during the 2007–2009 global financial crisis was one factor. Weak post-Brundtland leadership was another. When Ebola broke out in 2014, the WHO's response was, in the view of Council on Foreign Relations global health expert Laurie Garrett, "abysmal . . . shameful."

Were it not for NGOs like Médecins Sans Frontières (Doctors Without Borders) on the ground and the Bill and Melinda Gates Foundation providing funding, the Ebola pandemic would have been much worse. It is not only on this issue that NGOs have been playing crucial roles in global public health. We thus turn next to the Gates Foundation for its own work and as an example of the role of NGOs more broadly in global public health.

Gates Foundation and Global Health Philanthropy Statesmanship, 2000–

WHO are Bill Gates and Melinda French Gates?

William Henry Gates II was born in 1955. His mother, Mary, was a teacher, his father, William, a lawyer. The family lived in Seattle, Washington. "He was a nerd before the term was even invented," one of his teachers later remarked. By nine years old he was reading the World Book encyclopedia. In junior high, along with his friend Paul Allen, he got interested in a clunky ASR-33 Teletype linked to a General Electric computer system. He wrote his first computer program to play tic-tac-toe against the computer. He swapped computer time with a local company for helping the company find bugs in its systems. By high school he was writing programs for another company as well as ones to help the school principal with class scheduling. In his senior year he and Paul Allen created their own company, Traf-O-Data, for counting vehicle and pedestrian traffic.

In 1973 he went to Harvard. Initial interest in prelaw quickly shifted to mathematics and computer science. When in early 1975 he saw an article in *Popular Electronics* about a company called MITS (Micro Instrumentation and Telemetry Systems) and its Altair 880 personal home computer, he sent away for the $397 assembly kit. The Altair BASIC software he and Allen wrote landed them both jobs at MITS. Gates left Harvard for MITS's offices in Albuquerque, New Mexico (initially a leave of absence, he never returned as a student, although did get an honorary degree in 2007). He and Allen set up their own software company, originally named Micro-Soft, the hyphen dropped the following year. By 1978 Microsoft's sales were over $1 million. In 1979 they moved the company back close to home in Bellevue, Washington. In 1980 Microsoft signed a deal with IBM to produce what became the MS-DOS operating system. By 1984 Microsoft's software sales and other innovations were growing so fast that company revenue reached $100 million, double the previous year. Gates got the publicity trifecta of being featured on the covers of *Time*, *People*, and *Fortune*. The following year the first edition of Microsoft Windows was released. In 1987 at age 31, Bill Gates became the youngest billionaire ever. By 1995, with a fortune estimated at close to $13 billion (equivalent to about $20 billion today), he was the richest man in the world.

Melinda Ann French was born in 1964 in Dallas, Texas. Her father was an aerospace engineer. Her mother did not pursue a career but was a strong believer in one for her daughters as well as her sons. Melinda was high school valedictorian. She went to Duke and pursued a double major in economics and computer science, and then a Master's at Duke's Fuqua School of Business. In 1987, she was hired by Microsoft as a product manager in the multimedia division with a central role in development of the travel site Expedia, the digital encyclopedia Encarta, and other new products. She worked her way up to general manager of information products. She and Bill met at Microsoft. They married in 1994.*

That same year along with Bill's father they set up the William H. Gates Foundation. In 1999 it was merged with two other philanthropic ventures, Gates Library and Gates Learning, and renamed the Bill and Melinda Gates Foundation (BMGF). In 2000, Bill stepped down

---

* The story often told is that Bill first proposed a date two weeks later. Melinda said no. He revised his proposal for a more immediate date. They dated for about six years before getting married.

as Microsoft CEO while retaining the company chairmanship and taking on the role of chief software engineer. In 2006 Bill began fully phasing out as a Microsoft executive to focus more on the foundation. That same year Warren Buffett announced that he was giving the bulk of his fortune, over $30 billion, to the foundation. It was at that point that BMGF became the largest private philanthropic foundation in the world and greatly expanded its work, particularly in global health.

In terms of personal capital the Gateses carried enormous professional stature—indeed, star power. They could get meetings with world leaders that others working on global health could not. "If it's already on the agenda, we talk to them about what they're doing," Melinda Gates remarked. "If it's not on the agenda, I will bring it up." They had contacts across the public, private, and nonprofit sectors for partnerships. They tapped relationships with celebrities like U2 music star Bono to add luster and broaden public interest. The prestige they brought and the funding they provided attracted leading scientists and other talented people to BMGF projects. They quickly showed the authenticity of their commitment to their philanthropy, that they were invested with their time and ideas, not just their money, and interested in more than photo ops.

Moral capital was a tougher claim to stake. Would BMGF, as some critics warned, "bolster the same corporate, capitalist, neo-liberal agenda that has been so deleterious to health outcomes across the globe?" With accountability largely to their own board, could they be entrusted with such a broadly impactful role? Would BMGF's sheer size emanate a "Bill chill," pushing others' ideas off the global agenda and perversely incentivizing researchers, practitioners, affected populations, and others to mute criticism?

WHY: Helping all people lead healthy, productive lives

"I didn't do much philanthropy in my 20s and 30s," Bill Gates acknowledged in an interview. "I didn't believe in weekends, vacations. So philanthropy wasn't the only thing I didn't believe in. I was just fanatical." When he went with Melinda on a 1993 trip to Africa that was planned as a tourist safari, he was exposed to the realities of developing countries, staggering health inequalities in particular. "It's the right thing to invest back in society if we want to have an equitable and just world," was Melinda's view.

If you listen to National Public Radio, you likely have heard the "helping all people lead healthy, productive lives" motto in the acknowledgment of Gates Foundation support. Such a broad definition of mission and vision is common among philanthropic foundations. The Carnegie Corporation of New York, the main entity among the more than 20 foundations and other nonprofit entities spawned by Andrew Carnegie's philanthropy, seeks to "promote the advancement and diffusion of knowledge and understanding." For the John D. and Catherine T. MacArthur Foundation, it is "building a more just, verdant and peaceful world." The Gates Foundation's "productive lives" efforts have many aspects.* In making global health one of the priorities, "improving people's health and giving them the chance to lift themselves out of hunger and extreme poverty," BMGF builds on the linkage to poverty and development that Gro Brundtland emphasized in her commission and at the WHO.

Four aspects of global health particularly fit the profile of Melinda and Bill Gates. First, as businesspeople with a social conscience, they believe in markets but also acknowledge market failures. An oft-cited rough global statistic is that 80 percent of pharmaceutical spending is on illnesses and diseases prevalent in rich countries where 20 percent of the world population lives, and only 20 percent on those illnesses and diseases most common among the 80 percent of world population living in poor countries. Leveraging at least some leveling in this investment distortion is not just social altruism; it is business prag-

---

* Andrew Carnegie's funding of public libraries across America, over 2,500 of them, was one of the historically iconic acts of philanthropy. Following in that tradition, the Gates Global Libraries initiative seeks to bring the Internet to libraries serving one billion "information-poor" people around the world.

matism as well. "The poorest two-thirds of the world's population," Bill Gates stated in an interview with *Time* magazine, "have some $5 trillion in purchasing power . . . It would be a shame if we missed such opportunities." Some programs have had an estimated return on investment of $44 in economic benefits for every $1 spent on immunizing children.

Second, health is a policy area conducive to an approach grounded in science and technology. There are many knowledge gaps to be closed and technologies to be applied, plenty of room for the innovation that made Microsoft successful. A technological orientation is evident in BMGF grants like cellphone-based applications for preventive monitoring of disease outbreaks, new technologies to improve the health of mothers and newborns, next-generation sanitation technologies, vaccine development, control of disease-carrying mosquitoes, and "deliverable technologies" inexpensive to produce and simple to use. Some criticize the BMGF approach as overly technocratic and not sufficiently geared to the underlying social, economic, and political conditions that breed poverty. On the other hand, a technology-based approach fits the strengths and the comparative advantage the Gateses bring.

Third, BMGF focuses on grants that promise to be high impact. That was the insight that led to a fortune from software: find the leverage point that others don't see and for which you have expertise. Here it is in breaking the cycle of poverty. Over 75 percent of all BMGF grants go to global development and global health. This would be striking for any foundation. For the world's largest foundation, it amounts to $2.46 billion a year.* And its impact goes beyond its own funds. By leveraging its commitments to prompt other foundations as well as governments and international institutions to ante in, the

---

* The Gates Foundation 2015 annual report states the global health figure at $1.18 billion and global development at $2.06 billion. But 62 percent of the global development programs have substantial health components: for example, vaccine delivery, maternal and newborn health, and child nutrition, which are included in the $2.46 billion cited.

impact is even greater. BMGF provided $1.8 billion for polio eradication and leveraged another $4 billion from other donors. Its initial $50 million antimalaria grant in 1999 doubled the private money at the time and spurred numerous other commitments. As Helene Gayle, the head of CARE who previously worked at BMGF, put it, "I think people watch what the Gateses do and assume that if they're doing it, it's not only a smart humanitarian move, but a smart business move."

Fourth is the flexibility a foundation has compared to public-sector politics and bureaucracies. BMGF does have a policy advocacy division and maintains an office in Washington, DC, but with limited budgets. Most funds go directly into the research and programs that the foundation selects through its own review process and board decisions. In so doing BMGF and philanthropies in general can run risks and pursue issues that have public value that public officials, be they elected or appointed, may be reluctant to take on. "Don't just go for safe projects," Warren Buffett advised the Gateses as he entrusted his billions to them. "Take on the really tough problems." Bill Gates affirmed this advice. Yes, he acknowledged, "some of the projects we fund will fail." We not only accept that, we expect it: "because we think an essential role of philanthropy is to make bets on promising solutions that governments and businesses can't afford to make." On the other hand, the discretion foundations have raises issues of accountability and legitimacy that have brought BMGF some tough criticisms.

HOW does BMGF make a major impact on global health?

Whereas the problem on global environmental issues was about what was being done, on global health it was more about what was not being done. On climate change existing policies had to be reversed. On global health the policy void had to be filled. The World Health Organization had fallen off since Brundtland's directorship. Without her political skills and with member governments burdened by the 2007–2009 financial crisis, the WHO budget fell by more than 20 percent. It wasn't even that high to begin with and now was only about $2.3 billion—including the $257 million BMGF provided. With the interdependence of global health becoming increasingly evident, that left quite a bit not being done.

For funding as well as pooling expertise and other capacities, one of BMGF's main strategies is forging and strengthening public-private-nonprofit partnerships geared to particular global health problems. Take GAVI, for which, as noted in the previous chapter, Gro Brundtland provided the initial political leadership and BMGF the $750 million start-up grant. The BMGF grant in turn attracted funding from other foundations and from governments like Norway and the United Kingdom. Overall, BMGF has committed over $4 billion to GAVI. Whereas in 1990 only about 50 percent of children in low-income countries received DTP3 immunization (diphtheria, tetanus, and pertussis), 80 percent now do; close to 600 million children have been immunized. The under-five mortality rate has dropped 50 percent. At the same time, costs have been brought down from $35 per child to $20.

BMGF also has played a key role in the Global Fund to Fight AIDS, Tuberculosis, and Malaria. The Global Fund has even more partners than GAVI, yet as World Bank President Jim Yong Kim stated, "Without Bill Gates, we would never have had the Global Fund." Melinda Gates has been no less involved, in a speech at a major conference of malaria scientists challenging them to shift from control to eradication, which according to *Science* magazine greatly impacted the malaria community. BMGF also has played a key role in the Global Alliance to Improve Nutrition (GAIN), which includes six governments and five other NGOs attacking the malnutrition plaguing half the world's population, and Uniting to Combat Neglected Tropical Disease, which among other things on January 30, 2017, staged a "drug donation day," collecting over 207 million donations for distribution across four continents. One study found that of 23 global health partnerships analyzed, seven relied entirely on BMGF funding, and for another nine it was the largest donor.

Agenda-setting is another BMGF strategy, some of which is

accomplished through seats on the boards of partnerships that it helps fund. Some is through the DC office and other policy advocacy mentioned. Its Grand Challenges in Global Health initiative, launched in 2003, convened an international scientific board to assess the many ideas for impacting global health. Fourteen grand challenges were identified, backed by over $435 million initially and much more since. BMGF also was a major funder of Global Health 2035, a report by the blue-ribbon Lancet Commission on Investing in Health (*Lancet* being one of the world's leading medical-scientific journals), making the case for an even more ambitious global agenda going forward.

The 2014 Ebola pandemic brought BMGF more into pandemic prevention. In sharp contrast to the speed and effectiveness with which Brundtland's WHO had contained the 2003 SARS outbreak, the WHO was doing too little too late during the Ebola outbreak. The first Ebola cases were reported in late March. Doctors Without Borders (Médecins Sans Frontières), the leading NGO on the ground, kept sounding warnings. But budget cuts had shrunk the WHO's outbreak and emergency response division from 94 to 34 staff and its Africa regional office epidemic staff from 12 to 4. Between this reduced internal expertise and political delays, over four months elapsed until the WHO finally declared a global health emergency. Once it did, BMGF provided $75 million in emergency response funding.

The Ebola crisis prompted BMGF to make pandemic prevention a priority on an ongoing basis. It became one of the largest donors to the Coalition for Epidemic Preparedness Innovations (CEPI), which is developing and stockpiling vaccines against the pandemic threats of Lassa fever, MERS (Middle East Respiratory Syndrome), and Nipah virus. CEPI also is working on plug-and-play vaccine development techniques rapidly adaptable to the unpredictability of other pandemic threats. BMGF also supported the Commission on a Global Health Risk Framework for the Future, whose 2016 report made the case for substantially spanning local to global levels with roles for the public, private, and nonprofit sectors. Bill Gates also made pandemic prevention more of a theme in his own public statements. He gave interviews all over the media: national and international outlets, as well as general interest publications like *Time* and business journals like *Forbes*. He wrote on it in his blog, *GatesNotes*. He raised it in a speech at the 2017 Munich Security Conference, the Davos of the foreign policy–global security world. Whether through another "quirk of nature" like those that had produced Ebola and Zika and other outbreaks, or through intentional bioterrorism, "epidemiologists say a fast-moving airborne pathogen could kill more than 30 million people in less than a year. And they say there is a reasonable probability the world will experience such an outbreak in the next 10 to 15 years."

WHAT: Balance Sheet

Starting with an initial $10 million in 1997–1998, total BMGF global health funding thus far amounts to close to $20 billion. Adding in BMGF's leverage-generating funds from other philanthropies and from governments as well as its agenda-setting influence, there can be little doubt that BMGF has had a substantial impact on global health.

Whether that is a good thing has been a subject of debate. An "800-pound gorilla in the philanthrosphere" is how some critics characterize BMGF. The agenda-setting is agenda-skewing to the priorities BMGF sets and the strategies it has, on which other global health experts and NGOs do not always agree. The Bill chill risks crowding out ideas and programs that might be better, both directly in denying them funds and indirectly through trend-setting for other funders. Some go further, questioning the ethics of the BMGF endowment investing in oil companies and others whose profit-making operations contribute to public health problems and the more sweeping corporate-capitalist critique mentioned earlier. Some less ideological critics raise concerns about accountability and transparency, and especially the legitimacy of a private board exercising so much influence on matters of such importance to society.

No question there's plenty of room for criticism of BMGF. "The Foundation could do better with its money," a 2009 series of *Lancet* articles concluded. Among the *Lancet* points was that only 6 percent of BMGF grants had gone to organizations actually based in low- and middle-income countries, which "accentuated the dominance of Northern-based institutions in the determination of health programs and policies within low-income countries." Some programs have fallen short of goals, while others have been outright failures. BMGF's 2012 annual report acknowledged the need to bring in stronger leadership and make improvements in global programs. Endowment investments in tobacco companies were prohibited, with broader policy couched as being against "companies whose profit model is centrally tied to corporate activity that they find egregious."

These issues are not just ones for the Gates Foundation. They pertain broadly to policy philanthropy. Governments of various stripes are various mixes of unwilling and unable to address so many major societal concerns, nationally and globally. At the same time, more and more mega-donors are interested in dedicating part of their wealth to such issues. Over 170 millionaires and billionaires from 21 countries have signed the Giving Pledge (originated in 2010 by Bill Gates and Warren Buffett) committing more than half their wealth to philanthropy. Estimates run to $20 trillion in new mega-donor philanthropy over the next 50 years. Foundations need to "give smart," as Thomas Tierney and my Duke colleague Joel Fleishman title their book. Success in having made money does not necessarily guarantee success in applying it to policy goals. Kristin Goss, also a Duke colleague, poses the issue well as, on the one hand, such concentration of wealth reinforces social, economic, and political inequality, while on the other it provides capacity to at least partially offset those unable-unwilling governments.

While BMGF manifests many of the concerns of policy philanthropy critics, it also shows the benefits of being outside politics and large bureaucracies. Its $75 million emergency funding during the Ebola pandemic exemplified the agility to make quick decisions when needed. Its prestige attracts health professionals, scientists, and other experts. Partners can be convened based on shared interests and complementary capacities, with political affinities or animosities getting less in the way. Given the unlikelihood of governments and international institutions substantially increasing their resources for global health, BMGF continues to be needed to help fill the resource shortfall both directly and through its leveraging capacity. In these and other ways, as two experts in the field assess, "the Gates Foundation and other philanthropic organizations have come to be recognized by states, international organizations and others as important and legitimate [global health] governance actors."

BMGF has played a crucial role in the progress the world has made on global health. Its philanthropy statesmanship is essential to further progress.

EMD, DMD, AND GLOBAL SUSTAINABILITY

The EMD—environmental mass destruction—evidence gets stronger and scarier all the time.

2016 THE HOTTEST YEAR EVER:

Broke the record 2015 had set. Which broke the record 2014 had set. Once before, there were three hottest years in a row, 1939–1940–1941. Now, though, 1941 has fallen back to the thirty-seventh hottest year ever. Of the 17 hottest, 16 have been since 2000.

SEA LEVELS RISING AT THE FASTEST RATE IN 2,800 YEARS:

Even at the low end of projections (6 feet), let alone the high end (15–20 feet), with 40 percent of the U.S. population and eight of the world's ten largest cities along coasts, billions of people are at risk. Some island nations already are being inundated, their people climate change refugees.

OCEANS ACIDIFYING:

In 2016 the world's largest coral reef, Australia's Great Barrier Reef, had more coral die than in any previous year. This is not just a loss of beauty: coral reefs are vital incubators for marine ecosystems, including fish stocks that feed more than one billion people.

WEATHER WEIRDING:

Anyone who watches the Weather Channel or uses the app knows that while many factors determine extreme weather, climate change is a major one. Over the last two decades heat waves, droughts, wildfires, floods, hurricanes, tornadoes, and other weather weirding have caused over 600,000 deaths, damaged or destroyed 87 million homes, and injured and displaced over four billion people globally. Hurricanes Harvey, Irma, and Maria, which hit the United States and the Caribbean one right after the other in 2017 with devastating damage and death tolls, drove the point home.

COMPARATIVE DEATHS, TERRORISM AND CLIMATE CHANGE:

Deaths from terrorism are about 30,000 per year (close to 25 percent of which are the perpetrators themselves). At about 400,000 deaths per year, deaths from climate change are more than 13 times greater than deaths from terrorism and are projected to increase 50 percent by 2030.

CLIMATE CHANGE AS A MAJOR CAUSE OF INSTABILITY AND WAR:

"It degrades living conditions, human security and the ability of governments to meet the basic needs of their populations. Communities and states that already are fragile and have limited resources are significantly more vulnerable to disruption and far less likely to respond effectively and be resilient to new challenges." That's not a tree hugger speaking—that's from a Pentagon study.

This is but a sampling regarding climate change, let alone other EMD issues. All in all, not to put too fine a point on it, **what we're doing to the Earth has no parallel in 66 million years. That's 66,000,000 years.**

Incremental progress won't do. Even if all countries meet their Paris climate change agreement pledges, we still risk temperatures going up close to double the 2 degrees Celsius ceiling. And we know the United States won't meet the pledge since President Donald Trump, climate change denier in chief, reneged on the Paris agreement.

Breakthrough is needed. That requires statesmanship to raise the priority and urgency, make the case, and shape the narrative.

Al Gore tried. The ups and downs of his political career are telling. His first book on climate change, *Earth in the Balance: Ecology and the Human Spirit* (1992), came out of interests tracing back to his student days at Harvard. Having served as one of his foreign policy aides and advisors when he was a senator, I saw firsthand how intensely he worked and passionately believed in these issues. But while *Earth in the Balance* was well received by policy experts and environmental political activists, Gore was mocked by political opponents as "Senator Ozone." As Bill Clinton's vice president, he had the lead in U.S. diplomacy for the 1997 Kyoto climate change agreement and then took the political hit for the failure at Senate ratification. His own 2000 presidential campaign felt politically compelled to underemphasize his environmentalism. Even when he won the 2007 Nobel Peace Prize plus an Academy Award for his documentary *An Inconvenient Truth*, he couldn't shake the out-of-touch-wonk label. He has continued to work on climate change issues through his Climate Reality Project training environmental activists (www.climaterealityproject.org), private-sector sustainable capitalism ventures, and 2017's *An Inconvenient Sequel: Truth to Power*. But he never reached transformational statesmanship impact.

Pope Francis brought his enormous prestige to the issue with his 2015 encyclical "Laudato Si [Praise Be to You]: On Care for Our Common Home." We must, he implored, "bring the whole human family together to seek sustainable and integral development." His appeal was deeply spiritual, addressing people of every religion in the way that has become his trademark. On an issue like this, though, even such a popular Pope could but provide a small push. It has remained another issue fitting his lamentation, "I beg the Lord to grant us more politicians who are genuinely disturbed by the state of society, the people, and the lives of the poor!"

Constraints remain formidable. Corporations and other vested interests lobby hard. They propagate fake news, as a study by a Yale sociologist put it, using "their wealth to amplify contrarian views and create an impression of greater scientific uncertainty than actually exists." Political opponents make it into an issue of big government. And it is not just political jousting. The NGO Global Witness has documented over 1,200 environmental activists, "defenders of the earth," killed in 35 countries since it began gathering data in 2002, with a record 2,000 killed in 2016. In January 2017 a winner of the Goldman Environmental Prize, established by philanthropists to honor and support grassroots environmental activists, was assassinated in Mexico.

Yet a number of factors have become less constraining and more conducive. The old zero-sum trade-off between the economy and the environment, that policy could only be green in one way or the other, has opened up quite a bit. Cost curves are bending. Globally the average cost of generating electricity from solar panels fell 62 percent since 2009. Wind power costs also have dropped dramatically, so much so that wind surpassed hydroelectric as a power source for U.S. electric utilities. While renewables do get some subsidization, fossil fuel subsidies are four times as high. Calculations are being made of environmental debt along the lines of what economists long have called externalities.

Investors are showing confidence. The Financial Times Stock Exchange (FTSE) has created a green index. Goldman Sachs has established a fund prioritizing companies with smaller carbon foot-prints. Stock markets in Shanghai, São Paulo, and elsewhere globally have been setting their own reporting requirements to inform investors about companies' sustainability practices. *Entrepreneur* magazine sees such sustainable capitalism as "the next big thing." Bill Gates launched Breakthrough Energy Ventures, a more than $1 billion fund investing in technologies for clean energy innovation and commercialization. Sectors like the insurance industry are among the most ardent converts, as *Fortune* magazine puts it, to "climate change believers." With Zillow projecting $882 billion in risks to housing values from rising sea levels, being underwater is taking on a much more literal meaning. The chairman of Lloyd's of London has said that climate change is the company's number-one issue.

Even in the United States there are some political green shoots. In February 2017, a group of prominent Republicans including Secretaries of State James Baker (long associated with the Texas oil industry) and George Shultz (a distinguished economist before his foreign policy career), along with the Council of Economic Advisors chairs under Presidents Ronald Reagan and George W. Bush and the Wal-Mart CEO, issued a plan for a carbon tax. While short of what many environmentalists prefer, it shifted the debate to what, not if. When Trump renounced the multilateral Paris climate agreement, over 200 mayors, 1,600 businesses and investors, and numerous other organizations signed on to an open letter, "We Are Still In." "We are not waiting for Washington," Michael Bloomberg and California Governor Jerry Brown wrote, "America remains committed to our pledge under the [Paris] agreement." Polls show 62 percent overall support for the Paris agreement on climate change with Democrats at 83 percent, Independents at 60 percent, and "non-Trump Republicans" at 53 percent, but core Trump supporters at 24 percent. Yet of the 601 counties for which climate change is projected to cause a GDP loss of 10 percent or more by 2099, 82 percent voted for Trump in the 2016 presidential election. Faith-based groups motivated by "creation care" are providing some "purpling," bridging the conservative red and liberal blue divide.

China's politics also have been doing some greening. After years of resisting what it viewed as the international imposition of obligations, its national interest calculation has shifted. On an air quality index of anything over 200 being unhealthy and 301–500 as hazardous, Beijing's air has been measured at 623. Shanghai and other coastal cities face rising sea levels. Interior droughts pose water shortages that even the massive Three Gorges Dam cannot cover. China is now the leading investor in renewables, injecting more funds into solar and wind technologies than the United States and European Union combined. It hasn't been weaned from coal, but it has lowered targets for coal consumption.

India, by far the fastest-growing emitter based on business-as-usual projections, also is starting to reassess its interests. The WHO ranked Delhi "first" in air pollution among 1,600 cities worldwide. About half its school-age children already have incurred lung damage. In December 2015, right when the Paris talks were under way, the city of Chennai, that very year named one of the hottest cities in the world, suffered the worst flooding in over a century. Apple farmers in the Himalayan foothills must move their orchards as much as 2,000 feet higher to get to cool temperatures. The Jawaharlal Nehru National Solar Mission, named for the country's founding prime minister, seeks to establish India as a world leader in solar and other renewables.

It's not just now more than ever for transformational statesmanship on climate change. It's pretty close to now or never. This issue is so much at the heart of sustainability that little else matters without critical progress on climate change.

———

Messieurs c'est les microbes qui auront le dernier mot," the famed nineteenth-century French microbiologist Louis Pasteur warned. "Gentlemen, it is the microbes who will have the last word."

They have won in the past. The fourteenth-century bubonic plague killed at least 75 million people, some 17 percent of the world population at the time. The post–World War I Spanish flu killed 25 million in its first six months and spread to infect close to one-third of the world's

population. Those and other pandemics were in a much less interconnected world. Between 2013 and 2016, the Atlanta-based Centers for
Disease Control and Prevention monitored more than 300 outbreaks
of deadly pathogens in 160 countries. The world got lucky when the
2009–2010 H1N1 swine flu did not mutate to a more lethal strand.
No such luck with the 2014 Ebola pandemic or the 2015 Zika virus
outbreak, for which the worst effects may be over the long term with
a generation of children with microcephaly and other severe neuro-
logical disorders. Recent outbreaks of H7N9, an Asian bird flu, have
caused great concern because, based on the Influenza Risk Assessment Tool, H7N9 has "the greatest potential to cause a pandemic."
With many microbes developing resistance to antibiotics, one scientific study warned that by 2050 infectious diseases could kill more
people globally than cancer and diabetes combined, running as high
as 10 million deaths per year, with a $100 trillion economic toll. These
are numbers of DMD magnitude—diseases of mass destruction.

Pandemic prevention is a huge challenge. A revitalized World
Health Organization (WHO) has to be the key global institution. The
World Bank, UN Development Programme, and other international
organizations also have roles to play. So too does the philanthropy
statesmanship of the Gates Foundation and others in the nonprofit
sector. The 2016 Commission on a Global Health Risk Framework
for the Future was among those laying out sound policy proposals: for
example, a new Center for Global Health Emergency Preparedness
and Response, led by the WHO; more binding International Health
Regulations requiring governments to share outbreak information and
work with the WHO; strengthening public health infrastructure in
developing countries as a first line of defense; greater investment in
vaccines and other medical treatments; and other measures for which
the funding of the Gates Foundation and other philanthropies and
the expertise of NGOs are crucial. None of this will happen without statesmanship to raise the priority, give the issue a higher profile,
secure resource commitments, and motivate experts to engage.

"Leadership," as Gro Brundtland articulated it so well, "means taking the long view, inspired by our common needs and a clear sense of shared responsibility for taking the necessary action." While true throughout history, it is even more so today given "the evidence to show us that our human activities, the footsteps of our own time, will affect negatively the lives and choices we leave to future generations in a potentially disastrous way."

> We are all in this together, every human being. We all need to realize that time is running out, and that the only answer to give is to take commonly based actions, and take seriously our shared and combined responsibilities.

That is the essence of sustainability. The extinctions of Easter Island and other ancient societies, tragic for their own peoples, were largely within their own self-contained worlds. As we've been warned, "Globalization makes it impossible for modern societies to fail in isolation."

EPILOGUE

Twenty-First-Century Statesmanship: Difficult, Possible, Necessary

n closing, I reflect again on John F. Kennedy's *Profiles in Courage*. *The Peacemakers* is in some respects a global counterpart: world affairs, not just American politics, and world leaders, not just U.S. senators. In rereading *Profiles in Courage*, I was struck by the concern that "today" (i.e., 1956) "the challenge of political courage looms larger than ever before" and the reasons why:

> For our everyday life is becoming so saturated with the tremendous power of mass communications . . . Our political life is becoming so expensive, so mechanized and so dominated by professional politicians and public relations men that the idealist who dreams of independent statesmanship is rudely awakened by the necessities of election and accomplishment.

Kennedy, of course, didn't fully practice what he wrote (and some doubt how much of the book he actually did write). But if he thought it was hard then, many lament, he should see what it's like in our twenty-first-century media environment (blogs, iPhone cameras, social media, hackers, bots, cable TV, etc.) and multibillion-dollar political campaigns. There's been a spate of books telling us "historic greatness in the [American] presidency has gone the way of the dodo," that it's "the end of power from boardrooms to battlefields and churches to states," that it's "the end of leadership," and that we're descending into "global anarchy."

And then there is Donald Trump. That he has been a highly impactful leader cannot be denied. He won an election against the odds. His persona became the epicenter of American politics. He has challenged core norms, practices, and laws of the American political system and political culture. He has made America's relations in the world subject to his views and whims. In these and so many other ways he has tapped genuine concerns among citizens in ways intended more to foment grievances than to forge policy solutions. Indeed, we see a number of other leaders of this type in today's world. No wonder some question whether we would be better off if the end-of-leadership school were right.

Yet I come back to my earnest mid-1980s University of California-Davis students, whose hopes for peaceful ends to the Cold War and South African apartheid, seemingly so naïve, were borne out in reality. While many factors came into play, the extraordinary leadership of Mikhail Gorbachev and Nelson Mandela—exemplifying Isaiah Berlin's insight that "at crucial moments, at turning points . . . individuals and their decisions and acts . . . can determine the course of history"—was key. So, too, in the other cases profiled in our book.

None of these leaders were fully successful. Breakthroughs entail significant progress on issues long considered intractable. Further progress is made possible but it cannot be guaranteed. Backlashes and backsliding all too often follow. In none of these cases, though, was what had been achieved negated. The tensions in U.S.-China relations have been managed for close to a half century within the framework set by Henry Kissinger and Zhou Enlai back in 1971–1972. As bad as U.S.-Russia relations have become, they are not a new or renewed Cold War. Even though Dag Hammarskjöld's successors did not play comparable roles on issues of their day, Hammarskjöld's example of what the UN secretary-general can and needs to be bears on our day. South Africa has serious political and economic problems, Israeli-Palestinian peace has yet to be fully achieved, and Northern Ireland has yet to consolidate its political transition—but apartheid is no more, the progress Yitzhak Rabin made and the pro-security/pro-peace precedent he set still stands, and the violence in Northern Ireland has not again reached the levels of The Troubles. For all the challenges that freedom and human rights face, there are no more colonies in the world, very few communist countries, even fewer military governments, and a robust global human rights movement. We have a long way to go for global sustainability, but Gro Brundtland's common future and the Gates Foundation's global health initiatives have put the world in a better position than it otherwise would have been.

None of these accomplishments was achieved single-handedly. Other actors, other factors, and other forces came into play. Some provided conducive conditions. Some imposed constraints. Choices, though, had to be made—and were made in ways that others in the same position would be unlikely to have done or been as successful if they had: the basis for our diplo-ball statesman-above-replacement-leader (SARL) rankings.

The "impact had/not position held" approach keeps national leaders central—presidents, prime ministers, secretaries of state, foreign ministers—while also encompassing leaders of international institutions, social movements, and NGOs who did for peace and justice what governments were unable or unwilling to do. Hammarskjöld is our main international institutional case; Northern Ireland Women for Peace, Peter Benenson and Amnesty International, and the Gates Foundation are the social movement NGO ones. This more inclusive conception of statesmanship is likely to be borne out even more in the years ahead.

We also are likely to see more variation in the geography and gender of statesmanship. While some countries clearly have greater power and influence than others, more countries are playing more significant roles than in the past. Some of this is what *Financial Times* columnist Gideon Rachman calls "Easternization," with reference to the rise of

Asia generally and China and India in particular. Some variation is more broadly global, while some is a consequence of America First, Brexit, and other such policies ceding and discrediting statesmanship roles the United States, Great Britain, and other Western countries traditionally have had.

With regard to gender, there clearly is a long way to go. There has not yet been a female American president or a woman as the leader of China, Russia, or France, among others. A March 2017 study by the Pew Research Center identified 15 current female heads of state or heads of government, which was more than double the total in the year 2000 but still in less than 10 percent of countries. The United States did not have its first female secretary of state until 1997 (Madeleine Albright); since then there have been two others (Condoleezza Rice and Hillary Rodham Clinton). Federica Mogherini and Catherine Ashton have been the last two High Representatives of the European Union for Foreign Affairs and Security Policy. The United Nations has not yet had a female secretary-general. Women also have not been heads of the World Trade Organization or World Bank, although the International Monetary Fund has a woman at the top (Christine Lagarde). Although women are no more inherently inclined toward peacemaking than men, to engage only "half the sky," as Nicholas Kristof and Sheryl WuDunn put it in another context, makes finding quality leadership even more difficult.*

Both looking back and looking forward, the who-why-how-what framework hones in on keys to effective statesmanship. We see how early lives shape the personas but do not determine them. Mandela comes closest to a born leader, as to an extent does Zhou Enlai, the student radical leader. In most of the cases leadership qualities only develop over time and through events and circumstances. Kissinger was one among many foreign policy wonks. Gorbachev was an appa-ratchik, never a typical one but still coming up through the system.

---

* The academic world has its own long way to go. Along with statistics on women in the professoriate, one only needs to follow Twitter's #WomenAlsoKnowStuff.

Woodrow Wilson was a college professor. FDR was a patrician politician until his polio humbled him and helped develop his common touch. Hammarskjöld was regarded as just your average bureaucrat. Rabin was a soldier outside of politics until his midforties. Mairead Corrigan and Betty Williams were housewives and clerical workers. Gandhi started out as a London-educated barrister. Lech Walesa was a dockworker. Aung San Suu Kyi, while the daughter of Burma's independence leader, was out of the country for much of her life. Benenson had lost four times in bids for the House of Commons. Brundtland came from a politically prominent family and did become Norway's youngest and first woman prime minister but had limited involvement in global issues. Bill Gates was a full-on techie and businessman.

Whichever the path and whatever the source—moral beliefs, family roots, sacrifices made and courage shown for the cause, charisma, professional stature, and prestige—each accrued personal capital through qualities brought to their leadership positions that enhanced their capacity to be transformational. Their claims to personal capital weren't concocted consultant-style; they had authenticity in the eyes of those who would follow them.

This didn't require any to be a perfect person. Many had less than admirable aspects in how they led their personal lives. Leadership bona fides were more important than private life perfection. For anyone out there searching for that golden résumé, picture-perfect camera look, or other bases on which to anoint the next great peacemaker, there is a lesson here about what really is important for personal leadership capital.

People don't just follow an individual. They also have to have something to believe in—the "why." For transformational impact this has to be more than itemized lists of proposals. Some of the visions were about how international relationships are defined: U.S.-China, end of the Cold War, an empowered United Nations, Israel-Palestine peace, human rights, climate change, and global health. Some were about how societies organize themselves: end of apartheid, Catholic-Protestant peaceful coexistence, and transitions to democracy. All faced that analytic-prescriptive-normative challenge of sufficiently convincing people of what is wrong with the present to be motivated to pursue a better future, while also offering reassurance against the risks and uncertainties of that future. A formidable task, one for which Machiavelli's observation about the dangers of attempting "to initiate a new order of things" rang true time and again, as it does today.

The "how" varies across the different issue areas. The policy-politics-personal combination was crucial for major powers statesmanship. The common policy ground lay in prioritizing the transformational over the transactional. Conventional diplomacy posits the latter as dependent on the former: we can only have a new relationship if we first fully resolve the specific issues between us. Yet those very issues may become more resolvable, the transactions more open to compromise, if the overall relationship at least begins to be transformed and the domestic politics are effectively managed. This is how U.S.-China relations were opened, how the Cold War ended, and how renewed breakthroughs could be achieved in U.S.-China and U.S.-Russia relations. While the depth of the Kissinger-Zhou relationship and the genuine affection of the Gorbachev-Reagan relationship are unlikely among the major power leaders today, personal relations that build trust and mutuality remain a critical element.

Hammarskjöld proved the UN secretary-generalship did not have to be the "most impossible job in the world." He did so by stressing the authority inherent in the UN Charter for the secretary-general to initiate his own statesmanship, not just carry out the wishes of the Security Council P5. But he was unable to institutionalize a strong secretary-general role. The P5 ensured that successors would be more compliant. That protected P5 prerogatives. It also contributed to the UN's ineffectiveness. While the agenda for UN reform is long and cuts deep, unless there is strong leadership at the top, little else is likely to happen. The world, including the major powers, needs a Hammarskjöldian secretary-general for the UN to do for international peace and security what only the UN can do.

The politics of identity were precarious even in our cases in which there was significant reconciliation. The accolades about Mandela's extraordinary leadership, while richly deserved, implicitly acknowledge how unusual it is to have a leader of his nature and caliber. Rabin made the crucial breakthrough of validating that peace with the Palestinians was in Israel's interest, but by not abiding by the leadership tenets of "controlling the temperature" and "keeping the opposition close," he paid the ultimate price. Williams and Corrigan succeeded in catalyzing the end of The Troubles and bringing violence way down, but it still took more than 20 years to get the Good Friday Agreement; political tensions still remain another 20 years later. With identity driving so many twenty-first-century conflicts, ones that already have resorted to mass violence and ones that ominously raise that potential, reconciliatory statesmanship is essential. It has to start with leaders from within the parties to the conflicts, with support from the international community both instrumentally and inspirationally and with the overarching goal of "enlarging of that sense of We."

The main impetus for advancing freedom and democracy also has to come internally. The vision these leaders provide needs to combine the universal and the particular with values and practices that hold true for all peoples and ones rooted in their respective nations' history and culture. With Gandhi it was anticolonialism and *satyagraha*, with Walesa it was democracy and the Catholic Church, and with Aung San Suu Kyi it was democracy and Buddhism. The pattern of being much more effective in leading political transformation from the old order than in establishing political institutionalization of a new order is striking—especially so in the case of Aung San Suu Kyi's leadership. As to the international community, its role is one of amplification and insurance against internal repressive efforts to muffle the opposition, or worse, and then to provide support for institutionalization. While NGOs such as Amnesty International and the broader human rights movement cannot on their own change policy, they can catalyze governments and international institutions to act, often having more will to do so than officials with competing priorities and interests.

Global sustainability is the policy area that most requires the long view. That may be the hardest challenge in politics. The concern sustainable development emphasizes is about the world we leave for future generations: But I've got that next election to worry about. Climate change? What happens in 2050 is someone else's problem. Preventing the next pandemic? My inbox is full with more immediate issues, health and other. This is why it's been principally leaders outside formal political institutions, like the Brundtland Commission as an independent body and the Bill and Melinda Gates Foundation and its philanthropy statesmanship, that have been playing such important roles. It's why Al Gore has had more impact on climate change through his documentaries and activist training institute than in public office. It's why the private sector, increasingly convinced that what's good for the environment can also be good for the economy, is becoming more engaged, including the "We Are Still In" pledge by over 1,600 U.S. businesses and investors to abide by the Paris agreement even though President Trump officially pulled the United States out. The increasing realization that global health issues are "at the core of the development agenda . . . the key to poverty reduction," as Brundtland put it, has helped break out of issue stovepiping. The Ebola and Zika pandemics prompted some increase in attention and resources for pandemic prevention, not just reaction. But if we are to avoid the EMD and DMD threats, global sustainability needs to receive far greater commitment and priority.

The challenge of peacemaking has always been there. In every era. In every area of societal life. In every country. No question that it has been and continues to be difficult. But it has been and continues to be possible. And it has been and continues to be necessary. I hesitate to lapse into the "now more than ever" refrain. Suffice it to claim *as much as ever*. In drawing lessons from twentieth-century statesmanship for our twenty-first-century global challenges, I hope to have contributed to motivating and shaping the breakthroughs our era so greatly needs.

ACKNOWLEDGMENTS

At times it's been tempting not to finish this book. The stories for the most part are positive ones. The profiles are of largely admirable leaders. Compared to other work I do on issues like peace in the Middle East and genocide prevention, being immersed in researching and writing *The Peacemakers* has had its mental health benefits.

But finish it I have. I do so with the hope that the book will inspire readers, inform students, engage scholarly colleagues, and convey leadership lessons for twenty-first-century statesmanship.

And I do so with enormous thanks to so many who have contributed to the book.

My agent, Laura Yorke, and the team at the Carol Mann Agency helped to sharpen my approach, develop the proposal for the book, bring it to contract, and provided support and advice along the way. At W. W. Norton, Brendan Curry provided his insightful editing touch, especially his ideas for structuring the flow of the book. Nat Dennett has skillfully helped to manage the process, especially the final stages of manuscript preparation. If you're reading this book, it may be because of the publicity Rachel Salzman has helped to generate.

Special thanks go to the Woodrow Wilson International Center for Scholars and President Jane Harman, Rob Litwak, and Andrew Selee for Distinguished Scholar fellowship support, as well as to the many colleagues with whom I shared my residence, and also Janet Spikes, Kim Conner, and other supportive Wilson Center staff. I also was fortunate to hold the 2015–2016 Henry A. Kissinger Chair at the John W. Kluge Center at the Library of Congress. My thanks to Kluge Center Directors Jane McAuliffe, Bob Gallucci, and Ted Widmer and their staff and to many Kluge colleagues, including Marie Arana, Nathaniel Comfort, Mary Dudziak, David Hollenbach, and John Sexton. Thanks also to the Australia National University School of Politics and International Affairs and John Ravenhill, its director at the time, for hosting me as a Visiting Research Fellow. As valuable as these opportunities were, it's been Duke University and the Sanford School of Public Policy that have provided continued support and collegiality.

Thanks also to colleagues who were part of my presentations at the Wilson Center, Kluge Center, Australia National University, and Duke as well as the University of Virginia, University of Melbourne, Munk School of Global Affairs at the University of Toronto, Truman National Security Project, Congressional Research Service Foreign Affairs Division, University of Texas-Austin Summer Seminar in History and Statecraft, and various panels at the annual conferences of the American Political Science Association and the International Studies Association.

Much gratitude goes to colleagues whose expertise I have tapped: Alma Blount, Hal Brands, Dan Byman, Barbara Crossette, Frank Gavin, Jim Goldgeier, Joshua Goldstein, Lisa Morjé Howard, Michael Ignatieff, Will Inboden, James Joseph, Margaret Karns, Judith Kelley, Nan Keohane, Jonathan Kirshner, Joe Klaits, Anirudh Krishna, Fritz Mayer, Simon Miles, Joe Nye, Adam Roberts, Joel Rosenthal, Anne-Marie Slaughter, Patrick Smith, Jim Steinberg, Jordan Tama, Dominic Tierney, Steve Weber, and David West.

I've had one hardworking Duke research assistant after another. Jimmy Soni and Rachel Wald helped in the early stages; Danielle French has been here for these final stages; and along the way help has come from Chris Brown, Jenna Karp, Arden Kreeger, Breno de

Lima Maciel, Anand Raghuraman, and Aneesha Sehgal. Thanks also to my RAs while at the Wilson Center, Kimberly Hess and Savannah Schwing.

I was fortunate as a student, undergraduate and graduate, to have learned from such extraordinary teacher-scholars as Cornell's Peter Katzenstein, Walter LaFeber, and the late Theodore Lowi and Bud Kenworthy. And as I say at the start of the book, it was my own students who got me thinking.

I've been blessed with a wonderful family: Adam and Kate, tiny ones when I wrote my first book and now young adults with their own dynamic careers and fabulous families, their spouses Britt and Matt, and their children Danny and Mabel. Along with all the joys they all bring, I've had the added bonus of bouncing ideas and running my writing by a savvy political and communications strategist, a path-breaking museum curator, and two accomplished journalists. Let's just say quite a bit got sent to the cutting room floor, no doubt to the benefit of the reader.

Among the many things that made Lori such a great sister for me was that she was never shy about telling her older brother what she thought, good and bad, always in her own special loving way. We miss her terribly, as does her wonderful wife, Diane.

It's to Barbara Ann that I dedicate the book. I've been feeling a lot lately that there's no more meaningful word in the English language than "We." We experienced this. We worked through that. We persevered, we celebrated. We climbed that next hill, we enjoyed that next lush grove. We started, raised, and continue to nurture a family. We are proud of so much. Along with your own wonderful and deeply impactful career, this book—and so much else—would not have been possible without you.

NOTES

PREFACE:
MY STUDENTS GOT ME THINKING

xiii **On Gorbachev:** Archie Brown, *The Gorbachev Factor* (Oxford: Oxford University Press, 1996), 230; Margaret Thatcher, *The Downing Street Years* (New York: HarperCollins, 1993), 461.

xiv **Mandela exceeded the myth:** Interview with Ambassador James A. Joseph, September 11, 2006, Durham, North Carolina, conducted by research assistant Rachel Wald.

xiv **Isaiah Berlin quote:** Isaiah Berlin and Ramin Jahanbegloo, *Conversations with Isaiah Berlin* (New York: Charles Scribner's Sons, 1991), 34.

xv **Weak leadership:** Thomas Friedman, "Hard Lines, Red Lines and Green Lines," *New York Times*, September 22, 2012, http://www.nytimes.com/2012/09/23/opinion/sunday/friedman-hard-lines-red-lines-and-green-lines.html?mcubz=0.

INTRODUCTION:
DOES HISTORY MAKE STATESMEN OR DO STATESMEN MAKE HISTORY?

xvii **Carlyle, Spencer, Hook quotes:** Barbara Kellerman, ed., *Political Leadership: A Source Book* (Pittsburgh: University of Pittsburgh Press, 1986), 5, 10, 12, 25.

xviii **Notable exceptions:** For example, Elizabeth N. Saunders, *Leaders at War: How Presidents Shape Military Interventions* (Ithaca, NY: Cornell University Press, 2011); Barbara Kellerman, *The End of Leadership* (New York: Harper-Collins, 2012); Michael C. Horowitz, Allan C. Stam, and Cali M. Ellis, *Why Leaders Fight* (New York: Cambridge University Press, 2015); James M. Goldgeier, *Leadership Style and Soviet Foreign Policy: Stalin, Khrushchev, Brezh-*

nev, Gorbachev (Baltimore: Johns Hopkins University Press, 1994); Giacomo Chiozza and Hein Goemans, *Leaders and International Conflict* (Cambridge: Cambridge University Press, 2011); Keren Yarhi-Milo, *Knowing the Adversary: Leaders, Intelligence and Assessment of Intentions in International Relations* (Princeton, NJ: Princeton University Press, 2014).

xviii **Constraints, conducive conditions, choices:** In the more complex language of scholarly discourse, this is akin to "critical junctures," defined as "moments of relative structural indeterminism" (i.e., conducive conditions more than constraints) "when willful actors shape outcomes . . . these *choices* demonstrate the power of agency" (emphasis added); Giovanni Capoccia and R. Daniel Kelemen, "The Study of Critical Junctures: Theory, Narrative and Counterfactuals in Historical Institutionalism," *World Politics* 59, no. 3 (2007): 347.

xviii **"bad guy" leaders, Stalin:** Daniel L. Byman and Kenneth M. Pollack, "Let Us Now Praise Great Men: Bringing the Statesman Back In," *International Security* 25, no. 4 (Spring 2001): 107–146; David A. Bell, "Donald Trump Is Making the Great Man Theory of History Great Again," January 17, 2017, http://foreignpolicy.com/2017/01/12/donald-trump-is-making-the-great-man-theory-of-history-great-again/?utm_source=Sailthru&utm_medium=email&utm_campaign=New%20Campaign&utm_term=Flashpoints.

xviii **Burns, Nye:** James MacGregor Burns, *Leadership* (New York: Harper & Row, 1978) and *Transforming Leadership: A New Pursuit of Happiness* (New York: Atlantic Monthly Press, 2003); Joseph S. Nye, Jr., *Presidential Leadership and the Creation of the American Era* (Princeton, NJ: Princeton University Press, 2013) and *The Powers to Lead* (Oxford: Oxford University Press, 2008).

xix **Statesmanship Moneyball:** I adapt this from Gautam Mukunda, *Indispensable: When Leaders Really Matter* (Boston: Harvard Business Review Press, 2012), 6, along with a hearty dose of my love of baseball.

xix **Actor indispensability:** Fred I. Greenstein, *Personality and Politics: Problems of Evidence, Inference, and Conceptualization* (Chicago: Markham, 1971), 54.

xx **Twentieth-century leaders:** Writing in 1910 and working with similar criteria, Andrew Dickson White, historian and first president of Cornell University, identifies seven great statesmen who were not just interested in "winning a brief popular fame . . . but serving the great interests of modern states and, indeed, of universal humanity"; Andrew Dickson White, *Seven Great Statesmen: In the Warfare of Humanity with Unreason* (New York: Century, 1910), ix.

xxii **Observed and least understood phenomena, definition, elusive quality:** Burns, *Leadership,* 2; Howard Gardner, "Leadership: A Cognitive Perspective," *SAIS Review* 16, no. 2 (Summer–Fall 1996), https://muse.jhu.edu/article/30318; Walter Isaacson, ed., *Profiles in Leadership: Historians on the*

Elusive Quality of Greatness (New York: W. W. Norton, 2010); Kellerman, *End of Leadership*, xxi; Gabriel Sheffer, ed., *Innovative Leaders in International Politics* (Albany: State University of New York Press, 1993), viii.

xxiii **Leadership programs:** Tom Fox, "A Reading List to Strengthen Your Leadership Chops," January 21, 2016, https://www.washingtonpost.com/news/on-leadership/wp/2016/01/21/a-reading-list-for-strengthening-your-leadership-chops/?postshare=201453477632838&tid=ss_mail; George R. Goethals and Georgia L. J. Sorensen, eds., *The Quest for a General Theory of Leadership* (Cheltenham, UK: Edward Elgar, 2006), 12–13; Gordon Curphy, *Chief Learning Officer*, "The Problem with Leadership Development," May 22, 2014, http://www.clomedia.com/2014/05/22/the-problem-with-leadership-development.

xxiv **"rootage, leafage":** A. Scott Berg, *Wilson* (New York: G. P. Putnam's Sons, 2013), 49.

xxiv **"higher the position held":** Margaret G. Hermann, "Introduction: A Statement of Issues," in Margaret Hermann, with Thomas W. Milburn, eds., *A Psychological Examination of Political Leaders* (New York: Free Press, 1977), 20.

xxiv **"talismans":** Cited in "American Idols," *New York*, December 9, 2012, from Dixon Wecter, *The Hero in America: A Chronicle of Hero-Worship* (New York: Scribner, 1941).

xxiv **No perfect people:** Jonathan Tepperman makes the same point that in the leaders he studies "few were clearly marked for greatness at the start": *The Fix: How Nations Survive and Thrive in a World in Decline* (New York: Bloomsbury Press, 2016), Kindle Location 4187.

xxiv **Political psychology research:** Hermann, *A Psychological Examination of Political Leaders*; Jerrold Post, "Psychobiography: 'The Child Is the Father of the Man'," in Leonie Huddy, David O. Sears, and Jack S. Levy, eds., *The Oxford Handbook of Political Psychology* (Oxford: Oxford University Press, 2013).

xxiv **"There is no one recipe":** Isaacson, *Profiles in Leadership*, 11.

xxiv **all-of-these list, five-factor model:** Timothy Judge, "Personality and Leadership: A Qualitative and Quantitative Review," *Journal of Applied Psychology* 87, no. 4 (August 2002); Archie Brown, *The Myth of the Strong Leader: Political Leadership in Modern Politics* (New York: Basic Books, 2014), 1–2.

xxv **Personal capital, charisma:** On social capital, see Robert Putnam, *Bowling Alone: The Collapse and Revival of American Community* (New York: Simon and Schuster, 2000), and Anirudh Krishna, *Active Social Capital: Tracing the Roots of Development and Democracy* (New York: Columbia University Press, 2002). On moral capital, see John Kane, *The Politics of Moral Capital* (Cambridge: Cambridge University Press, 2001). On charisma, see Ann Ruth Willner, *The Spellbinders: Charismatic Political Leadership* (New Haven, CT: Yale University Press, 1984), and Micha Popper and Omri Castelnovo, "The Function of Myths about Great Leaders in Human Culture: A Cultural Evolutionary

Perspective," *Leadership* (August 2017), http://journals.sagepub.com/doi/abs/10.1177/1742715017720309.

xxv **Devise the right combination:** Nannerl O. Keohane, *Thinking about Leadership* (Princeton, NJ: Princeton University Press, 2010), 25–26.

xxv **Prior experience:** Saunders, *Leaders at War.*

xxv **"emotional intelligence":** Daniel Goleman, *Emotional Intelligence* (New York: Bantam Books, 2005).

xxvi **Narratives:** Thomas E. Cronin and Michael A. Genovese, *Leadership Matters: Unleashing the Power of Paradox* (Boulder, CO: Paradigm, 2012), 12. See also Frederick W. Mayer, *Narrative Politics: Stories and Collective Action* (New York: Oxford University Press, 2014); Ronald R. Krebs, *Narrative and the Making of U.S. National Security* (New York: Cambridge University Press, 2015).

xxvi **"navigators":** Robert I. Rotberg, *Transformative Political Leadership: Making a Difference in the Developing World* (Chicago: University of Chicago Press, 2012), 21.

xxvi **"harnessing its energy":** Elizabeth D. Samet, *Leadership: Essential Writings by Our Greatest Thinkers, A Norton Anthology* (New York: W. W. Norton, 2015), 124.

xxvi **"controlling the temperature, keeping the opposition close":** Ronald A. Heifetz and Marty Linsky, *Leadership on the Line: Staying Alive through the Dangers of Leading* (Boston: Harvard Business School Press, 2002), 85, 107–108.

xxvii **Machiavelli:** Lewis Edinger, "A Preface to Studies in Political Leadership," in Sheffer, *Innovative Leaders in International Politics*, 12.

INTRODUCTION: MANAGING MAJOR POWER RIVALRIES

2 **"reviled or revered":** Niall Ferguson, *Kissinger, The Idealist: 1923–1968* (London: Allen Lane, 2015), book jacket.

2 **"admirers marvel":** William Taubman, *Gorbachev: His Life and Times* (New York: W. W. Norton, 2017), 1.

CHAPTER 1:
HENRY KISSINGER, ZHOU ENLAI, AND THE U.S.-CHINA OPENING

4 **CBS Face of Red China:** "The Face of Red China," CBS News, December 28, 1958, transcript in David M. Rubenstein Rare Book and Manuscript Library, Duke University; see also https://archive.org/details/faceofredchina.

5 **"slave society":** "The Effect of Red China Communes on the United States: Hearing Before the Subcommittee to Investigate the Administration of the Internal Security Act and Other Internal Security Laws," Hearing Before the

Subcommittee to Investigate the Administration of the Internal Security Act and Other Internal Security Laws of the Committee on the Judiciary, United States Senate (Washington, DC: United States Government Printing Office, 1959), 4, 21.

5 **"sinister monster"**: *Congressional Record* 97 (April 19, 1951), 4261.

5 **"history will record"**: George F. Kennan, *Memoirs, 1925–1950* (Boston: Little, Brown, 1967), 493.

6 **"hearts," "vibration of the sound"**: Erez Manela, *The Wilsonian Moment: Self-Determination and the International Origins of Anticolonial Nationalism* (New York: Oxford University Press, 2007), 111, 191.

7 **Hammarskjöld, Kissinger quotes:** Cited in Brian Urquhart, *Hammarskjöld* (New York: Alfred A. Knopf, 1972), 117, and Henry A. Kissinger, *White House Years* (Boston: Little, Brown, 1979), 744.

7 **Zhou's early life:** Chae-Jin Lee, *Zhou Enlai: The Early Years* (Stanford, CA: Stanford University Press, 1994), 24, 30.

8 **depended on Zhou:** Dick Wilson, *Zhou Enlai: A Biography* (New York: Viking, 1984), 66.

9 **Winning across the negotiating table:** Cited in Wilson, *Zhou,* 166.

9 **Zhou and Great Leap Forward:** Gao Wenqian, *Zhou Enlai: The Last Perfect Revolutionary* (New York: Perseus Books Group, 2007), 96.

9 **"cold sweat, daughter, rode the tiger":** Gao, *Last Perfect Revolutionary,* 134, 140; Margaret MacMillan, *Nixon and Mao: The Week That Changed the World* (New York: Random House, 2007), 42.

10 **Zhou's report:** Li Jie, "Changes in China's Domestic Situation in the 1960s and Sino-U.S. Relations," in Robert S. Ross and Jiang Changbin, eds., *Re-Examining the Cold War: U.S.-China Diplomacy* (Cambridge, MA: Harvard University Press, 2001), 308, 311.

10 **"typical middle-class German":** Walter Isaacson, *Kissinger: A Biography* (New York: Simon and Schuster, 2005), 26.

11 **Serious student:** Isaacson, *Kissinger,* 35.

11 **"cheeky request":** Isaacson, *Kissinger,* 81.

12 **Grave doubts about Nixon:** Isaacson, *Kissinger,* 127.

12 **Leak to Nixon campaign:** John A. Farrell, *Richard Nixon: The Life* (New York: Doubleday, 2017), 341.

13 **James Reston comment:** Niall Ferguson, *Kissinger: The Idealist: 1923–1968* (London: Allen Lane, 2015), 857.

13 **Dysfunctional bureaucracy:** Henry A. Kissinger, *Nuclear Weapons and Foreign Policy* (New York: W. W. Norton, 1969), 407. See also Robert Litwak, *Detente and the Nixon Doctrine: American Foreign Policy and the Pursuit of Stability, 1969–1976* (New York: Cambridge University Press, 1984), 64–73; John Lewis Gaddis, *Strategies of Containment: A Critical Appraisal of Postwar*

American National Security Policy (New York: Oxford University Press, 1982), 299–305.

13   **Metternich:** Henry A. Kissinger, *A World Restored: Metternich, Castlereagh and the Problems of Peace, 1812–1822* (New York: Mariner Books, 1973), 319.

14   **"Political multipolarity," Rockefeller speech, "hold cards":** Henry A. Kissinger, "Central Issues of American Foreign Policy," in Kermit Gordon, ed., *Agenda for the Nation* (Washington, DC: Brookings Institution, 1968), 588–589; Kissinger, *White House Years*, 165; MacMillan, *Nixon and Mao*, 289–290.

14   **"judge other countries":** U.S. Department of State, Office of the Historian, *Foreign Relations of the United States, 1969–1976, Volume 1, Foundations of Foreign Policy, 1969–1972*, White House Background Press Briefing by the President's Assistant for National Security Affairs, December 18, 1969, https://history .state.gov/historicaldocuments/frus1969-76v01/d47.

14   **Bismarck:** Isaacson, *Kissinger*, 108.

14   **"dead weight":** Kissinger, *White House Years*, 165.

16   **"get ready for war":** William Kirby, Robert S. Ross, and Gong Li, eds., *Normalization of U.S.-China Relations: An International History* (Cambridge, MA: Harvard University Press, 2005), 151.

16   **Zhou study of international strategic situation:** Zhang Baija, "The Changing International Scene and Chinese Policy Towards the United States, 1954–1970," in Ross and Jiang, *Re-Examining the Cold War*, 70–71.

16   **ideologist in Zhou:** Yafeng Xia, *Negotiating with the Enemy: U.S.-China Talks during the Cold War, 1949–1972* (Bloomington: Indiana University Press, 2006), 156.

17   **"longest continual talks":** Kissinger, *White House Years*, 684.

17   *People's Daily*: Front page of *People's Daily*, translation of Richard Nixon's Inaugural Address, January 28, 1969, Library of Congress, National Security Archive, http://nsarchive.gwu.edu/NSAEBB/NSAEBB145/; Stephen E. Ambrose, *Nixon, The Triumph of a Politician, 1962–1972* (New York: Simon and Schuster, 1989), 253.

18   **Nixon 1970 foreign policy report, Zhou response:** President Richard M. Nixon, *First Annual Report to the Congress on United States Foreign Policy for the 1970s*, February 18, 1970, in Gerhard Peters and John Wolley, eds., *The American Presidency Project*, UC Santa Barbara, http://www.presidency.ucsb.edu/ ws/?pid=2835; Xia, *Negotiating with the Enemy*, 146–147.

18   **Intricate minuet, handwritten note:** Kissinger, *White House Years*, 187, 701.

19   **Ping-Pong diplomacy:** Nicholas Griffin, *Ping-Pong Diplomacy: The Secret History Behind the Game That Changed the World* (New York: Scribner, 2014), 202, 220.

20   **Zhou message:** Message from Premier Chou En Lai [*sic*] dated April 21, 1971, delivered to Dr. Kissinger 6:15 p.m., April 21, http://nsarchive.gwu.edu/ NSAEBB/NSAEBB145/06.pdf.

20   **Kissinger-Zhou first meeting:** The quotes that follow are drawn from the
      Memorandum of Conversation between Kissinger and Zhou, 9 July 1971, 4:35–
      11:20 p.m., with cover memo to Kissinger from Winston Lord, July 29, 1971,
      http://nsarchive.gwu.edu/NSAEBB/NSAEBB145/09.pdf; also Kissinger,
      White House Years, passim.

20   **Kissinger-Zhou October meetings:** U.S. State Department, Office of the
      Historian, *Foreign Relations of the United States, 1969–1976, Volume 17, China
      1969–1972*, Documents 161–165, https://history.state.gov/historicaldocuments/
      frus1969-76v17/ch4.

22   **"Come back soon, old friend":** Wilson, *Zhou*, 279; Marvin Kalb, *Kissinger*
      (Boston: Little Brown, 1974), 267.

22   **"settlement of fundamental questions":** Memorandum of Kissinger-Zhou
      Conversation, July 9, 1971.

22   **"PRC poses no significant threat":** Memorandum of Kissinger-Zhou Con-
      versation, July 9, 1971.

23   **Zhou's handwritten remarks:** Xia, *Negotiating with the Enemy*, 165.

23   **Shanghai Communiqué:** Joint Statement Following Discussions with Lead-
      ers of the People's Republic of China, February 27, 1972, Department of
      State, Office of the Historian, *Foreign Relations of the United States, 1969–1976,
      Volume 17, China 1969–1972*, https://history.state.gov/historicaldocuments/
      frus1969-76v17/d203.

24   **Zhou on Taiwan:** Memorandum of Kissinger-Zhou Conversation, July 9, 1971.

25   **Intelligence to China on Soviets:** The intelligence shared with the Chinese
      about the Soviets was, according to some accounts, quite extensive: William
      Burr, ed., *The Kissinger Transcripts: The Top-Secret Talks with Beijing and Mos-
      cow* (New York: New Press, 1999).

25   **"much unasked for advice":** Memorandum of Kissinger-Zhou Conversation,
      October 8, 1971.

26   **Revolutionary peoples, reactionary group:** John Garver, *China's Deci-
      sion for Rapprochement with the United States* (Boulder, CO: Westview Press,
      1982), 128; Memorandum of Conversation, President Nixon and Chairman
      Mao, February 21, 1972, USC US-China Institute, http://china.usc.edu/
      mao-zedong-meets-richard-nixon-february-21-1972.

27   **Secretary of State Rogers:** Kissinger, *White House Years*, 720, notes that,
      given that Secretary Rogers didn't know about the secret negotiations, these
      remarks were somewhat understandable, but this "did not diminish the
      impact."

27   **Agnew, Rose Mary Woods:** Jules Witcover, *Very Strange Bedfellows: The Short
      and Unhappy Marriage of Richard Nixon and Spiro Agnew* (New York: Public
      Affairs, 2007), 165; MacMillan, *Nixon and Mao*, 316.

27   **William Buckley:** Lee Edwards, *William F. Buckley Jr.: The Maker of a Move-
      ment* (Wilmington, DE: ISI Books, 2010), 115–116.

28   **Mao-Nixon:** USC US-China Institute, Mao-Nixon Conversation, February 21, 1972.

28   **"confirming what had already been negotiated":** MacMillan, *Nixon and Mao*, xvii.

28   **"no assurance that it would work out":** Cited in Gary J. Bass, *The Blood Telegram: Nixon, Kissinger and a Forgotten Crusade* (New York: Alfred A. Knopf, 2013), 145.

28   **Shanghai Communiqué:** "Joint Statement Following Discussions with Leaders of the People's Republic of China," February 27, 1972, https://history.state.gov/historicaldocuments/frus1969-76v17/d203.

29   **Zhou's toast:** "Toasts of the President and Premier Chou En-lai of the People's Republic of China at a Banquet Honoring the President in Peking," February 21, 1972, Peters and Wolley, *American Presidency Project*, http://www.presidency.ucsb.edu/ws/?pid=3748.

CHAPTER 2:
MIKHAIL GORBACHEV: ENDING THE COLD WAR

31   **Opening quotes:** Archie Brown, *The Gorbachev Factor* (Oxford: Oxford University Press, 1996), 317; Robert G. Kaiser, *Why Gorbachev Happened: His Triumphs and His Failure* (New York: Simon and Schuster, 1991), 12.

31   *Repentance:* Dusko Doder and Louise Branson, *Gorbachev: Heretic in the Kremlin* (New York: Viking, 1990), 3.

32   **"disgusting":** Brown, *The Gorbachev Factor*, 1996, 36.

32   **"rural banter":** Doder and Branson, *Gorbachev: Heretic in the Kremlin*, 31.

32   **"honest and unpretentious man":** Kaiser, *Why Gorbachev Happened*, 41.

33   **"question haunted me":** Mikhail Gorbachev, *Memoirs* (New York: Doubleday, 1995), 102–103.

33   **"He was smart":** Kaiser, *Why Gorbachev Happened*, 61.

34   **Margaret Thatcher on Gorbachev:** Margaret Thatcher, *The Downing Street Years* (New York: HarperCollins, 1993), 461.

35   **Gromyko nominating speech:** Central Intelligence Agency, "Memorandum: Gorbachev's Opening Gambit" (with Gromyko Nominating Speech as Attachment), September 9, 1985, https://www.cia.gov/library/readingroom/docs/CIA-RDP08S01787R000100030011-8.pdf.

35   **"How did Gorbachev become Gorbachev":** William Taubman, *Gorbachev: His Life and Times* (New York: Simon and Schuster, 2017), 1, 2, 5.

35   **"spell of Gorbachev's personal charm":** Archie Brown, *Myth of the Strong Leader: Political Leadership in the Modern Age* (New York: Basic Books, 2014), 172.

35   **Sagdeev's observations:** Roald Z. Sagdeev, *The Making of a Soviet Scientist* (New York: John Wiley and Sons, 1994), 272.

36   **Gorbachev's Czech friend:** Gail Sheehy, *The Man Who Changed the World: The Lives of Mikhail S. Gorbachev* (New York: HarperCollins, 1991), 76.

36   **New Thinking:** Mikhail Gorbachev, *Perestroika: New Thinking for Our Country and the World* (New York: Harper and Row, 1987), 21, 25, 44.

36   **"Wide, prompt and frank information":** Cited in Kaiser, *Why Gorbachev Happened,* 78.

37   **"You can return to Moscow":** Andrei Sakharov, *Memoirs* (New York: Knopf, 1991), 615.

37   **"economic and military might":** Brown, *The Gorbachev Factor,* 229.

37   **Andropov quote:** Anatoly Dobrynin, *In Confidence: Moscow's Ambassador to America's Six Cold War Presidents* (New York: Times Books, 1995), 511–512.

37   **"perestroika":** Cited in Janice Gross Stein, "Political Learning by Doing: Gorbachev as Uncommitted Thinker and Motivated Learner," in Richard Ned Lebow and Thomas Risse-Kappen, eds., *International Relations Theory and the End of the Cold War* (New York: Columbia University Press, 1995), 243.

38   **Gorbachev worldview:** Gorbachev, *Perestroika,* 11.

38   **Reagan speech quotes:** "Address to Members of the British Parliament," June 6, 1982, in Gerhard Peters and John Wolley, eds., *The American Presidency Project,* UC Santa Barbara, http://www.presidency.ucsb.edu/ws/index.php?pid=42614&st=British+Parliament&st1=, and "Remarks to the Annual Convention of the National Association of Evangelicals," American Presidency Project, http://www.presidency.ucsb.edu/ws/index.php?pid=41023&st=National+association+of+evangelicals&st1=.

39   **Secretary of State Shultz:** George P. Shultz, *Turmoil and Triumph: My Years as Secretary of State* (New York: Charles Scribner's Sons, 1993), 5.

39   **Able Archer:** President's Foreign Intelligence Advisory Board, The Soviet "War Scare," February 15, 1990, https://assets.documentcloud.org/documents/2484214/read-the-u-s-assessment-that-concluded-the.pdf; for a different interpretation, see Simon Miles, "The War Scare That Wasn't: Able Archer and the Myths of the Second Cold War" (unpublished manuscript).

39   **"Bear in the Woods":** Ronald Reagan TV Ad, "The Bear in the Woods," 1984, YouTube, https://www.youtube.com/watch?v=NpwdcmjBgNA.

39   **CIA report:** David E. Hoffman, *The Dead Hand: The Untold Story of the Cold War Arms Race and Its Dangerous Legacy* (New York: Anchor Books, 2009), 191.

39   **Gorbachev needed courage:** Brown, *The Gorbachev Factor,* 228.

40   **Gorbachev and Reagan quotes:** Kaiser, *Why Gorbachev Happened,* 119–120.

41   **"armed with a surprise":** James M. Goldgeier, *Leadership Style and Soviet Foreign Policy: Stalin, Khrushchev, Brezhnev, Gorbachev* (Baltimore: Johns Hopkins University Press, 1994), 111.

41   **Reagan and Gorbachev quotes:** Hoffman, *The Dead Hand,* 266–268.

42   **Akhromeyev quote:** Hoffman, *The Dead Hand,* 271.

42   *Krasnaya Zvezda* quote: Kaiser, *Why Gorbachev Happened*, 120.

42   **Perle, Shultz quotes:** Hoffman, *The Dead Hand*, 240.

43   **Gates quote:** Central Intelligence Agency, Director of Central Intelligence, National Intelligence Estimate, "Whither Gorbachev: Soviet Politics and Policy in the 1990s," November 1987, https://www.cia.gov/library/readingroom/docs/DOC_0000518059.pdf.

43   **Reagan quotes:** Stanley Meisler, "Reagan Recants 'Evil Empire' Description," *Los Angeles Times*, June 1, 1988, http://articles.latimes.com/1988-06-01/news/mn-3667_1_evil-empire; Don Oberdorfer, *From the Cold War to a New Era: The United States and the Soviet Union, 1983–1990* (Baltimore: Johns Hopkins University Press, 1991), 307.

44   **Rice, Baker quotes:** Condoleezza Rice, *No Higher Honor: A Memoir of My Years in Washington* (New York: Simon and Schuster, 2011), 23; James A. Baker III, *The Politics of Diplomacy: Revolution, War and Peace, 1989–1992* (New York: G. P. Putnam's Sons, 1995), 68.

44   **Matlock, Chernyaev books:** Jack F. Matlock, Jr., *Reagan and Gorbachev: How the Cold War Ended* (New York: Random House, 2004); Anatoly Chernyaev, *My Six Years with Gorbachev* (University Park: Pennsylvania State University Press, 2000).

45   **"reflection of current political thinking":** Sarah E. Mendelson, *Changing Course: Ideas, Politics and the Soviet Withdrawal from Afghanistan* (Princeton, NJ: Princeton University Press, 1998), 117.

45   **"International duty":** Chernyaev, *My Six Years with Gorbachev*, 42.

46   **"mixed bag at best":** Mendelson, *Changing Course*, 98.

46   **Gorbachev to Mlynar:** Brown, *The Gorbachev Factor*, 41.

46   **much harder to keep pushing glasnost:** Goldgeier, *Leadership Style and Soviet Foreign Policy*, 97.

47   **Tass quote:** Oberdorfer, *The Turn*, 364.

47   **Bush:** Oberdorfer, *The Turn*, 364.

47   **"Course of events":** Gorbachev, *Memoirs*, 516.

49   **Shevardnadze statement:** Baker, *Politics of Diplomacy*, 2.

50   **"We are Europeans":** Anthony D'Agostino, *Gorbachev's Revolution* (New York: New York University Press, 1998), 139–140.

50   **Thatcher:** Brown, *The Gorbachev Factor*, 243.

50   **New dialectics:** Gorbachev, *Perestroika*, 137.

50   **Shultz quote, Gorbachev quotes:** Shultz, *Turmoil and Triumph*, 1013; Gorbachev, *Memoirs*, 449; Gorbachev, *Perestroika*, 137.

51   **"as remarkable as any ever delivered at the UN":** Robert G. Kaiser, "An Offer to Scrap the Postwar Rules," *Washington Post*, December 8, 1988, A1.

53   **"when they woke me up":** Hoffman, *Dead Hand*, 360.

53   **Opinion polls:** Brown, *The Gorbachev Factor*, 271.

54 **On Gorbachev:** Brown, *The Gorbachev Factor*, 230; Taubman, *Gorbachev: Life and Times*, 1.

54 **"If we begin to make concessions":** Hal Brands, *What Good Is Grand Strategy? Power and Purpose in American Statecraft from Harry S. Truman to George W. Bush* (Ithaca, NY: Cornell University Press, 2014), 123.

55 **Evangelista quote:** Matthew Evangelista, *Unarmed Forces: The Transnational Movement to End the Cold War* (Ithaca, NY: Cornell University Press, 2002).

56 **Kennan:** Mr. "X," "The Sources of Soviet Conduct," *Foreign Affairs* (July 1947).

57 **CIA analysis:** Michael McFaul, *Russia's Unfinished Revolution: Political Change from Gorbachev to Putin* (Ithaca, NY: Cornell University Press, 2001), 37.

57 **Taking on Reagan's own political supporters:** Shultz, *Turmoil and Triumph*, 778, 1007.

57 **Gorbachev on Reagan:** Gorbachev, *Memoirs*, 405.

57 **Reagan on Gorbachev:** Ronald Reagan, *An American Life* (New York: Simon and Schuster, 1990), 707.

57 **"I gave him a pat":** Robert G. Kaiser, "Gorbachev: 'We All Lost Cold War,'" *Washington Post*, June 11, 2004, A1.

58 **"indispensable agent of change":** Melvyn Leffler, *For the Soul of Mankind: The United States, the Soviet Union, and the End of the Cold War* (New York: Hill and Wang, 2007), 466.

59 **Like the Pope and Luther:** Brown, *The Gorbachev Factor*, 127. See also James Graham Wilson, *The Triumph of Improvisation: Gorbachev's Adaptability, Reagan's Engagement, and the End of the Cold War* (Ithaca, NY: Cornell University Press, 2014).

59 **Leadership as dangerous activity:** Ronald A. Heifetz and Marty Linsky, *Leadership on the Line: Staying Alive through Dangers of Leading* (Boston: Harvard Business School Press, 2002), 11–12.

60 **Warnings to Gorbachev:** Jack Matlock, *Autopsy of an Empire: The American Ambassador's Account of the Collapse of the Soviet Union* (New York: Random House, 1995), 543; Chernyaev, *My Six Years with Gorbachev*, 352–355.

60 **Gorbachev farewell:** Gorbachev speech, "Dissolving the Soviet Union," Christmas 1991, http://www.publicpurpose.com/lib-gorb911225.htm.

60 **Nobel Peace Prize:** Nobel Peace Prize Ceremony, https://www.nobelprize.org/nobel_prizes/peace/laureates/1990/presentation-speech.html.

TRUMP-PUTIN, TRUMP-XI, AND MAJOR POWERS STATESMANSHIP

61 ***Destined for War:*** Graham T. Allison, *Destined for War: Can America and China Escape Thucydides's Trap?* (New York: Houghton Mifflin, 2017).

62 **Russian cyberspace proposal:** David Ignatius, "Russia Is Pushing to Control Cyberspace. We Should All Be Worried," *Washington Post*, Octo-

ber 25, 2017, https://www.washingtonpost.com/opinions/global-opinions/
russia-is-pushing-to-control-cyberspace-we-should-all-be-worried/2017/10/24/
7014bcc6-b8f1-11e7-be94-fabb0f1e9ffb_story.html?utm_term=
.c66ee1a74993.

62   **"The Putin Files"**: PBS, "The Putin Files," http://www.pbs.org/wgbh/
      frontline/interview-collection/the-putin-files/.

62   **GDP data:** FocusEconomics, "Economic Forecasts from the World's Leading
      Economists," http://www.focus-economics.com/countries/russia.

63   **Putin open to collaboration, "limits of partnership":** Fiona Hill and Clifford
      G. Gaddy, *Mr. Putin* (Washington, DC: Brookings Institution Press, 2015),
      394; Angela E. Stent, *The Limits of Partnership: U.S.-Russian Relations in the
      Twenty-First Century* (Princeton, NJ: Princeton University Press, 2015).

63   **Putin's approval rating:** Levada Center, "Indicators: Putin's Approval Rat-
      ing," https://www.levada.ru/en/ratings/.

63   **reports of Russian casualties in Syria:** Neil Hauer, "Putin Has a
      Secret Weapon in Syria: Chechens," May 4, 2017, http://foreignpolicy.
      com/2017/05/04/putin-has-a-new-secret-weapon-in-syria-chechens/.

63   **Those in the middle class:** Stephen Sestanovich, "The Two Putins," *New York
      Times,* November 25, 2016, https://www.nytimes.com/2016/11/25/opinion/
      sunday/the-two-putin-problem.html?emc=eta1&_r=0.

63   **Kissinger on U.S.-Russia relations:** "Kissinger's Vision for US-Russia Rela-
      tions," *National Interest,* February 4, 2016, http://nationalinterest.org/feature/
      kissingers-vision-us-russia-relations-15111.

64   **Democrats, Republicans on Putin, Russia:** Art Swift, "Putin's Image Rises
      in US, Mostly Among Republicans," February 21, 2017, http://www.gallup.
      com/poll/204191/putin-image-rises-mostly-among-republicans.aspx; Chi-
      cago Council on Global Affairs, "American Opinion on US-Russia Rela-
      tions, From Bad to Worse," August 2017, http://logon.thechicagocouncil.org/
      UserFiles/File/POS_Topline%20Reports/CCS2017/Russia_Brief/Topline_
      Russia_Brief_170802.pdf.

65   **"precarious crossroads":** Task Force on US-China Policy, *US-China Policy: Rec-
      ommendations for a New Administration,* Asia Society, Center on US-China Rela-
      tions, Executive Summary, http://asiasociety.org/center-us-china-relations/
      us-policy-toward-china-recommendations-new-administration.

65   **history's tense dance:** Allison, *Destined for War;* James Steinberg and Michael
      E. O'Hanlon, *Strategic Reassurance and Resolve: US-China Relations in the 21st
      Century* (Princeton, NJ: Princeton University Press, 2014); Aaron L. Friedberg,
      A Contest for Supremacy: China, America and the Struggle for Mastery in Asia
      (New York: W. W. Norton, 2011); John J. Mearsheimer, *The Tragedy of Great
      Power Politics* (New York: W. W. Norton, 2014).

67   **"becoming the strongest nation in the world":** Edward Wong, "Chinese Colo-
      nel's Views Seep into the Mainstream," *New York Times,* October 2, 2015, http://

www.nytimes.com/2015/10/03/world/asia/chinese-colonels-hard-line-views
-seep-into-the-mainstream.html; Liu Mingfu, *The China Dream: Great Power
Thinking and Strategic Posture in the Post-American Era*, http://www.amazon
.com/China-Dream-Thinking-Strategic-Post-American/dp/1627741402/ref
=sr_1_1?s=books&ie=UTF8&qid=1449077590&sr=1-1.

67 **Steve Bannon:** Mark Landler, "Next Stop for the Steve Bannon Insurgency:
China," *New York Times*, September 8, 2017, https://www.nytimes.com/
2017/09/08/us/politics/steve-bannon-china-trump.html.

67 **Chinese, American public opinion:** Richard Wike and Bruce Stokes, "Chinese Public Sees More Powerful Role in the World, Sees US as Top Threat,"
Pew Research Center, October 5, 2016, http://www.pewglobal.org/2016/10/05/
chinese-public-sees-more-powerful-role-in-world-names-u-s-as-top-threat/;
Richard Wike, "6 Facts about How Americans and Chinese See Each Other,"
Pew Research Center, March 30, 2016, http://www.pewresearch.org/fact
-tank/2016/03/30/6-facts-about-how-americans-and-chinese-see-each-other/.

68 ***Bu kaopu:*** Jane Perlez, "As Trump Unnerves Asia, China Sees an Opening,"
New York Times, August 10, 2017, https://www.nytimes.com/2017/08/10/
world/asia/north-korea-china-trump.html?_r=0.

68 **"Trump is too narcissistic":** Edward Luce, *The Retreat of Western Liberalism*
(New York: Atlantic Monthly Press, 2017), 170.

INTRODUCTION: BUILDING INTERNATIONAL INSTITUTIONS

70 **"A development unique":** Paul Kennedy, *The Parliament of Man: The Past, Present and Future of the United Nations* (New York: Random House, 2006), xiii.

70 **"international institutions":** Robert O. Keohane and Lisa Martin, "The Promise of Institutionalist Theory," *International Security* 20, no. 1 (Summer 1995): 50.

70 **"seals of approval":** Michael N. Barnett, "Bringing in the New World Order: Liberalism, Legitimacy and the United Nations," *World Politics* 49, no. 4 (July 1997): 541.

71 **"the most impossible":** Stanley Meisler, *United Nations: A History* (New York:
Grove Press, 1995), 73.

CHAPTER 3:
WILSON AND FDR: FAILURE OF THE LEAGUE OF NATIONS,
BIRTH OF THE UNITED NATIONS

72 **three core beliefs:** James David Barber, *The Presidential Character: Predicting
Performance in the White House*, 4th ed. (Englewood Cliffs, NJ: Prentice Hall,
1992), 93.

73 **political science Ph.D.:** A. Scott Berg, *Wilson* (New York: G. P. Putnam's
Sons, 2013), 95.

73   **ambitions to enter politics:** Alexander L. George and Juliette L. George, *Woodrow Wilson and Colonel House: A Personality Study* (New York: Dover Publications, 1964), 23.

73   **Not playing politics:** Berg, *Wilson*, 195.

75   **1913 inaugural speech:** Woodrow Wilson, "Inaugural Address," March 4, 1913, in Gerhard Peters and John T. Wolley, eds., *The American Presidency Project*, UC Santa Barbara, http://www.presidency.ucsb.edu/ws/index.php?pid=25832

75   **election reform bill, campaign manager:** Berg, *Wilson*, 252.

76   **"arrogant denial":** Edward C. Luck, *Mixed Messages: American Politics and International Organization: 1919–1999* (Washington, DC: Brookings Institution Press, 1999), 22.

76   **Medical:** Edwin A. Weinstein, *Woodrow Wilson: A Medical and Psychological Biography.* Supplementary volume to *The Papers of Woodrow Wilson* (Princeton, NJ: Princeton Legacy Library, 2014), 43; Barber, *Presidential Character*, 51.

76   **Wilson's racism:** Berg, *Wilson*, 309, 486.

76   **Wilson made the case:** "Wilson Accepts His Renomination," reprinted in Frances Farmer, ed., *The Wilson Reader* (New York: Oceana Publications, 1956), 129.

77   **Wilson's support for the Spanish-American War:** Erez Manela, *The Wilsonian Moment: Self-Determination and the International Origins of Anticolonial Nationalism* (Oxford: Oxford University Press, 2007), 28–29.

78   **"to elect good men":** Walter A. MacDougall, *Promised Land, Crusader State: The American Encounter with the World since 1776* (Boston: Houghton Mifflin, 1997), 131; Margaret MacMillan, *Paris 1919: Six Months That Changed the World* (New York: Random House, 2001), 9.

79   **Lodge, Lippmann:** Berg, *Wilson*, 438–439.

80   **"Every people has the right to choose":** Farmer and Wilson, *Wilson Reader*, 159–160.

80   **Outside Europe:** Manela, *Wilsonian Moment*, 41.

80   **"community of power":** "Peace Without Victory" speech, January 22, 1917, reprinted in Farmer, *Wilson Reader*, 156.

80   **ideas during his 1916 campaign:** Speech at the Willard Hotel, Washington, DC, May 27, 1916, reprinted in Farmer, *Wilson Reader*, 150–151.

81   **"indispensable instrumentality":** Barber, *Presidential Character*, 15.

82   **"like talking to Jesus Christ":** Norman A. Graebner and Edward M. Bennett, *The Versailles Treaty and Its Legacy: The Failure of the Wilsonian Vision* (New York: Cambridge University Press, 2011), 40.

83   **Poll data:** John Milton Cooper, *Breaking the Heart of the World: Woodrow Wilson and the Fight for the League of Nations* (Cambridge: Cambridge University Press, 2010), 58.

84   **"schoolmaster incarnate":** Gene Smith, *When the Cheering Stopped: The Last Years of Woodrow Wilson* (New York: Time-Life Books, 1984), 53–54.

84 **"anyone who opposes me"**: Nannerl O. Keohane, *Thinking about Leadership* (Princeton, NJ: Princeton University Press, 2010), 102 (italics in original).

84 **America's sense of mission, Pueblo speech**: Speech in Los Angeles, September 20, 1919, "Addresses of President Wilson on His Western Tour," U.S. Senate, Document 120, October 7, 1919; Pueblo speech, September 25, 1919, Voices of Democracy, http://voicesofdemocracy.umd.edu/wilson-the-pueblo -speech-speech-text/.

85 **"can always depend on Mr. Wilson"**: Cooper, *Breaking the Heart of the World*, 270.

85 **Quote from *Constitutional Government***: Woodrow Wilson, *Constitutional Government in the United States* (New York: Columbia University Press, 1961), 139–140.

85 **Senate defeat**: Cooper, *Breaking the Heart of the World*, 374.

87 **Keynes**: John Maynard Keynes, *The Economic Consequences of the Peace* (New York: Harcourt Brace Jovanovich, 1920), 211–216, and excerpts at http://www .pbs.org/wgbh/commandingheights/shared/minitextlo/ess_keynesversailles .html.

87 **"Not just wrong but wicked"**: MacMillan, *Paris 1919*, 7.

88 **"crowning act of his career"**: Stephen C. Schlesinger, *Act of Creation: The Founding of the United Nations* (Boulder, CO: Westview Press, 2003), 71–72.

89 **"folksy art of Washington politics"**: Jean Edward Smith, *FDR* (New York: Random House, 2007), 103.

91 **"Hudson River aristocrat"**: Smith, *FDR*, xii.

91 **Lessened tendency to arrogance**: Rose McDermott, *Presidential Leadership, Illness, and Decision Making* (Cambridge: Cambridge University Press, 2008), 13.

91 **"Franklin's disease"**: Shaila Dewan, "A Long-Ago Refuge Still Tends to the Needs of Polio Survivors," *New York Times*, April 30, 2005, http://www.nytimes .com/2005/04/30/us/a-longago-refuge-still-tends-to-the-needs-of-polio -survivors.html.

91 **"first-class temperament"**: Geoffrey C. Ward, *A First-Class Temperament: The Emergence of Franklin Roosevelt* (New York: Harper and Row, 1989), xiii.

92 **Lion and the Fox**: James MacGregor Burns, *Roosevelt: The Lion and the Fox* (New York: Konecky and Konecky, 1956), epigraph page.

93 **"I have read the draft"**: Smith, *FDR*, 176.

94 **"good intentions alone"**: Townsend Hoopes and Douglas Brinkley, *FDR and the Creation of the U.N.* (New Haven, CT: Yale University Press, 1997), 64, 68.

94 **Dumbarton Oaks declaration**: U.S. Department of State, Office of the Historian, *Foreign Relations of the United States: Diplomatic Papers, 1944, General, Volume I* (Washington, DC: Government Printing Office, 1966).

95 **"responsible participation," "freedom of action"**: Hoopes and Brinkley, *FDR and the Creation of the U.N.*, 86, 113.

95 **"We shall have to take responsibility"**: Franklin D. Roosevelt,

"Address to Congress on the Yalta Conference," March 1, 1945, in Peters and Wolley, *American Presidency Project*, http://www.presidency.ucsb.edu/ws/?pid=16591.

96 **public support:** Schlesinger, *Act of Creation*, 67–68.

96 **FDR to Churchill:** Henry Kissinger, *Diplomacy* (New York: Simon and Schuster, 1994), 401.

97 **Good start on the road to world peace:** Franklin D. Roosevelt, "Address to Congress on the Yalta Conference," March 1, 1945, in Peters and Wolley, *American Presidency Project*, http://www.presidency.ucsb.edu/ws/?pid=16591.

97 *Time* **magazine cover:** Hoopes and Brinkley, *FDR and the Creation of the U.N.*, 177.

98 **"buggy ride":** Steven Lomazow and Eric Fettmann, *FDR's Deadly Secret* (New York: PublicAffairs, 2011), 4.

98 **Truman:** President Harry S. Truman, "Address to the United Nations Conference in San Francisco," April 25, 1945, Peters and Wolley, *American Presidency Project*, http://www.presidency.ucsb.edu/ws/?pid=12391.

99 **"lifted himself from a wheelchair":** Smith, *FDR*, epigram.

99 **FDR's untimely death:** Frank Costigliola, *Roosevelt's Lost Alliances: How Personal Politics Helped Start the Cold War* (Princeton, NJ: Princeton University Press, 2012).

99 **Daisy Suckley diary:** Joseph Lelyveld, *His Final Battle: The Last Months of Franklin Roosevelt* (New York: Deckle Edge, 2016), 138. Lomazow and Fettmann say he "confided to Daisy on several occasions that he planned to resign the presidency in order to head the United Nations once it had been set up"; Lomazow and Fettmann, *FDR's Deadly Secret*, 3.

99 **Benjamin Cohen memo:** Lomazow and Fettmann, *FDR's Deadly Secret*, 117–118.

100 **Secretary-general active role:** Evan Luard, *A History of the United Nations: Volume 1: The Years of Western Domination, 1945–1955* (New York: St. Martin's Press, 1982), 12–13.

CHAPTER 4:

UN SECRETARY-GENERAL DAG HAMMARSKJÖLD: THE "SECULAR POPE"

101 **Opening quotes:** Henry P. Van Dusen, *Dag Hammarskjöld: The Statesman and His Faith* (New York: Harper and Row, 1964), 4; Dag Hammarskjöld, "Old Creeds in a New World," in Wilder Foote, ed., *Servant of Peace: A Selection of the Speeches and Statements of Dag Hammarskjöld* (New York: Harper and Row, 1962), 23.

102 **Edward R. Murrow interview:** Van Dusen, *Hammarskjöld: The Statesman and His Faith*, 12.

103 **"Sissy, sissy":** Kent J. Kille, *From Manager to Visionary: The Secretary-General of the United Nations* (New York: Palgrave Macmillan, 2006), 72.

103 **"did not suffer":** Brian Urquhart, *Hammarskjöld* (New York: Alfred A. Knopf, 1972), 31.

103 **"lack of close personal obligations"**: Urquhart, *Hammarskjöld*, 25–26.

103 **"quiet work of preparing the ground"**: Dag Hammarskjöld, "Introduction to the Annual Report 1956–57," in Andrew W. Cordier and Wilder Foote, eds., *Public Papers of the Secretaries General of the United Nations*, Volume 3: 1956–1957 (New York: Columbia University Press, 1973), 637.

104 **"universal organization"**: Dag Hammarskjöld, "Introduction to the Annual Report 1960–61," in Andrew W. Cordier and Wilder Foote, eds., *Public Papers of the Secretaries General of the United Nations*, Volume 5: 1960–1961 (New York: Columbia University Press, 1975), 125.

104 **"right of initiative"**: Mark W. Zacher, *Dag Hammarskjöld's United Nations* (New York: Columbia University Press, 1970), 36.

104 **"if the demand for neutrality"**: Dag Hammarskjöld, "The International Civil Servant in Law and in Fact," Lecture at University of Oxford, May 30, 1961, in Cordier and Foote, *Public Papers of the Secretaries General: 1960–1961*, 329–349.

104 **"keeping with the philosophy of the Charter"**: Dag Hammarskjöld, "Statement on Reappointment," in Cordier and Foote, *Public Papers of the Secretaries General: 1956–1957*, 665.

104 **"little more than an empty shell"**: Urquhart, *Hammarskjöld*, 18.

105 **"secular Pope"**: Roger Lipsey, *Hammarskjöld: A Life* (Ann Arbor: University of Michigan Press, 2013), 153; Kent J. Kille, "The Secular Pope: Insights on the Secretary-General and Moral Authority," in Kille, ed., *The UN Secretary-General and Moral Authority: Ethics and Religion in International Leadership* (Washington, DC: Georgetown University Press, 2007), 337–354.

105 **"dedicated professional service"**: Hammarskjöld, Oxford Lecture.

106 **Alma Myrdal**: Urquhart, *Hammarskjöld*, 64–65.

106 **"perseverance"**: Andrew W. Cordier and Wilder Foote, eds., *Public Papers of the Secretaries General of the United Nations*, Volume 2: 1953–1956 (New York: Columbia University Press, 1972), 28 (emphasis added).

107 **Hammarskjöld cable to Zhou Enlai, Zhou response**: Lipsey, *Hammarskjöld: A Life*, 211; Urquhart, *Hammarskjöld*, 103.

108 **Press conference**: "Transcript of Press Conference, Swedish Ministry of Foreign Affairs," December 17, 1954, in Cordier and Foote, *Public Papers of the Secretaries General*, Volume 2: 1953–1956, 426–433.

108 **Hammarskjöld-Zhou meeting**: Lipsey, *Hammarskjöld: A Life*, 220–221; Urquhart, *Hammarskjöld*, 112.

109 **Cable from Zhou**: Urquhart, *Hammarskjöld*, 126.

110 **Letter to brother Bo**: Lipsey, *Hammarskjöld: A Life*, 226.

110 **Diary**: Dag Hammarskjöld, *Markings* (New York: Alfred A. Knopf, 1965), 128.

112 **British Prime Minister Anthony Eden**: Lipsey, *Hammarskjöld: A Life*, 283.

112 **"As a servant of the Organization"**: "Suez Crisis" in Cordier and Foote, *Public Papers of the Secretaries General*, Volume 3: 1956–1957, 309.

115   **returned to the UN a hero:** Urquhart, *Hammarskjöld*, 194.

115   **"our supreme International Civil Servant":** Van Dusen, *Hammarskjöld: The Statesman and His Faith*, 147–148.

116   **Kasavubu, Lumumba:** Lipsey, *Hammarskjöld: A Life*, 396.

116   **"black defender of white capitalism":** Lipsey, *Hammarskjöld: A Life*, 397.

118   **Statement to Security Council:** "Opening Statement in the Security Council," August 21, 1960, in Cordier and Foote, *Public Papers of the Secretaries General*, Volume 5: 1960–1961, 101–102.

118   **dilemma of neutrality:** "Opening Statement in the Security Council," September 9, 1960, in Cordier and Foote, *Public Papers of the Secretaries General*, Volume 5: 1960–1961, 167.

118   **Dulles on Lumumba:** Odd Arne Westad, *The Global Cold War* (Cambridge: Cambridge University Press, 2007), 138.

119   **CIA station chief:** Larry Devlin, *Chief of Station, Congo: A Memoir of 1960–67* (New York: PublicAffairs, 2007), 67.

119   **"The more I considered Mobutu's plan":** Devlin, *Chief of Station*, 78.

119   **Khrushchev:** James Cockayne and David M. Malone, "Relations with the Security Council," in Simon Chesterman, ed., *Secretary or General? The UN Secretary-General in World Politics* (Cambridge: Cambridge University Press, 2007), 74.

120   **bold and full-throated defense:** "I Shall Remain in My Post—Second Statement of Reply," October 3, 1960, in Cordier and Foote, *Public Papers of the Secretaries General*, Volume 5: 1960–1961, 199–201.

121   **CIA role:** Devlin, *Chief of Station*, 94–99 and passim.

121   **"object of hatred":** Urquhart, *Hammarskjöld*, 507.

122   **Sabotage:** Susan Williams, *Who Killed Hammarskjöld? The UN, the Cold War and White Supremacy in Africa* (London: Hurst, 2011).

122   **Hammarskjöld Commission:** *Report of the Hammarskjöld Commission of Inquiry*, September 9, 2013, The Hague, http://www.hammarskjoldcommission. org/wp-content/uploads/2012/03/REPORT.pdf.

122   **2015 report:** UN News Centre, "UN Chief Urges States to Disclose Information Concerning the Death of Dag Hammarskjöld," http://www.un.org/apps/ news/story.asp?NewsID=56669#.WYHlRq3MxMU.

122   **Ban Ki-moon:** Melissa Kent, CBC News, "Dag Hammarskjöld Death Details May Still Be Sealed, UN Says," July 11, 2015, http://www.cbc.ca/news/world/ dag-hammarskjöld-death-details-may-still-be-sealed-un-says-1.3145238; Alan Cowell and Rick Gladstone, "Do Spy Agencies Hold Answer to Hammarskjöld's Death? U.N. Wants to Know," *New York Times*, July 15, 2017, https:// www.nytimes.com/2017/07/15/world/africa/dag-hammarskjold-united -nations-mohamed-chande-othman.html?_r=0.

122   **"plausible that an external attack or threat":** United Nations, "Investiga-
      tion into the Conditions and Circumstances Resulting in the Tragic Death of
      Dag Hammarskjöld and of the Members of the Party Accompanying Him,"
      September 5, 2017, https://documents-dds-ny.un.org/doc/UNDOC/GEN/
      N17/292/68/PDF/N1729268.pdf?OpenElement.

123   **Eulogies:** Kille, *From Manager to Visionary*, 67; Lipsey, *Hammarskjöld: A Life*,
      571, 576, 578.

123   **Adlai Stevenson:** Van Dusen, *Hammarskjöld: The Statesman and His Faith*, 4.

123   **Linnér meeting with JFK:** Sture Linnér and Sverker Åström, *UN Secretary-
      General Hammarskjöld: Reflections and Personal Experiences*, 2007 Dag Ham-
      marskjöld Lecture, Uppsala, Sweden, 2008, http://www.daghammarskjold.
      se/wp-content/uploads/2007/10/Dh_lecture_2007.pdf.

126   **"sound, hard realism":** Zacher, *Hammarskjöld's United Nations*, 46.

126   **"quiet but commanding personality":** Urquhart, *Hammarskjöld*, 176–177.

126   **Poem:** Hammarskjöld, *Markings*, July 6, 1961, 213.

A HAMMARSKJÖLDIAN SECRETARY-GENERAL

127   **"head waiter," not much of a splash:** James Cockayne and David M. Malone,
      "Relations with the Security Council," and James Traub, "The Secretary-
      General's Political Space," in Simon Chesterman, ed., *Secretary or General?
      The UN Secretary-General in World Politics* (Cambridge: Cambridge University
      Press, 2007), 70, 189.

127   **"sad day":** James Traub, *The Best Intentions: Kofi Annan and the United Nations
      in the Era of American Power* (New York: Farrar, Straus and Giroux, 2006), 185.

128   **Economist scoring:** "The UN Secretary-General: The Score at Half-Time,"
      Economist, June 11, 2009, http://www.economist.com/node/13825201.

128   **2016 report:** Kevin Rudd, "UN Reform Under the Trump Administration:
      The Way Ahead," *Washington Quarterly* 40, no. 1 (Spring 2017): 95–108.

128   **Antonio Guterres:** Yvonne Terlingen, "A Better Process, a Stronger Secretary-
      General: How Historic Change Was Forged and What Comes Next," *Ethics
      and International Affairs* 31, no. 2 (Summer 2017).

129   **"In no other hall, from no other platform":** Michelle Gorman and Polly Mosenz,
      "80,000 New Yorkers Watch the Pope in Central Park," *Newsweek*, Septem-
      ber 25, 2015, http://www.newsweek.com/pope-francis-central-park-376473.

130   **Oxford speech:** Dag Hammarskjöld, "The International Civil Servant in Law
      and in Fact," in Wilder Foote, ed., *Servant of Peace: A Selection of the Speeches
      and Statements of Dag Hammarskjöld* (New York: Harper and Row, 1962), 337.

132   **"A more independent U.N. leader":** Richard Gowan, "Yes Ban Ki-moon Is
      America's Poodle, and No That's Not a Good Thing," January 22, 2014, http://

www.politico.com/magazine/story/2014/01/ban-ki-moon-united-nations
-united-states-102491#ixzz3lLU3f1iE.

INTRODUCTION: RECONCILING THE POLITICS OF IDENTITY

134 *Romeo and Juliet*: Cited in Adrian Guelke, *Politics in Deeply Divided Societies* (Cambridge: Polity Press, 2012), 1.

134 **Bosnian schoolteacher quote**: Chris Hedges, "War Turns Sarajevo Away from Europe," *New York Times*, July 28, 1995, A4.

CHAPTER 5:
NELSON MANDELA: ICONIC STATESMAN OF RECONCILIATION

137 **"first white man to treat me as a human being"**: Anthony Sampson, *Mandela: The Authorized Biography* (London: HarperCollins, 1999), 34.

137 **"struggle is my life"**: Nelson Mandela, *The Struggle Is My Life* (London: Pathfinder Press, 1990), 13.

138 **"worst part of imprisonment"**: Martin Meredith, *Mandela: A Biography* (New York: PublicAffairs, 2010), 286.

139 **"Apart from the birthday of the Lord Jesus"**: Sampson, *Mandela: The Authorized Biography*, 363.

140 **"emerged from his two trials"**: Sampson, *Mandela: The Authorized Biography*, 198.

140 **Smile like the sun on cloudy day**: Richard Stengel, "Mandela: His 8 Lessons of Leadership," *Time*, July 9, 2008, http://www.dorrierunderwood.com/PDFs/Nelson%20Mandela%20on%20Leadership.pdf.

140 **"you don't address their brains"**: Bill Keller, "Mandela and Obama," *New York Times*, June 30, 2013, http://www.nytimes.com/2013/06/30/opinion/sunday/keller-mandela-and-obama.html.

140 **Tambo and Mbeki quotes**: Luli Callinicos, *Oliver Tambo: Beyond the Engeli Mountains* (Claremont, South Africa: David Philip Publishers, 2005), 300; Paul Taylor, "Mandela Takes Office: 'Let Freedom Reign,'" *Washington Post*, May 11, 1994, https://www.washingtonpost.com/archive/politics/1994/05/11/mandela-takes-office-let-freedom-reign/983a12fe-2127-45c7-b8a8-d75e4ae91f6a/?utm_term=.3ac869e14eb9.

141 **Clinton with Mandela**: John Kane, *The Politics of Moral Capital* (Cambridge: Cambridge University Press, 2001), 1.

141 **Mandela on his family life**: Nannerl O. Keohane, *Thinking About Leadership* (Princeton, NJ: Princeton University Press, 2010), 204.

142 **ANC Youth League 1948 Policy Document**: South African History Online,

"Basic Policy of Congress Youth League, Manifesto Issued by the National Executive Committee of the ANC Youth League, 1948," http://www.sahistory .org.za/archive/basic-policy-congress-youth-league-manifesto-issued -national-executive-committee-anc-youth-l.

142   **Freedom Charter:** South African History Online, "Congress of the People and Freedom Charter," http://www.sahistory.org.za/article/freedom-charter.

142   **"we felt":** South African History Online, "Nelson Mandela's Testimony at the Treason Trial 1956–1960," http://www.sahistory.org.za/archive/ nelson-mandelas-testimony-treason-trial-1956-1960.

142   **"If the government reaction is to crush by naked force":** South African History Online, "*Umkhonto we Sizwe (MK)*," http://www.sahistory.org.za/topic/ umkhonto-wesizwe-mk.

143   **"submit or fight":** Manifesto of Umkhonto we Sizwe, December 16, 1961, http://www.anc.org.za/content/umkhonto-we-sizwe-military-code.

143   **"First lesson in demolition":** Sampson, *Mandela: The Authorized Biography*, 168.

143   **"trial of the aspirations of the African people":** South African History Online, "Statements in Court October 22 and November 7, 1962," http://www.sahistory.org. za/archive/statements-court-nelson-mandela-october-22-and-november-7-1962.

143   **"lack of human dignity":** South African History Online, "I Am Prepared to Die, Rivonia Trial, Pretoria Supreme Court, April 20, 1964," http://www.sahistory .org.za/archive/i-am-prepared-die-nelson-mandelas-statement-dock-opening -defence-case-rivonia-trial-pretoria.

144   **"race maniacs who govern our beloved country":** South African History Online, "The Struggle Is My Life, Press Statement Issued on June 26, 1961," http://www.sahistory.org.za/archive/struggle-my-life-press-statement -issued-26-june-19611.

146   **"deep down in every human heart":** Nelson Mandela, *Long Walk to Freedom* (New York: Bay Back Books, 2013), 622.

146   **"choice is his":** John D. Battersby, "Johannesburg Journal: Nelson Mandela, 70, Captivates Even Those Who Jail Him," *New York Times*, July 18, 1988, http:// www.nytimes.com/1988/07/18/world/johannesburg-journal-mandela-70 -captivates-even-those-who-jail-him.html.

146   **"Only free men can negotiate":** South African History Online, "I Am Not Prepared to Sell the Birthright of the People to Be Free," February 10, 1985, http://www .sahistory.org.za/archive/i-am-not-prepared-sell-birthright-people-be-free.

148   **"deepening political crisis":** South African History Online, "Document 12 —Notes Prepared by Nelson Mandela for His Meeting with P. W. Botha," July 5, 1989, http://www.sahistory.org.za/archive/document-12-notes-prepared -nelson-mandela-his-meeting-p-w-botha.

149   **"a courtesy call":** Meredith, *Mandela: A Biography*, 388.

149   **De Klerk speech:** South African History Online, "FW de Klerk's Speech

to Parliament, 2 February 1990," http://www.sahistory.org.za/archive/fw-de-klerk's-speech-parliament-2-february-1990.

150 **favored option among Afrikaners:** Kate Manzo and Pat McGowan, "Afrikaner Fear and the Politics of Despair: Understanding Change in South Africa," *International Studies Quarterly* 36, no. 1 (March 1992): 21.

151 **"do not understand":** Tom Lodge, *Mandela: A Critical Life* (Oxford: Oxford University Press, 2006), 173.

151 **"nobody in the room had horns":** Sampson, *Mandela: The Authorized Biography*, 418.

153 **"A white man, full of prejudice and hate":** South African History Online, "Televised Address to the Nation by President Nelson R. Mandela on the Assassination of Chris Hani, 1 April 1993," http://www.sahistory.org.za/archive/televised-address-nation-president-nelson-r-mandela-assassination-chris-hani-13-april-1993.

153 **"will be a long and bitter struggle":** Sampson, *Mandela: The Authorized Biography*, 461–462.

154 **"accept that responsibility," "as long as I am your leader":** Meredith, *Mandela: A Biography*, 490–491.

154 **"shining example to the entire world":** Trudy Govler, *Forgiveness and Revenge* (London: Routledge, 2002), 69.

155 **"masterful stroke":** F. W. de Klerk, *The Last Trek—A New Beginning: The Autobiography* (New York: St. Martin's Press, 1998), 332.

155 **"We enter into a covenant":** South African History Online, "Statement of the President Nelson R. Mandela at His Inauguration, 10 May 1994," http://www.sahistory.org.za/archive/statement-president-anc-nelson-r-mandela-his-inauguration-president-democratic-republic-sout.

156 **"government stopped the gravy train":** Meredith, *Mandela: A Biography*, 544.

157 **"mutual trust and regard":** Meredith, *Mandela: A Biography*, 523.

157 **"I used to do it for the money":** Sampson, *Mandela: The Authorized Biography*, 489.

158 **"small minority in our midst":** South African History Online, "President Mandela State of the Nation Address, 17 February 1995," http://www.sahistory.org.za/archive/1995-president-mandela-state-nation-address-17-february-1995.

158 **"rid ourselves of the culture of entitlement":** South African History Online, "Mandela Address on Opening of Second Session of Democratic Parliament Cape Town," February 17, 1995, http://www.sahistory.org.za/archive/address-president-nelson-mandela-occasion-opening-second-session-democratic-parliament-cape-town.

159 **commended the TRC:** Lodge, *Mandela: A Critical Life*, 211.

160 **Ambassador Joseph interview:** Interview with Ambassador James A. Joseph, September 11, 2006, Durham, North Carolina, conducted by research assistant Rachel Wald.

160 **"can't think of anybody as a head of state":** Ambassador Joseph interview, September 11, 2006.

161 **"an old-fashioned aristocrat"**: Alec Russell, "Nelson Mandela: The Meaning of the Madiba Magic," *Financial Times*, December 6, 2013, https://www.ft.com/content/11bce4d2-37b0-11e1-897b-00144feabdc0.

162 **"I hold out my hand"**: Bill Keller, "The South African Vote; The Overview; Mandela Proclaims a Victory: South Africa Is 'Free at Last,'" *New York Times*, May 3, 1994, http://www.nytimes.com/1994/05/03/world/south-african-vote-overview-mandela-proclaims-victory-south-africa-free-last.html.

162 **"Apartheid was wrong"**: David Welsh and J. E. Spence, *Ending Apartheid* (London: Pearson Education Limited, 2011), 7.

162 **"allow time for me to fall flat on my face"**: Kane, *Politics of Moral Capital*, 135.

162 **"avalanche of information," "witch hunt"**: Sampson, *Mandela: The Authorized Biography*, 527; Meredith, *Mandela: A Biography*, 547.

163 **Obama on Mandela legacy**: "Obama Speech at Mandela Memorial," *Washington Post*, December 10, 2013, https://www.washingtonpost.com/world/obamas-speech-at-mandela-memorial-mandela-taught-us-the-power-of-action-but-also-ideas/2013/12/10/a22c8a92-618c-11e3-bf45-61f69f54fc5f_story.html?utm_term=.13c14b467c3f.

CHAPTER 6:
YITZHAK RABIN: SOLDIER AS PEACEMAKER

164 **his parents:** Yitzhak Rabin, *The Rabin Memoirs* (Berkeley: University of California Press, 1979), 3.

165 **"the Palmachnik"**: Rabin, *Rabin Memoirs*, 12.

166 **"there is only one army"**: David Horovitz, *Shalom Friend: The Life and Legacy of Yitzhak Rabin* (New York: New Market Press, 1996), 35.

169 **"You were the column of fire"**: "Eulogy Given by Granddaughter Noa Rothman (formerly Ben-Artzi Pelossof) at Yitzhak Rabin's Funeral," November 5, 1995, http://www.rabincenter.org.il/Items/01106/noarotman.pdf.

169 **"analytical brilliance"**: Dan Kurzman, *Soldier of Peace: The Life of Yitzhak Rabin 1922–1995* (New York: HarperCollins, 1998), 19.

170 **"a problem like none in our previous experience"**: Kurzman, *Soldier of Peace*, 410.

170 **"solution can only be a political one"**: Itamar Rabinovich, *Yitzhak Rabin: Soldier, Leader, Statesman* (New Haven, CT: Yale University Press, 2017), 158.

170 **here's our phone number:** Thomas L. Friedman, "Baker Rebukes Israel on Peace Terms," *New York Times*, June 14, 1990, http://www.nytimes.com/1990/06/14/world/baker-rebukes-israel-on-peace-terms.html.

171 **"special relationship is invaluable"**: David Makovsky, *Making Peace with the PLO: The Rabin Government's Road to the Oslo Accord* (Boulder, CO: Westview Press, 1995), 193.

171   **Rabin and AIPAC:** Clyde Haberman, "Rabin and Pro-Israel Group Off to Testy
      Start," *New York Times*, August 22, 1992, http://www.nytimes.com/1992/08/22/
      world/rabin-and-pro-israel-group-off-to-testy-start.html.

171   **Gush Emunim:** Dan Ephron, *Killing a King: The Assassination of Yitzhak Rabin
      and the Remaking of Israel* (New York: W. W. Norton, 2015), 68.

171   **IDF death toll rising:** B'Tselem, "Fatalities in the First Intifada," http://www
      .btselem.org/statistics/first_intifada_tables.

172   **Rabin speech after 1967 war:** Kurzman, *Soldier of Peace*, 231–232.

172   **"Peace you don't make with friends":** Dennis Ross, *The Missing Peace: The
      Inside Story of the Fight for Middle East Peace* (New York: Farrar, Straus and
      Giroux, 2004), 92.

173   **Rabin's initial reaction to Oslo talks:** Makovsky, *Making Peace with the PLO*,
      51, 66.

173   **Arafat and Rabin letters:** Israel Ministry of Foreign Affairs, "Israel-PLO
      Letters of Mutual Recognition," September 10, 1993, http://www.mfa.gov
      .il/mfa/foreignpolicy/mfadocuments/yearbook9/pages/107%20israel-plo%20
      mutual%20recognition-%20letters%20and%20spe.aspx.

174   **Rabin statement at White House signing ceremony:** "Mid East Accord:
      Statements by Leaders at the Signing of the Middle East Pact," *New York Times*,
      September 14, 1993, http://www.nytimes.com/1993/09/14/world/mideast
      -accord-statements-by-leaders-at-the-signing-of-the-middle-east-pact
      .html?pagewanted=all.

177   **Baruch Goldstein terrorism:** Ephron, *Killing a King*, 64.

177   **"What do you think":** Orit Shohat, "A Decade Without Him," November 4,
      2005, http://www.haaretz.com/news/a-decade-without-him-1.173229.

178   **"resisted as if they are soldiers of the Third Reich":** Kurzman, *Soldier of
      Peace*, 503.

178   **number of Israelis killed:** Israel Ministry of Foreign Affairs, "Fatal Ter-
      rorist Attacks in Israel (Sept. 1993–1999)," http://mfa.gov.il/MFA/Foreign
      Policy/Terrorism/Palestinian/Pages/Fatal%20Terrorist%20Attacks%20
      in%20Israel%20Since%20the%20DOP%20-S.aspx; and Johnston Archive,
      "Chronology of Terrorist Attacks in Israel, Part V: 1993–1995," http://www
      .johnstonsarchive.net/terrorism/terrisrael-5.html.

178   **"foiled attacks," "We did not return to an empty land":** Israel Ministry
      of Foreign Affairs, "Prime Minister Rabin in the Knesset—Ratification
      of Interim Agreement," October 5, 1995, http://mfa.gov.il/MFA/MFA
      -Archive/1995/Pages/PM%20Rabin%20in%20Knesset-%20Ratification%20
      of%20Interim%20Agree.aspx.

179   **"I'll never wear a bulletproof vest":** Ephron, *Killing a King*, 144–145.

179   **Rabin speech:** "The Last Speech—Address by Prime Minister Yitzhak Rabin
      at a Peace Rally, Kings of Israel Square, Tel Aviv," November 4, 1995, http://
      www.rabincenter.org.il/Items/01103/RabinAddressatapeacerally.pdf.

180 **"God decided Rabin would die"**: Ben Hartman, "Hagai Amir Questioned by Police for Allegedly Inciting Against Rivlin on Facebook," *Jerusalem Post*, October 27, 2015, http://www.jpost.com/Israel-News/Hagai-Amir-questioned-by-police-for-allegedly-inciting-against-Rivlin-on-Facebook-430211.

182 **what Abraham Lincoln's aides John Hay and John Nicolay remarked**: Terry Alford, "The Spiritualist Who Warned Lincoln Was Also Booth's Drinking Buddy: What Did Charles Colchester Know and When Did He Know It?" *Smithsonian* (March 2015): 45.

182 **American negotiator Aaron Miller**: Aaron David Miller, *The Much Too Promised Land: America's Elusive Search for Arab-Israeli Peace* (New York: Bantam Books, 2008), 261.

182 **"Arafat earned many points"**: Ephron, *Killing a King*, 128.

183 **"Of all the hands in the world"**: Efraim Inbar, *Rabin and Israel's National Security* (Washington, DC: Woodrow Wilson Center Press, 1999), 153.

183 **"It seems to me, Mr. Chairman"**: Ephron, *Killing a King*, 160.

183 **"Arafat seemed to revere Rabin"**: Ephron, *Killing a King*, 129.

183 **"Arafat's regard for Rabin"**: Bill Clinton, *My Life* (New York: Alfred A. Knopf, 2004), 545.

183 **"I've lost my partner"**: Kurzman, *Soldier of Peace*, 513.

184 **even if Rabin had lived**: Miller, *Much Too Promised Land*, 267.

185 **"Jerusalem must be united"**: Israel Ministry of Foreign Affairs, "PM Rabin Statements on Jerusalem June–August 1994," http://mfa.gov.il/MFA/MFA-Archive/1994/Pages/PM%20RABIN%20-%20STATEMENTS%20ON%20THE%20STATUS%20OF%20JERUSALEM%20-.aspx.

186 **King Hussein, President Mubarak statements**: Kurzman, *Soldier of Peace*, 514.

186 **Bill Clinton on Rabin and peace**: Daniel C. Kurtzer, Scott B. Lasensky, William B. Quandt, Steven L. Spiegel, and Shibley Telhami, *The Peace Puzzle: America's Quest for Arab-Israeli Peace* (Ithaca, NY: Cornell University Press, 2013), 113.

186 **"if Rabin had not been assassinated"**: Ari Shavit, *My Promised Land: The Triumph and Tragedy of Israel* (New York: Spiegel and Grau, 2013), 252.

186 **Amos Oz on peace**: Cited in Shavit, *My Promised Land*, 260.

CHAPTER 7:

MAIREAD CORRIGAN AND BETTY WILLIAMS:

NORTHERN IRELAND WOMEN FOR PEACE

188 **"It's not violence people want"**: Richard Deutsch, *Mairead Corrigan, Betty Williams: Winners of the Nobel Peace Prize & Norwegian Peoples Peace Prize* (Hauppauge, NY: Barron's, 1977), 4.

189   **"burst a dam inside me"**: Deutsch, *Mairead Corrigan, Betty Williams*, 5 and
       passim.

190   **"The threats will not stop me"**: Derek Brown, "Women of Peace Stage Second
       Rally in Ulster," *Guardian*, August 18, 1976, http://search.proquest.com.proxy
       .lib.duke.edu/docview/185849819?accountid=10598.

190   **"These people do not know"**: Derek Brown, "Savage Attack on Women's
       Peace Step by Provisionals," *Guardian*, August 21, 1976, http://search.proquest
       .com.proxy.lib.duke.edu/docview/185860226?accountid=10598.

191   **"The point of our campaign"**: Brown, "Women of Peace Stage Second Rally
       in Ulster."

191   **"We have a simple message"**: Peace People, "First Declaration of the Peace
       People," http://www.peacepeople.com/?page_id=10.

191   **"Sorry, we never talk politics"**: Deutsch, *Mairead Corrigan, Betty Williams*, 89.

193   **"vultures"**: Brown, "Savage Attack on Women's Peace Step by Provisionals."

193   **"an ideological weapon"**: Paul Bew and Gordon Gillespie, *Northern Ireland: A
       Chronology of the Troubles 1968–1999* (Lanham, MD: Scarecrow Press, 1999), 115.

193   **"refused to bow to bleak skepticism"**: Nobel Peace Prize 1976, "Award
       Ceremony Speech," https://www.nobelprize.org/nobel_prizes/peace/
       laureates/1976/press.html.

194   **"Religion"**: Conor Cruise O'Brien, *States of Ireland* (London: Panther Books,
       1974), 149.

195   **such differences**: Deutsch, *Mairead Corrigan, Betty Williams*, 90.

195   **exhilirated Mairead Corrigan mused**: Stephen Andrew, "Wives to Blow
       Whistle for Peace in Belfast," *Observer*, August 22, 1976, http://search.proquest
       .com.proxy.lib.duke.edu/docview/476337825?accountid=10598.

POLITICS OF IDENTITY'S ALTERNATIVE PLOTLINE

197   **South African polling data:** Jan Hofmeyr and Rajen Govender, Institute for Jus-
       tice and Reconciliation, *National Reconciliation, Race Relations and Social Inclu-
       sion*, South African Briefing Paper 1, December 8, 2015, http://reconciliation
       barometer.org/wp-content/uploads/2011/09/IJR_SARB_2015_.pdf.

198   **Support for peace with the Palestinians:** Commanders for Israel's Security,
       http://en.cis.org.il/about/; see also Amir Taboni, "Netanyahu vs. the Gener-
       als," *Politico*, July 3, 2016, http://www.politico.com/magazine/story/2016/06/
       netanyahu-prime-minister-obama-president-foreign-policy-us-israel-israeli
       -relations-middle-east-iran-defense-forces-idf-214004; http://www.imdb
       .com/title/tt2309788/.

200   **"enlarging the sense of 'we'"**: Howard Gardner, "Leadership: A Cognitive
       Perspective," *SAIS Review* 16, no. 2 (Summer–Fall 1996), https://muse.jhu
       .edu/article/30318.

200 **embodiments of mixed identities:** Mark Lefly, "Exclusive: London Mayor Sadiq Khan on Religious Extremism, Brexit and Donald Trump," *Time*, http://time.com/4322562/london-mayor-sadiq-khan-donald-trump/.

INTRODUCTION: ADVANCING FREEDOM AND PROTECTING HUMAN RIGHTS

202 **Things getting worse:** Danny Hakim, "The World's Dissidents Have Their Say," *New York Times*, October 25, 2014, http://www.nytimes.com/2014/10/26/sunday-review/the-worlds-dissidents-have-their-say.html?emc=eta1&_r=0.

202 **Orwellian technologies:** Amnesty International, *Annual Report 2015–16*, 16.

CHAPTER 8:
GANDHI: EXEMPLAR OF ANTICOLONIALISM, APOSTLE OF NONVIOLENCE

204 **Opening quotations:** Inscription on statue of Mahatma Gandhi, Glebe Park, Canberra, Australia; David Arnold, *Gandhi* (New York: Routledge, 2014), 11.

205 **in South Africa:** Robert A. Huttenback, *Gandhi in South Africa: British Imperialism and the Indian Question* (Ithaca, NY: Cornell University Press, 1971), 128.

206 **Nehru on Gandhi:** Jawaharlal Nehru, *The Discovery of India* (Delhi: Oxford University Press, 1985), 358.

206 **Gandhi as avatar:** Louis Fischer, *Mahatma Gandhi: His Life and Times* (London: Jonathan Cape, 1951), 258.

207 **"his smile":** Jawaharlal Nehru, *Toward Freedom: The Autobiography of Jawaharlal Nehru* (New York: John Day, 1941), 318.

207 **Churchill on Gandhi:** Johann Hari, "Not His Finest Hour: The Dark Side of Winston Churchill," *Independent*, October 27, 2010, http://www.independent.co.uk/news/uk/politics/not-his-finest-hour-the-dark-side-of-winston-churchill-2118317.html; Jad Adams, *Gandhi: Naked Ambition* (London: Quercus, 2010), 192; Tom Heyden, "The 10 Greatest Controversies of Winston Churchill's Career," *BBC News Magazine*, January 26, 2015, http://www.bbc.com/news/magazine-29701767.

207 **Letter to Hitler, views of Jews:** Adams, *Naked Ambition*, 220–221; Mohandas Gandhi, *Gandhi: Selected Writings*, ed. Ronald Duncan (Mineola, NY: Dover Publications, 2005), 91.

209 **Hind Swaraj:** Cited in Arnold, *Gandhi*, 65.

209 **"Every village will be a republic or *panchayat*":** Simone Panter-Brick, *Gandhi and Nationalism: The Path to Indian Independence* (London: I. B. Tauris, 2012), 26.

209 **"pursuit of truth":** Dennis Dalton, *Mahatma Gandhi: Nonviolent Power in Action* (New York: Columbia University Press, 2012), 38. Also in M. K.

Gandhi, *The Collected Works of Mahatma Gandhi* (Publications Division, Ministry of Information and Broadcasting, Government of India, 1961), 368–369.

210   **"snake":** *The Bhagavad Gita According to Mahatma Gandhi* (Berkeley, CA: North Atlantic Books, 2009), 13.

210   **Mountbatten quote:** Stanley Wolpert, *Gandhi's Passion: The Life and Legacy of Mahatma Gandhi* (Oxford: Oxford University Press, 2002), 241.

210   **"ineffaceable blot":** M. K. Gandhi, *The Collected Works of Mahatma Gandhi* (Publications Division Ministry of Information and Broadcasting, Government of India, 1967) 13, 232–233.

210   **"Shall we not have the vision":** Dalton, *Gandhi: Nonviolent Power in Action*, 55.

210   **Indian constitution:** David Hardiman, *Gandhi in His Time and Ours: The Global Legacy of His Ideas* (London: Hurst, 2003), 134.

210   **"India cannot cease to be one nation":** M. K. Gandhi, *Hind Swaraj or Indian Home Rule* (Ahmedabad, 1939), 44–45.

211   **Gandhi and Wilson's Fourteen Points:** Erez Manela, *The Wilsonian Moment: Self-Determination and the Internatinoal Origins of Anticolonial Nationalism* (New York: Oxford University Press, 2007), 159.

212   **"intrinsic violence of British rule":** Arnold, *Gandhi*, 111.

213   **"shaking the foundations of the British Empire":** Francis Watson, *The Trial of Mr. Gandhi* (London: Macmillan, 1969), 188.

215   **"We the undersigned":** Dalton, *Gandhi: Nonviolent Power in Action*, 149–167; Larry Collins and Dominique Lapierre, *Freedom at Midnight* (New York: Simon and Schuster, 1975), 353–367.

215   **"reunion of hearts":** Hardiman, *Gandhi in His Time and Ours*, 188.

216   **Gandhi assassination:** Abhishek Saha, "The Politics of an Assassination: Who Killed Gandhi and Why?" *Hindustan Times*, May 28, 2017, http://www .hindustantimes.com/analysis/the-politics-of-an-assassination-who-killed -gandhi-and-why/story-iUJqKjuw0sP9nAfc5KcOII.html.

216   **"most truly bright and precious jewel":** Carl Bridge, *Holding India to the Empire: The British Conservative Party and the 1935 Constitution* (New Delhi: Sterling Publishers, 1986), 62.

216   **"For large numbers of people":** Hardiman, *Gandhi in His Time and Ours*, 253.

217   **Success rate of nonviolent political resistance:** Erica Chenoweth and Maria J. Stepan, *Why Civil Resistance Works: The Strategic Logic of Nonviolent Conflict* (New York: Columbia University Press, 2011).

217   **Mandela and Gandhi:** Hardiman, *Gandhi in His Time and Ours*, 279.

217   **Dr. King's trip to India:** "Martin Luther King, Jr. and the Global Freedom Struggle: India Trip (1959)," *King Encyclopedia*, http://kingencyclopedia.stanford .edu/encyclopedia/encyclopedia/enc_kings_trip_to_india/.

217   **"joint family":** Harold Coward, ed., *Indian Critiques of Gandhi* (Albany: State University of New York Press, 2003), 194.

218   **Bangladesh commemoration of Gandhi**: Joseph Lelyveld, *Great Soul: Mahatma Gandhi and His Struggle with India* (New York: Alfred A. Knopf, 2011), 329–320.

CHAPTER 9:
LECH WALESA: FROM COMMUNISM TO DEMOCRACY

219   **"troublemaker"**: Tony Kaye, *Lech Walesa* (Langhorne, PA: Chelsea House, 1989), 28.
220   **"My worst fears had been realized"**: Lech Walesa, *A Way of Hope* (New York: Henry Holt, 1987), 70.
221   **Quote from Cardinal Wyszynski**: Mary Craig, *The Crystal Spirit: Lech Walesa and His Poland* (London: Hodder and Stoughton, 1986), 144.
221   **Church and Solidarity**: "An Interview with Lech Walesa," *Time*, January 4, 1982, http://content.time.com/time/magazine/article/0,9171,953279,00.html.
221   **"we eat the same bread"**: Special to the *New York Times*, "Walesa, a Calm Leader in a Dangerous Conflict," *New York Times*, March 28, 1981, http://www.nytimes.com/1981/03/28/world/walesa-a-calm-leader-in-a-dangerous-conflict.html.
221   **"Sometimes he doesn't even make any sense"**: Thomas A. Sancton, Richard Hornik, and Gregory H. Wierzynski, "He Dared to Hope," *Time*, January 4, 1982, http://content.time.com/time/magazine/article/0,9171,953276,00.html.
221   **"isn't capable of abstract thought"**: Victoria Pope, "Walesa, the Man Who Ignited Poland, Now Talks of Retiring from the Fray," *Wall Street Journal*, August 14, 1984, http://proxy.lib.duke.edu/login?url=https://search-proquest-com.proxy.lib.duke.edu/docview/134892938?accountid=10598.
222   **Assassination attempts**: United Press International, "Polish Underground Leader Lech Walesa Believes Three Different Assassination . . . ," March 24, 1983, http://www.upi.com/Archives/1983/03/24/Polish-underground-leader-Lech-Walesa-believes-three-different-assassination/8690417330000/.
222   **"stabbing the air"**: John Tagliabue, "Lech! Lech! Lech!" *New York Times*, October 23, 1988, http://www.nytimes.com/1988/10/23/magazine/lech-lech-lech.html?pagewanted=all.
222   **"consummate, even outrageous manipulator"**: Neal Ascherson, Introduction to *The Book of Lech Walesa* (New York: Simon and Schuster, 1982), 8.
223   **"bushy moustache, ever-present pipe"**: Robert Eringer, *Strike for Freedom! The Story of Lech Walesa and Polish Solidarity* (New York: Dodd, Mead, 1982), 91.
224   **Worker and GDP data**: Antoni Kuklinski, "Industrialization in Poland: Experiences and Prospects," *GeoJournal* 18, no. 2 (March 1989), http://www.jstor.org/stable/41144391?seq=3#page_scan_tab_contents.
224   **Nobel Peace Prize speech**: Lech Walesa, Nobel Peace Prize Lecture, Decem-

ber 11, 1983, http://www.nobelprize.org/nobel_prizes/peace/laureates/1983/walesa-lecture.html.

225 **Charter of Workers' Rights:** Daniel C. Thomas, *The Helsinki Effect: International Norms, Human Rights and the Demise of Communism* (Princeton, NJ: Princeton University Press, 2001), 203.

225 **Walesa on Father Popieluszko:** Interfaith Peacemakers, "Jerzy Popieluszko (1947–1984)," http://www.readthespirit.com/interfaith-peacemakers/jerzy-popieluszko/-.

226 **"Solidarity was born":** Walesa, *A Way of Hope*, 123.

227 **Pope John Paul II to Walesa:** H. Paul Jeffers, *Dark Mysteries of the Vatican* (New York: Citadel Press, 2010), 64.

227 **Brezhnev warning to Poland:** "Speech by Leonid Brezhnev at the Meeting of the Party and State Leaders of the Warsaw Pact," December 5, 1980, Wilson Center, International History Digital Archive, http://digitalarchive.wilsoncenter.org/document/112065.

227 **"Lead us, Walesa":** Tony Kaye, *Lech Walesa, World Leaders Past & Present* (New York: Chelsea House, 1989), 94.

228 **Lechia Gdansk football match:** Maciej Slominski, "The Power of Football: The Night Lech Walesa Changed Poland Forever," *Guardian*, September 27, 2013, https://www.theguardian.com/football/blog/2013/sep/27/football-lech-walesa-poland.

230 **"It wasn't that I wanted":** Lech Walesa, *The Struggle and the Triumph* (New York: Arcade Publishing, 1991), 281.

CHAPTER 10:

AUNG SAN SUU KYI: A CAUTIONARY TALE

233 **"Soon the world will witness a remarkable sight":** "Myanmar's Peace Prize Winner and Crimes Against Humanity," Nicholas Kristof, *New York Times,* January 9, 2016, http://www.nytimes.com/2016/01/10/opinion/sunday/myanmars-peace-prize-winner-and-crimes-against-humanity.html.

233 **UN Secretary-General Guterres on ethnic cleansing:** Margaret Besheer, "UN Chief Assails 'Ethnic Cleansing' of Myanmar's Rohingyas," Voice of America: Asia. September 13, 2017, https://www.voanews.com/a/united-nations-antonio-guterres-myanmar-rohingya-ehtnic-cleansing/4027395.html.

234 **"Vigorous, magnetic":** David I. Steinberg, *Burma/Myanmar: What Everyone Needs to Know* (Oxford: Oxford University Press, 2010), 42.

235 **"sincerity in her voice":** Aung Zaw, *The Face of Resistance: Aung San Suu Kyi and Burma's Fight for Freedom* (Chiang Mai: Mekong Press, 2013), 14.

235 **"could not, as my father's daughter":** Rod Troester, "Peacemaking in Burma:

The Life and Times of Aung San Suu Kyi," in Colleen E. Kelley and Anna L. Eblen, eds., *Women Who Speak for Peace* (Lanham, MD: Rowman and Little-field, 2002), 184.

237 **"our leader to get democracy"**: Rena Pederson, *The Burma Spring: Aung San Suu Kyi and the New Struggle for the Soul of a Nation* (New York: Pegasus Books, 2015), 358.

237 **"aura surrounding her"**: Jonathan Head, "Aung San Suu Kyi: From Icon to Political Player," *BBC News Magazine*, March 17, 2013, http://www.bbc.com/news/magazine-21802811.

238 **"moody, temperamental, difficult"**: Pederson, *Burma Spring*, 485.

239 **"freedom from fear"**: Aung San Suu Kyi, *Freedom from Fear and Other Writings* (London: Viking, 1991).

239 **"peaceful, stable and progressive society"**: "Open Letter to the UN Commission on Human Rights," in Suu Kyi, *Freedom from Fear*, 222.

239 **"spiritual renewal + political renewal = freedom"**: Pederson, *Burma Spring*, 63.

240 **1989 speech on ethnic minorities**: "The Need for Solidarity among Ethnic Groups," in Aung San Suu Kyi, *Freedom from Fear*, 226–231.

242 **ASEAN**: Alan Collins, *Building a People-Oriented Security Community the ASEAN Way* (London: Routledge, 2013), 40.

244 **"truly very risky"**: Thomas Fuller, "In Public Eye, Shining Star of Myanmar Loses Luster," *New York Times*, March 9, 2013, http://www.nytimes.com/2013/03/10/world/asia/in-public-eye-shining-star-of-myanmar-loses-luster.html.

247 **McKinsey $650 billion estimate**: McKinsey Global Institute, *Myanmar's Moment: Unique Opportunities, Major Challenges*, June 2013, https://www.mckinsey.com/global-themes/asia-pacific/myanmars-moment.

248 **"systematic rape"**: Michael Sullivan and Ashley Westerman, "Rohingya Fleeing Myanmar Describe Military Tactic of Systematic Rape," National Public Radio, April 13, 2017, http://www.npr.org/sections/parallels/2017/04/13/523418664/ngo-myanmar-forces-set-out-to-systematically-rape-rohingya-women-and-girls.

248 **Annan Commission report**: Final Report of the Advisory Commission on Rakhine State, *Toward a Peaceful, Fair and Prosperous Future for the People of Rakhine*, August 2017, http://www.rakhinecommission.org/the-final-report/.

249 **Aung San Suu Kyi response**: Rebecca Wright, Katie Hunt, and Joshua Berlinger, "Aung San Suu Kyi Breaks Silence on Rohingya, Sparks Storm of Criticism," September 19, 2017, http://www.cnn.com/2017/09/18/asia/aung-san-suu-kyi-speech-rohingya/index.html. See also Joshua Kurlantzick, "Why Aung San Suu Kyi Isn't Protecting the Rohingya in Burma," *Washington Post*, September 17, 2017, https://www.washingtonpost.com/outlook/why-aung-san-suu-kyi-isnt-protecting

-the-rohingya-in-burma/2017/09/15/c88b10fa-9900-11e7-87fc-c3f7ee4035c9
_story.html?utm_term=.b64f47c292a4.

249   **Satellite images of villages burned, *New York Times* reporter:** Human Rights
      Watch, "Burma: New Satellite Images Confirm Mass Destruction," October
      17, 2017, https://www.hrw.org/news/2017/10/17/burma-new-satellite-images
      -confirm-mass-destruction; Jeffrey Gettleman, "My Interview with a
      Rohingya Refugee: What Do You Say to a Woman Whose Baby Was Thrown
      into a Fire?" *New York Times*, October 19, 2017, A2.

249   **Fellow Nobel Peace Prize laureates statement:** Burma Task Force USA,
      "Press Release—7 Nobel Peace Laureates Call Rohingya Persecution a Geno-
      cide," May 28, 2015, https://www.burmamuslims.org/content/press-release
      -7-nobel-peace-laureates-call-rohingya-persecution-genocide.

249   **"Did the world get Aung San Suu Kyi wrong?":** Amanda Taub and Max
      Fisher, "The Interpreter: Did the World Get Aung San Suu Kyi Wrong?" *New
      York Times*, November 1, 2017, https://www.nytimes.com/2017/10/31/world/
      asia/aung-san-suu-kyi-myanmar.html.

249   **Roger Cohen leaves open:** Roger Cohen, "Myanmar Is Not a Simple
      Morality Tale," *New York Times*, November 25, 2017, https://www.nytimes
      .com/2017/11/25/opinion/sunday/myanmar-aung-san-suu-kyi-rohingya.html.

CHAPTER 11:
PETER BENENSON, AMNESTY INTERNATIONAL
AND THE GLOBAL HUMAN RIGHTS MOVEMENT

252   **W. H. Auden:** Flora Solomon and Barnet Litvinoff, *Baku to Baker Street: The
      Memoirs of Flora Solomon* (London: William Collins, 1984), 143.

252   **"revolutionary tendencies":** David Winner, *Peter Benenson: Taking a Stand
      against Injustice—Amnesty International* (Milwaukee: Gareth Stevens Publish-
      ing, 1991), 6–7.

253   **"I do not share his religious faith":** Solomon and Litvinoff, *Baku to Baker
      Street*, 225.

254   **"erratic actions":** Jonathan Power, *Like Water on Stone: The Story of Amnesty
      International* (Boston: Northeastern Press, 2001), 130.

254   **"re-kindle a fire in the minds of men":** Stephen Hopgood, *Keepers of the
      Flame: Understanding Amnesty International* (Ithaca, NY: Cornell University
      Press, 2006), 7; Amnesty International Archives, Oral History Pilot Project,
      Benenson to Baker, August 9, 1961.

255   **"strive to mobilize world opinion":** Hopgood, *Keepers of the Flame*, 24.

255   **"tired of polarized thinking":** Tom Buchanan, "'The Truth Will Set You
      Free': The Making of Amnesty International," *Journal of Contemporary History*
      37, no. 4 (2002): 579.

258 **"Amnesty International . . . carried the day":** Power, *Like Water on Stone*, 115.

258 **"When the two hundred letters came":** Power, *Like Water on Stone*, 134.

259 **Data:** Amnesty International Annual Report 1980, https://www.amnesty.org/en/documents/pol10/0003/1980/en/.

259 **"torch passed":** Stephen Hopgood, *The Endtimes of Human Rights* (Ithaca, NY: Cornell University Press, 2013), 112.

260 **Views from the global South:** Hopgood, *Keepers of the Flame*, 98.

261 **"NGO that made human rights important":** Wendy Wong, "Amnesty International: The NGO That Made Human Rights Important," Chapter 7 in *Internal Affairs: How the Structure of NGOs Transforms Human Rights* (Ithaca, NY: Cornell University Press, 2012), 84.

262 **Nobel Peace Prize:** "1977 Nobel Peace Prize Award Ceremony Speech," https://www.nobelprize.org/nobel_prizes/peace/laureates/1977/press.html.

BACKLASH AND BACKSLIDING, OR RENEWED BREAKTHROUGHS

263 **"threaten the constitutional order":** Freedom House, "Poland: Law and Justice Party Should Stop Constitutional Crisis," December 21, 2016, https://freedomhouse.org/article/poland-law-and-justice-party-should-stop-constitutional-crisis.

264 **"witch's brew":** Bruce W. Jentleson, "Western Democracies' Witch's Brew," April 6, 2016, http://thehill.com/blogs/pundits-blog/international/275306-western-democracies-witchs-brew.

264 **Harvard study:** Roberto Stefan Foa and Yascha Mounk, "The Signs of Deconsolidation," *Journal of Democracy*, http://www.journalofdemocracy.org/sites/default/files/02_28.1_Foa%20%26%20Mounk%20pp%205-15.pdf.

264 **"Western liberal democracy":** Edward Luce, *The Retreat of Western Liberalism* (New York: Atlantic Monthly Press, 2017), 184.

266 **"local ethics in a globalized world":** Michael Ignatieff, "Human Rights, Global Ethics and the Ordinary Virtues," *Ethics and International Affairs* (Spring 2017): 6, and *The Ordinary Virtues: Moral Order in a Divided World* (Cambridge, MA: Harvard University Press, 2017).

267 **American public opinion on human rights:** Chicago Council on Global Affairs, "Global Views 2017: US Public Topline Report," August 2017.

267 **"information power":** Margaret E. Keck and Kathryn Sikkink, *Activists Beyond Borders: Advocacy Networks in International Politics* (Ithaca, NY: Cornell University Press, 1998). See also Sarah S. Stroup and Wendy H. Wong, *The Authority Trap: Strategic Choices of International NGOs* (Ithaca, NY: Cornell University Press, 2017).

268 **"networked age":** Anne-Marie Slaughter, *The Chessboard and the Web: Strategies of Connection in a Networked World* (New Haven, CT: Yale University Press, 2017).

INTRODUCTION: FOSTERING GLOBAL SUSTAINABILITY

270 **"How could a society fail to have seen the dangers"**: Jared Diamond, *Collapse: How Societies Choose to Fail or Succeed* (New York: Penguin Books, 2011), 23.

CHAPTER 12:
GRO HARLEM BRUNDTLAND: OUR COMMON FUTURE

272 **"I was lucky"**: James Langton, "Norway's Iron Lady Honoured with Zayed Future Energy Prize," *National*, January 18, 2016, http://www.thenational .ae/uae/environment/norways-iron-lady-gro-harlem-brundtland-honoured -with-zayed-future-energy-prize.

272 **"radical students"**: Gro Harlem Brundtland, *Madam Prime Minister: A Life in Power and Politics* (New York: Farrar, Straus and Giroux, 2002), 26.

274 **earned environmentalist kudos**: Ulrich Grober, *Sustainability: A Cultural History* (Devon, UK: Green Books, 2010), 181.

274 **"her straight talk"**: Brundtland, *Madam Prime Minister*, 150–151.

274 *Limits to Growth*, **Club of Rome**: Donella H. Meadows et al., *The Limits to Growth: A Report for the Club of Rome's Project on the Predicament of Mankind* (New York: Universe Books, 1974).

275 **"The 'environment' is where we all live"**: World Commission on Environment and Development, *Our Common Future* (New York: Oxford University Press, 1987), xi, emphasis added.

276 **politics inside the commission, "considered me a relatively young and inexperienced woman"**: Iris Borowy, *Defining Sustainable Development for Our Common Future: A History of the World Commission on Environment and Development (Brundtland Commission)* (London: Routledge, 2014), 55–60; Brundtland, *Madam Prime Minister*, 194.

277 **prepared her own after-dinner speech**: Borowy, *Defining Sustainable Development*, 102–103.

278 **"stature and skill"**: Borowy, *Defining Sustainable Development*, vii.

278 **agency was demoralized**: BBC, "Special Report: 50 Years of the WHO— Successes and Failures," January 26, 1998, http://news.bbc.co.uk/2/hi/ special_report/1998/health/47191.stm.

279 **"undermine or subvert"**: WHO Framework Convention on Tobacco Control, "Achievements During 2016 and Expectations for the Coming Year," http:// www.who.int/fctc/mediacentre/news/2016/achievements-2016-expectations -2017-tobacco-control/en/.

280 **"at the core of the development agenda"**: Charles Clift, *The Role of the World Health Organization in the International System* (London: Chatham House, 2013), 8.

282 **"power of ideas"**: Heather A. Smith, "The World Commission on Environment and Development: Ideas and Institutions Intersect," in Ramesh Thakur,

Andrew F. Cooper, and John English, eds., *International Commissions and the Power of Ideas* (Tokyo: United Nations University Press, 2005), 77.

282 **Brundtland's skills:** Borowy, *Defining Sustainable Development*, 58.

284 **"abysmal, shameful":** Laurie Garrett, "Epic Failures Feeding Ebola Crisis," Council on Foreign Relations, September 18, 2014, http://www.cfr.org/public-health-threats-and-pandemics/epic-failures-feeding-ebola-crisis/p33465.

CHAPTER 13:
GATES FOUNDATION AND GLOBAL HEALTH
PHILANTHROPY STATESMANSHIP

285 **"a nerd":** Stephen Manes and Paul Andrews, *Gates: How Microsoft Mogul Reinvented an Industry—and Made Himself the Richest Man in America* (New York: Doubleday, 1993), 16.

287 **"If it's already on the agenda":** Dayo Olopade, "Gatekeepers," *American Prospect*, August 31, 2010, http://prospect.org/article/gatekeepers-0.

287 **"bolster the same corporate, capitalist, neo-liberal agenda":** Todd Faubion, Sarah B. Paige, and Amber L. Pearson, "Co-Opting the Global Health Agenda: The Problematic Role of Partnerships and Foundations," in Owain David Williams and Simon Rusthon, eds., *Partnerships and Foundations in Global Health Governance* (London: Palgrave Macmillan, 2011), 209.

287 **"I didn't do much philanthropy in my 20s and 30s":** David Callahan, *The Givers: Wealth, Power and Philanthropy in a New Gilded Age* (New York: Alfred A. Knopf, 2017), 20, 40.

289 *Time* **magazine interview:** Barbara Kiviat and Bill Gates, "Making Capitalism More Creative," *Time*, July 31, 2008, 30.

290 **Helene Gayle, the head of CARE:** Susan Okie, "Global Health: The Gates-Buffett Effect," *New England Journal of Medicine* (September 14, 2006): 1084–1088, http://www.nejm.org/doi/full/10.1056/NEJMp068186#t=article.

290 **"make bets on promising solutions":** "Who We Are: Letter from Bill and Melinda Gates," Bill and Melinda Gates Foundation, https://www.gatesfoundation.org/Who-We-Are/General-Information/Letter-from-Bill-and-Melinda-Gates.

291 **GAVI:** GAVI, The Vaccine Alliance, "2011–2015 Indicators," http://www.gavi.org/results/measuring/2011-2015-indicators/; UN Inter-Agency Group for Child Mortality Estimation, *Level and Trends in Child Mortality: 2015 Report*, http://www.childmortality.org/files_v20/download/IGME%20report%202015%20child%20mortality%20final.pdf.

291 **Melinda Gates speech:** Okie, "Gates-Buffett Effect."

291 **study of 23 global health partnerships:** K. Buse and A. M. Harmer, "Seven Habits of Highly Effective Global Public-Private Health Partnerships," *Social Science and Medicine*, 64, no. 2 (January 2007): 267.

293   **speech at the 2017 Munich Security Conference:** Bruce Y. Lee, "Bill Gates
       Warns of Epidemic That Could Kill Over 30 Million People," *Forbes*, Febru-
       ary 19, 2017, https://www.forbes.com/sites/brucelee/2017/02/19/bill-gates
       -warns-of-epidemic-that-will-kill-over-30-million-people/#30c064d6282f.

293   **"800-pound gorilla in the philanthrosphere":** Olopade, "Gatekeepers."

293   **questioning the ethics of the BMGF endowment:** Charles Piller, Edmund
       Sanders, and Robyn Dixon, "Dark Cloud Over Good Works of Gates Foun-
       dation," *Los Angeles Times*, January 7, 2007, http://articles.latimes.com/2007/
       jan/07/nation/na-gatesx07.

294   **"accentuated the dominance of Northern-based institutions":** David
       McCoy and Linsey McGoey, "Global Health and the Gates Foundation—In
       Perspective," in Owain David Williams and Simon Rushton, eds., *Partnerships
       and Foundations in Global Health Governance* (London: Palgrave Macmillan,
       2011), 151, 154.

294   **Endowment investments:** Bill and Melinda Gates Foundation, "Investment
       Policy," https://www.gatesfoundation.org/Who-We-Are/General-Information
       /Financials/Investment-Policy.

294   **Giving pledge:** David Callahan, "As Government Retrenches, Philanthropy
       Booms," *New York Times*, June 20, 2017, https://www.nytimes.com/2017/
       06/20/opinion/jeff-bezos-bill-gates-philanthropy.html?_r=0.

294   **"give smart":** Thomas J. Tierney and Joel L. Fleishman, *Give Smart: Philan-
       thropy That Gets Results* (New York: PublicAffairs, 2011).

294   **poses the issue well:** Kristin A. Goss, "Policy Plutocrats: How America's
       Wealthy Seek to Influence Government," *PS: Political Science and Politics* 49,
       no. 3 (July 2016): 442–448; also see Callahan, *The Givers*, 133.

295   **two experts in the field assess:** Owain David Williams and Simon Rush-
       ton, "Private Actors in Global Health Governance," in Williams and Rushton,
       Partnerships and Foundations in Global Health Governance, 4.

EMD, DMD, AND GLOBAL SUSTAINABILITY

296   **Deaths from terrorism, from climate change:** Rebecca Leber, "Obama
       Is Right: Climate Change Kills More People Than Terrorism," February 11,
       2015, *New Republic*, https://newrepublic.com/article/121032/map-climate
       -change-kills-more-people-worldwide-terrorism.

296   **Climate change a major cause of instability and war:** U.S. Department of
       Defense, "DoD Issues Report in Security Implications of Climate Change,"
       July 29, 2015, https://www.defense.gov/News/Article/Article/612710.

297   ***Earth in the Balance:*** Al Gore, *Earth in the Balance: Ecology and the Human
       Spirit* (Boston: Houghton Mifflin, 1992).

298   **Pope Francis encyclical:** Pope Francis, *Praise Be to You: Laudato Si, On Care
       for Our Common Home* (San Francisco: Ignatius Press, 2015).

298 **propagate fake news:** Justin Farrell, "Corporate Funding and Ideological Polarization About Climate Change," *Proceedings of the National Academy of Sciences* 113, no. 1 (2016): 92–97, http://www.pnas.org/content/113/1/92 .abstract.

298 **Killings of environmental activists:** Global Witness, "Defenders of the Earth," July 13, 2017, https://www.globalwitness.org/en/campaigns/environmental-activists/defenders-earth/.

298 **Cost curves bending:** Jess Shankleman and Chris Martin, "Solar Could Beat Coal to Become the Cheapest Power on Earth," *Bloomberg News*, January 2, 2017, https://www.bloomberg.com/news/articles/2017-01-03/for-cheapest -power-on-earth-look-skyward-as-coal-falls-to-solar.

298 **environmental debt:** Amy Larkin, *Environmental Debt: The Hidden Costs of a Global Economy* (New York: Palgrave Macmillan, 2013).

299 **"next big thing":** Tx Zhuo, "Sustainable Capitalism Is the Next Big Thing in Investing," *Sustainability*, February 3, 2016, https://www.entrepreneur.com/article/269813.

299 **"We Are Still In":** Open letter to the International Community and Parties to the Paris Agreement from U.S. State, Local, and Business Leaders, "We Are Still In," http://wearestillin.com.

299 **"We are not waiting for Washington":** Michael R. Bloomberg and Jerry Brown, "The U.S. Is Tackling Global Warming, Even If Trump Isn't," *New York Times*, November 14, 2017, https://www.nytimes.com/2017/11/14/opinion/global-warming-paris-climate-agreement.html.

299 **Polling data:** Coral Davenport and Marjorie Connelly, "Most Republicans Say They Back Climate Action, Poll Finds," *New York Times*, January 30, 2015, https://www.nytimes.com/2015/01/31/us/politics/most-americans-support -government-action-on-climate-change-poll-finds.html.

299 **GDP loss:** Chicago Council on Global Affairs, *What Americans Think of America First*, October 2017, https://www.thechicagocouncil.org/sites/default/files/ccgasurvey2017_what_americans_think_about_america_first.pdf; Matthew Shaer, "States of Denial," *New Republic* (November 2017): 16–25.

300 **Louis Pasteur quote:** Commission on a Global Health Risk Framework for the Future, *The Neglected Dimension of Global Security: A Framework to Counter Infectious Disease Crises* (National Academy of Sciences, 2016), Preface, v.

301 **H7N9:** Centers for Disease Control and Prevention, "Asian Lineage Avian Influenza a (H7N9) Virus," September 26, 2017, https://www.cdc.gov/flu/avianflu/h7n9-virus.htm.

301 **many microbes developing resistance to antibiotics:** Jim O'Neill (chair), *Tackling Drug-Resistant Infections Globally: Final Report and Recommendations*, May 2016, https://amr-review.org/sites/default/files/160525_Final%20 paper_with%20cover.pdf.

301   **"Leadership means"**: "Rare Interview with Gro Brundtland on Restorative
      Leadership for Sustainable Development," September 23, 2015, http://www
      .restorative-leadership.org/blog/brundtland-on-sustainable-development.

                          EPILOGUE:
            TWENTY-FIRST-CENTURY STATESMANSHIP:
               DIFFICULT, POSSIBLE, NECESSARY

303   **"challenge of political courage"**: John F. Kennedy, *Profiles in Courage* (New
      York: HarperCollins, 1984), 17.
303   **spate of books:** Aaron David Miller, *The End of Greatness: Why America Can't
      Have (and Doesn't Want) Another Great President* (New York: Palgrave Macmil-
      lan, 2014), 13; Moises Naim, *The End of Power: From Boardrooms to Battlefields
      and Churches to States, Why Being in Charge Isn't What It Used to Be* (New York:
      Basic Books, 2013); Barbara Kellerman, *The End of Leadership* (New York:
      HarperCollins, 2012).
305   **"Easternization"**: Gideon Rachman, *Easternization: Asia's Rise and America's
      Decline, From Obama to Trump and Beyond* (New York: Other Press, 2016).
306   **Female world leaders:** Abigail Geiger and Lauren Kent, *Number of Women
      Leaders Has Grown, But They're Still a Small Group,* March 8, 2017, http://www
      .pewresearch.org/fact-tank/2017/03/08/women-leaders-around-the-world/.
306   **"half the sky"**: Nicholas Kristof and Sheryl WuDunn, *Half the Sky: Turning
      Oppression into Opportunity for Women Worldwide* (New York: Vintage Books,
      2009).
308   **Machiavelli:** Lewis Edinger, "A Preface to Studies in Political Leadership,"
      in Gabriel Sheffer, ed., *Innovative Leadership in International Affairs* (Albany:
      State University of New York Press, 1993), 12.
309   **"controlling the temperature, keeping the opposition close"**: Ronald
      A. Heifetz and Marty Linsky, *Leadership on the Line: Staying Alive through
      the Dangers of Leading* (Boston: Harvard Business School Press, 2002), 85,
      107–108.
309   **"enlarging of that sense of We"**: Howard Gardner, "Leadership: A Cognitive
      Perspective," *SAIS Review* 16, no. 2 (Summer–Fall 1996), https://muse.jhu.edu/
      article/30318.
310   **"at the core of the development agenda"**: Charles Clift, *The Role of the World
      Health Organization in the International System* (London: Chatham House,
      2013), 8.

INDEX